▼ DATA SHARING
▼ USING A
▼ COMMON DATA
▼ ARCHITECTURE

Michael H. Brackett

JOHN WILEY & SONS, INC.

New York • Chichester • Brisbane • Toronto • Singapore

Publisher: Katherine Schowalter
Editor: Theresa Hudson
Managing Editor: Elizabeth Austin
Editorial Production & Design: Electric Ink, Ltd.

This text is printed on acid-free paper.

Library of Congress Cataloging-in-Publication Data

Brackett, Michael H.
    Data sharing using a common data architecture / Michael H. Brackett.
       p.   cm.
    Includes index.
    ISBN 0-471-30993-1 (pbk.)
    1. Data base management. 2. Data structures (Computer science)
   I. Title.
    QA76.9.D3B678   1994
    005.74'2—dc20
                                         93-33544
                                           CIP

Printed in the United States of America

10 9 8 7 6 5 4 3 2 1

To Juanita

CONTENTS

▼ LIST OF FIGURES
▼
▼

▼ ABOUT THE AUTHOR

Mr. Brackett is the Data Resource Coordinator for the State of Washington with the Department of Information Services. He has been in the data processing field over 30 years and has worked for the State for 27 years in a variety of agencies, including the Department of Natural Resources, Department of Fisheries, Employment Security Department, and Washington State University.

Mr. Brackett has developed many innovative concepts and techniques for designing applications and data. He is currently developing a common data architecture for the State that includes State agencies, cities, counties, Indian tribes, public utilities, and Federal agencies. That common data architecture covers large multi-jurisdictional areas, such as water resource, growth management, criminal justice, and health care.

Mr. Brackett has a BS in Forestry and an MS in Forestry (Botany) from the University of Washington, and an MS in Soils (Geology) from Washington State University. He has written and published three previous books on application and data design. He has also written many articles and given numerous presentations at local, national, and international conferences on the topic of application and data design.

Mr. Brackett is a past board member for the Seattle Chapter of the Data Resource Management Association. He teaches Data Modeling and Design in the Data Resource Management Certificate Program at the University of Washington. He also teaches Data Architecture classes for the State. He is listed in *Who's Who in the West* and *Who's Who in Education.*

▼ FOREWORD
▼
▼ BY JOHN A. ZACHMAN

When Michael Brackett initially suggested that I write a foreword to his latest book, I asked him to send me a copy of the manuscript so I could decide a.) whether I was competent to make a meaningful contribution, and b.) whether I actually liked the book. I am simply unable to write a foreword to a book unless I really like it. Needless to say, I really liked Michael's book.

I would call *Data Sharing Using a Common Data Architecture* a Vince Lombardi kind of a book. For those readers who are not football fans and don't know who Vince Lombardi was, what I mean by this metaphor is, this is a "block and tackle" book, a "back to the basics" approach to information systems and data architecture that is very refreshing.

From the very beginning of data processing, we have been inundated with technological panaceas, some kind of magic that would somehow obviate hard work...thinking-kind of hard work. My opinion is that not only are the users, in Michael's terminology, "clients," looking for "silver bullets," but those of us who are information professionals are equally culpable! Every time a new technology or a new tool comes on the scene, it always seems to be perceived to be the final word, the elixir that will forever make all pain go away. I think this "silver bullet" mentality has set very unrealistic expectations, and presently is causing severe problems for the information community.

As this book is published, it is my personal perception that the credibility of the information profession is at an all-time low. As the world moves relentlessly, at break-neck speed, into the Age of Information, public and private enterprises alike are finding themselves under enormous stress—restructuring, reengineering, downsizing, transforming, redefining their roles in a new and dynamic global marketplace. Unfortunately, I/S is being perceived as an inhibitor of the enterprise's efforts to survive the dramatic changes taking place all around and within it. It seems that it always takes I/S years and hundreds of thousands of dollars to respond to the enterprise's demands, or else "we can't even do it at all!"

I have had the opportunity to work with a very prestigious and very competent I/S organization that supports a major division of a very respected aerospace giant. They had one of the "Big Six Consulting Firms" analyze the quality of their information systems support of this division, and the final report basically said that I/S "takes too long, costs too much and doesn't meet expectations." Unfortunately, I think this is the rule rather than the exception for the information profession as a whole, and the root of the problem appears to be twofold: first, in the dynamic environment of the Information Age, *anything you do* is likely to seem to take too long, cost too much and not meet expectations; but second and more insidious, if your perception is that there is some kind of magic in the technology, *it is a guarantee* that it is going to take too long, cost too much and not meet expectations!

Clearly, my bias is that there is no magic. There is only creativity, ingenuity and a lot of hard work, both on the part of the client as well as on the part of I/S. We are in this Information Age game together and it is imperative that we work together if we expect the enterprise to emerge safely into the mainstream of the Information Age environment.

That is why *Data Sharing Using a Common Data Architecture* is such an important book. Michael Brackett is "telling it like it is." There is a lot of data out there in virtually every enterprise that is in sorry shape. It is not accurate, it is not consistent, it is not timely, it is not integrated, it is not accessible, it is expensive, and it is misleading to management. If it is ever going to be of any use to anyone outside of its immediate users, somebody is going to have to sit down and examine it element by element. Each element is going to have to be understood in terms of what it means and then be uniquely identified, named, defined, and related appropriately, Hard decisions and choices will have to be made and consensus reached between potential users. Incidentally, I particularly appreciated Michael's wisdom that "resolution of issues should not be forced." It takes time to reach consensus, and forcing resolution does not result in quality models. Also, "an integrated architecture cannot be build with automatic documentation and reengineering tools because there is a discovery process involved." That is, no tool is going to be able to do the work of analyzing all of the existing data elements and figuring out what the original programmers intended them to mean when they created them in the first place.

One might argue that it is not worth the time and money to invest the effort in the enterprise's existing data, but to focus only on new systems and new data. I would suggest that I have not yet encountered any enterprise that is ready to categorically dismiss its current investment in its existing systems. Even if the existing systems could be completely ignored, data in any new systems would ultimately have to receive the same element by element specification and consensus if its value is to be realized beyond merely a single implementation.

There is a good precedence in the world of linguistic studies for matters of this nature. Every culture that has been able to advance its body of knowledge and succeed in sophisticated undertakings, especially in the highly technical environment we associate with modern civilization, has done so on the basis of a formalized, well-documented language. For languages there are dictionaries, directories, thesauruses, indexes, glossaries, lexicons, concordances, and cross-references. The same concepts are relevant within the language (data) of an enterprise if it is to employ information technology and enterprise knowledge to its own advantage in the dynamics and vagaries of the Information Age. This may sound tedious, but nonetheless, it is a prerequisite. The book illustrates how to prepare each of these reference works (that is, the dictionaries, directories, thesauruses, indexes, glossaries, lexicons, concordances, cross-references, and so on) in support of the management and preservation of value for the data of the enterprise.

Data Sharing Using a Common Data Architecture is an exhaustive reference, defining every data concept I have ever encountered plus concepts I have never even thought of that are relevant to the management of data. For example, Michael points out that "data accuracy is a new category of data quality in the architectural infrastructure," and includes things like precision, scale, resolution, level of detail, frequency of collection, volatility, method of capture, degree of reproducibility, confidence, and so on. The book is not only a comprehensive source for subjects related to data, but it also contains concise definitions for those subjects.

It is clear that Michael Brackett has had an enormous amount of experience in doing the actual work of architecting data, not only because of the exhaustive definitions or the explicit instructions on how to handle every anomaly, but also because of the richness and diversity of his illustrations and his pragmatic methodological suggestions.

For anyone who is merely involved in a reverse engineering project or a data warehouse project (that is, even something far short of an enterprise-wide, common data architecture strategy), *Data Sharing Using a Common Data Architecture* will be an invaluable aid.

I believe this book will stand as a foundation work. It is very detailed and explicit, yet it is very readable. It is very technical, yet it is intelligible to the non-technical reader. It suggests approaches that require nothing more than a word-processor and a data base management system to implement. No special tools are required to employ the concepts and address/solve the enterprise data problem. It would be nice if some better tools were available and I am sure that it is only a matter of time, but in fact, there is no magic in the tools in themselves. The tools merely support the people who have to do the actual work of defining, naming, identifying, and relating.

You might not agree with every single idea or technique or definition or even the methodological approach Michael takes. Still, *Data Sharing Using a Common Data Architecture* is a valuable reference where it comes to managing data.

I think we tend to become overwhelmed by the magnitude and complexity of the "data problem," particularly in enterprises of any size and any sizable inventory of existing systems. However, it only takes time and costs money. If you don't start, you will never finish. Clever ideas and tools will come and go. There still will be a lot of data out there that is not clearly understood and therefore whose value is not at all leveragable. But any enterprise that wants to exist over the next few years and needs to retain any of its current knowledge-base is going to have to buckle down and do this data work sooner or later. Once again, I am sure it will be argued that you need only to "build new" and ignore what is already out there—and it might work. In this case, one would only have to define the "common data architecture" and go from there. However, the practicality of the matter is it will be hard to get around the substantial investment already made in the current systems—plus, the enterprise will have to continue to operate in some fashion for some period of time during the transition to the new environment. If this is true, then it only stands to reason that someone is going to have to do the work of mapping the existing data elements to the "common data architecture."

It appears to me that this is a universal issue and sooner or later, everyone is going to have to get back to the basics and "(block and) tackle" this formidable data problem. But Michael says, "just when it appears that the job is insurmountable, the critical mass of information is achieved and disparate data fall into place within the common data architecture." That sounds like some pretty good news to me.

I think you will find this book valuable, informative, readable, and an excellent reference.

LaCanada, California
May 20, 1993

▼ ACKNOWLEDGMENTS
▼
▼

The author thanks Bruce Jorgensen and Tim Feetham for their ideas and comments about how the current environment can be improved. The author thanks Joe Oates and Tom Haughey for their input about the implementation of new technologies to solve our current problems. The author thanks Gary Guinotte for his review of the book and the publishers for their reviews and comments about the content and the method of presentation. Their input helped make this book a polished product.

The author thanks the students in his classes, the conference attendees, and data refining project team members who provided input about the current problems they face and how the new techniques described in this book help solve their problems. Their input helped make the techniques people-oriented and client-friendly. The author also thanks Denise Prowse for her comments about the techniques and features of the Data Resource Guide, and Barb Malen for her help in developing the Data Resource Guide and making it a useful product.

Special thanks go to Carey Clark and Tom Crawford for the time spent discussing different approaches for controlling disparate data and managing an organization's data resource, and for their reviews of the book. Without their thoughts and comments, many of the concepts and techniques presented in this book would not be available.

Finally, with deep respect, the author thanks Mr. John Zachman for his intuitive insight into understanding and resolving many of the problems we face today. Through several long discussions with Mr. Zachman, the author has gained some of that insight and applied it to understanding and resolving the disparate data situation.

▼ ▼ ▼ PREFACE

Wouldn't it be a pleasure to know and understand all the data in your organization? Wouldn't it be great to easily identify and readily share those data to develop information that supports business strategies? Wouldn't it be wonderful to have a formal data resource that provides just-in-time data for developing just-in-time information to support just-in-time decision making?

That's what this book is about. It defines a common data architecture, its contents, and its uses. It describes how a common data architecture is developed for defining disparate data in a common context and sharing those data across projects within an organization and across organizations. It explains how a common data architecture is used to achieve short-term, incrementally cost-effective benefits with minimum impact on business operations, while achieving long-term goals.

Let's face reality! The data in most organizations are disparate data. They are poorly named, defined, structured, and documented. They are highly redundant, and redundant versions are often inconsistent. They are highly variable in their format, content, and meaning. They cannot be readily identified, easily accessed, or properly used. Large quantities of useful data already exist, and people are not aware of these hidden data or their value. The reality for most organizations is a large quantity of disparate data.

Organizations are basing their existence on these disparate data. They have a rapidly increasing demand for information, often on short notice. This information is often critical to their success in a dynamic business world. However, the information cannot be prepared quickly from the existing disparate data. The conflict between existing disparate data and the high demand for information are creating a crisis in many organizations.

The crisis can be resolved by developing a common data architecture for understanding and sharing disparate data. The vision is a formal data resource where all data are defined in a common context. The formal data resource evolves to a mature data resource that has less variability and all the data necessary to support rapid development of critical information for a dynamic organization. The common data architecture provides a base for achieving the vision. It helps people build incrementally toward the vision. It gives people the courage to face the reality of today's situation and stop the trend of continuing to develop disparate data.

Developing a common data architecture is relatively easy for new data at the project level. However, it is more difficult to develop a data architecture for new data that is consistent across several large projects, across an organization, or across several organizations. It is extremely difficult to develop a data architecture that integrates disparate data within an organization or across organizations. Many of the techniques and tools that work well for new data at the project level do not work for disparate data.

A common data architecture helps people understand and share disparate data within an organization, and across organizations where there is no point of common authority. It helps people manage data in purchased applications. It helps people manage multiple, conflicting mandates from other organizations. It increases productivity, because real productivity comes from understanding and reusing existing data, not creating new data. It improves data quality so that data directly support business activities. It provides visibility and credibility for both clients and executives.

If this sounds like the approach you need—read on!

There are no global, one-shot, overnight cure-alls for the current disparate data situation. Many people believe that tools can build an architecture, align existing data to that architecture, and clean up the current situation. This is not true! Tools don't build architectures, and tools will not solve the problems with existing data. People build architectures, and people align existing data with architectures. Only people can clean up disparate data. Tools only support the efforts of people, just like a carpenter's toolbox supports the carpenter. The knowledge and skills are in the people, not in the tools.

Building a common data architecture does not require changing existing applications or databases. It does not require changing existing data names or formats. It does not prevent the acquisition or continued use of purchased applications. It does provide a way to define all existing and new data in a common context so they can be easily understood and readily shared.

This book presents a practical, real-world approach for developing and using a common data architecture to define all data in a common context. It paints the vision of a formal data resource library and provides techniques for building incrementally toward that vision. It provides simple concepts, terms that are easy to understand, and techniques that are easy to follow. It explains pitfalls that may be met and how they can be avoided. It emphasizes people and technology equally, because it is the people who make or break any technology. It unfolds an new way of thinking about data that breaks the continuing tradition of developing disparate data.

This book is not about designing and modeling data or constructing databases. It is not about traditional data resource management or data administration. It is not about the use of CASE tools or information engineering techniques. It is about understanding existing data within the context of a common data architecture. It is about using data engineering techniques to understand and share data, and to develop a data resource that supports information engineering. This book builds on a previous book by the author, titled *Practical Data Design.* The concepts and techniques for modeling and designing data are explained in detail in that book

Chapter 1 describes the current disparate data situation, an engineering perspective to solving that situation, and a vision for sharing data. Chapter 2 explains the concepts of a common data architecture and how it fits into the information technology infrastructure. Chapters 3, 4, 5, 6, and 7 explain the individual components of the common data architecture: data naming, data definition, data structure, data quality, and data documentation.

Chapter 8 describes the concepts and techniques for refining data to a common data architecture. Chapters 9, 10, and 11 describe the description, structure, and quality of disparate data. Chapter 12 describes techniques for cross referencing disparate data to the common data architecture. Chapter 13 describes techniques for identifying official data variations and developing data translation schemes. Chapter 14 describes the entire process for identifying disparate data, developing a formal data resource, and evolving to a mature data resource.

Chapter 15 explains the concepts and techniques for ensuring that the formal data resource is complete and contains all the data necessary to support information engineering. Chapter 16 explains how the data sharing reality is achieved. It emphasizes the importance of people and the creation of a win–win situation. An extensive Glossary is provided. Appendices provide a data lexicon that supports the data naming taxonomy, data names and descriptions, data resource survey questions, data cross reference criteria, and data structure criteria.

This is not a book about the future. It's about today and getting to the future. It's about people surviving their disparate data situations. It's about people sharing the problems they face with data and sharing the resolution of those problems. Most people want to change the current situation; they just don't know how to change without adversely affecting the business. They are wary of past cure-alls and vendor hype. They are unsure about how to approach the uncertainty and variability of disparate data to gain control of their data

There is a window of opportunity for organizations to gain control of their data. The rate at which an organization gains control of its data is its own choice. However, control must be gained before open systems, decentralization, and further fragmentation close that window. Control can be gained by developing a common data architecture that provides a central architecture to support decentralized use and deployment information systems. An organization must step ahead to gain control of its data. There is a risk and cost for stepping ahead, but the risk and cost are far greater if nothing is done and disparate data proliferate.

Is it possible to gain control of your disparate data? The answer is a resounding *Yes!* The common data architecture provides an approach that ensures a win–win situation for clients, executives, and the organization.

Olympia, Washington
August, 1993

▼
▼ **1**
▼

SHARED DATA VISION

A vision for integrating and sharing data is the first step toward understanding the current data situation and gaining control of data.

Most organizations have large quantities of data that are fragmented across a variety of files, redundant and inconsistent, poorly named and defined, poorly structured, and not well documented or understood. These disparate data do not adequately support the information needs of an organization operating in a dynamic business environment. The existing disparate data, and any new data, need to be identified, described, understood, and integrated within a common context so they can be readily shared throughout the organization, and between organizations, to support business activities.

Most organizations want to gain control of their data. They can't afford to continue operating with the existing disparate data, or to continue developing additional disparate data. They just don't know how to gain control of their data, or how to gain control without impacting business operations. They need a new approach to identify all existing data and new data in a common context so they can be integrated and shared without impacting the business.

The chapter begins with an explanation of the current data situation in most organizations, the information technology trends and business trends in progress today, and the crisis faced by organizations resulting from a conflict between the current data situation and the trends. The opportunity for organizations to take the initiative and gain control of their data is described. An engineering perspective is presented for developing a formal data resource to provide data that support delivery of just-in-time information. Finally, a vision is presented for using an engineering perspective to resolve the crisis, build a data resource, and begin sharing data.

▼ THE CURRENT SITUATION

The current situation is a crisis created by the existence of massive quantities of disparate data, a high rate of data capture and increasing data redundancy, rapidly evolving technologies for using and managing data, and a dynamic business environment that is creating a high demand for information.

Disparate Data

Disparate refers to things that are essentially not alike, or are distinctly different in kind, quality, or character. They are things that are fundamentally different and are often incompatible. In other words, they are basically unequal. *Disparate data* are data that are essentially not alike, or are distinctly different in kind, quality, or character. They are fundamentally different and are often incompatible. They are unequal and cannot be readily integrated to adequately support the business activities of an organization. They are heterogeneous data.

Disparate data do not adequately support the business.

Disparate data are not identified, named, defined, structured, or maintained by the same set of rules as other data. They are inconsistently named, poorly defined, improperly structured, and incompletely documented. Their meaning, content, and format are highly variable, and they have low integrity and unknown accuracy. They are fragmented in different locations, on different databases, with different structures, and are often stored redundantly. They are often in a raw, unorganized state, and frequently do not exist in electronic form. They are generally unreliable, incompatible, incomplete, and inaccurate. They are difficult to understand, identify, and access, and they are expensive to maintain.

Data Deluge

Massive quantities of data are being captured and stored at an alarming rate. These data are being captured by traditional means, by scanning, by imaging, by remote sensing, and by derivation. They are being stored on personal computers, networks, departmental computers, and mainframes. The quantity of data in many organizations is increasing exponentially, and is bordering on data pollution. If this data proliferation continues, the data deluge of the '90s will put the '80s to shame.

A deluge of data is virtually inundating organizations.

People often cannot find or access existing data because the true content and meaning of those data are unknown. In many situations, the people are not even aware that the data already exist. So they capture or create additional data, often redundantly, adding to the data deluge. Some estimates for redundant data in an organization run as high as a factor of ten. That means, on the average, each piece of data is stored in ten different places! Known and managed redundancy is acceptable for back-up and recovery, and for optimization on a network. But unknown or inconsistent redundancy is disastrous.

Technology Trends

Information technology is evolving at a rapid rate. Advancements are being made in the price-performance and capacity of hardware and networks, and in software development technology and databases. However, these advancements may be adding disparate data rather than reducing disparate data.

Advancements in technology are adding to the disparate data problem, not resolving it.

Client/server is a technology that allows multiple clients to access shared data stored on one or more databases on a server. It is an environment where computing is shared between many front-end clients and a back-end server. Open systems is an open architecture that allows seamless integration across different platforms and gives people unlimited ability to produce new and innovative applications. Ultimately, anybody will be able to access any data or application without knowing its location.

Client/servers and open systems provide the mechanism for electronic connection of a wide variety of data, but they often increase disparate data. They only solve half of the problem: the electronic connection. The other half is the real problem of integrating disparate data. This problem is not solved as easily as electronic connection. It requires a deep understanding of the true content and meaning of the data being integrated.

Electronic data interchange (EDI) is the electronic exchange of data between two or more applications, often in two or more hardware environments, without manual intervention. It connects wide-ranging, but functionally related, business activities in separate organizations through standard interfaces to share data between applications running on different hardware. However, the use of electronic data interchange is being hampered by the existence of disparate data.

Executive information systems (EIS) provide financial, marketing, operational, personnel, and competitive information to executives in summary form. They support the management of an organization by adding value to the data that support the operational aspects of an organization. They are becoming very popular and are used by more than executives. In some organizations EIS means "Everybody's Information System."

Successful executive information systems require the integration of a wide variety of data to support their summarization and drill-down features. However, disparate data cannot be easily integrated, and this problem contributes to the high failure rate of executive information systems. The content and meaning of existing data must be thoroughly understood to support successful executive information systems.

Geographic information systems (GIS) are gaining wide popularity for storing, manipulating, and retrieving large quantities of spatial data in many disciplines. Remote sensing and remote photography also provide large quantities of data for many disciplines. The integration of geographic information systems and executive information systems provide a new dimension to executive information. The problem is that these technologies cannot integrate disparate data. In addition, they are creating additional disparate data.

Expert systems and object-oriented technology contain data the same way conventional systems do. However, many of the design techniques concentrate on the design of rules and processes and ignore the design of data. This omission further perpetuates disparate data.

Data are becoming more decentralized with the evolution of servers, networks, and open systems. They are often decentralized across mainframe computers, departmental computers, and personal computers, and are located in different database management systems. Most decentralization is done randomly, based on client needs and available software and hardware, because most people are just trying to stay on top of their workloads. The result is an increase in disparate data.

Business Trends

The business environment is increasingly dynamic and complex, and constantly creates the need for new information. It used to be that the only thing that was constant was change. However, the rate of change is accelerating, and now the only thing that is constant is the acceleration. The rate of change will not decrease in the foreseeable future, and the corresponding need for new information will not decrease, either: it will increase.

> *The increasingly dynamic and complex business environment is increasing the need for new information.*

Organizations are merging and splitting at an increasing rate to take advantage of business opportunities. Many organizations are changing or realigning their activities to be successful and profitable. The identification, evaluation, planning, execution, and control of these activities further increases the need for new information. These activities will not decrease in the near future.

Many clients are developing their own information systems and databases because they need information. This trend will continue at an increasing rate as the price performance of hardware improves, open systems mature, and software becomes less expensive and more friendly. However, this trend is also creating additional disparate data.

The Crisis

Organizations are facing a crisis. The need for information is increasing at an accelerated rate and the time frame for receiving the information is increasingly shorter. The quantity of disparate data is increasing at an exponential rate and new technology is increasing, not reducing, the quantity of disparate data. Disparate data cannot be readily integrated and do not adequately support the increasing need for information in a shorter time frame.

This is a grim and intolerable situation for many organizations. There is literally more data and less information. Organizations are drowning in a sea of disparate data, and the sea is rising. Yet they cannot produce the information they need in a timely manner.

The increasing need for new information on short notice is incompatible with the growing volume of disparate data.

Technology has wreaked havoc with data over the past 10 or 15 years and left a base of disparate data that is difficult to change. It has provided a capability without a corresponding engineering rigor. It is continuing to make things easier, faster, and cheaper, but it still lacks a corresponding engineering rigor to prevent the proliferation of disparate data.

Organizations are throwing technology at the problem without understanding the problem. They are doing what vendors have told them is right according to the tools those vendors have. They ignore the future in the name of current technology. Many organizations are continuing to throw technology at the problem, but are only making the problem worse. Until the trend is reversed, the problems will continue to get worse, and they will get worse faster.

An Opportunity to Change

There is an opportunity to change the current situation and take control of the data, to stop the proliferation of disparate data and start integrating data into a formal data resource that supports the information needs of an organization. There is an opportunity to uncover the value of disparate data and refine those data into a formal data resource.

There is an opportunity to understand the true content and meaning of data, and to reuse those data to continually develop new information.

Most organizations have a hidden data resource that needs to be discovered.

Most organizations have no idea of the hidden data resource they have in their disparate data. There are large quantities of data that are largely unknown, unavailable, and unused because there is no easy way to identify the their content and meaning. The data just sit in databases or filing cabinets. If the true content and meaning of disparate data were known and those data were refined into a formal data resource, they would be readily available to meet information needs.

▼ AN ENGINEERING PERSPECTIVE

Engineering is the use of science and mathematics to put scientific knowledge to practical use. It is the process of planning, designing, constructing, and managing something. Engineering generally applies to chemistry, physics, machinery, and so forth. It also applies to data and information, and can be used both to develop a formal data resource and to develop information.

Data

Although it may be startling in the information age, many people do not know the difference between data and information. In an age where information is a major commodity, people do not know what is the resource and what is the product. The terms *information* and *data* are often used interchangeably without definition. Below, these terms are defined as they are used by data engineers.

Data are the individual facts and the raw material for producing information.

Data are individual facts with specific meaning at a point in time or for a period of time. Data include the atomic level, known as primitive data, and derived data. For example, a person's birth date is *primitive data*, because it is obtained directly from the person. A person's age is *derived data*, because it is derived from his or her birth date and the current date. Even though the person's age is derived, it is still data, not information.

Data also include both elemental and combined data. *Elemental data* are individual facts that cannot be subdivided and still retain meaning. *Combined data* are a concatenation of individual facts. For example, a person's birth date is combined data consisting of four pieces of elemental data: century, year, month, and day. It is not information just because there is a concatenation of elemental data.

Data are the basic building blocks used to develop information, like Lego blocks are the basic building blocks for children's toys. The information built from data is limited only by the need and imagination of the client, like the toys built by Lego blocks are limited only by the need and imagination of the child who builds them.

Information

The rapidly changing business environment causes uncertainty, which creates a need for information to resolve or reduce the uncertainty, as shown in Figure 1.1. The more dynamic a business environment is, the more rapid the change, the greater the uncertainty, and the greater the need for information. Since the trend is toward accelerated change, there will be an accelerated need for new information.

A *message* is a communication containing a collection of data in some order and format. If that message meets the information need, it contains information, as shown in Figure 1.2. If it does not meet the need, it is simply noise; it is useless or less than fully useful. Therefore, *information* is a collection of data in the form of a message that is relevant to the recipient at a point in time. It must be meaningful and useful to the recipient at a specific time for a specific purpose. If the

Figure 1.1 *The dynamic business environment creates a need for information.*

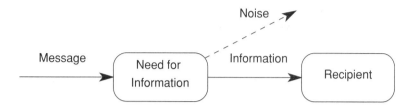

Figure 1.2 *A message that meets an information need contains information.*

message is not relevant to the recipient, it does not contain information. Only the recipient determines whether the message contains information.

For example, a person who is going clam digging on Washington's coast on the Fourth of July needs to know the time for low tides. If that person were given precise tide tables for the Atlantic coast, the data would be useless and would not be information. If that person were given winter tide tables for Washington's coast, that data would also be useless. However, if that person were given tide tables for Washington's coast in July, and those tables were provided before the trip, they would meet a need and would be information.

> *Information is a collection of data that is relevant to the recipient at a specific time for a specific purpose.*

Under this definition of information, there can be no information overload. There can only be a data overload. If people need information and receive messages that meet that need, they are not overloaded. A person is only overloaded by too much data and too little information.

Also, there can be no information resource management. Since the need for information changes with the changing business environment, and those changes cannot be managed as a resource, the need for information cannot be managed as a resource. Therefore, a message containing information to meet a need cannot be managed as a resource. Managing a dynamic business environment is difficult; managing a person's need for information as a resource in that environment is impossible.

In addition, there can be no information base. Some information systems, such as executive information systems, provide data to people in a specific context to meet an information need. However, those information systems do not access information bases. They access databases that contain primitive and derived data. Those data are used to prepare a message that meets an information need. Similarly, reports, documents, and other transactions stored electronically are data, not information.

Information Engineering

Messages are produced by information systems, as shown in Figure 1.3. One of the major problems today is that messages contain too much noise and too little information. To resolve this problem, messages that contain maximum information and minimum noise must be prepared. The information need that exists, or could exist, must be identified, and messages must be prepared to meet that information need. The success of information systems is measured, in part, by how well the information needs are identified and whether those needs are fully met in a timely manner.

Information engineering is the discipline for identifying information needs and developing information systems that produce messages providing information. It is a manufacturing process that uses data as the raw material to construct and transmit a message. It is a filtering process that reduces masses of data to a message providing information. The objective of information engineering is to ensure that a message maximizes information and minimizes noise.

> *Information engineering is the discipline for producing messages that contain maximum information and minimum noise.*

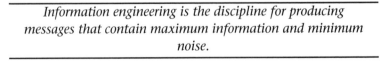

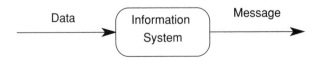

Figure 1.3 *Messages are produced by information systems.*

Very few organizations, perhaps 10 to 20 percent, are using a formal information engineering discipline today to deal with the massive quantities of disparate data. Information engineering is a formal discipline that requires a formal data resource. Since most organizations have large quantities of disparate data that do not form a formal data resource, information engineering cannot be fully implemented. Information engineering can only be fully implemented when there is a formal data resource.

Information systems take too long to develop. Typically, it takes 9 to 12 months just to locate data. It takes 18 to 24 months to get to disparate data consolidated. It often takes three to five years to get consistent information from disparate data. These times are not acceptable in today's dynamic environment. Data need to be identified, located, and accessed in 3 to 6 months, maximum.

> *An organization needs just-in-time information to be successful.*

Executives and managers often need information on a daily or hourly basis to make informed decisions, support business strategies, and respond to change. They need *just-in-time information* that is current, timely, and meets their information needs. This information can only be provided if there is a formal data resource containing the data necessary to produce the information.

Formal Data Resource

The *total data resource* for an organization is the total of all data available to the organization. All data in filing cabinets, data files, database management systems, text, hypertext, geographic information systems, executive information systems, and so on, are part of the total data resource. All disparate data are part of the organization's data resource.

A *formal data resource* is an integrated, comprehensive data resource that makes data readily identifiable and easily accessible by information engineering. It is a subset of the total data resource. It contains data that are identified within a common context so that people can understand their full content and meaning. The data are formally named, comprehensively defined, well structured, and properly documented. They have high integrity and known accuracy. The data are organized by subject independent of their use, just like the books in a library are organized by subject independent of their use.

The formal data resource contains data defined within a common context.

A formal data resource integrates disparate data and new data. The formal data resource is comprehensive. It contains all data needed to meet information needs. Since an organization cannot predict all its information needs, it is difficult to predict all the data needed in the formal data resource. However, good business planning provides insight into the types of data that may be needed and results in just-in-time data.

Data Engineering

Data engineering is the discipline that designs, builds, and maintains the formal data resource and refines data into that data resource. It is the formal process of identifying both disparate data and new data, bringing them into the formal data resource, and making them available to information systems, as shown in Figure 1.4. It is the responsibility of data engineering to make the formal data resource available to information systems. It is not the responsibility of information engineering to go and find the appropriate data for information systems.

Data engineering provides a formal data resource for information engineering.

Data engineering is also a data refining process. *Refining* removes impurities from crude or impure material to form useful products, such

Figure 1.4 *A comprehensive data resource provides data to information systems.*

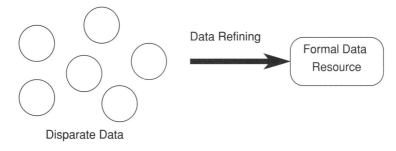

Figure 1.5 *Disparate data are refined for the formal data resource.*

as the refined oil produced from crude oil. *Data refining* takes disparate data, refines them within a common context, and stores them in the formal data resource, as shown in Figure 1.5. Disparate data are the raw material and the formal data resource is the product. The process is similar to the oil refining process that takes crude oil, refines it into usable products, and stores those products for future use.

> *Data refining is a filtering process that finds the hidden value in disparate data.*

Data engineering is largely undefined and unsupported by automated tools. Most techniques and tools, including CASE tools, concentrate on information engineering rather than data engineering, because it is relatively easy to work with new data and produce good results at a project level. It is also easier to define and automate the information engineering process.

Data engineering, however, is much more difficult and cannot be fully automated. It is a discovery process that relies largely on people to determine the true meaning of disparate data. It takes real thought, analysis, intuition, and consensus by knowledgeable people to identify the true content and meaning of disparate data. Automated tools can support people, but they cannot perform the discovery process or gain consensus. A new class of *computer aided data engineering* (CADE) tools need to be developed to support data engineering.

There is considerable hype and misinformation about data engineering and development of a formal data resource. Numerous products and methods are promoted to resolve the disparate data problems. But there are no quick fixes, no magic formulas, no tools to develop a formal data resource and resolve the problems overnight. There is no panacea, in spite of the current level of vendor hype.

Many organizations are gridlocked in their own data because people cannot assimilate data at the rate they are produced, or because the cost of assimilation is unreasonably high. *Information refining* is a process that takes undifferentiated raw data, extracts the content into elemental units, and recombines those elemental units into usable information. It removes the impurities from the raw data and recombines the basic usable components into new end products. *Intelligent databases* provide data compression techniques that filter raw data, remove unnecessary data, and produce information. They can also guide clients to the data they need. However, both information refining and intelligent databases require refined data in a formal data resource.

Meta-Data

Meta-data are data about the data. They are data in their own right, but they describe the actual data representing the real world. Meta-data include the names and definitions of data, the logical and physical structure of data, data integrity, data accuracy, and any other information about the data resource. The total design and documentation of the data resource is meta-data.

Meta-data include all data describing the data resource.

For example, the name and definition of Employee are meta-data. A diagram showing the relationship between Employee and Position is meta-data. Rules for maintaining the integrity of Employee data are meta-data. Any other statements about data, such as the evaluation of data accuracy, are meta-data. Any information about identifying and accessing data is meta-data.

Meta-data also include coded data values. The names and definitions of coded data values are just as important as the names and definitions of Employee data or Position data. Coded data values are often used to maintain data integrity, and must be part of the design of the data resource. The definition of coded data values is critical to a thorough understanding of the data resource. Therefore, they must be included as meta-data. They are not considered actual data until they are stored with data representing the real world.

The meta-data in most organizations are as disparate as the real data. They must be refined within the common data architecture, just like real data. It does very little good to refine real data into a formal data resource and ignore the meta-data. The meta-data must be refined and maintained with the same rigor and emphasis as real data.

Meta-data are as disparate as real data.

Information engineering develops and maintains actual data about the real world. It captures data, store them in the data resource, and retrieves them to produce information, as shown in Figure 1.6. It is responsible for the maintenance of all data representing the real world. Information engineering develops both data and information.

Data engineering develops and maintains meta-data. It uses information systems to capture meta-data, store them in the formal data resource, and retrieve them to produce information about the data resource. These information systems are built within the same information engineering discipline as other information systems, but are managed within the data engineering discipline.

▼ THE VISION

The vision for integrating and sharing data consists of a data resource library, an extensive data resource guide to that library, a common data architecture for defining all data in a common context, a concept for

Figure 1.6 *Disparate data are refined for the formal data resource.*

sharing data, and an evolution to a mature data resource. It is a future-oriented vision that helps make integrating and sharing data a reality.

The Data Resource Library

A *library* is a place where literary, musical, artistic, or reference materials are kept for use, but are not for sale. The library is a resource of works organized by subject and cross referenced by subject, title, and author. The works are organized independently of how people will use those works to obtain information. People go to the library and check the cross references to find the information they need. In most cases, people need only a fraction of the data they find about one subject. They take only the data that are meaningful to them and ignore the rest. The library contains data for everyone, but one person does not use all data.

The *data resource library* is a library for the formal data resource. Data are organized independently of how people use those data. People go to the data resource library, just like a regular library, to find the data they need. When they find the data they're looking for, they usually don't need all the data that is available. They take only what they need and ignore the rest. As in a regular library, the data are available for the next person.

A data resource library contains the formal data resource.

A data resource library may be decentralized, particularly when there are large volumes of data, the organization is decentralized, or the library represents several organizations. The data in the data resource library, like the books in a regular library, need not be in one location. However, the location for all data is known and those data can be readily accessed.

The library concept is better for the formal data resource than a warehouse or a supermarket. For example, a library contains summary data, while a warehouse or supermarket does not contain summary items. Also, a library does not have turnover, reorder, or back order processes like warehouses or supermarkets. A library contains historical items, and a warehouse or supermarket does not. Items from a library are used and then returned for others, as they are not in a warehouse or supermarket.

Data Resource Guide

The formal data resource needs a formal index if the data are to be fully understood and utilized. A comprehensive *data resource guide* provides extensive information about all data in the data resource library. It is an information system that maintains meta-data about the formal data resource. It is the card catalog for the formal data resource, just like a card catalog for a normal library.

A data resource guide can, and should, be automated so that it can be kept current, like the on-line card catalogs in a normal library. It is nearly impossible to maintain a current data resource guide on paper, because of its size and the rate at which it changes. A data resource guide can, and should, be located on a network, decentralized to allow access by anyone interested in the data resource. Ultimately, a data resource guide could be used to locate and order data, in a manner similar to the way books are ordered through an inter-library loan network.

Common Data Architecture

A *common data architecture* is the common context within which all data are defined. It provides a context for identifying the true content and meaning of data and improving the value of data. It is the base for refining and integrating disparate data and new data into the formal data resource so they can be shared and reused.

> *The common data architecture is the common context for defining all data so they can be readily identified and easily shared.*

The common data architecture transcends all data, whether they are disparate, in the data resource, or in a message, as shown in Figure 1.7. It encompasses all data regardless of where they reside, who uses them, how they are structured, or how they are used. It often includes data from many organizations. It is not limited to automated data in the formal data resource.

The common data architecture ensures that data are integrated within an organization and across organizations, not just at the project level. It enables a shift from reactive data resource management to

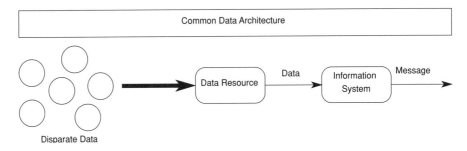

Figure 1.7 *The common data architecture transcends all data.*

proactive data resource management by allowing people to check and see whether the data already exist before they create redundant data. It enables the refinement of disparate data and their integration into the formal data resource. It helps make the integration and sharing of data a reality.

> *The common data architecture changes the current situation of* what data do you think you got *to a situation of knowing* I got exactly the data I needed.

Mature Data Resource

Disparate data are highly variable; there are many variations in format, content, and meaning for a specific piece of data. For example, a date could be month–day–year, day–month–year, and so on. A person's name could be in the normal sequence or an inverted sequence, and it could have several different lengths. These variations in format, content, or meaning are referred to as *data variations*.

Official data variations are those data variations that have been selected by consensus of knowledgeable people as the data variations to be used for short-term data sharing and for long-term evolution to a mature data resource. The designation of official data variations establishes the base to which all non-official data variations are ultimately converted. Data translation schemes are developed for translation between the official data variations and non-official data variations until the non-official data variations are converted.

A mature data resource is the ultimate goal.

A *mature data resource* is the ultimate goal for a data resource. It is a formal data resource that contains all official data variations with minimum non-official data variations. Data variability and data translation schemes are reduced to a minimum. Data redundancy is reduced to a known and manageable level. Data accuracy is known and is at the desired level. Clients can readily identify and access data with a minimum of effort.

The diagram in Figure 1.8 shows the relationships among an organization's three data resources. The total data resource is all data, manual or automated, that are available to an organization. The formal data resource is a subset of the total data resource, representing data that have been refined within the common data architecture. Data outside the formal data resource have not been refined within the common data architecture. The mature data resource is a subset of the formal data resource that contains official data variations.

The mature data resource will not be achieved overnight. The current disparate data situation will get worse before it gets better. How bad it gets depends on how quickly an organization takes the initiative and begins developing a formal data resource. The more quickly an organization begins, the more quickly it will understand its data

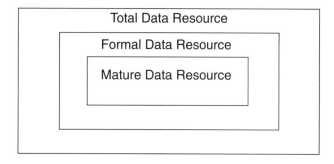

Figure 1.8 *An organization's three data resources.*

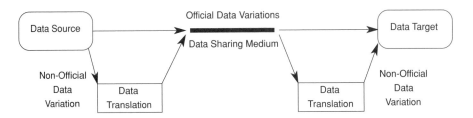

Figure 1.9 *Sharing official data.*

and begin integrating, sharing, and reusing those data to their full potential.

Data Sharing Concept

The concept for data sharing is shown in Figure 1.9. Data are shared over a *data sharing medium*. This can be a network, a tape, a diskette, or any other mechanism for sharing data. The data shared over the medium must be the official data variations. If the data source does not have the official data variation, it must translate its non-official data variation to an official data variation by accepted data translation schemes before sharing. If the data targets do not use the official data variation, they must translate the official data variation to their non-official data variation by accepted data translation schemes.

This concept is better than the current practice of developing individual physical files and independent translation schemes that are useful only as long as the source and target databases retain the same structure. The current practice results in a proliferation of data sharing files that often require high maintenance. It also adds to the disparate data problem. One proactive approach to resolving the disparate data problem is to share data only through the official data variations. Each organization is then free to change its data resource without impacting other organizations.

▼ SUMMARY

The existence of large quantities of disparate data keeps an organization from exploiting data to their full advantage. Disparate data are growing at an exponential rate and organizations' ability to deal with disparate data is decreasing. Organizations need new information, on shorter notice, at an ever increasing rate to continue operating in an increasingly dynamic and complex business environment. A crisis of too much data and not enough information is crippling organizations.

Most organizations have a large hidden data resource they could draw on if they only knew it existed. They need a way to explore these data, find their true meaning and content, and use them to full advantage. They need a way to understand the data and the business knowledge hidden in the data. They need a way to gain control of their data, stop the proliferation of disparate data, and develop a data resource that supports development of just-in-time information.

Control of data can be achieved by taking an engineering approach that provides more rigor, stops the proliferation of disparate data, and assures that no more disparate data will be created. A common data architecture needs to be developed, and disparate data need to be refined within this architecture and integrated into a formal data resource. Short-term data sharing can be enhanced through a concept of official data variations and data translation schemes. Data can be maintained and reused rather than captured, used once, and discarded or forgotten. A mature data resource can be achieved through a long-term evolution from the formal data resource.

Is the cost of gaining control of data and providing just-in-time information worthwhile? Each organization must answer that question individually, after carefully weighing the cost of changing against the cost of not changing. Only the organization can determine whether implementing a formal data resource and developing it into a mature data resource will be necessary for survival. Most progressive organizations cannot afford to wait.

▼ QUESTIONS

The following questions are designed to provide a review of Chapter 1 and to stimulate thought about the current data situation and the vision for resolving that situation.

1. What are disparate data?

2. Why is the volume of disparate data increasing at an exponential rate?

3. Why is there an increasing need for new information on shorter notice?

4. What is the hidden data resource?

5. What are the differences between data, meta-data, and information?

6. What are the responsibilities for data engineering and information engineering?

7. What is a formal data resource?

8. How do data refining and information refining differ?

9. What is a data resource library?

10. How does a data resource guide support the data resource library?

11. How does a common data architecture help gain control of data?

12. What are official data variations?

13. How does a mature data resource differ from a formal data resource?

14. How is the data sharing concept different from current data sharing practices?

15. What is the shared data vision?

16. Is it worthwhile for an organization to gain control of its data?

▼▼▼ 2

COMMON DATA ARCHITECTURE

---

*A common data architecture is the common context for refining
data to achieve the shared data vision.*

The current data resource of most organizations resembles a typical
mini-storage facility. Each person's belongings are dumped into a mini-
storage in a relatively unorganized manner, depending on the size of
the storage and how things were brought to the storage. Separate mini-
storages are organized differently and are not easily integrated. It is
very difficult for a person to find anything in another person's mini-
storage. Sometimes it is even difficult for people to find anything in
their own storage spaces.

Many organizations store their data in much the same way. People
dump their data into different files and databases, according to their
current needs. Organizations need to bring their data under control so
they can achieve a shared data reality. That control can best be gained
by defining all data within the context of a common data architecture.

This chapter begins with an explanation of an architectural infrastructure for information technology consisting of four frameworks for
business activities, a platform resource, a data resource, and information systems. The data resource framework is described in detail, with
emphasis on the data architecture component. The common data
architecture is defined and its scope, uses, and benefits are explained.
The chapter ends with a brief description of the base for building a

common data architecture. The remainder of the book explains the techniques for building a common data architecture.

▼ INFORMATION TECHNOLOGY INFRASTRUCTURE

An *infrastructure* is an underlying foundation or framework for a system or an organization. The term generally refers to the basic installations and facilities for community development or military operations. For example, roads, schools, power, transportation, and communication are all part of a community infrastructure. The concept of an infrastructure can also be applied to information technology. An *information technology infrastructure* is shown in Figure 2.1. It consists of four *information technology frameworks* for business activities, a data resource, a platform resource, and information systems.

Information Systems Framework

An information systems framework is shown in the center of the information technology infrastructure. It represents integration of the business activities, data resource, and platform resource needed to support an organization's business strategies. These three frameworks are used

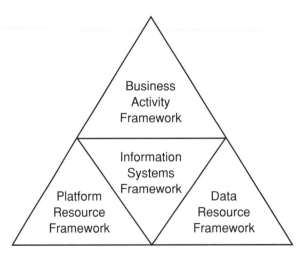

Figure 2.1 *An information technology infrastructure.*

to develop information systems. In other words, an *information system* is the integration of the business activities, the data resource, and the platform resource.

John Zachman presents an excellent framework for information systems in his "Framework for Information Systems Architecture." That framework consists of a matrix of columns and rows. The columns represent architectures for data, processes, and network—the three major architectures in the information technology infrastructure. The rows represent development steps for information systems. Progression down the rows represents a transformation from more general models to more detailed models.

The Zachman Framework is a powerful paradigm for development of information systems.

The rows in the Zachman Framework represent techniques for developing and maintaining information systems. The techniques contained in each row produce models that help develop architectures, and they use those architectures to develop information systems. Progression down the rows represents a sequence of one model driving development of the next model to final implementation. The Zachman Framework is a powerful paradigm for information system development and fits well with the information technology infrastructure presented above. It helps form a stable foundation that maintains an organization's competitive advantage.

Business Activity Framework

The business activity framework represents the business activities of an organization and the automation of those activities into business processes. It is the most dynamic framework in the infrastructure because it is closest to the changes that occur in the business world. Any change in the business world usually results in a change to one or more business activities.

Gaining control of disparate data helps in gaining control of disparate business processes.

The implementation of business activities into business processes is about as disparate as data are, and the increase in disparate business processes is increasing about as fast as disparate data. Disparate business processes need to be brought under control just like disparate data does. Any discussion of how control of disparate business processes can be gained is beyond the scope of this book. However, bringing disparate data under control will reduce the complexity and ease the process of bringing disparate business processes under control.

Platform Resource Framework

The platform resource framework represents the hardware and system software in an organization or between organizations. It is a resultant framework that is dependent on data, business activities, and information systems. It is responsive to the demands for storing, retrieving, processing, and communicating data. A detailed discussion of the platform resource is also beyond the scope of this book.

> *Data must be brought under control before open systems are*
> *fully implemented.*

The platform resource is also disparate, like data and business processes, and needs to be brought under control. It differs from data and business processes in that client/servers, open systems, and other efforts are attempting to resolve the disparate platform resource to provide open communications across heterogeneous platforms. The problem is that if these technologies are developed and fully implemented before data are brought under control, the proliferation of disparate data may be so great that data may never be brought under control. This is one compelling reason that data need to be brought under control as soon as possible.

Data Resource Framework

A data resource framework is a discipline for complete management of the data resource. It consists of three components for data management, data architecture, and data availability, as shown in Figure 2.2.

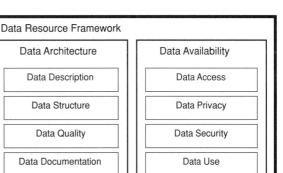

Figure 2.2 *The data resource framework.*

The goal of the data resource framework is:

> *The cooperative management of an enterprise-wide data architecture that ensures readily available data to support the enterprise's mission, goals, and business activities.*

The Data Management component contains all activities related to management of the data resource. The goal of the data resource management component is:

> *To develop a plan for building and managing a formal data resource that will lead an enterprise toward control of its data.*

The Data Management component contains four activities:

- Enterprise Resource ensures that data are managed as an enterprise resource.

- Management Principles ensures that data are managed by the same management principles as other resources.

- Cooperative Management ensures cooperative management of the data resource by the stakeholders.

- Business Integration ensures that data resource management plans are integrated with the business and information technology plans of the enterprise.

The Data Architecture component contains all the activities related to describing, structuring, maintaining quality, and documenting the data resource. The goal of the data architecture component is:

To develop an organization-wide data resource of well-described, properly structured, high-quality data that are properly documented.

The Data Architecture component contains four activities:

- Data Description ensures the formal naming and comprehensive definition of all data.

- Data Structure ensures the proper logical and physical structure of data.

- Data Quality ensures the maintenance of high-quality data.

- Data Documentation ensures current, complete, continuing documentation of the entire data architecture component.

The Data Availability component contains all activities related to making data available while properly protecting and securing those data. The goal of the data availability is:

To provide easily accessible data that are properly protected, adequately secured, and effectively and efficiently used.

The Data Availability component contains four activities:

- Data Access ensures rapidly identifiable, easily accessible, and readily shared data.

- Data Security ensures protection from unauthorized alteration, deletion, or destruction, and appropriate back-up and recovery procedures.

- Data Privacy ensures a person's or organization's right to privacy.

- Data Use ensures appropriate and ethical use of data.

All three components of the Data Resource Framework are important for managing data as a resource. However, the Data Management component and the Data Availability components are useless without the Data Architecture component. If there is no data architecture, there is nothing to manage and nothing to make available. Therefore, the emphasis is on the Data Architecture component.

Data Resource Management

Data resource management is the business activity responsible for designing, building, and maintaining the data resource of an organization and making data readily available for developing information. It is responsible for shifting an organization from being information-poor to being information-rich. Data resource management uses data engineering principles and techniques to build a formal data resource and ensures that those data evolve to a mature data resource.

> *Data resource management promotes an information-rich organization.*

The major purpose for data resource management in most organizations today is getting disparate data under control. Identifying, defining, and refining disparate data is time-consuming and costly. It is an enormous task to refine data, remove redundancies, identify variability and designate official data variations, and develop a formal data resource while continuing to support business operations. The task requires a chief data architect supported by a staff of data architects and data engineers to face the challenges and build a common data architecture.

▼ COMMON DATA ARCHITECTURE CONCEPT

Organizations need a common view across all their data so they can integrate those data and readily share them. They need a creative solution to their disparate data problem that provides short-term, incrementally cost-effective benefits while achieving the long-term goal of a mature data resource. A common data architecture provides that creative solution and helps achieve the reality of shared data.

Data Architecture Definition

The term *data architecture* has been defined narrowly as being synonymous with a data structure, and broadly as being anything associated with managing data as a resource, including strategic planning, tactical planning, personnel, and so on. The term has been defined so many times and used in so many ways without definition that it has become quite confusing.

Based on the definition of the Data Architecture component of the Data Resource Framework above, an initial definition of a data architecture is:

> *The component of the data resource framework that contains all activities, and the products of those activities, related to the identification, naming, definition, structuring, quality, and documentation of the data resource for an enterprise.*

However, this definition is not good enough for developing the data architecture of a formal data resource. A more formal definition is needed.

The term *architecture* has several definitions. First, it is the art, science, or profession of designing and building structures. Second, it is a structure or set of structures as a whole, such as the frame, heating, plumbing, or wiring in a building. Third, it is the style of structures and method of design and construction, such as Roman or Colonial architecture. Fourth, it is the design or system perceived by people, such as the architecture of the Solar System. *Architecture* is a term generally used in reference to buildings, bridges, and other structures, but it can apply to data as well.

These basic definitions for an architecture can be adjusted for a more formal definition of a data architecture. First, it is the art, science, or profession of designing and building a data resource. Second, it is the structure of the data resource as a whole. Third, it is the style or type of design and construction of the data resource. Fourth, it is a system perceived by people that represents the real world. Based on these adjustments, the formal definition of a data architecture is:

> *The science and method of designing and constructing a data resource that is business-driven, based on real world subjects, and implemented into appropriate operating environments; the overall structure of a data resource that provides a consistent foundation across organizational boundaries to provide easily identifiable, readily available, high-quality data to support business activities.*

A data architecture is similar to a building architecture. A building has a description that consists of the names and definitions of all the elements, such as pipes, wood, paint, windows, roofing, and so on. A building has a structure that shows the relationship of the elements and how they fit together, such as heating, wiring, plumbing, and phone through the walls, floors, and ceilings. A building has integrity that ensures the quality of the building, such as size and type of lumber, use of steel-reinforced concrete, type of paint, required maintenance, and so on. A building also has documentation in the form of plans, blueprints, specification sheets, and so on, about the other three components.

> *An entity-relationship diagram does not a data architecture make.*

Like the building architecture, a complete data architecture includes all the components, not just a one or two of them. A common perception of a data architecture is the traditional entity-relationship diagram prominent in data modeling. The entity-relationship diagram is only one technique for defining the structure of the data resource. It does not represent the total data architecture.

Common Data Architecture Definition

A *common data architecture* is a data architecture that provides a common context within which all data are defined to determine their true content and meaning so they can be integrated into a formal data resource and readily shared to support information needs. It is consistent across all data so they can be refined within a common context. It is a common base for formal naming, comprehensive definition, proper structuring, maintenance of quality, and complete documentation of all data.

> *A common data architecture is the common context for integrating and sharing widely disparate data.*

A common data architecture is structurally stable. It does not change for individual events. Projects come and go, schedules come and go, information systems come and go, people come and go, the data use changes, and data values go through their life cycle, but the architecture remains structurally stable.

A common data architecture is extensible and enhancable. It can be extended into new areas, such as finance, marketing, and personnel. Its contents can be enhanced by adding new data that are needed and removing old data that are no longer needed. A common data architecture evolves with the organization and its changing information needs.

The common data architecture is vendor-neutral, hardware-neutral, application-neutral, and platform-independent. It represents both the logical data that represent the real world and the physical data that exist in any operating environment. It is also development method– and CASE tool–independent.

Building and implementing a common data architecture does not require restructuring all existing databases or converting existing data files. It does not require changing data names in programs or data dictionaries. It does not require changing all documentation that refers to data. It represents all data and all references to data through cross references.

Common Data Architecture Scope

The common data architecture encompasses the formal data resource. It includes disparate data within an organization and across many organizations. It includes primitive and derived data; tabular and non-tabular data; elemental and combined data; automated and non-automated data; historical, current, and projection data. It includes data used by traditional information systems, expert systems, executive information systems, geographic information systems, and object-oriented systems. It includes data in purchased software, home-built applications, databases, programs, screens, reports, and documents. It includes centralized and decentralized data. It is common across all business activities, all projects, and all information systems.

The common data architecture transcends all data.

The specific use of data is outside the scope of the common data architecture. The common data architecture documents only the true meaning and content of data and does not include the use of data. The actual use of data is defined during a specific project and is documented in the information system.

Common Data Architecture Use

A common data architecture has many uses that may vary with each organization. A few of the more prominent uses are described below.

- Disparate data are refined and integrated into the formal data resource within a common data architecture. Many data integration efforts fail because there is no common base for integration. Any attempt to integrate disparate data without a common data architecture is a high-risk effort.

- Data variability is identified and official data variations are easily designated within a common data architecture. Data translation schemes are developed quickly.

- Redundant data are reduced to a known and manageable level: all redundant data is identified, and unnecessary redundant data is removed. The primary source of redundant data is identified and becomes the repository of record for all other secondary existences of redundant data.

- Data can be readily shared within an organization and between organizations using a common data architecture. Data collected and used for one purpose can be reused for other purposes. Many data sharing attempts fail because there is no common context for sharing. Any attempt to share disparate data without a common data architecture is a high-risk effort.

- Data surveys and inventories of existing data are conducted within a common data architecture to provide a portfolio of the data resource; this portfolio shows what data exist and where they are located.

- Data needs are identified within a common data architecture. The data needs are easily compared with data inventories to determine what data exist and what data need to be collected or acquired.

- Organizations can collaborate and cooperate on the collection of new data and exchange data they have already collected. They can leverage limited funding by coordinating their data collection efforts.

- Data design and modeling for information systems at the project level is done within the common data architecture to ensure that existing data are used and that only unavailable data are collected or acquired.

- A common data architecture assists with development of decentralized databases through the proper deployment of data on a network.

- Re-engineering data from one database management system to another, known as *forward and reverse engineering*, is accomplished much more easily within a common data architecture.

- Sharing data readily across organizational boundaries minimizes the impact of organizational changes. The existence of common data allows people to concentrate on realigning business activities and other aspects of organizational changes.

- Priorities are set within the common data architecture so that due consideration is given to other non-priority data. If the common data architecture is prioritized, due consideration may not be given to unprioritized data. It is easier to extend priority when it is established within the common data architecture than when the architecture itself is prioritized.

Common Data Architecture Benefits

A common data architecture provides many benefits for an organization. The prominent benefits are described below.

- People have a better understanding of data when those data are defined in a common data architecture. They also have a better understanding of the business through a better understanding of the data.

- People have a better understanding of the current state of the data resource. A common data architecture increases awareness and reduces uncertainty about the data resource. People accept the current state of the data resource and begin to improve data to meet their needs.

- A common data architecture ensures consistency across the data resource. It ensures that data are formally named, comprehensively defined, and properly structured, that they have high quality and known accuracy, and that they are properly documented.

- A common data architecture provides stability across dynamic business activities. Business activities change frequently in a rapidly changing business environment. A stable data resource ensures that data are available to meet information needs.

- A common data architecture allows an organization to achieve short-term, incrementally cost-effective benefits from a formal data architecture while achieving the long-term goal of a mature data resource. It helps managers focus on the critical data first and leverage limited funding to develop an effective formal data resource.

- People knowledgeable about data and the business can reach consensus about the true meaning and content of data, and about the designation of official data variations when data are defined within a common data architecture. A common data architecture facilitates consensus from below, rather than allowing mandates from above.

- Integrating data within a common data architecture reduces the volume of data in the mature data resource by 20% to 60% through the removal of unnecessary redundant data and converting non-official data variations to official data variations.

- A common data architecture stabilizes the data resource so that more effort can be spent on the dynamic architectures in the infrastructure, such as business activities and information systems. Many business activity and organization issues are often masked by disparate data.

- A common data architecture makes the task of building information systems easier by providing common data and allowing them to be structured by business activities. It helps avoid inflexible, interface-bound bridges between information systems. Information systems can use subsets of a common data architecture rather than developing separate, disjoint data architecture.

They can be built in shorter time, with reduced risks, and they require less maintenance.

- A common data architecture allows people to make more informed decisions. It does not improve the decision making process, but it does provide a better understanding of the data. This allows the right information to be developed from the right data and results in more informed decisions.

- The common data architecture improves productivity by allowing people to spend more time on performing their business activities and less time on finding data, because data can be easily identified and readily accessed.

- A common data architecture supports innovative and creative solutions to business problems by allowing people to spend more time on understanding the business and improving business processes than on identifying and understanding data.

▼ BUILDING A COMMON DATA ARCHITECTURE

Many organizations today are data-rich and information-poor. They have tremendous quantities of data, but very little information. They need to shift to an information-rich organization by building a formal data resource under a common data architecture. However, building a formal data resource under a common data architecture on a project by project basis will take a long time, and may never be completed.

Many projects today develop formal, but disjoint, data architectures that are not compatible across projects. Most of these data architectures are for new data, not disparate data. Occasionally, these data architectures are integrated across several projects and a few are integrated within the organization, usually for small organizations. Very few data architectures are integrated for large organizations and virtually none are integrated across multiple organizations.

Most projects today are propagating the disparate data situation.

The only way all new and disparate data can be integrated within an organization and across organizations is through a common data architecture. Building a common data architecture is not easy, but it is not impossible. It requires a whole different set of techniques to deal with the uncertainty and variability inherent in disparate data, and a tremendous amount of thought and intuition. But even more than new techniques, thought, and intuition, it requires an understanding of the business, a way of viewing the real world, and an approach to structuring data by subjects.

Business Understanding

Building a common data architecture to support an organization's information needs requires a thorough understanding of the business. A common data architecture is *meta-data*—data about the data that support the business activities of an organization. If the people building a common data architecture do not understand the business, they cannot understand the data supporting the business, and they certainly cannot develop meta-data about those data.

> *Understanding the business ensures that the formal data resource will support the business.*

Development of traditional information systems is process-driven, based on the activities an organization performs. This approach is weak, because data cross business activities. The data-driven approach to developing information systems attempts to correct this weakness, but it is also weak for the same reason. A business-driven approach uses an understanding of the organizations business to drive the development of information systems and the data to support those information systems. This *business-oriented information engineering* approach is the only way information engineering will be successful.

A business understanding requires direct client involvement—the direct involvement of people knowledgeable about the business and the data supporting the business. The best approach to building a common data architecture is a partnership between data architects, data engineers, and knowledgeable clients. This partnership allows clients to exploit their knowledge of the business and the data supporting the business to build a common data architecture.

Real World

Understanding an organization's business requires a understanding of the real world where that business is operating. It requires an understanding of the way an organization views the real world, identifies objects in the real world, and interacts with those objects. It is the understanding of the organization's view of real-world objects and interactions with those objects that drives the basic structure of the common data architecture.

One problem with understanding an organization's view of the real world is that different organizations have different views of the real world. For example, different organizations may see the same people as patients, drivers, students, home owners, employees, and so on. Different organizations may look at vehicles as motorized and unmotorized, as commercial and non-commercial, or as licensed and unlicensed. These different views often result in identification of different objects and different interactions with those objects, and often result in different data architectures. Integrating these different data architectures within large organizations or across many organizations is difficult.

> *A common data architecture integrates objects identified from different views of the real world.*

A common data architecture integrates different views of the real world and the objects identified by those different views. It allows different views of the same real-world object to be placed in their proper perspectives so that one organization can understand another organization's view. Understanding different views of real-world objects helps organizations cooperate in the collection, exchange, and use of data.

Subject Data

Objects identified in the real world and an organization's interactions with those objects provide the basic structure of a common data architecture. The objects and interactions are used to identify data subjects and characteristics about those data subjects. These data subjects and characteristics form the core of the common data architecture.

Data cannot be organized by business activities because data cross business activities. Structuring data by one business activity could limit use of those data by other business activities, and could result in unnecessarily redundant data. Data must be organized by data subjects based on objects and interactions in the real world. These data cross business activities so they remain stable and reusable by many business activities.

Subject data consist of data subject, data characteristics, data values, and data occurrences. These terms are defined below and are used throughout this book.

- A *data subject* is a person, place, thing, event, or concept about which an organization collects and manages data. Data subjects are identified by the organization's view of the real world. For example, employee, city, vehicle, traffic accident, and customer account are data subjects as perceived by the organization. A data subject is also known as a *data entity*. Either term is acceptable, but *data subject* is more acceptable and less technical.

- A *data characteristic* is an individual feature or trait of a data subject. A data subject is described by a set of data characteristics. For example, birth date, height, weight, and Social Security Number are characteristics of an employee. Make, model, and color are characteristics of vehicles. A data characteristic is also known as a *data attribute*. Either term is acceptable, but *data characteristic* is more people-oriented and less technical.

- A *data value* represents the individual facts and figures contained in data characteristics. An *actual data value* is an actual measurement, value, or description of a trait or feature of a data subject. For example, *12/24/87* is an employee's birth date, *blue* is the color of a vehicle, and *127.36* is the balance in a customer's account. A *coded data value*, referred to as a *data code*, is actual data that have been codified in some way. For example, codes *1, 2,* and *3* represent *Probationary Employees, Temporary Employees,* and *Permanent Employees*, respectively.

- A *data code set* is a set of data codes that are closely related. For example, all of the data codes pertaining to types of vehicles belong together as a set of Vehicle Type Codes, and all the data codes pertaining to land use belong together as a set of Land Use Codes.

- A *data occurrence* is a logical record that represents one existence of a data subject in the real world. For example, employee *John J. Smith* is represented by a data occurrence in the Employee data subject. A data occurrence is sometimes referred to as a *data instance*. However, *data instance* is used to refer to a period of time, not to an occurrence in a data subject.

▼ SUMMARY

When electricity first became available, it required an expert to come to the office, home, or factory to do special wiring, because there were no common voltages, plug sizes, or wire sizes. Eventually, common voltages, plugs, and wires were established and a whole set of plug-compatible equipment became available. This equipment can now be purchased and installed by any novice. An expert is no longer required.

The same situation is true with data today. Disparate data require an expert to perform special modeling for each project because there is no common context for defining data. Special modeling is expensive and continues to create additional disparate data. It does not solve the problem any more than the electrical expert solved the problem. A common base is required so that all data can be defined and shared within a common context. Clients can then use data to support their information needs without the constant services of an expert.

A common data architecture provides that common base. It provides a base for identifying the true content and meaning of disparate data in a common context and integrating them, along with new data, into a formal data resource. It provides an evolutionary path from a formal data resource to a mature data resource. It provides a way for organizations to resolve their disparate data situations and prevent those situations from ever happening again.

Building a common data architecture is a real change for most people. It requires a new way of thinking about data, and involves understanding the business and viewing the real world where that business operates. It requires cooperation by all stakeholders to develop a credible formal data resource consisting of data subjects. It requires new concepts and techniques that are technologically sound and readily accepted.

The last chapter posed the question of whether building a formal data resource within a common data architecture is worthwhile. Is a change worth the cost and effort? After reviewing the trends, the state of an organization's data resource, the information needs of an organization in a rapidly changing world, the evolution of open systems and client/servers, and the capabilities of a common data architecture, the answer should be a resounding *Yes!*

Building a common data architecture may seem expensive, but not building one is even more expensive. However, organizations should not be concerned with the expense of building or not building a common data architecture. Instead, they should be concerned about building a common data architecture that provides short-term, incrementally cost-effective deliverables; it must pay its way. They should also be concerned about achieving the long-term vision of a mature data resource that provides data for every information need. They should be concerned about making the shared data vision a reality.

▼ QUESTIONS

The following questions are designed to provide a review of Chapter 2, and to stimulate thought about how to build a common data architecture, what problems it resolves, and whether the effort is worthwhile.

1. What is an infrastructure and how does it apply to information technology?

2. Why are business activities and the platform resource as disparate as data?

3. What is the Data Resource Framework?

4. Why is emphasis placed on the Data Architecture Activity of the Data Resource Component?

5. What is Data Resource Management?

6. What is a data architecture?

7. What is a common data architecture?

8. What is the scope of a common data architecture?

9. How can a common data architecture be useful to an organization?

10. What are the benefits of a common data architecture to an organization?

11. Why is it important to understand the business when building a common data architecture?

12. Why is it necessary to have direct client involvement when building a common data architecture?

13. Why is a view of the real world important for building a common data architecture?

14. Why are different views of the real world a problem?

15. Why is it important to build a data resource based on subject data?

16. Is it worthwhile for an organization to build a common data architecture?

▼▼▼ 3

DATA NAMES

A formal data naming taxonomy and supporting vocabulary
provide the base for uniquely identifying all data.

Data Description is the first activity in the Data Architecture component of the Data Resource Framework. It includes the formal naming and comprehensive definition of data. All data, regardless of their location, regardless of their use, whether they are automated or manual, and whether they are primitive or derived, must have a formal name and a comprehensive definition.

Developing formal data names is a relatively easy, though often ignored, process. Failure to formally name all data leads to disparate data. Proliferation of additional disparate data can be avoided and existing disparate data can be uniquely identified if a few simple principles are followed for properly naming data.

This chapter presents a formal data naming taxonomy that was originally presented in a previous book (Brackett, 1990). It begins with an explanation of semiotic theory and existing data naming conventions. A set of criteria for developing a formal data naming taxonomy are presented, followed by an explanation of the data naming taxonomy and its supporting vocabulary. Next, the process for naming data repositories, data subjects, data characteristics, data characteristic variations, data codes, data name substitution, and data name abbreviations is explained.

▼ DATA NAMING CONCEPT

A data name is the first thing people see when dealing with data. They may be clients, programmers, or database analysts, and they may see a report, a screen, a document, a program, a file listing, or a data dictionary. Regardless of who they are or what they see, the data name is what they use to identify, understand, and use data.

> *The data naming taxonomy and vocabulary provide unique*
> *names for all logical and physical data.*

Data in a common data architecture have formal data names based on a data naming taxonomy and a data naming vocabulary that supports that taxonomy. The data naming taxonomy and vocabulary are based on semiotic theory that provides a formal syntax for the name, enhanced meaning through common words, and practical value. They provide a unique label for every piece of logical and physical data in the data resource.

Definitions

The terms *data subject*, *data characteristic*, *data occurrence*, and *data value* were defined in the last chapter. Several additional terms need to be defined before the data naming taxonomy and vocabulary are discussed.

A *data repository* is a specific location where data are stored. That location may be a manual filing cabinet, a data file, or a formal database management system. It may be located in a city, in a building, or on a computer. For example, data may be stored in the Employee file, in the Equipment file in Chicago, or in archive boxes in the main office basement. Each of these data storages is a data repository.

A *data characteristic variation* represents a difference in the format, content, or meaning of a specific data characteristic. It does not represent a different data characteristic or an alias of a data characteristic. For example, the depth of a well is a data characteristic about a well. However, the depth of that well could be measured in feet, yards, or meters. Each of these variations in measurement is a data characteristic variation. Similarly, a person's name is a characteristic about that person. However, the name could be in either a normal or an inverted sequence; each sequence is a variation of the same name.

A *data name* is a label for a data repository, data subject, data characteristic, data characteristic variation, or data code. Ideally, a data name should be unique within the common data architecture, it should be meaningful, and it should be developed within a formal taxonomy.

An *actual data value* is an actual measurement, value, or description of a trait or feature of a data subject. For example, a customer's name and an employee's height are actual data values. A *coded data value* is a coded form of an actual data value. For example, disabilities might be coded such that *1* represents a *Speech Disability*, *2* represents a *Sight Disability*, and so on.

Coded data values are commonly referred to as *data codes*. A *data code value* is the value of the code, such as *1* and *2* in the example above. A *data code name* is the formal name of the data code, such as *Speech Disability* and *Sight Disability* in the example above. A *data code definition* is the comprehensive definition of a data code.

Logical data are references to data that appear on a data resource model, in a data architecture, or in other documentation about the data resource. They represent the existence of physical data or a plan for development of physical data. All logical data must be formally named by the data naming taxonomy so they can be uniquely identified.

Physical data are data that actually exist in a data file, database, database management system, or manual storage. All physical data must be formally named so they can be uniquely identified, and so the data repository where they reside is known.

Semiotic Theory

Semiotics is the general theory of signs and symbols and their use in expression and communication. *Semiotic theory* is the branch of philosophy dealing with semiotics. It consists of syntatics, semantics, and pragmatics. *Syntatics* deals with the relation between signs and symbols and their interpretation, specifically the rules of syntax for using signs and symbols. *Semantics* deals with the relation between signs and symbols and what they represent, specifically their meaning. *Pragmatics* deals with the relations between signs and symbols and their uses, focusing specifically on their usefulness.

A common data architecture is a set of signs and symbols that expresses and communicates the design of a formal data resource. It is therefore part of semiotics, and should include all three parts of semiotic theory. A common data architecture must have specific rules for syntax, an explicit meaning, and a practical value. Formal data names are part of a common data architecture and must also have specific rules for syntax, explicit meaning, and practical value.

Formal data names are based on semiotic theory.

Syntatics requires that a formal data name have a specific, consistent format. If the format varies from one data name to another, it is very difficult for people to understand those data names. One of the worst things in a common data architecture is to have inconsistent data name formats. Therefore, all formal data names must have a specific, consistent format so that they can be readily understood.

Semantics requires that a formal data name have a specific meaning. If the meaning is unclear or varies from one data name to another, it is very difficult for people to understand those data names. Therefore, a formal data name must have a specific meaning.

Pragmatics requires that the formal data name have practical value. If a data name does not have a practical value, it is not useful. Therefore, a formal data name must have practical value.

Data Naming Conventions

Traditional data names are usually abbreviations and truncations developed on-the-fly as programs are written or data files are defined. They are usually abbreviated because of physical limitations and are not consistent across programs or data files. There is usually no convention or structure to the names, and often there is no meaning. Consequently, there are many homonyms and synonyms. Most of us are painfully aware of this situation.

Traditional data names provide no support for a common data architecture.

A variety of data naming conventions have evolved to resolve problems with traditional data names, and many of these conventions are in use today.

The *Of Language* was an early attempt to put structure and formality into data names by progressing from the specific to the general and placing the word *of* between each pair of words. For example, an employee's birth date would be Date of Birth of Employee. This data naming convention provided a structure and formality that did not exist in many traditional data names. However, it resulted in longer data names that often exceeded length restrictions, and the data names were in a sequence that was foreign to most people. As a result, this data naming convention is not commonly used today.

Data naming conventions provide more structure and meaning than traditional data names.

The *entity–attribute–class* data naming convention consists of an entity name, an attribute name, and a class word. The *entity* is the subject about which data are collected and stored by the organization. The *attribute* is a characteristic that describes the entity. The *class* is a standard keyword that indicates the type and general format of the attribute, such as *date, number, description,* and so on. For example, an employee's birth date would be Employee Birth Date, where Employee is the *entity,* Birth is the *attribute,* and Date is the *class.* The same is true for Employee Social Security Number: Employee is the *entity,* Social Security is the *attribute,* and Number is the *class.*

The *role–type–class, prime–descriptor–class, entity–adjective–class, entity–attribute–class word, entity–description–class, entity keyword–minor keyword–type keyword,* and *entity keyword–descriptor–domain* are similar data naming conventions. The difference is the words representing the components of the data name. *Role, prime, entity,* and *entity keyword* identify the data subject. *Type, descriptor, adjective, attribute, minor keyword,* and *description* identify the data characteristic. *Class, class word, minor keyword,* and *domain* identify the class.

Although these data naming conventions provide data names that have more structure and meaning than traditional data names, none of these conventions is robust enough for a common data architecture. They do not meet the requirements of semiotics for the following reasons:

- The names of the data name components do not provide any real meaning about the structure of a data name. Most clients do not understand what *role, prime, descriptor, class, class word, minor keyword*, and *domain* mean. If they don't understand the components of a name, they won't understand the name.

- The words used to form the data name are often abbreviated, and those abbreviations are often inconsistent. These problems limit the meaning of a data name. Although this may not be a fault of the data naming convention itself, it is a fault of the implementation of the convention, meaning that the convention is not robust enough to enforce consistent abbreviations.

- Data names often indicate the use of data. Data could have many different uses, which could result in many different names for the same data. This practice leads to synonyms and redundant data. Even though this problem may be the fault of the implementation of a data naming convention, it means that the convention is not robust enough to enforce data names that do not indicate the use of the data.

- Data names do not always indicate the structure of data. The purpose of the first component of most data naming conventions is to identify the data subject. If those names were properly developed, they would indicate the structure of the data subjects in the data resource. However, most data naming conventions are not robust enough to enforce data names that indicate the structure of data.

- Physical data names do not indicate the data repository. Most data naming conventions apply only to logical data modeling and design, without concern for how data are physically implemented, or they assume only one physical implementation. Therefore, they do not include a component for defining the physical location. As data are deployed over a network, it is important to know the data repository. It is also important to know the exact location of existing disparate data when they are refined into the common data architecture.

- Data names do not identify variations of the same data characteristic. New logical data seldom have variations in data characteristics. However, existing disparate data often have many variations of the same data characteristic that need to be uniquely identified.

- Data names do not apply to data codes. Data codes need to be formally named so they can be uniquely identified and readily understood.

> *Current data naming conventions are not robust enough for unique identification of all logical and physical data.*

Therefore, the existing data naming conventions are not acceptable for the common data architecture. Although they may be acceptable for logical design and modeling of new data on small projects, they are not robust enough for unique identification of all logical and physical data in a common data architecture.

Data Naming Criteria

The new approach for naming data in the common data architecture is a formal data naming taxonomy and supporting vocabulary based on semiotics. The approach consists of a goal and a set of criteria to assure consistent, meaningful names that uniquely identify all logical and physical data in a common data architecture. The goal is:

> *To provide consistent, unique, and meaningful names for all existing and new data repositories, data subjects, data characteristics, data characteristic variations, and data codes in a common data architecture.*

The criteria to meet this goal are:

- Each data repository, data subject, data characteristic, data characteristic variation, and data code must have one and only one primary data name.

- The primary data name must be the real-world, fully spelled out name that is not codified or abbreviated and is not subject to any length restrictions. There a few exceptions, explained later, that allow abbreviations.

- The primary data name for logical data must uniquely identify each data subject, data characteristic, data characteristic variation, or data code within the common data architecture.

- The primary data name for physical data must uniquely identify each data repository, data subject, data characteristic, data characteristic variation, or data code within the common data architecture.

- The primary data name must provide consistency throughout the common data architecture.

- The primary data name must be fully qualified, meaningful, understandable, and unambiguous.

- The primary data name must indicate the true content and meaning of data, not the use of the data.

- The primary data name must identify variations in form, content, and meaning.

- The primary data name must indicate the logical structure of data subjects, data characteristics, and data characteristic variations in the common data architecture.

- The components of the primary data name must progress from the general to the specific.

- All other names are secondary data names that are cross referenced to the primary data name.

Data Naming Taxonomy

Taxonomy is the science of classification, a system for arranging things into natural, related groups based on common features. Plants and animals are classified and uniquely named according to a taxonomy initially developed in the 1730s by Carolus Linnaeus. It is a robust taxonomy that has lasted for several hundred years and includes thousands of organisms. The Dewey Decimal system, the ZIP code system, and chemical names are examples of robust classification systems.

The *data naming taxonomy* for a common data architecture is based on the goal and criteria described above. It provides a system for arranging data into related groups and uniquely naming them that is consistent throughout the common data architecture. It provides a common language for naming data.

A formal data naming taxonomy is based on the goal and criteria for naming data in a common data architecture.

The data naming taxonomy establishes common data names that can be used by anyone. The situation is similar to using a common language for air traffic control. Air traffic controllers world-wide use English regardless of the country where the air traffic controller is located or the native language of the pilots. All spoken communication from the pilot to the air traffic controller is in English. Translation to the language of the country is done on the ground and translation to the language of the cockpit is done in the plane. English is the common communication between the cockpit and the air traffic controller.

The same situation is true with common data names. As existing disparate data are identified and documented, their local names are cross referenced (translated) to the primary data name. As new logical data are identified, they are named according to the data naming taxonomy. As new data are decentralized or deployed on a network, the data repository name is added to their logical data name to make a unique physical data name. This approach allows people familiar with their local data to work with those data using their local data names. It also allows people using different local data names to work with each other through a common data name.

The data naming taxonomy consists of four components: the data repository, the data subject, the data characteristic, and the data characteristic variation.

Repository: Subject.Characteristic,Variation

A colon follows the repository name, a period follows the subject name, and a comma follows the characteristic name in the formal data naming taxonomy. However, in common practice, the punctuation is often left out of the name.

The data naming taxonomy provides unique data names for all logical and physical data within the common data architecture.

The components of the data naming taxonomy can be used in several combinations. The data repository, data subject, and data characteristic components are used to uniquely identify disparate data that currently exist. The data subject, data characteristic, and data characteristic variation components are used to uniquely identify all logical data in the common data architecture. All four components are used to uniquely identify all new physical data deployed throughout an organization or on a network within the common data architecture. Each of these uses is explained in more detail throughout the book.

Data Naming Vocabulary

The biggest problem with implementing the data naming taxonomy is the use of class words. There is very little concern over the use of data subject and data characteristic names rather than the data naming convention component names, or with the addition of data repository or data characteristic variation names. The most concern, and the most resistance, comes from changing the concept of a class word.

The most resistance to a formal data naming taxonomy comes from changing the concept of a class word.

Class words provide a standard structure and format for data values by using standard words to represent classes of data, such as integer, string, date, or name. They increase the meaning of a data name over that of traditional data names and provide preliminary data editing rules. They originated as an early attempt to define data domains and data integrity rules. They resolve many of the problems with traditional data names. However, there are several problems with the use of class words:

- Class words apply only to the data characteristic component of a data name. All four components of the data naming taxonomy could have their own class words to provide the same benefits as the class word for the data characteristic component.

- The requirement for one and only one class word may cause unnecessary words in a data name. There are situations where the class word is strongly implied by other words in the data characteristic name, and addition of a required class word is redundant and makes a longer data name. For example, *Amount* is a class word meaning a monetary amount, not a quantity or capacity. It should be used whenever a data characteristic represents a monetary amount. However, *Depreciation, Price,* and *Charge* imply that an amount is involved, so it is not necessary to add the class word *Amount.*

- The class word does not show variations in format, content, or meaning. For example, a class word indicates that a data characteristic is a date, but does not indicate the format of that date. It could also indicate that the data characteristic is text, but not specify the length of the text. Therefore, several data characteristics that contain the same class word may be variations of a data characteristic.

- The requirement for a class word at the end of the data name gets in the way of the data characteristic variation name. The general-to-specific rule for a data name requires that the data characteristic variation component follow the data characteristic component.

The class word concept is expanded to a data naming vocabulary to support all components of the data naming taxonomy.

For these reasons, the class word concept is expanded to a full data naming vocabulary to support all components of the data naming taxonomy. A *vocabulary* is a set of words or phrases used for a particular purpose. The *data naming vocabulary* is a set of common words for each component of the data naming taxonomy. Each common word has a specific meaning that is consistent whenever that word is used in a data name.

The term *common word* is used rather than *keyword* because it is compatible with the common data architecture concept. *Class word* is avoided because of the current class word concept. *Standard word* is avoided because of the implication that standards are mandated. *Common word* implies a consensus and a willingness to create common words for data names within a common data architecture.

The data naming vocabulary provides common words with common meanings for all data names.

The data naming vocabulary is much like the vocabulary for naming chemicals. For example, *methyl, ethyl, propyl, butyl,* and *pentyl* identify the number of carbon atoms in a ring, *ol* indicates an alcohol, and *ane* indicates a gas. The combination of these words produces *methanol, ethanol, propanol, butanol,* and *pentanol,* which identify a series of alcohols formed by carbon rings, and *methane, ethane, propane, butane,* and *pentane,* which identify a series of gases formed by carbon rings. The structure and contents of chemical compounds are also indicated in the name. For example, *n-butane, 2,4,5-trichloro-phenoxy-acetic-acid,* and *2,4-dichloro-phenoxy-acetic-acid* indicate the structure and contents of those chemical compounds.

Even though this example uses words rooted in Latin or Greek, they are useful for uniquely naming chemicals. The data naming vocabulary could have been rooted in Latin or Greek, or it could have had a purely mathematical base, but these approaches would have been confusing to many clients. Clients would have had to learn something new just to understand the data. The criteria for a data naming taxonomy, based on semiotics, are oriented toward maximum understanding with minimum additional learning. Therefore, the class word concept was expanded to the four components of the data naming taxonomy.

An initial set of common words for the four components of the data naming taxonomy is shown in Appendix A. Each organization should enhance this initial set and develop a data naming vocabulary that supports its own common data architecture. As additional words are encountered during development of a common data architecture, they should be added to the vocabulary.

▼ DATA NAMING PROCESS

Formally naming data is the first step in building a common data architecture. However, formally naming data often requires comprehensive definition and proper structuring. In many cases, these processes form a cyclic process of discovery. A formal data name depends on comprehensive definition and proper structuring, proper structuring often depends on comprehensive definition, a comprehensive definition often depends on proper structuring, and so forth. The best place to start this discovery cycle is with a thorough understanding of how to formally name data.

Data Repository Names

A *data repository name* consists of one or more words that uniquely identify a specific data repository. Generally, one to four words are sufficient to uniquely name a data repository. For example, Payroll, Seattle Payroll, Dallas IBM 3090 Payroll, and New York Personnel identify specific data repositories.

Data repository names are used whenever physical data are documented. They uniquely identify the physical location of existing disparate data, and they uniquely identify the physical location of data deployed throughout an organization or on a network. Most data naming conventions concentrate on the logical design of new logical data and don't consider naming existing disparate data or deploying new physical data. However, a data repository name is needed to uniquely identify and document existing disparate data and to uniquely identify the deployment of new physical data.

> *A data repository name is necessary to properly document existing disparate data and to document the deployment of new data.*

Common words add consistency and meaning to data repository names. Cities, buildings, computers, files, reports, screens, and documents can provide common words for data repository names. For example, if data were located in three cities, such as *Chicago, Los*

Angeles, and *Dallas,* those city names would be data repository common words.

Data repository common words may vary from one organization to another. A set of data repository common words should be defined and maintained for naming data repositories in a common data architecture. If the common data architecture includes more than one organization, the data repository name must uniquely identify each data repository across all those organizations.

Data Subject Names

A *data subject name* consists of one or more words that uniquely identify each data subject in the common data architecture and indicates the structure of the formal data resource. The name must be long enough to be meaningful and unique, but not so long that it becomes a definition. Generally, one to four words is sufficient to uniquely identify a data subject and to indicate its meaning and structure. More than four words becomes excessive and adds little to the meaning. For example, Appointment is not unique because there could be a variety of appointments, such as medical appointments, meeting appointments, or employee appointments to positions or committees. Unique data subject names would be Doctor Appointment, Meeting Appointment, Employee Appointment, Committee Appointment, and so on.

---

*Each data subject must be uniquely named within the common
data architecture.*

Common words may be used in data subject names to add consistency and meaning across data subjects, and to indicate the structure of data in the organization's common data architecture. Common words like *Activity, History, Suspense, Validation,* and *Authorization* could be data subject common words. For example, Student, Employee, and Customer data subjects each might have Activity, Suspense, and History data. The combination of the data subjects and the common words produces nine data subjects that provide consistency and meaning and indicate the structure of data.

Data subject common words may vary from one organization to another. Each organization should develop and maintain a set of data subject common words. If a common data architecture includes more than one organization, the data subject common words must include all the organizations.

Data Characteristic Names

A unique *data characteristic name* consists of the data subject name followed by the data characteristic name. The data subject name provides uniqueness within the common data architecture and the data characteristic name provides uniqueness within the data subject. Together they provide uniqueness for each data characteristic in the common data architecture.

Each data characteristic must be uniquely named within a data subject.

The data characteristic name must be long enough to be unique within a data subject, but not so long that it becomes a definition. Generally, one to five words are sufficient to uniquely identify a data characteristic within a data subject. A name longer than five words is excessive and becomes a definition. For example, Equipment Date is not unique or meaningful because there could be many different dates for a piece of equipment. Better data characteristic names might be Equipment Manufacture Date, Equipment Purchase Date, or Equipment Install Date. A data characteristic name like Date Salesman Said Equipment Would Be Shipped is too long. It could be shortened to Equipment Salesman Ship Date and provide the same meaning and uniqueness.

The words in a data characteristic name should progress from general to specific, like the sequence of components in the data naming taxonomy. For example, a person's name could be complete or abbreviated. The general-to-specific sequence places the words Complete and Abbreviated after the word Name because they are more specific qualifications of a person's name, producing Person Name Complete and Person Name Normal.

Another way to understand the sequence of words in a data characteristic name is with implied words that are not shown. For example, Day Number Calendar Year is the number of the day within a Calendar Year. Putting *Number* at the end would form Day Calendar Year

Number, but it is not the Calendar Year Number, it is the Day Number. *Number* belongs with Day, not with Calendar Year. The name would certainly not be Calendar Year Day Number because the data subject is not Calendar Year. In this situation, the implied words might be Day Number **within a** Calendar Year, or Day Number **in** Calendar Year **sequence**.

Data characteristic names must be fully qualified to avoid any confusion or uncertainty. For example, Equipment Ship Date appears to be fully qualified. However, there could be a planned ship date as stated by the salesman, a planned ship date as confirmed by the factory, and the actual ship date. To be fully qualified, the names could be Equipment Salesman Ship Date, Equipment Factory Ship Date, and Equipment Actual Ship Date.

Some adjustment of the general-to-specific rule is acceptable for normal English usage. In the example above, the data characteristic names could have been Equipment Ship Salesman Date, Equipment Ship Factory Date, and Equipment Ship Actual Date if they followed the general-to-specific rule. However, these data names just don't sound right to many people and were adjusted for maximum understanding.

> *An organization must plan ahead when developing a common data architecture to ensure that all data characteristic names are fully qualified.*

Common words may be used to add consistency and meaning across data characteristic names. Common words like *Date, Number, Quantity, Identification, Value, Amount,* and *Description* are data characteristic common words. For example, Equipment Purchase Date, Class Description, and Part Order Quantity use the common words *Date, Description,* and *Quantity.*

Combined is a common word meaning that a data characteristic is a concatenation of several other data characteristics. For example, date and time may be combined into a single data characteristic that might be named Chronology Combined. The data definition would explain the combination. *Combined* is not used for an expected combination of data characteristics, such as a date consisting of century, calendar year, month, and day. It is also not used when another word indicates a combination, such as Employee Name Complete.

There is one problem with an absolute, rigid implementation of data characteristic common words. Some common usages that violate the common words are very difficult to change. For example, license places on vehicles contain a License Number that is often not a number, such as *XYZ 123*. The value of the license number violates the definition of the common word *Number.* However, it may be difficult to change the data characteristic name to License Identifier because of common usage. Therefore, when common usage violates the definition of a common word, and it would be difficult to alter common usage, it is better to accept the violation.

An organization should develop and maintain a set of data characteristic common words and use them consistently for naming data in the common data architecture. If a common data architecture includes more than one organization, the data characteristic common words must include all the organizations.

Data Characteristic Variation Names

A *data characteristic variation name* consists of one or more words that uniquely identify a variation of a data characteristic. The data characteristic variation name follows the data characteristic name. The name must be long enough to be meaningful and uniquely identify the variation, but not so long that it becomes a definition. Generally, one or two words are sufficient to uniquely identify a data characteristic variation. For example, an employee's complete name may be in several different forms, such as the normal sequence, *John William Smith*, and the inverted sequence, *Smith, John William.* The data characteristic is Employee Name Complete and the data characteristic variations are Employee Name Complete Normal and Employee Name Complete Inverted.

Each variation of a data characteristic must be uniquely identified in a common data architecture.

The same data characteristic often exists in many different lengths that can be identified by the data characteristic variation. For example, City Name is a data characteristic, but it can exist both as 20 characters and as 35 characters. The data characteristic variation names are City Name 20 and City Name 35.

More than one data characteristic variation can be used in a data name. For example, if Employee Name Complete Normal existed in two different lengths of 42 characters and 56 characters, the data characteristic variation names would be Employee Name Complete Normal 42 and Employee Name Complete Normal 56.

A data characteristic variation can designate the format of the data. For example, Employee Birth Date CYMD and Employee Birth Date MDY provide explicit information about the format variations of an employee's birth date.

A data characteristic variation can indicate accuracy, resolution, units of measurement, source of data, meaning, content, and a variety of other criteria. For example, Vehicle Speed Estimated and Vehicle Speed Measured, Employee Height Inches and Employee Height Centimeters, County Code Numeric and County Code Alpha, and Person Birth Date CYMD Certificate and Person Birth Date CYMD Verbal are examples of data characteristic variations indicating these criteria.

Abbreviations and numbers are acceptable in the data characteristic variation name, as shown in the examples above. Although the data naming taxonomy usually requires fully spelled out names, the use of numbers and abbreviations in selected cases provides the same meaning and keeps the data name from being unreasonably long. For example, Person Birth Date Century Year Month Day or Person Name Complete Normal Fifty Six are very long and probably cannot be understood quickly.

A data characteristic variation name should not be used to indicate a standard. For example, State Code Standard or State Code Official should not be used to indicate the accepted set of state codes. All sets of state codes should be identified and documented, and then one of those sets designated as the official variation. The word *Standard* or *Official* should not be used in a data characteristic name to indicate that its form and content are the official data variation.

All of this detail about data characteristic variation names may seem unnecessary and purely academic. However, as disparate data are identified and refined to the common data architecture, their variability must be identified so that official data variations can be designated. For example, what does the birth date 06/05/11 mean, particularly when there are people still living who were born in the early part of this century? The data characteristic variation name provides unique identification of all these variations.

---

*The data characteristic variation name uniquely identifies all
the variations of a data characteristic in disparate data.*

Common words can be used in data characteristic variation names
like they are for data subjects and data characteristics. Common words
like *Feet, Meters,* and *Yards* provide consistency and meaning to data
variations. For example, Well Depth Feet, Well Depth Meters, and Well
Depth Yards indicate variations in the data characteristic for Well Depth.

Irregular is a common word showing that the format or meaning is
not consistent. It means that the data characteristic format or meaning
is likely to change and is unpredictable. It indicates that some type of
analysis is necessary to bring this data characteristic into conformity.
For example, Employee Name Irregular indicates that the content of the
name is variable and inconsistent—it could be a mixture of complete
and abbreviated names, and normal and inverted sequences.

Multiple is a common word showing that a data characteristic contains multiple values. For example, Project Participant Name Multiple
indicates that several participants' names, such as *J. Smith* and *S. Jones,*
can be included. More than one common word can be used in a data
characteristic variation name. For example, Project Status Date Multiple
Irregular indicates that multiple status dates are included and that those
dates are in an irregular format.

Usually, many data characteristic variations are encountered when
disparate data are documented. As these variations are encountered, an
organization needs to maintain a set of the data characteristic variation
common words and use them consistently to identify specific data variations.

Data Code Names

Actual data values may be coded for a variety of reasons, such as reduced
data entry time, reduced disk storage, and reduced report size. Each set of
data codes, such as disability codes or land use codes, is defined as a separate data subject in the common data architecture. Each data code in a
data code set must be formally named, like data subjects and data characteristics, because data codes are considered meta-data just like data
subjects and data characteristics. This level of detail is often ignored in
many data naming conventions and data design methods.

Each data code must be uniquely named in the common data architecture.

A *data code name* uniquely identifies each data code within the common data architecture, not just within the data subject. The data code names must be long enough to be unique, but not so long that they become definitions. For example, Student Admission Codes of *1, 2,* and *3* mean *New Student, Returning Student,* and *Continuing Student*, respectively, and are acceptable data code names. A data code name like A Student Returning To School After A Lapse of One or More Terms is too long.

Generally, two to five words are sufficient for a unique data code name. However, more than five words may be necessary in some situations. The data subject name, or an indication of the data subject, should be added as a suffix to make the data code name unique. For example, the data code names of disability codes for speech, hearing, and sight might be Speech Disability, Hearing Disability, and Sight Disability rather than just Speech, Hearing, and Sight.

Data Name Substitution

As the common data architecture evolves, there could be a proliferation of data characteristic variations. For example, Person Birth Date might be defined as *The date a person was born as shown on a birth certificate or other legal document.* However, Person Birth Date could have many format variations, such Person Birth Date CYMD, Person Birth Date YMD, or Person Birth Date MDY.

Having a scheme for substituting data characteristic variation names prevents the development of numerous data names that vary only in their format. A *data characteristic variation substitution* is a data characteristic name that represents a variety of format variations. The variation is identified by parentheses around the word or words in the data characteristic name that represent the substitution. In the example above, the data characteristic name is Person Birth (Date), where (Date) represents the substitution. Any formally defined Date variation can be substituted for (Date), such as Date CYMD, Date YMD, or Date MDY. These formally defined Date variations are explained further under Fundamental Data Definitions.

Alias Data Names

An *alias* is an alternate or assumed name for the same thing, usually for a person. However, aliases can apply to data names. An *alias data name* is an alternate name, a different name, a synonym for the same piece of data. It does not represent a data variation.

> *An alias data name is an alternate name for the same data.*

Almost all disparate data names are alias data names, because they do not meet the criteria for primary data names. These alias data names are cross referenced to the primary data name, so all existing data are defined in a common context. This process is explained in more detail in the Data Cross Reference chapter.

Data Name Abbreviations

Many software products, such as application languages, database management systems, and CASE tools, have data name length restrictions, and will continue to have those restrictions for some time. Many primary data names exceed these length restrictions and need to be abbreviated for use in software products. Ideally, primary data names should be abbreviated in a consistent manner so they can be easily unabbreviated to the primary data name. However, this is not the case with disparate data, where many different abbreviations exist.

> *Ideally, primary data names should be automatically abbreviated and unabbreviated as necessary to meet software product length restrictions.*

All data names within the common data architecture should be abbreviated in a consistent manner, based on a set of common abbreviations. An organization needs to develop a set of common abbreviations and use them consistently. Any new data name abbreviations should use the set of common abbreviations. A variety of approaches to developing data name abbreviations are explained in a previous book (Brackett, 1990).

Data names abbreviated according to common abbreviations do not need to be cross referenced to the primary data name, because they can be readily unabbreviated to the primary data name. Disparate data, however, do need to be cross referenced to the primary data name.

Since length restrictions vary with software products, there may need to be different algorithms for abbreviating a primary data name, depending on the software product. Each organization needs to determine how many different data name lengths it will support, and define the algorithms for developing those abbreviations from a set of common abbreviations. One approach to developing a set of common abbreviations is to document existing sets of abbreviations. These sets can be reviewed and merged into one integrated set of common abbreviations.

▼ SUMMARY

Traditional data names were incomplete and inconsistent, and were often developed on-the-fly as programs and databases were developed. Formal data naming conventions evolved to provide structure and consistency to data names. However, these data naming conventions are not robust enough for managing a wide variety of highly variable disparate data within a common data architecture. A full data naming taxonomy and supporting vocabulary provide formal data names for all data in the common data architecture.

The data naming taxonomy and supporting vocabulary were developed to meet a goal and a set of criteria, based on semiotics, that require a primary data name for all data in the common data architecture. The primary data name is the fully spelled out, real-world name that uniquely identifies each data repository, data subject, data characteristic, data characteristic variation, and data code within the common data architecture. It indicates the true content and meaning of the data, the structure of the data, and any variations in the data. All other data names are aliases of the primary data name.

The data naming taxonomy consists of the data repository name, data subject name, data characteristic name, and data characteristic variation name. The data repository name uniquely identifies the location of physical data, whether they are disparate data or data deployed within the common data architecture. The data subject name, data characteristic name, and data characteristic variation name uniquely identify all logical data within the common data architecture.

The data naming vocabulary is an expansion of the class word used in most data naming conventions. It contains a set of common words for each of the four components in the data naming taxonomy. These common words are used to develop formal data names that provide consistent meaning across all data names in the common data architecture. A set of common abbreviations allows the primary data name to be abbreviated easily to meet software product length restrictions, and the abbreviated data names to be easily unabbreviated to the primary data name.

The data naming taxonomy provides the general-to-specific sequence for data names, and the data naming vocabulary adds consistent meaning to the words in the primary data name. Developing primary data names is the first step in building a common data architecture, and is a critical success factor for a common data architecture.

▼ QUESTIONS

The following questions are designed to provide a review of Chapter 3 and to stimulate thought about how data are formally and uniquely named in the common data architecture.

1. What is a data name?

2. What is wrong with traditional data names?

3. What did formal data naming conventions provide?

4. What is wrong with these formal data naming conventions?

5. What did the class word concept provide?

6. What is the goal for formal data names?

7. What are the criteria for formal data names?

8. What is the data naming taxonomy?

9. What is the data naming vocabulary?

10. How does the data naming vocabulary support the data naming taxonomy?

11. How are data repositories named?

12. How are data subjects named?

13. How are data characteristics named?

14. What is meant by fully qualified data characteristic names?

15. What is a data characteristic variation?

16. Why must each data code be formally named?

17. Why must all data be uniquely named within the common data architecture?

18. What is meant by data characteristic variation name substitution?

19. What are alias data names?

20. Why is it so important to name data formally and uniquely?

▼ 4

DATA DEFINITION

*Comprehensive data definitions explain the true content and
meaning of data in the formal data resource.*

The Data Description activity in the Data Architecture component of
the Data Resource Framework includes the formal naming and comprehensive definition of all data. The last chapter explained the need and
process to formally name all data. Like data names, all data must have
a comprehensive data definition for people to thoroughly understand
and fully utilize the formal data resource.

Developing comprehensive data definitions, like developing data
names, is a relatively easy, though often ignored, process. Defining
data comprehensively helps resolve the disparate data situation and
prevents it from happening again. It also increases use of the formal
data resource by improving data sharing and results in more informed
business decisions.

This chapter begins with an explanation of the concepts for defining
data. It presents guidelines for developing comprehensive data definitions and describes how definitions are developed for data repositories,
data subjects, data characteristics, data characteristic variations, and
data codes. Data definition reference and inheritance are explained, the
use of common words is described, and an approach is presented for
managing data definition conflicts. The Disparate Data Description
chapter explains how data definitions are applied to disparate data.

▼ DATA DEFINITION CONCEPTS

Most disparate data definitions are superficial and provide very little information about the data, such as *Customer name is the name of the customer,* or *Student status shows the status of the student.* These data definitions originated when many original data names were limited to six or eight characters, so a further explanation of an abbreviated data name was needed. For example, CUSNAM is not readily understood, so the definition *CUSNAM is the name of the customer* provides more meaning.

> *Comprehensive data definitions are necessary to fully understand and utilize the data in a formal data resource.*

This practice continues today in most organizations, even though some software products have increased the size of data names they allow and have provided more space for data definitions. However, one-sentence definitions and truncated phrases are not appropriate for the common data architecture. They just do not provide enough understanding to build and fully utilize a formal data resource.

Definitions

A *comprehensive data definition* is a formal data definition that provides a complete, meaningful, easily read, readily understood, real-world definition of the true content and meaning of data. Comprehensive data definitions are based on sound principles and a set of guidelines. These ensure that they provide enough information to clients so the formal data resource can be thoroughly understood and fully utilized to meet information needs.

An *elemental data characteristic* is an atomic level data characteristic that cannot be further subdivided and retain any meaning. For example, century number or a person's first name cannot be further subdivided and retain any meaning. Ideally, all data characteristics should be elemental. However, this is not always practical, and elemental data characteristics are often combined into more useful forms. A *combined data characteristic* is a practical, useful combination of two or more closely related elemental data characteristics. For example, Date CYMD is a combined data characteristic consisting of a Century Number, Calendar Year Number, Month Number, and Day Number.

Semiotic Theory

Semiotic theory was explained in the last chapter as it related to naming data. Semiotic theory also applies to defining data. A comprehensive data definition must have a precise syntax, must be meaningful, and must have a practical use to be comprehensive.

Comprehensive data definitions are based on semiotic theory.

The precise syntax for a data definition is a specific, consistent format. If the format varies from one data definition to another, it is very difficult for people to read and understand those definitions. One of the worst techniques for building a common data architecture is to have widely different data definition formats. Therefore, comprehensive data definitions must have a consistent format so that they can be easily read and understood.

Semantics includes both denotative and connotative meanings. The denotative meaning is the direct, explicit meaning provided by a data definition. The connotative meaning is the idea or notion suggested by the definition that a person interprets in addition to what is explicitly stated. Since the connotative meaning may be different for each person, a comprehensive data definition must be as direct and explicit as possible.

Data definitions must be as explicit as possible to limit any implicit meanings.

Pragmatics requires that a data definition have practical value. If a data definition, or any part of it, is not of practical value, it is not useful. Therefore, anything that is not of practical value must be removed from the definition. Also, anything of practical value that is not in the data definition must be added.

Real World

A comprehensive data definition must reflect the real-world definition of an object. Since a formal data resource is a model of the real world, and data in the formal data resource represent objects in the real world, the definitions of the data in the formal data resource must reflect the real-world definitions of those objects.

Data definitions must reflect the real-world definitions of their objects.

A data definition must apply to the entire common data architecture, whether that architecture represents a single organization or several organizations. It must be consistent across all uses and all business activities. There is only one data definition that applies wherever the data are used. The situation is like the definition of Lego blocks. Each Lego block has one definition, and that definition applies whether that block is used to build a boat or a space ship.

Content and Meaning

A comprehensive data definition must explain the true content and meaning of the data and must not explain the use of data. One problem with many traditional data definitions, if they exist at all, is that they explain the use of data. Three problems occur with data definitions based on the use of data.

A comprehensive data definition explains the true content and meaning of data, not the use of data.

First, explaining the existing use or uses of data could limit new uses of the data. If people are searching for data to meet their own needs, and the definitions they see explain someone else's use of the data, those definitions could limit their ability to identify data they need. However, data definitions that explain the true content and meaning of data, independent of current uses, make it easier for people to identify data they need.

For example, the definition for an automobile might be *A vehicle that is used to transport employees to and from work on a daily basis.* This explains one use of an automobile, but doesn't explain what an automobile is. Since an automobile can be used for more than transporting employees to and from work on a daily basis, this definition could limit another person's use of an automobile. A data definition that describes what an automobile is helps people see all types of uses for an automobile.

Second, defining data based on use usually results in disagreements that may never be resolved. For example, Employee Name might be defined as *Data used to print paychecks*. This could cause immediate disagreement with people who use Employee Name for training schedules, affirmative action, project assignments, or tracking assigned inventory. To satisfy these uses, the definition needs to be expanded. The expanded definition only causes more disagreement, which results in an expanded definition, and so forth. It is extremely difficult to get consensus on a data definition that has a wide, and often expanding, range of uses. Concentrating on the true content and meaning promotes agreement on data definitions.

Third, the use of data changes over time, depending on the business activities those data support and the business needs of those activities. Since data have different uses in different business activities, and since business activities frequently change, the use of data changes over time. Even a very comprehensive data definition that includes all uses will deteriorate as the use of data changes. Keeping data definitions current with their true content and meaning is difficult enough, but keeping data definitions current with actual use is impossible

---

The actual use of data is documented in business process definitions, not in data definitions.

The actual use of data is shown in detailed data models and explained in business process descriptions. Each business process uses data in a particular way, and a comprehensive definition of that process includes an explanation of the data use. Defining data use in the business process allows the data definition to focus on the true content and meaning of data, and to remain stable over time.

Complete and Meaningful

A comprehensive data definition must be complete and meaningful. It must completely define and explain the data and any similarities to—

or differences from—closely related data. It must include anything that is pertinent to a thorough understanding of the data.

> *Comprehensive data definitions must be complete and meaningful enough to ensure a thorough understanding of the data.*

An excellent guideline for developing data definitions that are complete and meaningful is to prepare definitions people would like to see when they view data for the first time. What would newcomers like to see in a definition to help them understand the data? What information do they need to make the data explicitly clear?

▼ DATA DEFINITION GUIDELINES

A comprehensive data definition is developed for each data repository, data subject, data characteristic, data characteristic variation, and data code in the common data architecture. The guidelines below show what is contained in a comprehensive data definition and how one is developed.

General Guidelines

The following general guidelines are useful for preparing all comprehensive data definitions. Detailed guidelines for preparing specific data definitions are presented after these general guidelines.

- A data definition should fully explain the true content and meaning of the data. It should not contain any reference to specific data uses, processes using the data, or physical storage for the data.

- A data definition should be one to three paragraphs of three or four sentences each. Some data definitions may be completely stated in one or two sentences, and others may require up to a page of explanation.

- A data definition should contain any prominent alias data names that are commonly used, but it should not contain all possible synonyms or aliases. For example, *The Vehicle Identifier is also known as 'VIN' or 'Vehicle Identification Number'.*

- A data definition should include responsibility for identifying or maintaining the data. For example, *The Financial Transaction Codes are designated by the Controller* shows who is responsible for designating the financial transaction codes for the organization.

- A data definition should include a reference to the source of the definition if the definition comes from outside the organization. For example, the U.S. Postal Service should be referenced for a definition of ZIP codes.

- A data definition should include similarities to—or differences from—closely related data. For example, *An Employee is not the same as a **Contractor*** indicates a difference between employees and contractors. The client can review the definition of a contractor to determine the exact differences.

- A data definition may include history or rationale if it is pertinent to a thorough understanding of the data. However, a data definition should not be a complete chronology of events leading to a comprehensive data definition.

Data Definition Status

A comprehensive data definition must have a status and a date for that status. *Proposed, Interim,* and *Accepted* are good statuses for data definitions. When the data definition is first prepared, its status is *Proposed,* meaning that it is open to adjustment by anyone. As the data definition becomes more refined and the data appear in a data model, its status is raised to *Interim.* A data definition with an *Interim* status can be changed only by a project leader. When the data definition is complete and represents real data in a data file or database, its status is raised to *Accepted* and can be changed only by the data administrator.

Each organization should establish the status levels for its data definitions and designate the people who may change data definitions at each level. Any change to an existing data definition must be analyzed for the impact on current use or understanding. Generally, changes that improve or correct grammar and punctuation, or that clarify meaning, are readily accepted. Changes that alter the definition must be reviewed carefully.

Data Repository Definition

Each data repository must have a comprehensive data definition. Since disparate data can exist in a variety of physical locations, and data may ultimately be deployed on a network for optimum performance, it is very important to have a comprehensive definition of each data repository. A typical comprehensive data repository definition contains the data repository name, a definition, the status, and the status date, as shown in Figure 4.1. The data repository name is shown in bold type font; bold names in the definition are references to other comprehensive data definitions.

Data Subject Definition

Each data subject must have a comprehensive data definition that contains the data subject name, a definition, the primary key, its status and status date, and any other information that ensures a thorough understanding. A typical comprehensive data subject definition is shown in Figure 4.2. The data subject name is shown in bold type font; bold names in the definition are references to other comprehensive data definitions.

A data subject definition may contain additional items to make the definition more comprehensive. These items are described below:

- A definition can state exactly what each data occurrence represents, if it is not explicitly clear in the definition. For example, *Each data occurrence represents one trip taken by one Vehicle.*

Seattle Payroll

The Seattle Payroll is a payroll database located on an IBM 3090 computer in a Seattle office. It contains payroll data for all employees in the western region of its organization. It is not the same as the **Dallas Payroll** or the **New York Payroll**.

Status: Proposed 6/09/91

Figure 4.1 *Data repository definition example.*

Vehicle

A piece of **Equipment** that is capable of moving from one location to another, under its own power, or under the power of another Vehicle, a Person, or the natural elements. It may move on the ground, in the water, or in the air. A Vehicle may transport people or cargo, or may provide other specific services.

Primary Key: Vehicle Identifier

Status: Proposed 6/09/91

Figure 4.2 *Data subject definition example.*

- A definition can include the time period the data represent, if that time frame applies to all or most of the data characteristics in the data subject. For example, *The data have been collected at the end of every month since December 1967.*

- A definition can include the geographic extent of the data, if that extent applies to all or most of the data characteristics in the data subject. For example, *Data are collected for all counties in Eastern Washington,* or *Data are collected for all rivers in Western Washington.* If there are different geographic extents for different data occurrences, those extents should be explained. For example, *Data are collected for Employees in the Eastern Region prior to January 1, 1990, and for all Employees in the company after January 1, 1990.*

Data Characteristic Definition

Each data characteristic must have a comprehensive data definition that contains the data characteristic name, a definition, its status and status date, and any other information that ensures a thorough understanding. A typical comprehensive data characteristic definition is shown in Figure 4.3. The data characteristic name is shown in bold type font; bold names in the definitions are references to other comprehensive data definitions.

> **Vehicle Identifier**
>
> A Vehicle Identifier is a unique number affixed to a Vehicle by the **Manufacturer**. It is often refereed to as a VIN or Vehicle Identification Number. On later model motor vehicles, a plate is affixed to the dashboard on the driver's side of the vehicle so that it is readily visible from the outside.
>
> Status: Proposed 7/12/89; Interim 8/01/91

Figure 4.3 *Data characteristic definition example.*

A data characteristic definition may contain additional items to make the definition more comprehensive. These items are described below:

- The definition should show the length of the data characteristic and indicate whether it contains characters or numbers. For example, *A 3-character code representing...* or *A 5-digit count of the ...* might begin the data definition.

- If the data characteristic is a character string or a number that does not need to be completely filled, the definition should include the word *maximum*. For example, *The maximum 30-character name of the City* or *The maximum 5-digit number...*

- If the data characteristic contains a decimal point, the definition should show the format in a manner that clients understand. For example, *A 6-digit distance (3.2) in feet...* meaning the first three digits represent feet, the next digit is the decimal point, and the last two digits represent hundredths of a foot.

- The definition should contain the units of measurement, such as linear, angular, surface, volume, and so on. For example, *The 6-digit volume in gallons of...*

- If the data characteristic is a combination of several other data characteristics, it should include the word *combined* and include the names of those data characteristics in the sequence in which they appear. For example, the definition of Employee Name Complete Normal might be *A combined data characteristic consisting of the Employee Name Individual, Employee Name Middle, and Employee Name Family.*

- If the data characteristic is derived or calculated, it should include the word *derived* and the method or algorithm for derivation, including other data characteristics involved. For example, the definition of an employee's age might be *A maximum 3-digit derived data characteristic obtained from the difference between the Employees Birth Date and the current date.* The time and location of the derivation is a process issue, but knowing the method or algorithm is part of a comprehensive data definition.

- The definition should include how the value was determined, or how the question was asked to obtain the value. For example, *the disability as stated by the individual* and *the disability as determined by a physician according to a set of formal rules provided by...* indicate different methods of determination.

- The definition should include how the value was measured. For example: *...determined by the Global Positioning System.*

- The definition should include any information relating to how accurately the data represent the real world, such as precision, resolution, scale, and so on. For example, *The data were interpreted from 1:100,000 aerial photos* or *The distance was measured with a Theodolite.*

- The definition should include the time period the data represent, if that time period is different than the time period for the data subject or there was no time period for the data subject. For example, *Data were collected daily since 1971.*

- The definition should include the geographic extent of the data, if that extent is different than the geographic extent for the data subject or there is no geographic extent for the data subject. For example, *Data were collected for every land parcel in Eastern Washington* or *Data were collected for every mile of the Nooksack River.*

- The definition should include an explanation of alternatives for variable data characteristics. For example, *...may be either the Person Name Complete Normal or the Person Name Complete*

Inverted or A combined data characteristic consisting of the Date YMD before January 1, 1990 or Date CYMD after January 1, 1990.

Data Characteristic Variation Definition

Each data characteristic variation must have a comprehensive definition that looks the same as a data characteristic definition but explains the specific variation. Definition of the variation may be extensive if it explains a content and meaning variation, or it may be short if it explains a format variation. A typical comprehensive data characteristic variation definition is shown in Figure 4.4. The data characteristic variation name is shown in bold type font; bold names in the definitions are references to other data definitions.

The data characteristic variation definition should repeat the full definition of its parent data characteristic and add an explanation of the variation. Including only an explanation of the variation in the data characteristic variation definition is not acceptable, even though it reduces the size of the definition. The full data definition is needed in case a person extracts a data characteristic variation definition without its parent data characteristic definition. In other words, each data characteristic variation must be complete.

Data Code Definition

Each data code must have a comprehensive data definition that contains the data code value, the data code name, the definition, its status and status date, and any additional information necessary to a thorough understanding. Typical comprehensive data code definitions are shown in Figure 4.5.

Person Birth Date CYMD

The **Date CYMD** a **Person** was born as shown on a birth certificate or other legal document.

Status: Accepted 10/11/91

Figure 4.4 *Data characteristic variation definition example.*

01	Emergency Appointment	An appointment made without regard to normal hiring rules when such an appointment is necessary for emergency or immanent emergency situations.
		Status: Proposed 4/23/89
02	Exempt Appointment	An appointment to a position that is officially designated as being exempt from the normal hiring rules.
		Status: Proposed 4/23/89

Figure 4.5 *Data code definition example.*

Additional Data Definition Items

Additional comments, notes, questions, and issues may be recorded during the development of data definitions. These are usually listed below the definition of the data.

- A *data definition comment* is a comment about a data definition made by a reviewer. It appears after the word *Comment* and shows the date, the name of the individual making the comment, and the individual's organization if more than one organization is involved. Comments are usually removed before the definition becomes final.

- A *data definition note* is a fact or statement that clarifies something about the data definition. It is documented after the word *Note.* Notes are more permanent than comments and usually stay with the data definition.

- A *data definition question* is something about the data definition that needs to be answered. It is documented after the word *Question.* Questions are generally easy to answer after checking a reference or source. When the question is answered, the definition is adjusted accordingly and the question is removed.

- A *data definition issue* is something about the data definition that needs further analysis or a decision. It is documented after the word *Issue.* Issues are generally more difficult to answer than questions. When the issue is resolved, the definition is adjusted accordingly and the issue is removed.

Data Definition Document

Data definitions must be presented in a consistent format so they can be easily read and understood. A format that works well for data definitions is described below. Sample data definitions are shown in Appendix B.

- A table of contents lists the data subject and data characteristic contained in the document.

- The data subjects are placed in alphabetical order within the document for quick location. Beginning a new page for each data subject is helpful during the review process. It allows people to separate the document by data subject, and to insert or delete data subjects easily.

- Data characteristics are placed in alphabetical order within each data subject for quick location. The data characteristic definitions are indented to help separate data characteristics from data subjects.

- Data code definitions are placed in data code value order within their data subject. They are usually listed in a separate section after the data subject and data characteristic definitions.

- Page numbers can be used if they are beneficial. If pages are frequently inserted, moved, or deleted during preparation of data definitions, it is best not to use page numbers.

- The date of printing should be shown on each page to identify each version of the data definitions and prevent confusion.

▼ DATA DEFINITION REFERENCE

Any data definition can contain references to any other data definition. A *data definition reference* is a connection between two data definitions so that one can be clarified by the other, or each can be clarified by the other. A data definition reference is indicated by a data name in bold type font within a data definition, as shown in several of the examples above.

Data definitions can refer to other data definitions for clarity.

For example, the statement *An Employee is not the same as a* **Contractor** in the Employee data subject definition refers to the Contractor data subject definition for the definition of a Contractor. The Contractor data subject definition contains a similar statement about an Employee: *A Contractor is not the same as an* **Employee**. A person can review both data definitions for a better understanding of the similarities and differences between employees and contractors.

▼ DATA DEFINITION INHERITANCE

Inheritance is the situation where something is received from a predecessor, ancestor, or other type of contributor, such as money or property from a relative or a personal characteristic that is passed on genetically. *Data definition inheritance* is the situation where some portion of a data definition is received from another data definition. It provides the maximum amount of information with a minimum of wording. It provides consistency among data definitions and helps people better understand the data.

Data Subject Inheritance

A data subject can inherit data definitions from parent data subjects, but those definitions are not repeated. For example, Student contains data about each student, such as the student's name, and Academic Term contains data about each term, such as begin and end dates. Student Term contains data about a particular student for a particular term, such as the number of credit hours for which the student is registered. The definition of Student Term inherits the data definitions of both Student and Academic Term. It cannot be defined as something larger or smaller than Student or Academic Term.

A data subject does not inherit the definition from a data repository. The data repository name is an indication of the deployment of a particular data characteristic in a data file or database. It does not help qualify the definition of a data subject or a data characteristic.

Fundamental Data

Fundamental data are data that do not exist in databases and are not used in applications. They provide a foundation for defining specific data. *Specific data* are data that do exist in databases and are used in applications. For example, Date CYMD is a fundamental data characteristic because it does not appear in a database and is not used in applications. Employee Birth Date CYMD is a specific data characteristic because it appears in data bases and is used in applications. Employee Birth Date CYMD inherits the definition of Date CYMD.

> *A full set of fundamental data supports development of a common data architecture.*

Fundamental data are like Lego blocks that can be used to build an infinite variety of things. They can be used as necessary to support specific data. Some fundamental data are used frequently; other fundamental data are used seldom. They are a set of data definitions available for people to draw on when defining specific data. Each organization should develop an initial set of fundamental data and continue to enhance that set to provide consistency within the common data architecture.

Data Characteristic Inheritance

Each data characteristic inherits the data definition of its parent data subject, but it does not repeat that definition. For example, the definition of Vehicle was shown in Figure 4.2 and the definition of Vehicle Identifier was shown in Figure 4.3. Vehicle Identifier inherits the definition of Vehicle through the data definition reference, but it does not repeat that definition.

If a data characteristic repeats the definition of its parent data subject, as shown in Figure 4.6, it creates extensive and redundant definitions. Also, if the definition of Vehicle is adjusted, all the corresponding data characteristic definitions in Vehicle need to be adjusted. This either

Vehicle Identifier

The unique identification of a piece of **Equipment** that is capable of moving from one location to another under its own power, or under the power of another Vehicle, a **Person**, or the natural elements, and that may move on the ground, in the water, or in the air.

Figure 4.6 *Redundant data definition for Vehicle Identifier.*

increases the maintenance effort or results in inconsistent data definitions. Therefore, it is better to inherit the definition of the parent data subject through a data definition reference and add a definition that is specific to the data characteristic. This approach reduces maintenance, reduces the amount of wording, and increases the meaning.

A data characteristic can also inherit data definitions from fundamental data. For example, Well Latitude Degrees is defined as *The Latitude Degrees of a well head.* It inherits the definition of Latitude Degrees through a data definition reference, but does not repeat that definition.

The inheritance of data characteristic definitions can be shown on a *data definition inheritance diagram.* A rectangle represents a data definition with the name of the data inside the rectangle. A dashed line with an arrowhead on one end shows the direction of inheritance between data definitions. Generally, the diagram is arranged so that inheritance is from the bottom.

For example, an inheritance scheme is defined for the components of a person's name, as shown in Figure 4.7. A person's individual name, middle name, and family name are defined as elemental fundamental data characteristics. These elemental data characteristics are combined to form a combined fundamental data characteristic for Person Name Complete Normal, which inherits the definitions of the three elemental components and adds a definition of the sequence. The Customer Name Complete Normal data characteristic inherits the definition of Person Name Complete Normal.

Data Characteristic Variation Inheritance

A data characteristic variation inherits the data definition of its parent data characteristic, and it repeats that definition. For example, Well

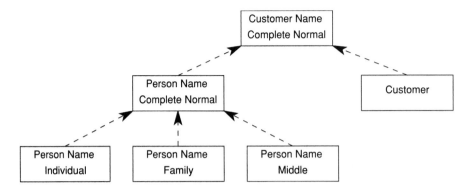

Figure 4.7 *Inherited data characteristic definition diagram example.*

Depth Meters inherits the data definition of Well Depth. The data defini-tion of the parent data characteristic is repeated because the data char-acteristic variation may be removed and used for a specific project without its parent data characteristic. If the data definition of the par-ent data characteristic variation were not repeated, that definition would be lost. For example, the definition of Well Depth is *The depth of a well as measured from the top of the well head to the bottom of the well shaft.* The definition of Well Depth Feet is *The depth in feet of a well as measured from the top of the well head to the bottom of the well shaft.*

A data characteristic variation can inherit a fundamental data defini-tion, but does not repeat that definition. For example, Employee Birth Date CYMD is defined as *The **Person Birth Date CYMD** of an Employee.* It inherits the definition of Date CYMD through a data definition refer-ence to Date CYMD. When a data characteristic variation definition inherits a fundamental data definition, the data name must be fully qualified to show the variation. In the example above, the data charac-teristic variation is Employee Birth Date CYMD, not just Employee Birth Date.

Data Code Inheritance

Each set of data codes is defined as a separate data subject in the common data architecture. That data subject contains two data characteristics rep-resenting the value and the name of the data code. The data code defini-

Employee Appointment Status

A Code Table containing a set of codes designating the **Employee's** personal status during the period of a specific **Employee Appointment**. It has no bearing on the Employee's overall status within the organization.

> **Employee Appointment Status Code**
>
> The maximum 2-digit code uniquely identifying an Employee Appointment Status.
>
> **Employee Appointment Status Name**
>
> The maximum 20-character unique name of an Employee Appointment Status.

Figure 4.8 *Data subject definition for Employee Appointment Status.*

tion inherits both the parent data subject definition and the definitions of the two data characteristics that represent the value and the name.

For example, employees are appointed to positions. Each employee has a status during an appointment, and those statuses are coded. Therefore, a data subject is identified for Employee Appointment Status and data characteristics are identified for Employee Appointment Status Code and Employee Appointment Status Name, as shown in Figure 4.8. Each of the Employee Appointment Status codes shown in Figure 4.5 inherits the definition of Employee Appointment Status, Employee Appointment Status Code, and Employee Appointment Status Name.

▼ DATA DEFINITION COMMON WORDS

A comprehensive data definition inherits the definition of the common words used in data names. One reason for establishing a data naming taxonomy and supporting vocabulary is to provide inheritance of the data name. When a data name contains common words like *Seattle, Dallas,* or *New York* in data repository names; *Account, Detail, History,* or *Suspense* in data subject names; *Number, Quantity,* or *Identifier* in data characteristic names; and *Feet, Inches, Yards,* or *Meters,* in data characteristic variation names; the data definition inherits the meaning of those words. It can also explain the meaning in more detail.

Common words provide consistency in data definitions.

A comprehensive data definition can also contain common words other than those used in the data name, such as *maximum, elemental, combined,* and *derived.* A *data definition common word* is a word that is commonly used in data definitions to provide consistent meaning. Each organization should maintain a set of data definition common words the same as they maintain a set of common words for data names. An initial list of data definition common words is shown in Appendix A.

▼ DATA DEFINITION CONFLICTS

Frequently there are multiple, conflicting data definitions in common use. Comprehensive data definitions cannot resolve these discrepancies because they exist in the real world. Since data definitions represent the real world, and discrepancies exist in the real world, the data definitions reflect those discrepancies. Ignoring these discrepancies limits understanding of the data and the real world the data represent. It may even result in the improper use of data.

Data definition conflicts must be documented for proper use of the data.

Conflicting data definitions must be thoroughly documented to alert people to their existence. The data name should be unique and should identify the specific situation that the comprehensive data definition explains. When people use the data, they can indicate which definition they are using. For example, there are several conflicting definitions for Wetlands. Each of these conflicting definitions is isolated, uniquely named, and precisely defined, such as Wetlands Growth Management, Wetlands Habitat, and so on. The comprehensive data definition explains each of these situations.

Conflicting data definitions should contain references to other data definitions and explain the conflict, differences, and similarities. They should contain a statement about the most commonly used data definitions and the circumstances under which each data definition is used. The source of each definition should also be explained, along with any other information that ensures a thorough understanding.

It is not the intent to resolve the real-world conflict through documenting conflicting data definitions. Changing a data definition cannot change the real world those data represent. It can, however, point out the conflicts and help people approach a resolution. Awareness of a conflict is the first step to resolving that conflict.

▼ SUMMARY

Traditional data definitions are an extension of the data name and provide little understanding of the data. They do not support development of a formal data resource within a common data architecture. Comprehensive data definitions are based on semiotic theory, like data names. They must represent the real world, explain the true content and meaning of data, and be complete and meaningful for a formal data resource to be fully utilized.

Comprehensive data definitions are prepared for all data repositories, data subjects, data characteristics, data characteristic variations, and data codes within the common data architecture. Comprehensive data definitions are also prepared for fundamental data to provide a foundation for consistent definitions of specific data with maximum meaning and minimum wording.

Since data represent the real world, any conflicts in the real world result in conflicts in data definitions. These conflicts are documented in comprehensive data definitions so that people are aware of the conflict and can state explicitly which definition they are using.

Data definitions, along with data names, form the Data Description activity of the Data Architecture component of the Data Resource Framework. One of the critical success factors for a formal data resource is comprehensive data definitions. If the true content and meaning of data are not completely defined, all the other components of the common data architecture will have little meaning.

▼ QUESTIONS

The following questions are designed to provide a review of Chapter 4 and to stimulate thought about developing comprehensive data definitions within a common data architecture to ensure that a formal data resource is fully utilized.

1. What is wrong with traditional data definitions?

2. How can this problem be corrected?

3. How does semiotic theory apply to data definitions?

4. Why is the real-world definition important in forming data descriptions?

5. What is meant by complete and meaningful data definitions?

6. Why should data definitions explain the true content and meaning, but not the use, of data?

7. Why are data definition statuses and status dates important?

8. What information should be included in a data definition?

9. Why are more things included in a data characteristic definition than in the other data definitions?

10. Why is the data characteristic definition repeated in a data characteristic variation definition?

11. How are data codes defined?

12. How are data definitions formatted for review and updating?

13. How are conflicts in data definitions managed?

14. What is a data definition reference?

15. How are data names involved in data definition references?

16. What is data definition inheritance?

17. How are fundamental data definitions involved in data definition inheritance?

18. How are inherited data definition references shown graphically?

19. Why are comprehensive data definitions a critical success factor for the common data architecture?

20. What happens when there are comprehensive data definitions?

▼ ▼ ▼ 5

DATA STRUCTURE

*A data structure shows the relationships between data subjects
and the content of each data subject in the formal data resource.*

Data Structure is the second activity in the Data Architecture component of the Data Resource Framework. It is the second most important activity in data resource management, and is closely integrated with the Data Description activity in the development of a common data architecture. The naming, definition, and structuring of data are closely integrated in a discovery process to build a formal data resource.

A data structure defines the arrangement and relationships of data subjects, and the contents of the data subjects. It includes both a logical and a physical data structure. Normally, a logical data structure is developed first and is transformed into a physical data structure for implementation. However, with disparate data, the physical data structure already exists, usually without a corresponding logical data structure. Refining disparate data involves identifying physical data, cross referencing them to the common data architecture, and developing a logical data structure that covers those physical data.

This chapter explains the concepts and terms associated with developing a logical data structure for data. It does not cover development of a physical data structure or transformation of the logical data structure to a physical data structure. Data relation diagrams and data structure charts for documenting the logical data structure are presented.

Data relations and data keys are explained. Finally, the different types of data are described and approaches to data classification are explained. The Disparate Data Structure chapter explains how a data structure is developed for disparate data.

▼ DATA STRUCTURE CONCEPT

A data structure is shown in two different types of diagrams. The formats of these diagrams have been repeatedly refined so they are both technically correct and are acceptable to all clients involved in building a common data architecture and using the formal data resource. Each of these diagrams is explained below.

Definitions

The term *data structure* is used in many contexts and has many definitions. In the common data architecture, a *data structure* is a representation of the arrangement, relationship, and contents of data subjects and data files. It includes all logical and physical data in the common data architecture, and both working levels and categorical levels of data classification.

A *logical data structure* is a data structure representing logical data. It is generally developed to show how the formal data resource supports business activities. A *physical data structure* is a data structure representing physical data. It is generally developed from a logical data structure to show how data are physically stored in files and databases.

Data Relation Diagram

A *data relation diagram* shows the arrangement and relationship of data subjects in the common data architecture, but does not show any contents of a data subject. A data relation diagram is traditionally known as an *entity-relationship diagram,* or *ER diagram.* However, these terms are avoided because of they cause confusion with the entity-relationship diagram that pertains to behavioral entities and their relations in the real world.

Data relation diagrams follow semiotic theory like data names and data definitions. Each symbol used on a data relation diagram is part of

Figure 5.1 *Symbols used on a data relation diagram.*

a set of symbols that are used consistently across all models. Each symbol has a formal syntax, an explicit meaning, and a practical value that do not change from one type of model to another.

A data relation diagram contains four symbols, as shown in Figure 5.1. A *box with bulging sides* indicates a data subject with the name of the data subject inside the symbol. A *dashed line* connecting two data subjects indicates a data relation between those data subjects. The dashed line may have no arrowheads, an arrowhead on one end, or an arrowhead on both ends, and it may be branched or unbranched.

The dashed line signifies a relation between data subjects, not a flow of data between data subjects. A solid line, such as a data flow on a data flow diagram, indicates a flow. Since there is only a relation between data subjects, not a flow of data, a dashed line is used rather than a solid line.

Data relation diagrams must be acceptable to people, as well as technically correct. Making the data relation diagrams technically correct is relatively easy, but making them readily acceptable is often difficult. Many data analysts just get the data subjects and data relations recorded and forget the arrangement of the data subjects for maximum meaning. CASE tools often do not produce an acceptable data relation diagram.

A few simple guidelines for developing acceptable data relation diagrams are listed in Appendix C. If these guidelines are followed, data relation diagrams will provide maximum meaning.

Data relation diagrams can be created at three levels of detail. Each level has a specific content and is useful to a particular audience. All are important and no single level meets the needs or interests of all people.

- The *strategic data relation diagram* consists of a data relation diagram that shows the common data architecture on a page or two. It consists of the major data areas within the scope of the common data architecture and provides an overview of the common data architectures for executives and administrators. The data subjects usually represent the behavioral entities managed or monitored by the organization.

- The *tactical data relation diagram* consists of a data relation diagram that shows the major data subjects in the common data architecture and their relationships. The major data subjects are grouped according to their relations and are shown on a single page, or on a few pages. Major data subjects are those of primary importance, such as customer, employee, or equipment. They do not include detailed data subjects, such as transactions or code tables. The tactical documentation is useful for identifying the backbone of a common data architecture.

- The *detail data relation diagram* consists of a data relation diagram that shows all the data subjects and all the data relations between those data subjects. The data subjects are grouped according to their relations and are placed on as many pages as necessary to show the detail. The detail documentation is a blueprint for the data resource.

Data Structure Chart

A *data structure chart* shows the contents of each data subject, but not the arrangement or relationship of those data subjects. A *logical data structure chart* is a data structure chart that shows the primary keys, foreign keys, secondary keys, and data characteristics contained in a data subject. A *physical data structure chart* is a data structure chart that shows the data keys and data items contained in a data file. Physical data structure charts are explained in the Disparate Data Structure chapter.

There are several formats for displaying a logical data structure chart, including a modified set theory format, a table format, and an outline format. All three formats have advantages and disadvantages, and neither is acceptable for all situations. However, the most useful and meaningful for developing a common data architecture is the *data structure outline* format. It is used throughout this book.

The *data structure outline* format for a logical data structure chart is shown in Figure 5.2. It consists of the data subject name, usually in bold type font, followed by the primary key or keys, any foreign keys,

Employee

Primary Key
 Employee Social Security Number

Alternate Key
 Employee Name Complete Normal
 Employee Birth Date

Employee Management Level
 Employee Management Level Code

Employee Status
 Employee Status Code

Secondary Key
 Employee Social Security Number

Secondary Key
 Employee Name Complete Normal

Characteristic List
 Employee Birth Date
 Employee Management Level Code
 Employee Name Complete Normal
 Employee Social Security Number
 Employee Status Code

Figure 5.2 *Format of the data structure chart.*

any secondary keys, and a complete list of the data characteristics in the data subject.

The official primary key is designated with the label *Primary Key*, followed by the data characteristics comprising the primary key. Alternate primary keys are designated with the label *Alternate Key*, followed by the data characteristics comprising the alternate primary key. Limited primary keys are designated with the label *Limited Key* followed by the data characteristics comprising the limited primary key. Obsolete primary keys are designated with the label *Obsolete Key*, followed by the data characteristics comprising the obsolete primary key. Each of these primary keys is explained in more detail below.

Foreign keys are designated with a label showing the name of the parent data subject referred to by the foreign key. The name of the parent data subject helps verify the data relations on the data relation diagram. The data characteristics comprising the foreign key are listed below the label in the same order they are listed in the parent data subject's primary key. The foreign keys are placed in alphabetical order by parent data subject name for quick reference.

Secondary keys are designated with the label containing either *Secondary Key* or the specific name of the secondary key. The data characteristics comprising the secondary key are listed below the label. If the secondary keys are named, they are placed in alphabetical order according to that name.

The complete set of data characteristics is designated with the label *Characteristic List.* The data characteristics contained in the data subject are listed in alphabetical order below the label. This list contains all data characteristics in the data subject, even if they are already listed in primary keys, foreign keys, or secondary keys. It provides a complete reference to all data characteristics contained in the data subject.

A data structure chart is usually developed as information is available. It is best to keep the logical data structure current to represent the current state of the data. It is very difficult to develop a data structure chart after-the-fact. The criteria for keeping a data structure chart current during data remodeling are listed in Appendix C.

▼ DATA RELATIONS

A *data relation* is an association between data occurrences in different data subjects or within the same data subject. It provides the connections between data subjects for building the structure of a common data architecture. Data relations are only an association, are not named, and do not contain any data characteristics. Anytime a data relation contains data characteristics, a data subject must be defined for those data characteristics. Definition of the three types of data relations is an important step in developing the structure of a data common architecture.

Data Relation Types

A *one-to-one data relation* occurs when a data occurrence in one data subject is related with only one data occurrence in a second data subject, and that data occurrence in the second data subject is related to only one data occurrence in the first data subject. For example, an employee of a medical clinic may also be a patient in that clinic. Since an employee can be only one patient and that patient can be only one employee, there is a one-to-one data relation between Employee and Patient, as shown in Figure 5.3. A one-to-one data relation is designated by a dashed line between two data subjects without any arrowheads.

A *one-to-many data relation* occurs when a data occurrence in one data subject is related to more than one data occurrence in a second data subject, but each data occurrence in that second data subject is related to only one data occurrence in the first data subject. A one-to-many data relation is shown by a dashed line between two data subjects with an arrowhead on one end. The arrowhead points to the data subject containing the many data occurrences. The end of the dashed line with no arrowhead identifies the data subject with only one data occurrence involved in the relation, and the end of the dashed line with an arrowhead identifies the data subject with the multiple data occurrences involved in the relation.

For example, a vehicle may have many repairs, but each repair applies to only one vehicle, as shown in Figure 5.4. The data relation points from Vehicle to Vehicle Repair, indicating that for each data

Figure 5.3 *A one-to-one data relation example.*

Figure 5.4 *A one-to-many data relation example.*

occurrence in Vehicle, there can be many data occurrences in Vehicle Repair.

A *many-to-many data relation* occurs when a data occurrence in one data subject is related to more than one data occurrence in a second data subject, and each data occurrence in that second data subject is related to more than one data occurrence in the first data subject. A many-to-many data relation is shown by a dashed line with an arrowhead on each end. For example, a vehicle can have many traffic accidents and each traffic accident can involve many vehicles, as shown in Figure 5.5. The data relation points to both Vehicle and Traffic Accident, indicating that there are many data occurrences on each end of the data relation.

A many-to-many data relation needs to be resolved by adding a third data subject that is subordinate to the two data entities involved in the many-to-many data relation. For example, the many-to-many data relation shown in Figure 5.5 is resolved with the addition of Vehicle Accident, as shown in Figure 5.6. Two one-to-many data relations are created from the original parent data subjects to the new subordinate data subject.

A many-to-many data relation is really two one-to-many data relations pointing in opposite directions between the data subjects. For

Figure 5.5   *A many-to-many data relation example.*

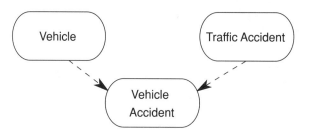

Figure 5.6   *Resolution of a many-to-many data relation.*

convenience, these two one-to-many data relations were collapsed into a single many-to-many data relation. Resolution of the many-to-many data relation is accomplished by taking the two one-to-many data relations and pointing them to the new subordinate data subject.

Reducing One-to-Many Data Relations

One-to-many data relations may be reduced in certain situations. For example, an employee may have many phone numbers contained in Employee Phone. Phone Type indicates the type of each phone number, such as home or work. Employee Phone and Phone Type can be reduced by adding specific data characteristics to Employee for each phone, such as Employee Work Phone, Employee Home Phone, and so on.

Reducing one-to-many data relations is not recommended for a logical data structure of the common data architecture. It is acceptable for a physical data structure following a formal denormalization of the logical data structure. However, this situation is common with disparate data, and must be recognized so that it can be resolved when a logical data structure is developed for disparate data.

Recursive Data Relations

A *recursive data relation* is a data relation between data occurrences in the same data subject. A recursive data relation may be one-to-one, one-to-many, or many-to-many, the same as data relations between data subjects.

A *one-to-one recursive data relation* means that a data occurrence within a data subject is related to only one other data occurrence in that data subject. A one-to-one recursive data relation is shown as a one-to-one data relation from the data subject to itself. For example, if spouses worked for the same organization, each would have a data occurrence in Employee, as shown in Figure 5.7. Each data occurrence would refer to the other data occurrence. A one-to-one recursive data relation is also known as a *closed recursive data relation* because it forms a closed loop between two data occurrences.

A *one-to-many recursive data relation* means that a data occurrence within a data subject is related to two or more other data occurrences in that data subject. A one-to-many recursive data relation is shown as

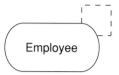

Figure 5.7 *A one-to-one recursive data relation example.*

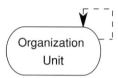

Figure 5.8 *A one-to-many recursive data relation example.*

a one-to-many data relation from the data subject to itself. For example, the organizational structure in an organization can be represented in a one-to-many recursive data relation, as shown in Figure 5.8. Each parent Organization Unit can have many subordinate Organizational Units, but each Organizational Unit has only one parent Organization Unit. A one-to-many recursive data relation is also known as an *open recursive data relation* because one can navigate either up or down through the relations and never come back to the original data occurrence.

Cyclic Data Subjects

A *many-to-many recursive data relation* means that each data occurrence in a data subject can be related to many other data occurrences in that data subject. That many-to-many recursive data relation is resolved with the addition of another data subject, just like a many-to-many data relation between two data subjects.

For example, Network Component has a many-to-many recursive data relation, as shown in Figure 5.9. Network Component shows how various components on a network are connected to form the network. Each data occurrence in Network Component is related to many other data occurrences in Network Component, and each of those is related to many other data occurrences.

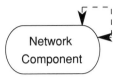

Figure 5.9 *A many-to-many recursive data relation example.*

Figure 5.10 *Resolution of a many-to-many recursive data relation.*

The many-to-many recursive data relation is resolved with the addition of another data subject, like a many-to-many data relation between two data subjects. Network Component Connection is added with two one-to-many data relations between Network Component and Network Component Connection, as shown in Figure 5.10. Each component on the network can have many other components connected to it. Each of those connections is identified by the network component, which identifies the two components, and any other data regarding the connection. The resolution of a many-to-many recursive data relation is called a *cyclic data subject.*

The resolution of a recursive many-to-many data relation produces two one-to-many data relations between the parent data subject and the resolution data subject. Each one-to-many data relation represents a recursive one-to-many data relation that formed the recursive many-to-many data relation.

Data Subject Hierarchy

A *data subject hierarchy* is a hierarchical structure of data subjects with branched one-to-one relations. It represents mutually exclusive, or *can-only-be,* situations between data subjects at each level in the hierarchy. A data subject hierarchy is traditionally known as an *entity type hierarchy*, and consists of super-types and sub-types. However, in the common data architecture, each super-type and sub-type is considered a

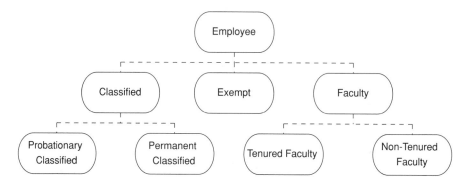

Figure 5.11 *Data subject hierarchy example.*

data subject, regardless of its level in the hierarchy. Therefore, the hierarchical structure is referred to as a *data subject hierarchy.*

For example, employees in a university may be classified, faculty, or exempt, as shown in Figure 5.11. Classified employees may be probationary or permanent, and faculty may be tenured or non-tenured.

Inheritance is an important feature in data subject hierarchies. Each subordinate data subject inherits the definition of its parent data subject. For example, Probationary Classified Employees and Permanent Classified Employees inherit the definition of a Classified Employee.

There are three forms of a data subject that may appear in a data subject hierarchy. A *virtual data subject* is a data subject that has no data characteristics and represents a broad classification of subordinate data subjects. A *true data subject* is a data subject that contains one or more data characteristics that describe the data subject. A *data subject type* is a breakdown of a true data subject that either has no data characteristics of its own, or has data characteristics that inherit their data names and definitions directly from a true data subject.

All three forms of a data subject may exist in the same data subject hierarchy. If a virtual data subject exists, there is only one, and it is the top level. There may be many levels of true data subjects, and there may be many levels of data subject types. Data subject types must be subordinate to true data subjects or other data subject types, not to a virtual data subject. True data subjects may be subordinate to a virtual data subject, but not to a data subject type.

Data subject forms are not identified on a data relation diagram because their identification requires another set of symbols. The intent of a data relation diagram is to keep the format simple so that people can readily understand the structure of data subjects in the common data architecture. Data subject forms are readily identified in their data definition through the use of common data definition words, such as *A virtual data subject representing...* or *A subtype of the Employee data subject that...*

There can be one-to-many data relations between data subjects or data subject types in a data subject hierarchy. This situation was not accepted in the traditional entity type hierarchy, but is allowed in the common data architecture. For example, the financial structure of an organization might consist of divisions, resource units, and financial centers. The same data are collected about each of these financial units, resulting in definition of a Financial Unit data subject with three subordinate data subject types, as shown in Figure 5.12. However, one-to-many data relations still exist between the individual financial units and are shown on the data subject hierarchy. When a data subject has subordinates with data relations between them, the parent data subject is shown as a recursive data subject.

The parent data subject in a data subject hierarchy may have data relations to other data subjects, as shown in Figure 5.13. Data relations with a parent data subject apply to all subordinate data subjects or data subject types, unless shown otherwise in a data subject hierarchy. This situation was not accepted in the traditional entity type hierarchy, but is allowed in the logical data structure for a common data architecture.

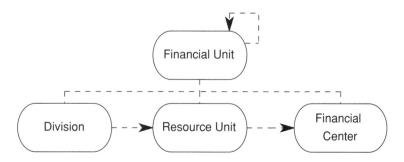

Figure 5.12 *Data relations between subordinate data subjects.*

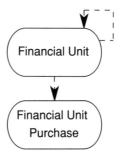

Figure 5.13 *Data relations from outside the data subject hierarchy.*

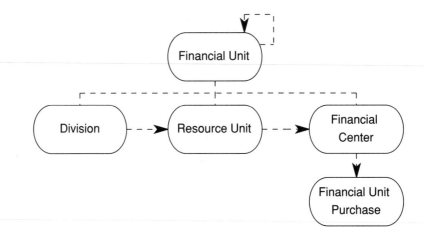

Figure 5.14 *Explicit data relations to subordinate data subjects.*

For example, the data relation between Financial Unit and Financial Unit Purchase in the example above applies only to Financial Center. It is shown explicitly in the data subject hierarchy, as shown in Figure 5.14. It is not subordinate to Division or Resource Unit.

Data subject hierarchies can have many branches at any level in the hierarchy. Although this situation is not common, it is possible, and was not accepted in the traditional entity type hierarchy. It is acceptable in the logical data structure for a common data architecture.

When a data subject hierarchy represents types of a data subject, a code table identifies the types. The code table becomes a parent of the

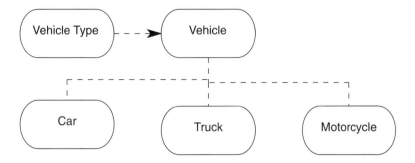

Figure 5.15 *Code table for a data subject hierarchy.*

parent data subject in the hierarchy. For example, Vehicles may be Trucks, Cars, or Motorcycles. A code table for Vehicle Type identifies which type of vehicle each data occurrence represents, as shown in Figure 5.15. However, the existence of a code table does not always mean that there is a data subject hierarchy. For example, a code table showing the type of chemical analysis performed on water samples does not represent a data subject hierarchy.

Data characteristics may be named according to each data subject in the data subject hierarchy, or they may be named by the parent data subject. Generally, when subordinate data subjects are types of the parent data subject, as in the vehicle example above, the data characteristics are named by the parent data subject. A *data characteristic matrix* shows which data characteristics are valid for each subordinate type, but they are all named by the parent data subject. The data characteristics are listed down the left side of the matrix, and the data subject types are listed across the top. An *X* in the cell indicates that the data characteristic belongs in the data subject type.

When subordinate data subjects are substantially different, the data characteristics are contained in, and are named by, the subordinate data subjects. In this situation, the parent data subject usually has no data characteristics and is a virtual data subject.

The situation may be found where the same data characteristic exists in the parent data subject and in one or more subordinate data subjects. The data characteristic is named by the parent data subject, and the data characteristic in the subordinate data subject inherits the definition of the parent data subject. This approach allows flexibility during data refining. If the parent data subject becomes a virtual data subject, the definitions are moved to the subordinate data characteristics and the reference is removed. If the subordinate data subjects are data subject types and the parent data subject contains all data characteristics, the data characteristics in the subordinate data subject are removed.

Ideally, when the same data characteristic exists in two or more subordinate data subjects, it should be factored to a parent data subject. However, this situation is only valid when both the parent and the subordinate data subjects contain data characteristics. If the parent data subject is a virtual data subject and the subordinate data subjects contain all the data characteristics, there is no factoring.

Data Categories

A *data category* is a data subject that is in a mutually inclusive, or *can-also-be,* relation with other peer data subjects, all of which are subordinate to a parent data subject. For example, an educational institution could have associations with students, employees, and alumni. Any person could have any combination of these associations with the educational institution. Associate is defined as a parent data subject and Student, Employee, and Alumnus are defined as data categories, as shown in Figure 5.16. There are one-to-one data relations between the parent Associate and the data categories. Data categories may also have one-to-one data relations between them, as shown in Figure 5.17.

Each data category contains data unique to that data category. Any data that are common to two or more data categories are placed in the parent data subject to reduce or eliminate redundant data. If common

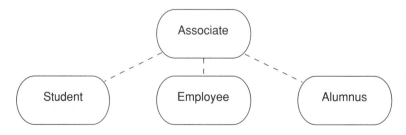

Figure 5.16 *Data categories for people data subjects.*

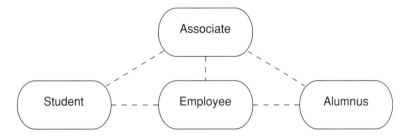

Figure 5.17 *Data relations between data categories.*

data are left in two or more data categories, those data are redundant and must be properly maintained to ensure integrity of the data resource.

Mutually Exclusive Parents

Mutually exclusive parents is a situation where a data subject has two or more parent data subjects that are mutually exclusive. Mutually exclusive parents are shown by a branched one-to-many data relation from the parent data subjects to the subordinate data subject. Each occurrence in the subordinate data subject belongs to only one parent data subject. This situation is not common, but does occur. For example, a Vehicle may be owned by either a Person or an Organization, never both, as shown in Figure 5.18.

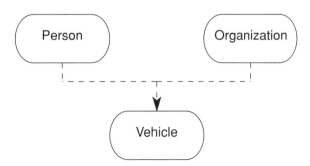

Figure 5.18 *Mutually exclusive parents.*

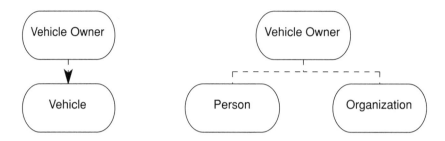

Figure 5.19 *Resolution of mutually exclusive parents.*

This situation is usually resolved by adding another data subject that shows the role played by the two parent data subjects. The two parent data subjects then become subordinate to the new data subject and form a data subject hierarchy. In the example above, Vehicle Owner is the new data subject. Person and Organization form a data subject hierarchy with Vehicle Owner, and Vehicle is subordinate to Vehicle Owner, as shown in Figure 5.19.

Inherent and Acquired Data Relations

Data relations may be inherent in the definition of data subjects, or they may be acquired, depending on how those data subjects are connected. An *inherent data relation* is a data relation that exists between two data subjects, based on the definition of those data subjects. It always exists, whether or not it is used. For example, an employee receives many paychecks from an employer, and each paycheck belongs to only one employee. A comprehensive definition of Employee Paycheck gives a reference to Employee that establishes the data relation, as shown in Figure 5.20.

An *acquired data relation* is a data relation that exists between two data subjects only when it is defined. It does not exist by reason of the definition of a data subject. For example, Disability is a table of disability codes.

Figure 5.20 *An inherent data relation example.*

Figure 5.21   *An acquired data relation example.*

There is no inherent data relation with other data subjects in the definition of disability codes. A data relation exists only when Disability is connected to another data subject like Customer, as shown in Figure 5.21.

Explicit and Implicit Data Relations

Data relations may be shown explicitly on a data relation diagram, or they may be implicit in the primary keys but not shown on the data relation diagram. An *explicit data relation* is a data relation that is shown on a data relation diagram. The diagrams above are examples of explicit data relations.

An *implicit data relation* is one that exists between two data subjects by the existence of data characteristics in the primary key, but is not shown on the data relation diagram. A data relation is implicit when one or more data characteristics in the primary key of a subordinate data subject match the primary key of a parent data subject, but that relation is not shown on a data relation diagram.

> *All data relations must be shown explicitly on a data relation diagram.*

All implicit data relations must be identified and shown explicitly on the data relation diagram in a common data architecture. Anytime one or more data characteristics in the primary key of a data subject match the primary key of another data subject, there is a data relation that must be shown explicitly on the data relation diagram.

▼ DATA KEYS

A *data key* is a set of one or more data characteristics that have a special meaning and use, in addition to describing a feature or trait of a data subject. The unqualified term *key* is frequently used in data design, and usually refers to a primary key. However, to avoid any confusion, and to adhere to semiotic theory, qualified terms are used in this book.

Primary Key

A *primary key* is a set of one or more data characteristics whose values uniquely identify each data occurrence in a data subject. A primary key is also known as a *unique identifier*. Each data occurrence in a data subject must have a different value in the primary key. If two or more data occurrences in a data subject have the same value in the primary key, there is no uniqueness and the primary key is not valid. This concept is very important for identifying and integrating disparate data into a common data architecture.

> *Every data subject must have a primary key that uniquely identifies each data occurrence in that data subject.*

Many data subjects have more than one primary key, particularly data subjects in a common data architecture that represents disparate data. When there is more than one primary key in a data subject, an official primary key is usually designated. An *official key* is a primary key that is designated as the dominant, outstanding, preferred primary key for a data subject in the mature data resource. All other primary keys are either alternate, limited, or obsolete primary keys.

There are several criteria for identifying a primary key and assuring its validity across the full range of data occurrences. If a primary key meets these criteria, it is a *valid primary key*. If it does not meet these criteria, it is an *invalid primary key*. Official primary keys adhere to these requirements. The criteria for identifying an official primary key are listed in Appendix C.

An *alternate primary key* is a primary that uniquely identifies all occurrences in a data subject, but was not designated as the official primary key. For example, the combination of an employee's name and birth date uniquely identifies each employee. However, the employee's social security number was designated the official key, so the combination of an employee's name and social security number becomes an alternate primary key.

Ideally, a primary key is unique for all data occurrences in a data subject. However, there are situations with disparate data where a primary key is not unique for all data occurrences. This situation usually occurs when the scope of a data subject is expanded. For example, if the scope were a single state, a Vehicle License Number would uniquely identify each vehicle. Therefore, Vehicle License Number would be a primary key for Vehicle. However, if the scope were the entire United States, Vehicle License Number would not uniquely identify a vehicle, because the same license number exists in many different states. A State Name or State Code needs to be added to make the primary key unique. A *limited primary key* is a primary key that is valid for a limited set of data occurrences in a data subject within the common data architecture.

> *Primary key uniqueness depends on the scope of the data.*

An *obsolete primary key* is a primary key that no longer uniquely identifies each data occurrence in a data subject within the common data architecture. Obsolete primary keys usually result from integrating disparate data into a formal data resource, and from the determination that an existing primary key is obsolete.

A primary key should contain elemental data characteristics whenever possible. It is easier to identify unique data subjects when the primary key contains elemental data characteristics rather than combined data characteristics. For example, if a college class is uniquely identified by the Department Name, Class Number, and Academic Term Identifier, the primary key should consist of these three individual data characteristics. One exception to this rule is data characteristics that are common combinations of elemental data characteristics, such as dates.

Foreign Key

A *foreign key* is the primary key of a parent data subject that is placed in a subordinate data subject. Its value identifies the data occurrence in the parent data subject that is the parent of the data occurrence in the subordinate data subject. A foreign key must be defined for each data relation to a parent data subject. If there are two data relations to the same parent data subject, such as the resolution of a recursive many-to-many data relation, there will be two foreign keys to the parent data subject. When there is a one-to-one data relation, a foreign key is defined in each data subject.

There must a foreign key defined for each data relation to a parent data subject.

Foreign keys are redundant data, but they are a necessary and known form of redundant data. It is often said that proper data design eliminates all redundant data. This is not true, because foreign keys are a form of redundant data. Proper data design does, however, eliminate unnecessary and unknown forms of redundant data.

A foreign key may contain fully qualified data characteristics that are not fully qualified in the parent data subject. For example, a Vehicle may have two different Vendors, one from whom the vehicle was purchased and one who performs the maintenance. This situation is shown by two one-to-many data relations from Vendor to Vehicle. Since there are two data relations, there will be two foreign keys. The data characteristics in the foreign keys will be fully qualified as Vendor Identifier Purchase and Vendor Identifier Maintenance.

However, the primary key of Vendor contains Vendor Identifier. This is not a problem, because the sequence of data characteristics in the foreign key matches the sequence of data characteristics in the primary key of the parent data subject. Vendor Identifier Purchase and Vendor Identifier Maintenance both point to Vendor Identifier. It is not necessary to identify alternate primary keys in Vendor to represent the two foreign keys in Vehicle.

Two fully qualified data characteristics in Vehicle, Vendor Identifier Purchase, and Vendor Identifier Maintenance are defined in Vendor as variations of Vendor Identifier. They inherit the definition of Vendor Identifier, and their specific roles of identifying the vendor from whom the vehicle was purchased and the vendor who performs the maintenance are added to the definitions.

Secondary Key

A *secondary key* is a set of data characteristics that provide physical access to a data file. Secondary keys are important for developing information systems and physical databases and for defining data navigation between data files, but they are not necessary for developing a logical data structure in the common data architecture or for documenting disparate data. They will not be discussed further in this book.

▼ DATA TYPES

Developing a common data architecture that integrates a wide range of disparate data requires a thorough understanding of the different types of data that can exist.

Elemental and Combined Data

Elemental data characteristics that form a combined data characteristic must always be in the same sequence. For example, Date CYMD must always have the elemental characteristics in the sequence of Century Number, Calendar Year Number, Month Number, and Day Number. If they occur in a different sequence, it is a different data characteristic with a different name, such as Date YMD.

The elemental data characteristics in a combined data characteristic may have a fixed or variable length. For example, the elemental data characteristics in Date CYMD are each two characters in length. However, the lengths of the elemental data characteristics in Person Name Complete Normal (Person Name Individual, Person Name Middle, Person Name Family) vary from one person's name to another.

Combined data characteristics should not be a combination of unrelated elemental data characteristics. For example, the license number and make of a vehicle should not be used to form a combined data characteristic. It is very difficult to name and identify data properly in the formal data resource when unrelated elemental data characteristics are combined.

Primitive and Derived Data

A *primitive data characteristic* is a data characteristic whose value represents a feature or actual measurement of a feature in a data subject. It is usually the data characteristic that is captured or received about an object in the real world. It is not derived in any manner. For example, a person's height or a vehicle's color is a primitive data characteristic. A *derived data characteristic* is a data characteristic whose value is derived, generated, summarized, or otherwise formed by some algorithm. For example, yearly rainfall and a customer's account balance are derived data.

Active derived data is derived data based on contributing data characteristics that exist and could change. The derived data characteristic must be rederived to remain current. *Static derived data* are derived data that will never change because their contributing data characteristics are static or no longer exist.

Traditionally, emphasis was on placed on naming, defining, and structuring primitive data. Statements like *Take care of the primitive data and the derived data will take care of themselves* and *Identify the key 500 primitive data elements in an organization and you have control of the organization* are frequently heard. Statements like *You will never identify all the derived data because they keep changing, so why even try* are also heard. Very little emphasis has been placed on derived data.

A common perception is that derived data are always calculated when needed and are never stored in the database, and therefore never need to be named, defined, or structured. This perception is not true. Derived data are frequently stored, particularly in executive information systems. They are not always derived at the time they are needed because repeated derivation is too time-consuming and too expensive, and because much of the contributing data may be gone.

A problem with ignoring derived data is in determining which data are really primitive and which are derived. In many cases, one person's derived data is another person's primitive data. For example, a customer's bank account balance is derived from all the transactions a customer makes, and is therefore derived data. However, if the account balances of all customers are taken at the end of the month to determine the average account balance, the account balances are primitive data, and the monthly average is derived data.

Derived data must be named, defined, and structured, like primitive data.

Since it is difficult to distinguish between primitive and derived data, since derived data may be stored in databases, and since many organizations are managed by derived data, it is mandatory that derived data be formally named, comprehensively defined, and properly structured in the same manner as primitive data in a common data architecture.

Fundamental Data

There is a common perception that fundamental data, such as Calendar Year Number, do not belong to a data subject. This perception is wrong, because all data, regardless of whether they are fundamental or specific data, belong to some data subject. Calendar Year Number is a data characteristic of Calendar Year, and Century Number is a data characteristic of Century. Just because an organization does not track data for Calendar Year or Century does not mean those data are not data subjects.

Furthermore, one person's specific data may be another person's fundamental data. For example, Post Office Box is a data subject containing many specific data characteristics, such as Post Office Box Number, Post Office Box Size, Post Office Box Fee, and so on, for the U.S. Postal Service. However, Post Office Box Number can also be a fundamental data characteristic that is inherited by Address Post Office Box Number for many organizations. Therefore, all data, including fundamental and specific data, are formally named, comprehensively defined, and properly structured in the common data architecture.

Tabular and Non-Tabular Data

Tabular data are data that exist in tables, such as characteristics describing people or equipment. Most disparate data that exist today are tabular data. *Non-tabular data* are data that do not exist in tables, such as imaging data, spatial data, remote sensing data, voice data, and textual data. Non-tabular data are becoming more popular every day, and the volume of non-tabular data is growing rapidly.

Non-tabular data must be managed with the same intensity and by the same rules as tabular data. If they are not, the situation with non-tabular data just a few years from now will be the same as the situation with old tabular data today. There will be large quantities of disparate non-tabular data that must be refined into a common data architecture. Therefore, non-tabular data must be managed in the same way as tabular data and integrated with tabular data in the common data architecture.

Non-tabular data are designed and managed in the same way as tabular data.

Non-tabular data belong to data subjects just like tabular data, and they are named and defined in the same way. Common data subject words identify the specific type of non-tabular data subject, such as Layer or Image. Non-tabular data are remodeled in the same way as tabular data, although there are slight differences.

For example, vendor invoices contain tabular data in a tabular Vendor Invoice data subject. Vendor invoices can also be stored as an image in a non-tabular Vendor Invoice Image data subject. The common data subject word *Image* indicates that the data subject contains non-tabular image data. A one-to-one data relation exists between Vendor Invoice and Vendor Invoice Image, as shown in Figure 5.22.

Spatial data, such as data in geographic information systems, are contained in data layers. A *data layer* is a specific grouping of data in a geographic information system, such as timber stands, topography, or school districts. A *data topic* is a one or more closely related data characteristics used in a geographic information system, such as species, site, and size class for timber stands. The data characteristics composing a data topic must be named and defined in the same manner as tabular data. A *primitive data layer* contains a single data topic. A *derived data layer* contains two or more data topics.

Ideally, a geographic information system should be designed with primitive data layers, which are then combined to form derived data layers that meet a particular need. A finite number of primitive data layers could produce an unlimited number of derived data layers to

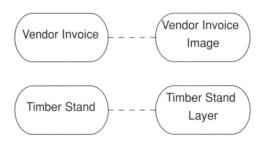

Figure 5.22 *Data Relations between tabular and non-tabular data.*

support different business activities. For example, a geographic information system contains two data layers for timber stands and soil units. Each data layer consists of polygons that represent timber stands and soil units respectively. Each polygon has a unique identifier, such as Timber Stand Identifier or Soil Unit Number, and may have other data related to that polygon.

Home and Foreign Data

Data characteristics may exist in the data subject that they characterize, or they may exist in another data subject. A *home data characteristic* is a data characteristic that exists in the data subject it characterizes. For example, Vehicle License Number in the Vehicle data subject is a home data characteristic. A *foreign data characteristic* is a data characteristic that exists in a data subject other than the one it characterizes. For example, Vehicle License Number in the Traffic Citation data subject is a foreign data characteristic.

> *All data characteristics are defined in their home data subject,*
> *regardless of where they appear in logical data structures.*

Ideally, foreign data characteristics should be limited to the data characteristics in primary and foreign keys. However, there are situations where it is desirable to have foreign data characteristics that are not part of a primary key or foreign key. These situations should exist in a physical data structure for a specific implementation, not in a logical data structure for the common data architecture. The use of formal data names and comprehensive data definitions helps to identify foreign data characteristics that are not part of a primary or foreign key.

Code Table Data Subjects

The contents of a data characteristic may be actual data values or data codes. Ideally, actual data values should be used whenever possible, particularly when the values are measurements. Too often actual measurements, such as a person's height, are coded into arbitrary groups, such as short, medium, and tall, that had meaning for a specific use. However, those groupings might be useless for another use of a person's height, such as a statistical analysis. Therefore, actual measurements should not be coded into arbitrary groups in the common data architecture.

Actual data values should be used whenever possible.

A *data code set* is a set of data codes that are closely related. For example, all the properties related to disability, such as speech, hearing, and so on, become a set of disability codes. Each data code set is defined as a separate data subject in the common data architecture. A *code table data subject* is a data subject containing a set of data codes. For example, the set of disability codes becomes the Disability data subject.

Each data code set must be defined as a separate code table data subject independent of its use.

Each code table data subject contains at least two data characteristics representing the data code value and the data code name. For example, Disability contains two data characteristics for Disability Code and Disability Name. The primary key for a code table data subject is the data characteristic representing the data code value. For example, Disability Code is the primary key for Disability.

If there are different levels of detail for data codes, a separate data subject is defined for each level. For example, land use might have three levels of detail, from general land use to specific land use. A separate data subject is established for each level of land use codes, such as Land Use Category, Land Use Group, and Land Use Type. The Land Use Category might be *Agriculture* or *Manufacturing*. The Land Use Group might be *Crops* or *Livestock*, within *Agriculture*. The Land Use Type might be *Potatoes* or *Corn*, within *Crops*.

A general guideline is to establish a common hierarchy to show levels of detail for code tables. For example, a hierarchy of *category*, *group*, *class*, and *type* might be established, where *category* is the highest level of summarization and *type* is the most detailed. This common hierarchy adds uniformity to the common data architecture. The words become common data subject words and are placed in the data resource lexicon.

If there are two or more different higher level groupings for a set of data codes, a parent data subject is defined for each of those groupings.

For example, a set of specific Building Use Codes must be grouped one way for fire protection and another way for valuation. A parent data subject is defined for each of these groupings, such as Building Use Fire Protection Group and Building Use Valuation Group.

A code table may be attached to one or more data subjects to characterize the occurrences of that data subject. For example, Disability Type can be attached to Employee, Customer, Student, or Vendor to identify a disability. Defining a one-to-many data relation from Disability Type to Employee identifies one disability for an Employee, as shown in the diagram on the left in Figure 5.23. However, an Employee may have many disabilities, resulting in a many-to-many data relation. This many-to-many data relation is resolved by adding Employee Disability, as shown in the diagram on the right in Figure 5.23.

The data analyst must carefully review the use of data codes to determine whether there are one or many occurrences. If a data subject can have only one occurrence of a data codes, a one-to-many data relation is defined. If a data subject can have more than one occurrence of a data code, an additional data subject is defined.

Indicators

An *Indicator* is a data characteristic that identifies a binary situation, such as 0/1, on/off, yes/no, true/false, and so forth. For example, Employee might have an Employee Voice Mailbox Indicator showing whether that employee's phone line has a voice messaging capability.

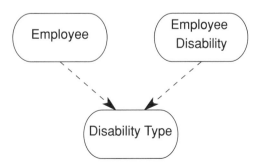

Figure 5.23 *Attaching coded table data subjects.*

Indicators represent the existence of another data subject, which may be visible or hidden. In the example above, there is really a Voice Mailbox data subject. Each data occurrence in Voice Mailbox represents the voice mailbox for an employee and contains all the data required for managing that voice mailbox. The existence of a data occurrence in Voice Mailbox for an employee results in the Employee Voice Mailbox Indicator having a value of *Yes*, and the absence of a data occurrence for an employee results in the indicator having a value of *No*.

> *Indicators represent another data subject that may be visible or hidden.*

There can be more than one indicator for a data subject. For example, Phone Line contains data about each phone line, and Phone Feature contains data about features that could be on a phone line. These two data subjects are in a many-to-many data relation. In other words, a phone line can have many features, and a feature can exist on many phone lines. This many-to-many data relation is resolved by the addition of Phone Line Feature. Each data occurrence in Phone Line Feature identifies the existence of a specific feature on a specific phone line.

Determining all the features on a particular phone line requires a search of Phone Line Feature. It would be easier to create a set of indicators in Phone Line showing which features exist on a phone line. The name of each of these indicators begins with Phone Line, followed by the feature name from Phone Feature. For example, there might be Phone Line Stutter Indicator, Phone Line Call Forward Indicator, Phone Line Call Waiting Indicator, and so on, representing various Phone Features that can be placed on a Phone Line. The definition of each indicator references the Phone Feature.

> *Indicators represent derived data that must be maintained to ensure integrity of the data resource.*

Since an indicator represents the existence of a data occurrence in another data subject, it is derived data. Its value is derived from the existence of another data occurrence. If that data occurrence can change, the indicator represents active derived data. Therefore, the indicator must be kept synchronized with its corresponding data occurrence or the integrity of the data resource deteriorates.

▼ DATA CLASSIFICATION

Classification is a method or scheme to arrange things in classes according to some established criteria. A classification scheme progresses from generalization to specialization, like the animal and plant kingdoms, chemicals, minerals, and so on. For example, Ursus Horribilis, commonly known as a grizzly bear, fits into a classification scheme for animals, as shown in Figure 5.24. The animal classification scheme has a formal naming taxonomy and supporting vocabulary.

Data can be classified like animals. The *data classification scheme* is a scheme for classifying data that progresses from general levels to specific levels. It includes categorical levels and working levels of data. The general data classification scheme is shown in Figure 5.25. It is supported by a formal data naming taxonomy and supporting vocabulary, just like the animal classification scheme.

The *working levels of data classification* are the lower three levels, consisting of data subjects, data characteristics, and data characteristic variations. They represent the operational level of data classification, like genus, species, and subspecies in the animal and plant kingdoms.

Kingdom Animale (animals)
Phylum Chordata (spinal cord)
Subphylum Gnathostomata (jawed vertebrates)
Superclass Tetrapoda (four legged land vertebrates)
Class Mammalia (mammals)
Subclass Theria (marsupials and placental mammals)
Infraclass Eutheria (placental mammals)
Order Carnivora (carnivores)
Suborder Fissipedia (dogs, cats, bears)
Family Ursidae (bears)
Genus Ursus (bears)
Species Horribilis (grizzly bear)

Figure 5.24 *Classification scheme for the grizzly bear.*

Data Discipline
Data Area
Data Group
Data Class
Data Subject
Data Characteristic
Data Characteristic Variation

Figure 5.25 *The data classification scheme.*

These three levels are used for building the common data architecture and designing the formal data resource.

The *categorical levels of data classification* are abstract groupings of data above the working level that provide a broader perspective of data. They are used to emphasize the importance of data, to determine priorities, and for strategic planning. They are used during surveys to determine the existence of broad groupings of data. They are used to begin the definition of data from very diverse disciplines and very diverse uses.

Each categorical level must have a formal name and a comprehensive definition, just like the working levels. The categorical levels are named and defined just like data subjects, except that a suffix defines the level in the categorical hierarchy. For example, part of the categorical levels of data classification for water resources is shown in Figure 5.26. Sample definitions of the categorical levels are shown in Appendix B.

The general guideline is to develop categorical levels of data classification as necessary to help people understand the data. Developing categorical levels should not be a major effort, particularly if it will not help development or understanding of the common data architecture. Only the number of categorical levels that are necessary for meaning and understanding need be developed. People should not be forced to classify data unless there is a tangible benefit from that classification. If development of the categorical levels of data classification gets in the way of developing a common data architecture, it should be abandoned. In other words, developing the categorical levels is a technique to help people understand data at a higher level. It is not a requirement

```
Water Resource Data Discipline
    Stream Data Area
        Stream Quality Data Group
            Stream Biological Quality Data Class
            Stream Chemical Quality Data Class
            Stream Physical Quality Data Class
        Stream Quantity Data Group
        Etc.
    Lake Data Area
        Etc.
```

Figure 5.26 *Categorical data classification example.*

for developing a common data architecture, nor is it a purely academic exercise.

> *Developing categorical levels of data classification is done to help people understand data, not as an academic exercise.*

Data themes are specific groupings of data subjects for a specific purpose. They are identified within some scope, such as a major project, and are based on the way people view the grouping of data subjects for that project. Data themes can cross the groupings in the categorical level of data classification and can change easily. There can be many different data themes crossing the data classification scheme, and a data subject can be in many different data themes. For example, there are data subject groups for Lake Quality, Reservoir Quality, and Stream Quality. A data theme for water quality could cross the Lake, Reservoir, and Stream data subject groups to include all water quality data.

▼ SUMMARY

A data structure shows the arrangement and relations among data subjects and their contents in the common data architecture. It includes both the logical data subjects and the implementation of those data subjects into physical data files. Data subjects and data relations form the structure of the formal data resource. Primary keys, foreign keys, secondary keys, and other data characteristics form the contents of a data subject. The logical data structure is documented on a data relation diagram, and the contents of data subjects are documented on a logical data structure chart.

Data relations can occur between data occurrences in different data subjects or within the same data subject. Data relations can be inherent in the definition of data, or they can be acquired through the connection of data subjects. All data relations must be identified and stated explicitly on a data relation diagram.

Data keys are data characteristics that have a special use in addition to defining the characteristic of a data subject. Primary keys uniquely identify each data occurrence in a data subject and are required for every data subject in the data resource. Foreign keys identify the parent data occurrence in a parent data subject for each data occurrence in the subordinate data subject. Secondary keys provide access to a data subject for storing or retrieving data. Only primary and foreign keys are used to document disparate data and define a formal data resource.

Various types of data characteristics, such as elemental and combined, primitive and derived, actual and coded, home and foreign, tabular and non-tabular, and fundamental and specific, exist in disparate data and in the common data architecture. Each of these data characteristic types must be understood so that it can be easily recognized and used to build a common data architecture.

A data classification scheme provides higher levels of classification above data subjects. These levels of classification are useful for identifying broad groupings of data for a variety of purposes. Data themes are groupings of data for a specific purpose; they may cross the data classification scheme.

A thorough understanding of all these data structure components is necessary to identify and define both new and disparate data within a common data architecture, to build a formal data resource, and to evolve to a mature data resource.

▼ QUESTIONS

The following questions are designed to provide a review of Chapter 5 and to stimulate thought about what the data structure for a common data architecture contains.

1. What are the two formats for documenting a data structure?

2. What does a data relation diagram represent?

3. What does a logical data structure outline represent?

4. What is a data relation?

5. What are the three basic types of data relations?

6. What is a primary key?

7. What is an alternate primary key?

8. What is a foreign key?

9. What is the difference between elemental and combined data characteristics?

10. What is the difference between home and foreign data characteristics?

11. What is the difference between primitive and derived data characteristics?

12. Why is documenting derived data important?

13. What is the difference between tabular and non-tabular data?

14. What is the difference between fundamental and specific data?

15. Why is it necessary to define fundamental data?

16. What are recursive data relations?

17. What is a data subject hierarchy?

18. What are data categories?

19. How is inheritance helpful in developing a data structure?

20. Why is it helpful to classify data?

▼▼▼ 6

DATA QUALITY

Data quality ensures that the formal data resource supports an organization's information needs.

Data Quality is the third activity in the Data Architecture component of the Data Resource Framework. Its purpose is to ensure high quality data in the formal data resource. The integration of highly variable disparate data into the formal data resource increases the importance of data quality. Initial work integrating disparate data shows that disparate data are far more variable and have much lower quality than was first thought. This variability must be identified and data quality must be improved to have a formal data resource that supports the organization's information needs.

Data quality is often talked about but, like a data architecture, is seldom defined. It has received limited interest in most organizations, and most of that interest has been in measuring various aspects of data quality. One of the reasons for the limited interest has been the lack of a formal data architecture within which data quality could be defined and implemented. Now that a common data architecture has been formally defined, data quality can be defined and implemented within that architecture.

This chapter begins with the concept of data quality and the three components of data quality: data integrity, data accuracy, and data completeness. It provides an explanation of data integrity, followed by a brief discussion about normalizing data and approaches to managing data integrity. Next, data accuracy and data completeness are described. Finally, the approaches to managing data quality are presented.

▼ DATA QUALITY CONCEPT

Data quality is how well data in the formal data resource support the business activities of an organization. It is both a measure of that support and an activity to ensure that the data resource contains high quality data. Data quality includes data integrity, data accuracy, and data completeness. *Data integrity* deals with how well data are maintained in the formal data resource. *Data accuracy* deals with how well data in the formal data resource represent the real world. *Data completeness* ensures that all the data needed to support business activities are available in the formal data resource.

Maintaining high quality data in the formal data resource, just like formally naming and comprehensively defining data, requires a recognition and understanding of the real world. The formal data resource represents the real world and how an organization operates in the real world. Recognizing and understanding that real world and an organization's business activities ensures that the formal data resource adequately represents the real world and supports the organization's business activities.

Since organizations perform different activities, they have different views of the real world; they identify, monitor, and manage different things in the real world. Developing a formal data resource for an organization must include all views of the real world for that organization. Developing a formal data resource for more than one organization requires inclusion of the real-world views for all those organizations. Integrating different real-world views helps people understand the real world better and helps them share data.

Integrating disparate data that represent different views of the real world means integrating data with different data quality. Disparate data have widely different integrity, accuracy, and completeness. An understanding of these data quality components helps people integrate data within a common data architecture and build a formal data resource that provides high quality data.

▼ DATA INTEGRITY

The first component of data quality is data integrity. *Data integrity* is the formal definition of comprehensive rules and the consistent application of those rules to ensure high quality data in the formal data resource. It deals with how well data are maintained in the formal data resource. It is both an indication of how well data are maintained in the formal data resource and an activity to ensure that the formal data resource contains high-quality data.

There are four categories of data integrity: data values, data structure, data derivation, and data retention. Each of these categories is explained below.

Data Value Integrity

Data value integrity specifies the allowable values for each data characteristic and each relation between data characteristics in the formal data resource. Data value integrity can be specified as data integrity values or data integrity rules. A *data integrity value* is an actual data value or a data code value that is allowed in the formal data resource. A *data integrity rule* is a statement that defines the actual data values or data code values that are allowed in the formal data resource.

Data integrity values can be specified for a single data characteristic. For example, the data code values for Disability specify the allowable values when those codes are in another data subject, such as Employee. If the data code value appears in Disability, it can appear in Employee. If it does not appear in Disability, it cannot appear in Employee.

Data integrity values can also be specified for a relation between data characteristics. For example, there is a relation between Employee Type and Employee Seniority. Certain employee types can only exist with certain employee seniorities. The data value integrity for the relation between Employee Type Code and Employee Seniority Code is specified in the first two columns of the table in Figure 6.1. Additional columns can be added for begin and end dates, or for any other data characteristics relating to the relation between Employee Type Code and Employee Seniority Code.

Data integrity rules can be specified for data characteristics. For example, *Maximum 3-digit numeric* is a data integrity rule for Employee

Employee Type Code	Employee Seniority Code	Begin Date	End Date
1	A	10/1/91	
1	B	10/1/91	
2	B	10/1/91	
2	C	10/1/91	
3	A	10/1/91	
3	B	10/1/91	
3	C	10/1/91	12/31/92
4	A	08/1/92	
4	C	08/1/92	

Figure 6.1 *Data value integrity table.*

Age, and *Maximum 34-character alphabetic right justified* is a data integrity rule for Organization Name.

Conditional data value integrity specifies whether the values in data characteristics are required, optional, or prevented under certain conditions. For example, a student's name and birth date are required; a customer's name is required, but a customer's monthly income is optional; and a vehicle's horsepower is required for motorized vehicles, but prevented for non-motorized vehicles. These conditions are specified in a *conditional data value integrity table,* as shown in Figure 6.2.

Conditional data value integrity can also be specified as a data integrity rule. The rule form is useful when a condition is involved. For example, Vehicle Horsepower in the example above involves a condition. The conditional data value integrity rules for those conditions are shown in Figure 6.3.

Data Domains

Traditionally, data value integrity was embedded in application programs, if it was even defined and documented. In the common data architecture, data value integrity is defined in data subjects like any other data, and it becomes part of the formal data resource. A *data domain* is a data subject that contains data integrity values or data

Student
Student Name	Required
Student Birth Date	Required

Customer
Customer Name	Required
Customer Monthly Income	Optional

Vehicle
Vehicle Horsepower	
Motorized Vehicles	Required
Non-Motorized Vehicles	Prevented

Figure 6.2 *Conditional data value integrity table.*

If Vehicle is Motorized	Then Vehicle Horsepower is Required
If Vehicle is Non-Motorized	Then Vehicle Horsepower is Prevented

Figure 6.3 *Conditional data value integrity rules.*

integrity rules. A *data value domain* is a data domain that contains data integrity values. A *data rule domain* is a data domain that contains data integrity rules.

Data domains contain the data integrity for actual data values and data code values.

Every data characteristic must have a corresponding data domain that specifies the values it can have. In the examples above, data domains are defined for Disability Codes, for the relation between Employee Type Code and Employee Seniority Code, and for the three data subjects with conditional data values. The data subject names for those data domains are Disability, Employee Type Seniority Integrity, Student Integrity, Customer Integrity, and Vehicle Integrity, respectively. Notice the use of a common data subject word *Integrity* for those data subjects.

Data value domains must have a data domain for their data characteristics. For example, Disability contains a set of Disability Codes that is the data domain for any data subject containing disability codes, such as Employee. However, Disability has at least two data characteristics for Disability Code and Disability Name. Each of these data characteristics requires a data domain defining the allowable values. The data rule domain for Disability Code is *A 1-digit number* and the data rule domain for Disability Name is *A maximum 16-character alpha-numeric string.*

Data domains are defined until they contain a rule.

Data value integrity in the formal data resource must be carried to a data integrity rule. In the example above, Employee Disability Code contains a disability code for an employee. The valid set of disability codes allowed are specified in Disability, which is the data value domain for Employee Disability Code. However, Disability Code contains two data characteristics that must have data integrity rules covering their values. This process continues until all data value integrity is specified by data integrity rules. The implied data integrity rule for these data integrity rules is *An alpha-numeric string of unlimited length.*

The data subject representing a data value domain is a code table data subject, and is designed like any other data subject. A data subject representing a data rule domain is also designed like any other data subject. It has a primary key and data characteristics representing the data value integrity rules. For example, the data value integrity rules for Student are specified in Student Integrity, as shown in Figure 6.4. The pri-

Student Integrity

    Primary Key
        Data Characteristic Name

    Characteristic List
        Data Characteristic Name
        Data Characteristic Integrity Rule
        Data Characteristic Integrity Condition

Figure 6.4 *Data domain structure.*

mary key is Data Characteristic Name, which contains the name of the data characteristic for which integrity is being specified. Data characteristics are defined for the data value integrity rule and for any conditional data value integrity.

Data Structure Integrity

Data structure integrity specifies the data integrity for data relations. Data structure integrity may be documented in a diagram, a matrix, or a table. A *data structure integrity diagram* shows data structure integrity as a diagram. For example, the existence of an Employee requires the existence of a Person, but existence of a Person does not require the existence of an Employee, as shown in Figure 6.5. Existence of a Student prevents existence of a Prospective Student and existence of a Prospective Student prevents existence of a Student. Existence of an Employee does not require existence of a Paycheck, but existence of a Paycheck requires existence of an Employee.

A *data structure integrity matrix* shows data structure integrity in a matrix. For example, the same data structure integrity shown in Figure 6.5 is shown in a matrix in Figure 6.6. The data structure integrity matrix is not as graphical as the diagram, but it shows the possibility of other conditions, such as those between Student and Person, and between Prospective Student and Person.

A *data structure integrity table* shows data structure integrity in a table. For example, the same data structure integrity shown in Figure 6.5 is shown in a table in Figure 6.7. The data structure integrity table is not as graphical as the data structure diagram and does not show other pos-

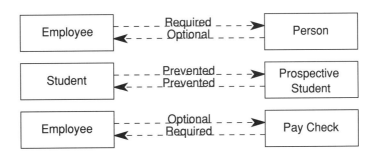

Figure 6.5 *Data structure integrity diagram.*

	Employee	Person	Pay Check	Student	Prospective Student
Employee		Required	Optional		
Person	Optional				
Pay Check	Required				
Student					Prevented
Prospective Student				Prevented	

Figure 6.6 *Data structure integrity matrix.*

Person
    Employee   Optional

Employee
    Person   Required
    Pay Check   Optional

Pay Check
    Employee   Optional

Student
    Prospective Student   Prevented

Prospective Student
    Student   Prevented

Figure 6.7 *Data structure integrity table.*

sibilities like the data structure matrix, but it takes less space. Usually, a data structure integrity diagram or data structure integrity matrix is used to identify structural data integrity, and a data structure integrity table is used for documentation.

Conditional data structure integrity specifies the cardinality for data relations. For example, Students can have zero, one, or many Degrees. However, Undergraduate Students cannot have any Degrees, and

Student
Undergraduate	Degree Prevented
Graduate	Degree Required

Figure 6.8 *Conditional data structure integrity table.*

Graduate Students must have one or more Degrees. Cardinality can be documented in a data structure integrity table or as data structure integrity rules.

A *conditional data structure integrity table* for the cardinality between Student and Degree is shown in Figure 6.8. The number of degrees for an Undergraduate Student is *0*, or *Prevented*. The number of degrees for a Graduate Student is one or more, commonly shown as *1,M*, or *Required*.

Conditional data structure integrity can also be documented as rules. A *conditional data structure integrity rule* shows the conditional data structure integrity in rule form. For example, the rules for the cardinality between Students and Degrees are shown in Figure 6.9. Either the tabular form or rule form is useful for documenting conditional data structure integrity. The cardinality can even be shown on a data relation diagram, if desired, by using the symbols *0, 0,1, 0,M,* or *1,M* meaning *zero, zero or one, zero-to-many,* or *one-to-many,* respectively. However, placing cardinality on a data relation diagram may make the diagram difficult for people to understand.

Referential integrity is part of data structure integrity that ensures a parent data occurrence exists for each subordinate data occurrence. A subordinate data occurrence cannot be added if there is no parent data occurrence, and a parent data occurrence cannot be deleted if subordinate data occurrences still exist. For example, a Customer Order cannot be added without a corresponding Customer, and a Customer cannot be deleted if there are corresponding Customer Orders. Referential integrity

If Student is Undergraduate	Then Degree Prevented
If Student is Graduate	Then Degree Required

Figure 6.9 *Conditional data structure integrity rule.*

is required in the common data architecture. It does not need to be stated explicitly for every data relation.

Referential integrity is required in the common data architecture.

Data structure integrity is maintained in a data subject similar to data value integrity, so that all data integrity is part of the formal data resource and can be used to maintain its integrity.

Data Derivation Integrity

A formal data resource contains a considerable quantity of data that is derived from other data. These derived data need to be properly maintained through data integrity rules. A formal data resource may also contain a considerable quantity of redundant data that must be maintained to be consistent. *Data derivation integrity* specifies the procedure for maintaining derived data and redundant data in the formal data resource. For derived data, the specification includes the contributing data characteristics, the procedure for deriving data, and the timing for derivation and rederivation. For redundant data, the specification includes identification of the official version and the timing for maintaining redundant data.

Derived data values are developed from a data derivation procedure and one or more contributing data characteristics. *Active derived data* are derived from contributing data characteristics that still exist and whose values can change. They must be rederived on a regular basis. *Static derived data* are derived from contributing data characteristics that no longer exist or whose values will never change. They are always valid and never need to be rederived.

The problem with most active derived data is that once they are derived, they are usually not updated when the values of their contributing data characteristics change, or they are updated inconsistently. When the values of contributing data characteristics change, the values of the active derived data characteristics must be rederived to be remain valid. Data derivation integrity specifies when the rederivation occurs, such as immediately, daily, or monthly.

---

*Active derived data must be routinely updated when the values
of their contributors change.*

Data derivation integrity is specified with a data derivation diagram
and a data derivation procedure. A *data derivation diagram* specifies the
data characteristics contributing to the derived data characteristic. For
example, a data derivation diagram for deriving an Account Balance
from Account Transactions, and for deriving Well Type from Well Casing
Material and Well Depth, are shown in Figure 6.10. The arrows point
from the contributors to the derived data characteristics.

A d*ata derivation procedure* is an algorithm, equation, logical expression, or matrix that specifies the procedure for deriving data. For example, the derivation of kilometers from miles could easily be
documented as an equation. The data derivation procedure for Account
Balance is shown in Figure 6.11.

The data derivation procedure for Well Type is shown in Figure 6.12.
It is a matrix showing the conditions of Well Casing Material and Well
Depth for deriving Well Type. A statement about the timing of rederiva-
tion appears below the matrix.

Redundant data often exist in the formal data resource, even though
the objective is to limit redundant data to foreign keys. Redundant

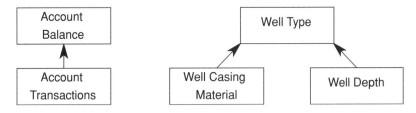

Figure 6.10 *Data derivation diagram.*

The new **Account Balance** is derived at midnight of each working day
by applying **Account Transactions** for the working day to the previous
day's **Account Balance**.

Figure 6.11 *Data derivation procedure for Account Balance.*

Well Casing Material	Well Depth	Well Type
Black Steel	< 10 Feet	1
Black Steel	11 to 100 Feet	2
Black Steel	> 100 Feet	3
Stainless Steel	< 50 Feet	4
Stainless Steel	50 Feet +	5

Well Type is rederived immediately when either **Well Casing Material** or **Well Depth** changes.

Figure 6.12 *Data derivation algorithm for Well Type.*

data are also very prominent in disparate data. These redundant data must be identified, documented, and properly maintained. *Data redundancy integrity* is the proper maintenance of consistent values in each existence of a redundant data characteristic.

Data redundancy integrity can be documented in a diagram or a table. A *data redundancy diagram* specifies the data characteristics containing the official version of data and the redundant data characteristics that are maintained from the official version as a diagram. For example, an employee's birth date may exist in the employee file, the payroll file and the training file. The employee file is designated as the official version and the other two files must be updated based on the official version, as shown in Figure 6.13. The arrow points from the official version to the redundant versions. Whenever Employee Birth Date is entered or changed in the Employee file, it is immediately changed in the Payroll file and the Training file.

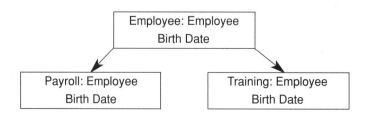

Figure 6.13 *Data redundancy diagram.*

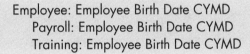

Employee: Employee Birth Date CYMD
Payroll: Employee Birth Date CYMD
Training: Employee Birth Date CYMD

Immediate update to Payroll and Training.

Figure 6.14 *Data redundancy table.*

A *data redundancy table* specifies the data characteristics containing the official version and the redundant data characteristics that are maintained from the official version as a table. For example, the data redundancy table for employee birth dates is shown in Figure 6.14. The timing of the update is shown in a statement at the bottom of the table.

Data derivation integrity and data redundancy integrity are maintained in a data subject the same as other data integrity specifications. They are readily available for maintaining integrity in the formal data resource.

Data Retention Integrity

Data are often changed or discarded according to current business operations, without consideration for the future value of those data. *Data retention integrity* specifies criteria for preventing the loss of critical data through updates or deletion. It considers the future value of data to determine which data should be retained and how they should be retained. It looks to the future to determine the unknown or hidden usefulness of the data.

Data retention integrity is best specified in narrative form. A *data retention statement* describes exactly what is done to existing data occurrences before they are deleted and to data characteristics before they are updated. The data retention statements for Employee are shown in Figure 6.15.

Data retention integrity is defined for the data occurrences in each data subject and for each data characteristic. Data retention integrity is maintained in a data subject the same way as any other data integrity, so the integrity of the formal data resource can be readily maintained.

Employee

An **Employee** data occurrence may be deleted after January 31st of the year following the end of the employment.

Employee Birth Date may be updated without retaining the previous value.

Employee Name may be updated after the existing value is placed in **Employee Audit Name** with a corresponding **Employee Audit Date**.

Figure 6.15 *Data retention integrity statements.*

▼ NORMALIZING DATA

Normalizing data is a way to manage data so that they meet the needs of business activities in the real world, the design requirements of a formal data resource, and the operational requirements of a database management system. It is a way to manage unnormalized data in the real world, normalized logical data, and denormalized physical data.

Unnormalized Data

Unnormalized data reflect the way data are used in the real world. They are structured by business needs, not by data subjects. For example, a student's class list contains data about the student, the classes that student is taking, the instructors teaching those classes, the location of those classes, and the term in which those classes are taken. The data are presented in a form that is meaningful to the student. If data were presented by data subject, they would be useless. Therefore, they are presented in an unnormalized form that is useful to the student in the real world.

Normalized Data

The unnormalized form is not acceptable for storing data in a formal data resource structured by data subjects. The data must be normalized by data subject to be properly stored in the formal data resource. *Normalized data* refers to the way data are stored by data subject in the formal data resource. *Data normalization* is a process to bring data into a normal form according to data subjects. Storing data in the unnormalized form created most of the disparate data problems that exist today.

Traditionally, data normalization is used to design or adjust the data structure based on precise criteria. However, the problem with data normalization in a common data architecture is a rigid adherence to pure data normalization criteria. It often alters the data structure in a way that does not correspond to the real world, particularly when disparate data are refined to a common data architecture.

The problem is with primary keys. Traditional data normalization says that if candidate data subjects have the same primary key, they are the same data subject. If they have different primary keys, they are different data subjects. The data subjects are structured according to the primary keys.

A more appropriate approach is to identify major data subjects based on the real world and use data normalization to validate those data subjects. If multiple existences of the same data subject have different primary keys, those primary keys are documented as multiple primary keys of one data subject. For example, Employee might have one primary key of Employee Social Security Number and another primary key combining Employee Name Complete Normal and Employee Birth Date CYMD. This does not mean that there are two different data subjects.

If different data subjects have the same primary key, they remain separate data subjects with identical primary keys. For example, Employee and Retiree may each have Social Security Number as the primary key. This does not mean they are the same data subject. Separation and combination of data subjects should only be done based on the real world.

> *Data normalization is only a tool to help identify and define data subjects based on the real world.*

Multiple primary keys usually do not occur in a traditional project. For this reason, pure data normalization has survived. However, data subjects with multiple primary keys are frequently found in disparate data and in the common data architecture. To avoid altering the data structure to conform to the primary key requirement, the data normalization process is used only as a tool to identify truly different data subjects within a common data architecture.

Denormalized Data

Data denormalization is the formal process of transforming the logical data resource model to operate in a specific operating environment without compromising that logical model. The resulting physical data resource model is used to define physical data files and data items. A logical data resource model can be denormalized in several different ways to operate in several different operating environments. This multiple data denormalization is common in today's disparate operating environment. It will also be common as data are formally deployed on an open network.

When the operating environment changes to an open network, data may be automatically reverse-engineered (normalized) to the logical data resource model and forward-engineered (denormalized) to another operating environment. This automatic re-engineering process will become routine as data are moved around a network for optimization. Data must be well structured and data integrity rules must be clearly defined to assure that automatic re-engineering maintains high-quality data.

▼ MANAGING DATA INTEGRITY

Managing data integrity is an important part of building a common data architecture. Proper management of data integrity requires an understanding of the use of data integrity rules, the inheritance involved in data integrity, the use of data integrity constraints, and the processes to identify existing data integrity and develop appropriate data integrity for the formal data resource.

Data Integrity Rules

Fundamental data integrity rules are data integrity rules that apply to fundamental data. They usually have wider limits—for example, Calendar Year may be *00* through *99*—and are developed from an analysis of possible values. They apply to all specific data based on fundamental data. *Specific data integrity rules* are data integrity rules that apply to specific data. They may be a subset or further qualification of the fundamental data integrity rules if the specific data are based on fundamental data.

Specific data integrity rules cannot alter or violate the limits of fundamental data integrity rules, but they may constrain them. For example, a specific data integrity rule might specify a valid Calendar Year of 62 through 90 for Service Contracts, or a subset of Disability Codes might be valid for school-age children. However, a specific data integrity rule can not allow a value of AX for Calendar Year when the fundamental data integrity rules limit the value to 00 through 99.

Specific data integrity rules are subsets of fundamental data integrity rules for specific business activities.

Data integrity can be inherited in the same way as data descriptions. *Data integrity inheritance* is the situation in which data integrity is obtained from parent data subjects and fundamental data characteristics. Any data characteristic may inherit data integrity from its parent or a fundamental data characteristic, and may have its own unique data integrity. For example, data integrity rules for a Date CYMD are inherited from the data integrity rules for Century Number, Calendar Year Number, Month Number, and Day Number. Employee Birth Date CYMD inherits the data integrity rules for Employee Birth Date and for Date CYMD. Additional data integrity rules might be added for valid ranges of an employee's birth date.

Data integrity can be inherited in the same way as data descriptions.

Required data integrity rules are specific data integrity rules that are mandatory and must be applied in all situations. Data that do not meet the specific data integrity rules must not be allowed in the formal data resource. For example, a Calendar Year of AB should not be allowed in the formal data resource.

Optional data integrity rules are specific data integrity rules that are optional in certain situations. For example, a specific data integrity rule for Person Name Complete Normal may be optional for a person's name on a phone list, even though it is required for that person's name in payroll. An optional data integrity rule does not alter the specific data integrity rule, it just makes the implementation of that rule optional. Optional data integrity rules are the exception in the formal data resource, but they can occur and should be documented.

Data Integrity Constraints

Data integrity rules become data integrity constraints following the data denormalization. *Data integrity constraints* represent specific data integrity rules that are implemented for data files and data items. They are derived from a formal denormalization of specific data integrity rules.

> *Data integrity constraints are the physical implementation of data integrity rules.*

All specific data integrity rules must be implemented, except as modified during denormalization. There is no discretion about eliminating specific data integrity rules, or adding data integrity constraints that are not defined as specific data integrity rules.

Improving Data Integrity

Data integrity is specified as data are described and the data structure is developed. It evolves as the common data architecture evolves.

Data integrity control is the reactive process of determining the existing level of data integrity for the formal data resource. It is a process to determine the existing data integrity that is being applied to the formal data resource. If the true data integrity is known, people can use the data appropriately.

Data integrity assurance is the proactive process of ensuring that the formal data resource contains the appropriate data integrity. It is a process to determine the appropriate level of data integrity and ensure that the appropriate level of data integrity is achieved. Defining data integrity within a common data architecture helps determine the current level of data integrity and achieve the level of data integrity desired.

▼ DATA ACCURACY

The second component of data quality is data accuracy. *Data accuracy* is how well data stored in the formal data resource represent the real world. It includes both a definition of the current data accuracy and the adjustment in data accuracy to meet the business needs. It ensures that the current level of data accuracy is known and that the appropriate level of data accuracy can be achieved. The level of data accuracy must be known and must be adjusted to meet the needs of an organization.

> *The data accuracy must be known and must meet an organization's needs.*

Data accuracy issues were always present but were masked by a lack of a formal data architecture. Very little effort was made to determine how well data represented the real world. Implementing common data architectures across widely disparate data brought up data accuracy issues and forced inclusion of data accuracy as part of data quality. Data accuracy includes many different things.

Data accuracy includes the method used to identify objects in the real world and the method of collecting data about those objects. For example, it describes how an object was identified and the means by which data were collected about that object, such as remote sensing, air photo interpretation, or ground measurement.

Data accuracy includes precision, scale, and resolution. *Precision* indicates how precisely the measurement was made and how many significant digits are in the measurement. For example, a distance could be measured to the nearest 100 feet, the nearest one foot, or the nearest 0.01 foot. The location could be to the nearest 40 acres or the nearest square foot. A survey could be first order, second order, or third order.

Scale is the ratio of real-world distance to map distance, such as 1:12,000 or 1:100,000. A scale of 1:12,000 means that one inch on the map represents 12,000 inches on the ground, or one inch on the map represents 1000 feet on the ground. A 1:12,000 scale is a larger scale than 1:100,000 (one inch on the map represents a little over a mile and a half on the ground).

Resolution is the degree of granularity of the data, indicating how small an object can be represented with the current scale and precision.

For example, the resolution of remote sensing might be ten acres, one acre, or 0.1 acres. Ten acres would be course granularity and 0.1 acres would be fine granularity. Resolution is the precise measurement and granularity is a relative indication.

A relationship exists among precision, scale, and resolution. For example, a scale of 1:100,000 with a resolution of 0.001 inches on a map represents a resolution of 1:100 on the ground, or about eight feet. Anything smaller than eight feet will not be identified. If the precision of a measurement on the ground is one foot, that precision will not appear on the map. If the precision is greater than eight feet, it will appear on the map.

A relationship also exists between precision and format. For example, time might be captured to the nearest hour and stored to the nearest 0.01 hours. A person looking at the time as it is stored would assume that time was measured to the nearest 0.01 hours, which is not true. The format must match the precision, or a separate data characteristic must indicate the actual precision for the measurement.

Data accuracy includes the level of detail. Data can be stored at a very detailed level or at a summary level. For example, the flow of a river might be measured hourly in gallons per minute, and then summarized to acre feet per month. The individual measurements are detailed data, and the monthly total is a summary. This range of detail is common in executive information systems that allow drill-down and summary capabilities to provide information at the desired level.

Data accuracy includes collection frequency, data instance, and data volatility. The *collection frequency* is how often data are collected. For example, a patient's vital signs during heart surgery might be collected every second, while the population of a city might be collected every ten years. The collection frequency must be known for all data collected from the real world.

Data instance is the time frame the data represent in the real world. For example, the data for a heart patient during surgery represents a few seconds, and the cost-of-living index represents a specific month. The data instance must be known for all data.

Data volatility is the measure of how quickly data in the real world change. For example, data for a patient during heart surgery might change every few seconds, but a person's name often remains unchanged for an entire lifetime. The volatility of all data must be known to define its accuracy.

A relationship exists between collection frequency and data volatility. For example, if a patient's vital signs were taken every hour during heart surgery, the patient might die before the change was noticed and corrective action taken, but measuring the population of a city every day would not show significant changes. Therefore, the frequency of data collection must match the volatility of the data. Data that are not kept fresh will deteriorate, and spoiled data result in less accurate formal data resource.

Data accuracy includes the method of capture and degree of reproducibility of data. Who captured the data, what method was used to capture the data, how were data input, who is authorized to collect and input data, and who can declare a data value to be correct, are all data accuracy issues. They must be known for all data collected from the real world.

Confidence is an important consideration for data accuracy. Every person has a level of confidence about data. Confidence in the person or organization collecting data, or the method of collection, is reflected in confidence about the data, regardless of the true accuracy. Loss of confidence in a few pieces of data might destroy confidence in the formal data resource. Any issue with the confidence of data must be identified and resolved.

Data accuracy is documented in both the data name and the data description, as described in the Data Name and Data Definition chapters. The common data architecture identifies the range of data accuracy variability and allows an adjustment of data accuracy to meet an organization's needs.

Data accuracy is documented in the data name and data definition.

Data accuracy control is the reactive process of determining how well data in the formal data resource represent the real world. It determines the existing level of data accuracy. It is very important for people to know the true accuracy of data. If the true data accuracy is not known, it makes little difference how well the data represent the real world.

Data accuracy assurance is the proactive process of ensuring that data in the formal data resource represent the real world as closely as the organization desires for support of its business activities. It determines the desired level of data accuracy and ensures that the desired level of accuracy exists in the formal data resource. In many situations, data accuracy needs to be increased, but in some situations data accuracy may be reduced and still meet an organization's needs. It is important to have the desired level of data accuracy in the formal data resource.

▼ DATA COMPLETENESS

The third component of data quality is data completeness. *Data completeness* is how available data are to support the business needs of an organization. It includes an inventory of existing data and an analysis of the data required to meet an organization's data needs. It ensures that all required data are available in the formal data resource when an organization needs those data. It ensures just-in-time data to develop just-in-time information.

> *The formal data resource must completely meet the data needs of an organization.*

Data suitability is how suitable data are for a specific purpose. It varies with the use of data. The same data may be suitable for one use and unsuitable for another. Data suitability is a subset of data completeness. The total of data suitability for all uses determines data completeness.

Data completeness control is the reactive process of determining what data are available and how completely they support an organization's business activities. It's a process to inventory existing data and determine how often they are being used. It is important that people first know what data are available before they begin collecting additional data. In many situations, the desired data actually exist, but people do not know they exist and begin collecting additional data.

Data completeness assurance is the proactive process of analyzing the data needs of an organization's business activities and ensuring that those data are available when needed. In many situations, additional data are needed to support business activities, but in other situations, data may be discarded because they are not needed for any of the organization's business activities. It is important to have all the data, and only the data, needed to support business activities in the formal data resource.

▼ MANAGING DATA QUALITY

Managing data quality includes managing data integrity, data accuracy, and data completeness to ensure that the formal data resource adequately supports the business activities of an organization. It is possible to have data with high integrity, high accuracy, and low quality. For example, a system is developed to track employee sock color. Data are updated every hour the employee is on the job and are highly accurate. However, there is absolutely no need for data on employee sock color to support any business activity in the organization. Therefore, the data are low quality.

The formal data resource must have the data quality necessary to support the organization's business activities.

The opposite situation is also true. Data can have low accuracy and high quality. For example, general population trends are not very accurate because the exact number of people is not known. However, population trends are frequently used in analyzing and predicting many things related to the population, which makes them high quality data. Data accuracy is at the level needed to support business activities, not the highest accuracy possible.

Clients will ultimately maintain the quality of the data resource, including definition and implementation of data integrity rules. Data architects will design and maintain the common data architecture and build the formal data resource, but clients will use that architecture and populate the data resource to support their business activities. Defining data integrity in an understandable way helps clients become involved in defining and implementing data integrity.

Direct client involvement substantially improves data integrity.

Data quality control is the reactive process of determining how well data in the formal data resource support business activities. It's a process to review the formal data resource and the business activities to determine how well the data support the business activities. It includes data integrity control, data accuracy control, and data quality control.

Data quality assurance is the proactive process of ensuring that data in the formal data resource adequately support business activities. It includes data integrity assurance, data accuracy assurance, and data completeness assurance. It's a process to identify the data needs of business activities and ensure that the formal data resource contains the appropriate data.

▼ SUMMARY

Data quality is a major activity in the Data Architecture component of the Data Resource Framework. It includes data integrity, data accuracy, and data completeness. Development of a common data architecture across widely disparate data shows that existing data have widely varying and very low quality. The data quality of a formal data resource must be known and improved to meet the data needs of an organization. The common data architecture provides the base for identifying existing data quality, defining the desired data quality, and ensuring that the desired data quality is achieved.

Data integrity is how well data are maintained in the formal data resource. It includes identifying and implementing data integrity rules for data values, data structure, data derivation, and data retention. Data accuracy is how well the data represent the real world. Data accuracy has been masked by data integrity issues, but development of a common data architecture brought out the varying degrees of data accuracy and led to a formal definition of data accuracy. Data completeness is how available data are to support business activities. Once it was apparent that data completeness was important for development of a formal data resource, the availability of data could be defined and managed.

Data quality is managed through data quality control and data quality assurance. Data quality control determines the level of data quality for existing data, including data integrity control, data accuracy control, and data completeness control. Data quality assurance determines the desired level of data quality for the formal data resource and ensures that the desired level is achieved, including data integrity assurance, data accuracy assurance, and data completeness assurance.

Data quality management starts with an understanding of the business activities and the data required to support those business activities. It also requires an understanding of the real world where the business operates. It directly involves clients who are knowledgeable in business activities and the data needs of those business activities. It results in a formal data resource that meets an organization's data needs and is fully utilized.

▼ QUESTIONS

The following questions are designed to provide a review of Chapter 6 and to stimulate thought about what data quality includes, how existing data quality is identified, and how appropriate data quality is achieved.

1. What is data quality?

2. What does data quality include?

3. Why is data quality important?

4. What does data integrity include?

5. What is a data domain?

6. Why is it important to manage derived data?

7. Why is it important to manage redundant data?

8. What is data integrity inheritance?

9. What is the difference between data integrity rules and data integrity constraints?

10. What is the difference between fundamental data integrity rules and specific data integrity rules?

11. What is the difference between required data integrity rules and optional data integrity rules?

12. What is the difference between data integrity control and data integrity assurance?

13. How has the use of data normalization changed in the common data architecture?

14. What is data accuracy and what does it include?

15. What level of accuracy should data characteristics have?

16. What is data completeness?

17. How is data completeness improved?

18. Why are different views of the real world so important?

19. What is client involvement necessary in defining data quality?

20. Why is it important to understand the real world?

▼7
DATA DOCUMENTATION

A comprehensive Data Resource Guide contains documentation of the formal data resource.

Data Documentation is the fourth, and last, activity of the Data Architecture component of the Data Resource Framework. Even though it is the last activity, it is certainly not the least important. All too often there is no documentation about the data resource, or the existing documentation is either not readily available or so poor that it is useless. All of these situations result in a less than effective formal data resource. The purpose of data documentation is to document the other three activities of the Data Architecture component as they are developed.

Data documentation provides complete, accurate, readily available documentation about the formal data resource. It includes documentation of existing disparate data and new data. It is an ongoing activity with all other activities in the Data Architecture component. It provides a complete, comprehensive picture of the formal data resource so that it can be fully utilized to support business activities.

This chapter explains documentation of the common data architecture and the formal data resource. It begins with an explanation of the data documentation concept. The use of semiotics to develop comprehensive data resource models is explained. The concept of a comprehensive data resource guide is presented and its components are described in detail.

▼ DATA DOCUMENTATION CONCEPT

Data documentation is the last activity in the Data Architecture component of the Data Resource Framework. Even though it is the last activity listed in the Data Architecture Component, it is not the least important. It supports the first three components, as shown in Figure 7.1.

Data documentation is *meta-data*—data about the common data architecture and the formal data resource. However, meta-data are no different from the data they define. They are analyzed, designed, and managed like any other data. The problem with meta-data about disparate data is that there are few commercial products available to support the identification and documentation of disparate data. Text processors, hypertext, and utility diagramming applications are the best tools available.

Data documentation is an important and indispensable part of the common data architecture. Good data documentation begins by capturing meta-data when they first become available, formatting them properly, and storing them where they are readily available to everyone. It is an effort that is ongoing with development of the common data architecture.

Client involvement is critical for developing useful documentation.

Good data documentation requires client involvement. Clients generally have a better knowledge and understanding of the business and data that support the business than the data processing staff. They also generally have better writing skills, and this combination of knowledge and writing skills helps them write better data documentation. In addition, client involvement increases acceptance and use of data documentation, which leads to better use of the formal data resource.

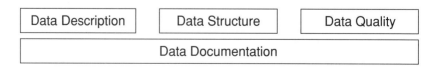

Figure 7.1 *Data documentation support for data architecture activities.*

Documentation Tools

There are many different techniques and tools for capturing, storing, and retrieving data documentation, such as data dictionaries, CASE tools, and repositories. They are good for designing and documenting new systems containing new data, and they are good for detail at a project level. However, most of these techniques and tools do not handle documentation of disparate data. They are generally weak on text processing, formal names, and data cross-referencing.

A whole new set of integrated Computer Aided Data Engineering (CADE) tools are needed for analyzing and documenting both new and disparate data within the common data architecture. These tools do not exist today, but a variety of other non-integrated tools can be used for analyzing and documenting the common data architecture.

> *A new set of Computer Aided Data Engineering tools is needed to support data engineering.*

The first and simplest tool that is available is a text processor. A text processor is good for developing data descriptions and logical data structures when there are frequent changes. Another useful tool that provides the capability of a text processor and a hot-key capability is hypertext. Hypertext is also good for data entity relation diagrams and references between the diagrams and data descriptions. A third useful tool is a utility diagrammer that provides a wide range of symbols that support semiotics. A fourth useful tool is a good database management system that stores text and graphics.

Documentation of the common data architecture must be readily available, easily accessible, and understandable. Initially, documentation can be in a paper form that is readily accessible by clients. As the common data architecture grows and people become familiar with documentation techniques, paper becomes cumbersome, and some form of automation is needed. Documentation can be automated in a variety of ways on personal computers, local area networks, or mainframe computers. The best approach for comprehensive data documentation is the Data Resource Guide described below.

Documentation Design

Design of meta-data is no different from the design of any other data. Organizations must develop a meta-data resource model for the meta-data, just as they develop a data resource model for the data used in information systems. When the meta-data resource model is developed, an organization can either build its own data documentation system or buy one. Either way, there must be a design for the data documentation system.

Meta-data are designed and managed the same as any other data in the formal data resource.

There is considerable hype about a meta-data resource model as the design for meta-data, and some suggestions that the data resource model supporting the meta-data resource model be called the *meta-meta-data resource model*. Most of this hype is unnecessary and is making documentation of the formal data resource more difficult than it needs to be. Meta-data are designed and documented like any other data. The meta-data resource model is simply another part of the formal data resource model for an organization.

Data Resource Model

There are two basic models for managing data. A *data model* is the mathematical construct of a database management system, such as a hierarchical, network, inverted, or relational construct. It represents the physical implementation of the organization's data resource. It does not represent the logical design of a formal data resource or the physical design of the database following denormalization.

A *data resource model* is a comprehensive model of the formal data resource. It contains both the logical design of the data resource based on the real world and the physical design of the data resource following denormalization. The denormalization process considers the mathematical construct of the database management system that will hold the data, but the physical design of the database is documented in the data resource model.

Unfortunately, the term *data model* is often used to represent both the logical and physical design of the formal data resource and the mathematical construct of the database management system. It would be better if the term were abandoned in favor of *database model* and *data resource model* to prevent confusion. The term *data resource model* will be used in this book.

Semiotic Modeling

The data resource model is a set of signs and symbols that communicate the design of the data resource. It is part of semiotics and includes specific rules for syntax, explicit meaning, and practical value. If any of these components are lacking, the model is weak and provides a poor representation of the formal data resource.

Traditional data resource models provide strong syntax and emphasize structure more than meaning. Semantic data resource models provide unambiguous sentences that describe the data resource and emphasize meaning more than structure. Neither of these approaches provides a robust model for the formal data resource.

A combination of the two approaches emphasizes structure and meaning equally, and when oriented to producing a model of practical value, becomes a full semiotic data resource model. A *semiotic data resource model* is a model of the formal data resource that provides equal emphasis on syntax, meaning, and practical use. It is more robust than a traditional data resource model, and increases the clarity and usefulness of the formal data resource.

Semiotic data modeling produces a comprehensive data resource model.

Semiotics applies to all models used in information technology and emphasizes the consistent use of symbols across all those models. A data resource model is one of those models and must conform to the consistent use of symbols. The symbols explained in previous chapters conform to the common set of symbols used across all information technology models.

Some people argue that symbols do not need to be consistent across all models. However, when information technology evolves to the point where one model drives development of the next model, the consistent use of symbols will be extremely important.

A good analogy is a hypothetical system that uses red lights to mean *stop* on four-lane paved roads, *caution* on two-lane paved roads, and *go* on unpaved roads. This standard should be no problem for drivers because they obviously know the type of road they are using. However, this standard is weak because it places an unnecessary burden on drivers to remember the type of road they are using and what the red light means. It could lead to serious traffic accidents. The unnecessary burden of remembering different symbols on different information technology models is as serious as the burden of remembering the meaning of red lights, and could lead to serious model accidents. Therefore, symbols must be used consistently across all models.

Symbols must be used consistently across all models.

Developing a data resource model is much like developing a house, as John Zachman emphasizes in his "Framework for Information Systems Architecture." Different models are developed for different levels of detail during the transformation from concept to design, construction, and implementation. Each model is a transformation of a previous model and provides more detail than that previous model. The use of common symbols across all models helps the transformation from one model to the next.

Data Resource Model Development

Data resource models must be developed within a common architecture. A prominent approach today is to develop individual data resource models at the project level and then integrate those models into a common data resource model for the formal data resource. This approach has not worked and will not work because of the variability created in the individual models. The time required to integrate individual models often exceeds the time required to develop the model, and often integration is not even attempted. Even if individual models were integrated and then altered during integration, they would not represent the information systems built from the initial model. This approach only perpetuates the disparate data situation.

An organization must build a common data architecture for its formal data resource. Data resource models must draw on data already defined in the common data architecture. Any new data must be defined and immediately placed in the common data architecture for others to use. This is the only approach that ensures consistent, efficient development of a formal data resource.

A data resource model must be built within the common data architecture.

Using the common data architecture as a base for developing project level data resource models avoids specific use bias in the model. It ensures that all specific uses of the data resource are consistent with the content and meaning of data in the common data architecture. It ensures that the common data architecture encompasses all data, regardless of their specific uses.

▼ DATA RESOURCE GUIDE

Comprehensive data documentation is based on standard methods of storing, locating, and presenting information, such as indexes, thesauruses, dictionaries, directories, catalogs, and lexicons. Libraries have used these techniques for years to guide people to the information they need. These techniques can be applied to documentation of a formal data resource.

The *Data Resource Guide* is a repository for meta-data about a formal data resource and the common data architecture. It contains the logical and physical data resource models for the formal data resource. It shows data that exist, where they are located, who to contact to obtain the data, and how the data can be accessed and shared. Clients access the Data Resource Guide to determine whether the data they need exist, where they exist, and how they can be obtained.

The Data Resource Guide is very powerful when it documents all data in the formal data resource. It is even more powerful when it documents data across multiple organizations and the primary sources of data. It changes the situation of *I didn't know those data were available* and *Whose data did I get* to the situation of *I know I have the data, I know what they are and where they are, and I know how to get them.*

The Data Resource Guide may eventually use expert systems to help clients identify data they need based on their terms. It can help them acquire those data to support business activities. Expert systems can

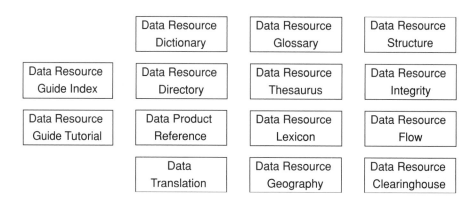

Figure 7.2 *Data Resource Guide components.*

also help clients share data by identifying source and target data variations and implementing appropriate data translation schemes. Tutorials can be enhanced to include multi-media presentations about the data resource and help clients understand both the data resource and the nature of the organization's business.

The Data Resource Guide consists of 14 components, as shown in Figure 7.2. Each component contains specific meta-data about the data resource. Relationships and navigation between the components provide access to meta-data about the formal data resource. Each of the components is described below.

Data Resource Guide Index

The *Data Resource Guide Index* is an index to the components of the Data Resource Guide. It helps clients quickly find the component they need to obtain the desired information about the formal data resource. It provides quick access to each component and to the data contained in each component.

Data Resource Guide Tutorial

The *Data Resource Guide Tutorial* provides a tutorial for using the Data Resource Guide and on-line help during use of the Guide. It provides information about all components of the Guide and explains how clients can use those components to understand the data resource.

Data Resource Dictionary

A *dictionary* is an alphabetical list of words in a language; it provides definitions, origins and developments, pronunciations, punctuation, usage guidelines, and other information. A *data resource dictionary* is an alphabetical list of data repositories, data subjects, data characteristics, data characteristic variations, and data codes in the formal data resource, with comprehensive definitions about their content and meaning. It contains no information about use of the data.

The Data Resource Dictionary component contains formal names and comprehensive definitions for all data repositories, data subjects, data characteristics, data characteristic variations, and data codes in the common data architecture. It does not contain the existing definitions of disparate data. They are contained in the Data Product Reference component.

The Data Resource Dictionary is maintained by constant addition and adjustment of data definitions. The common data architecture continues to grow as data are identified and cross referenced to the common data architecture. Whenever new data are defined or existing data definitions are enhanced, those changes must be made in the Data Resource Guide. Data descriptions may be removed from the Data Resource Guide, but only when those data no longer exist.

Data Resource Directory

A *directory* is a book of directions or a listing of names and locations for a specific group of people or organizations. A *data resource directory* is a directory that indicates who has data and how those data can be acquired. It provides a listing of data sources, the data available at those sources, organizations controlling those data, contact points in those organizations, availability of the data, formats and other physical parameters about data storage, terms and conditions for accessing or acquiring data, and any other useful information. The Data Resource Directory component contains the data resource directory.

The Data Resource Directory requires constant maintenance. New organizations are constantly being added as data are identified and cross referenced to the common data architecture. In addition, contact people within organizations are constantly changing. Frequently, information about the availability of data changes, as do the terms and conditions for accessing or acquiring those data. All of these changes need to be made to the Data Resource Directory so that it provides current information to clients.

Data Product Reference

Cross references are made between disparate data and the common data architecture so that all data are defined in a common context. Those cross references are placed in a database to provide two-way cross references between disparate data and the common data architecture. Two-way cross references allow a client to identify the common data architecture equivalent of disparate data, or all existences of disparate data in the common data architecture. The Data Cross Reference chapter explains cross references in more detail.

The Data Product Reference component contains the definitions, integrity rules, and the structure of disparate data, along with all cross references between disparate data and the common data architecture. Most of the cross references are for data characteristics and data codes. However, there are optional cross references for data subjects.

Data cross references are maintained through constant modification. Whenever new data are cross referenced to the common data architecture, those cross references are added to the Data Resource Guide. Whenever cross references are adjusted, adjustments are also made in the Data Resource Guide. Whenever the disparate data cease to exist, the cross references are removed from the Data Resource Guide.

Data Translation Schemes

A data translation scheme provides translation between common data characteristic variations when those data characteristic variations represent measurements or format variations. They are not used to translate data between data characteristic variations that represent differences in content or meaning. Data translation schemes usually translate data between official data characteristic variations and non-official data characteristic variations. They may translate data between official data variations if more than one official data variation has been designated, or between non-official data variations if the need exists.

The Data Translation Schemes component contains the data translation schemes. These schemes are used to facilitate data sharing by allowing data to be translated to the official data variation, shared through the official data variation, and then translated to a non-official variation. They enable short-term data sharing and provide long-term transition to the mature data resource. The Data Translation chapter explains the data translation schemes in more detail.

Data translation schemes are maintained by the constant addition of new translation schemes. Whenever official data variations are designated and translation schemes are developed and accepted, they are added to the Data Resource Guide. Clients can readily access those translation schemes to support their data sharing activities. Data translation schemes may be removed when the data characteristics being translated no longer exist.

Data Resource Glossary

A *glossary* is an alphabetical listing of words or abbreviations. A *data resource glossary* is an alphabetical listing of definitions for words, terms, and abbreviations used in data definitions in the common data architecture.

The Data Resource Glossary component contains the data resource glossary. It does not contain abbreviations for words used in data names. Those are contained in the Data Resource Lexicon. It does not contain definitions of common data subjects, data characteristics, or data codes. Those are contained in the Data Resource Dictionary. An example of a definition in the Data Resource Glossary is shown in Figure 7.3.

The Data Resource Glossary may be partitioned by data discipline or data subject area. For example, terms related to personnel may be maintained separately from terms related to education.

The Data Resource Glossary is maintained by the continual addition of new definitions and enhancement of existing definitions. Whenever a new word, term, or abbreviation in a data definition may not be clear

Water Diversion—The removal of water from a stream, lake, reservoir, or any other surface water body into a canal, pipe, or other conduit.

Figure 7.3 A data resource glossary entry.

to clients, or may require further explanation, it is added to the glossary. Whenever an existing definition is unclear or confusing, it is enhanced so that clients thoroughly understand all words, terms, and abbreviations used in data definitions.

Data Resource Thesaurus

A *thesaurus* is a book containing a store of words, specifically a book of synonyms and antonyms. It is a treasury of words and information. It is a book of selected words or concepts, often for a given field, for use in information retrieval. A *data resource thesaurus* is a set of data name synonyms to help people locate the particular data they need. It provides a reference between similar names or business terms and the true data names. It is also useful for determining whether data already exist when developing cross references between disparate data and the common data architecture.

The common data architecture for an organization, or for multiple organizations, can become very large very fast. The quantity of references can grow at an exponential rate and become larger than any one person can comprehend. The data resource thesaurus provides a place to document all references to true data names. The Data Resource Thesaurus component contains the data resource thesaurus. It does not contain any data definitions.

The Data Resource Thesaurus is maintained by the addition of new references each time new data are defined or each time new references are identified for existing data. Most of the new references are identified when new data are defined. The three techniques of identifying data resource thesaurus entries are explained below.

First, a data name is broken down into keywords that could be used in the thesaurus. There are usually more keywords than there are data names. Typically, a data name may be referenced by two to ten keywords. For example, Employee Appointment is broken down into Employee and Appointment, and Employee Performance Evaluation is broken down into Employee, Performance, Evaluation, Performance Evaluation, and Employee Evaluation. Each of these keywords is entered into the thesaurus, as shown in Figure 7.4.

Each organization must decide the extent of keywords used in its Data Resource Thesaurus. For example, words like Type, Class, Status, and so on, which are common in many data names, should not be

Appointment	Employee Appointment
Employee	Employee Appointment
Employee	Employee Performance Evaluation
Evaluation	Employee Performance Evaluation
Performance	Employee Performance Evaluation
Performance Evaluation	Employee Performance Evaluation
Employee Evaluation	Employee Performance Evaluation

Figure 7.4 *Data resource thesaurus example.*

placed in the thesaurus. They are too common and not useful to locating specific data.

Second, related data names are identified and documented. For example, Employee Appointment places Employees in Positions. References should be entered from Employee Appointment to Position and from Position to Employee Appointment. It is helpful to review each data definition to determine these additional references.

Third, references from words or phrases used by clients are added to the thesaurus. Clients frequently use business terms that are different from the formal data names. These terms need to be added to the thesaurus. For example, Staff, Worker, and Personnel are words that clients might use when referring to Employees, and Job, Responsibility, and Duties might refer to Position. These references should be added to the thesaurus, as shown in Figure 7.5. Reviewing the Data Resource Glossary may also provide terms that could be added to the thesaurus.

The Data Resource Thesaurus needs constant maintenance when data names are changed. All references must be changed from the old

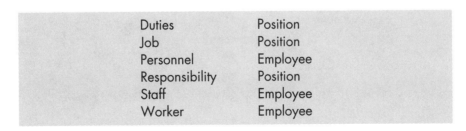

Duties	Position
Job	Position
Personnel	Employee
Responsibility	Position
Staff	Employee
Worker	Employee

Figure 7.5 *Additions to data resource thesaurus.*

data name to the new data name. This process requires careful searching of the thesaurus for all references to the old data names and alteration of those references to the new data names. Old data names used as references to other data names must also be found and replaced. If this maintenance is not done, the thesaurus rapidly deteriorates.

The Data Resource Thesaurus is usually developed for data subjects and data characteristics. Data subject references are entered first, followed by data characteristic references.

Data Resource Lexicon

A *lexicon* is a special vocabulary of a particular author or field of study. The *data resource lexicon* is a special vocabulary of common words used to form data repository, data subject, data characteristic, data characteristic variation, and data code names. It is a list of definitions for the common words in the data naming vocabulary. The Data Resource Lexicon component contains the data resource lexicon.

Several common words used in data characteristic names are shown in Figure 7.6. A more complete data characteristic lexicon is contained in Appendix A.

The Data Resource Lexicon also contains a list of the common abbreviations for words in a data name. Ideally, there is only one set of abbreviations. However, if an organization allows multiple length abbreviations, there could be more than one set of abbreviations for each word. The Data Resource Lexicon contains all these abbreviations.

Data Characteristic Lexicon

Count—The number of objects that exist or have occurred. Not the same as Amount or Number.

Number—A number that identifies an object. Not an Amount, Capacity, Code, or Quantity.

Quantity—The capacity or count of something. Not a Value, Amount, or Number.

Figure 7.6 *Common data word definitions example.*

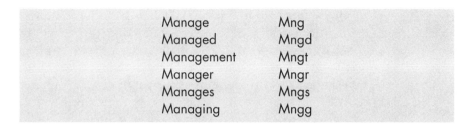

Manage	Mng
Managed	Mngd
Management	Mngt
Manager	Mngr
Manages	Mngs
Managing	Mngg

Figure 7.7 *Data name word abbreviation example.*

An example of word abbreviations is shown in Figure 7.7. Whenever a word (e.g., *management*) is used in a data name, the root word (e.g., *manage*) is identified, all manifestations of that word are identified, and all those words are abbreviated. This procedure ensures that words are abbreviated in a consistent manner.

The Data Resource Lexicon contains all the algorithms for abbreviating data names and a definition of when each algorithm is used. If the abbreviation algorithms use different word abbreviations, these are indicated in the definition of the algorithm. The lexicon can assist automatic abbreviation and unabbreviation of data names by passing the full data name through the algorithm to obtain the abbreviated data name or vice versa.

The Data Resource Lexicon is maintained by adding new common words and new word abbreviations whenever they are identified. Every time a new common word is identified for a data repository, data subject, data characteristic, data characteristic variation, or data code, it is entered into the Data Resource Lexicon.

Data Resource Geography

A considerable amount of spatial data is stored in geographic information systems. As the price performance of geographic information systems improves, there will be increasing use of those systems and increasing volumes of spatial data. These spatial data are designed and documented like traditional tabular data.

One method of documenting spatial data is to use a geographic information system to show the extent of spatial data. Each layer shows the extent of one specific type of data, such as soil classification, voting districts, or wildlife habitats. Clients can work between the layers to identify geographical areas where data they need are available. They can then consult the Data Resource Directory to determine how those data can be obtained, as with tabular data.

The Data Resource Geography component contains references to the existence of spatial data. It may be a geographic information system as described above, or it may be tabular data referencing the existence of spatial data. Anytime new spatial data are designed and documented, the Data Resource Guide is updated.

Data Resource Structure

The data resource model has data relation diagrams and logical data structure charts for the logical data resource, and data file diagrams and physical data structure charts for the physical database. The Data Resource Structure component contains all of these charts and diagrams. It contains strategic and tactical data relation diagrams that provide overviews of the formal data resource for planning purposes, and detailed diagrams for developing the formal data resource. The Data Structure and Disparate Data Structure chapters explain data structures in more detail.

The Data Resource Structure component is maintained through constant addition and enhancement. Whenever new data structures are defined or existing data structures are changed, the Data Resource Guide is enhanced.

Data Resource Integrity

Data integrity rules are very important for maintaining integrity of the formal data resource. The Data Resource Integrity component contains all data integrity rules for the formal data resource. It does not contain data integrity rules that exist in disparate data. Those are contained in the Data Product Reference component.

Data integrity rules are maintained through constant enhancement. Generally, few data integrity rules are placed in the Data Resource Guide during documentation and cross referencing of disparate data. Most of the data integrity rules are entered during development of new information systems.

Data Resource Availability

Primary data sources are organizations that collect or develop new data. Data are disseminated from these primary data sources to organizations that need the data to support their business activities. In many cases, organizations receiving data modify them in some way or add additional data and become primary sources for the modifications. These new or modified data are then disseminated to other organizations. This value-added process forms a network of data flowing between organizations. The Data Sharing Strategy chapter explains primary data sources and major data flows in more detail.

The Data Resource Availability component contains data about primary data sources. It contains a high level inventory of data that exist in organizations that are primary sources of data. It does not carry a detailed inventory of data. That is shown in the Data Product Reference component.

The Data Resource Availability component is maintained by constant adjustment of the data that are maintained at primary data sources. Organizations are constantly changing the data they capture, create, and maintain, and they are constantly changing the data they have available to other organizations. Whenever an organization adjusts the data it has available, enhancements are made to the Data Resource Guide. Periodic data resource surveys or data resource inventories should be conducted to ensure that the Data Resource Guide is current.

Data Resource Clearinghouse

Data sharing within and between organizations involves both the sharing and exchange of existing data and cooperation on the collection of new data. Considerable emphasis is being placed on the identification and sharing of existing data. However, limited emphasis is placed on cooperation to collect new data. Data sharing can be increased by emphasizing cooperation on the collection of new data.

Many organizations are collecting high-priority data redundantly and ignoring lower priority data. If these organizations could cooperate on the collection of new data, they would be able to extend data collection to lower priority data. The result would be increased data collection for the same expenditure. This is one approach to using limited funding to expand and enhance the formal data resource.

The Data Resource Clearinghouse component contains information about projects that are completed, in progress, or planned for the documentation of existing data, or for the collection and development of new data. It contains a description of all data resource projects and studies that explains the project, the dates, the objectives, and the deliverables. It also contains a bibliography of studies, reports, and other publications pertaining to the data resource.

The Data Resource Clearinghouse is maintained by constant enhancement. Data resource projects are constantly being completed, implemented, and planned, and reports and other publications are constantly being produced. Keeping the Data Resource Clearinghouse current ensures that organizations can share existing data and cooperate on the collection of new data.

▼ SUMMARY

The Data Documentation activity maintains meta-data about the common data architecture and the formal data resource, and provides complete, accurate, readily available documentation. It contains the data resource model for the formal data resource. It directly supports the other activities in the Data Architecture component of the Data Resource Framework.

Development of the data resource model is based on semiotics to ensure that the model emphasizes syntax and semantics equally, and that it produces a product that has a practical use. The combination of semiotics with data resource modeling produces semiotic data resource models. These semiotic data resource models are built within the common data architecture. They are not developed separately and then incorporated into a common model.

Data documentation may be produced by CASE tools, CADE tools, or a variety of other tools and techniques. Data documentation is maintained in a comprehensive Data Resource Guide consisting of 14 components that provide assistance to clients using the formal data resource. An index and a tutorial help clients use the data resource guide. The dictionary, structure, integrity, and geography components document the data resource. The thesaurus, lexicon, and glossary help users find data they need to support their business activities. The directory, product references, translation schemes, and data availability help clients identify where data are located and learn to to access and share those data. The clearinghouse helps clients identify data resource projects and maximize limited resources.

The Data Resource Guide must be constantly maintained to be useful. Client involvement in the development and maintenance of data documentation ensures that the appropriate meta-data will be available for client use. A properly designed and maintained Data Resource Guide maximizes use of the formal data resource. It is a powerful tool for strategic management of a critical resource.

▼ QUESTIONS

The following questions are designed to provide a review of Chapter 7 and to stimulate thought about how to develop and manage a comprehensive data resource guide.

1. How does data documentation support other activities in the data resource framework?

2. Why is good documentation management important?

3. What is the difference between CASE and CADE?

4. What are meta-data?

5. Why are meta-data designed like any other data?

6. What is the difference between a data model and a data resource model?

7. Why is semiotics important in data modeling?

8. Why should data resource models be developed within the common data architecture?

9. What is a data resource guide?

10. What does a data resource guide provide that CASE tools and repositories do not?

11. What are the components of a comprehensive data resource guide?

12. What is the difference between the dictionary and the directory?

13. What does the glossary provide?

14. What is the difference between the thesaurus and the lexicon?

15. How is the thesaurus maintained?

16. How is the lexicon maintained?

17. What are the benefits of a clearinghouse?

18. Why is it beneficial to know primary data sources and major data flows?

19. How can a data resource guide help clients?

20. Why is it important to have a comprehensive data resource guide?

▼ 8
▼
▼

DATA REFINING

---

*Data refining begins by understanding the disparate data
syndrome and the evolutionary stages to a formal data resource.*

Disparate data have been created for so long that the process has
become a self-perpetuating syndrome. The existence of the syndrome
must be recognized and the causes must be understood so that the syndrome will be broken, disparate data will no longer be created, and
existing disparate data will be corrected.

Breaking the disparate data syndrome is not easy, but it is not
impossible. The common data architecture provides the base for defining new data and refining disparate data. Defining new data within the
common data architecture stops the creation of disparate data. Refining
disparate data within the common data architecture corrects the existing situation. The result is the integration of all data within a common
context. The process is evolutionary, as disparate data move into the
formal data resource and the formal data resource evolves to a mature
data resource.

This chapter explains the concept of refining data. It begins with an
explanation of the disparate data syndrome and how that syndrome
can be broken. A remodeling analogy is presented. Data products are
introduced and basic data refining concepts are explained. Finally, the
evolutionary stages that an organization goes through are described.

▼ DISPARATE DATA SYNDROME

Refining data begins with a recognition of the disparate data situation and an understanding of how disparate data are created. When the disparate data situation is understood, it can be stopped. New data can be defined properly and existing data can be refined within a common data architecture. All data can be integrated into a formal data resource so that they can be fully utilized.

The Syndrome

Large quantities of disparate data have been created since the beginning of data processing. Disparate data have been so actively created that a syndrome has formed that perpetuates the creation of disparate data. A *syndrome* is a group of signs or symptoms that usually occur together and characterize a particular abnormality. It is a set of concurrent things that form an identifiable pattern. The *disparate data syndrome* is a set of signs and symptoms about the creation of an organization's data that form an identifiable pattern of disparate data. This syndrome still exists today, in spite of many new techniques and tools.

> *The disparate data syndrome is a set of signs and symptoms that identify a pattern of disparate data.*

Disparate data are created when different groups in an organization take small subsets of data, name and define those data according to their own use of the data, and place them in files to support specific applications. In this situation, data names are oriented toward a specific use and are constrained by physical limitations. The formats meet specific needs of the application and cannot be easily integrated to meet the needs of other applications. Data definitions and data integrity are not required and are seldom prepared.

Some organizations attempt to resolve the disparate data situation by developing cross references. However, these cross references are between sets of disparate data, not between disparate data and a common data architecture. Also, the cross references are often limited to data exchanged through bridges and feeds between information systems. The result is multiple cross references between sets of disparate data, giving layer upon layer of cross referenced data.

Many of these cross references connect data characteristics with different formats, different meaning or content, or different sets of data codes. Cross referencing data characteristics in this way results in comments like *similar to...*, *nearly the same as...*, *most of the codes used in...*, and so on. These are not robust cross references and only add to the disparate data problem.

Breaking the Syndrome

Organizations must break this syndrome if they want to stop creating disparate data and start building a formal data resource. Most organizations recognize the disparate data situation. However, recognizing the syndrome is only the beginning. Stopping the continued creation of disparate data and refining existing disparate data is where the real work starts. The problem is how an organization can stop creating disparate data, start defining new data properly, and start refining disparate data. How can an organization that recognizes the disparate data situation start changing the situation?

The common data architecture is the base for changing the disparate data situation. All new data are defined within the common data architecture, which stops the trend of continuing to create disparate data. Existing data are refined within the common data architecture. The result is the definition of all data within a common context.

Refining data within a common data architecture is a real change for most people, and it causes them to procrastinate. However, the problem is not whether to build a common data architecture and refine data, but rather how to start refining data. The problem is understanding how to build a common data architecture and refine disparate data to that common data architecture. The problem is how to set a new strategic direction for the organization.

It is not important whether an organization starts the common data architecture with the definition of new data or the refining of disparate data. It is easier to start defining new data within the common data architecture based on the techniques explained in the previous chapters. It is more difficult to start with disparate data because of the variability and uncertainty in their content and meaning. Nevertheless, it is important that an organization does start. Usually, the organization starts with a combination of defining new data and refining existing data, beginning with the data most critical to the organization's major business activities.

Remodeling Analogy

Refining data is much like remodeling a house. When people start remodeling a house, they have no idea where the plumbing, electrical, phone, and heating ducts are located. They can observe plumbing fixtures, electrical outlets, phone jacks, light fixtures, heat registers, but these terminations don't identify where things are routed in the walls. People can crawl under the house or in the attic to get a better idea of where things are located. They can pull circuit breakers and turn off water valves, but they are still not sure where everything is located until they begin to tear out the walls. There are always surprises.

The same situation is true for refining data. People can observe documents, screens, and reports. They can look at application listings and database structures. They can run automated documentation tools. They still have very little idea about the true content and meaning of disparate data until they begin to tear those data apart. There are always surprises.

Wouldn't it be nice to know all the things about a house—its structure, anomalies, plumbing, wiring, heating, quality of lumber, roofing, paint, and so forth? Wouldn't it be nice to have a comprehensive architecture for a house that contained the description of all components, the structure of those components, and the integrity of those components? Wouldn't it be nice to have a comprehensive blueprint of the house? Wouldn't that blueprint make use and maintenance of the house much easier?

The same situation applies to data. Wouldn't it be nice to know all the things about data, their structure, and their anomalies? Wouldn't it be nice to have a comprehensive blueprint so that people do not have to make assumptions about data? Wouldn't it be nice to be able to readily identify, locate, and access the data needed to support business activities?

A house is remodeled by making an initial model of what exists; this model is based on perceptions, assumptions, and available documentation. As the process continues, things are discovered, perceptions change, and assumptions are proven or changed. The initial model is enhanced to represent the current state of knowledge. When the process is completed, the house is remodeled and an accurate model of the house is available.

That is exactly what data refining accomplishes. It starts with an initial common data architecture based on perceptions and assumptions about disparate data, and on whatever documentation is available. As data refining continues, new things are discovered, perceptions change, and assumptions are proven or changed. The initial common data architecture is enhanced to represent current knowledge about disparate data, and it continues to evolve until all disparate data are refined. When the process is completed, there is one accurate model of all disparate data, and they are all part of the formal data resource.

▼ DATA REFINING CONCEPT

Data refining is a process to define disparate data within the common data architecture and make them part of the formal data resource. It is based on several concepts that ensure success.

Data Product Concept

Disparate data may be semi-structured or unstructured. *Semi-structured disparate data* are disparate data that were structured at a project level, but not at the common data architecture level. They conform to some type of naming, definition, structure, and quality criteria, but not to the criteria of the common data architecture. Therefore, they are considered disparate data and are cross referenced to the common data architecture. *Unstructured disparate data* are disparate data that do not conform to any type of naming, definition, structure, or quality criteria and have no similarity to the common data architecture.

Disparate data are named and defined in a variety of different products, such as data files, data dictionaries, programs, reports, screens, and documents. Each of these products is referred to as a *data product*.

- A *data product* is a major, independent piece of documentation of any type that contains the names and/or definitions of disparate data. It may be a data dictionary, a major project, a major information system, or a small organization or organizational unit.

- A *data product subject* is a major grouping of data within a data product, such as record, screen, report, or data subject. Typical unstructured data product subjects are records, screens, and reports. Semi-structured data product subjects are closer to data subjects in the common data architecture, but are not exactly aligned with the common data architecture.

- A *data product characteristic* is an individual element of data in a data product subject, such as a field in a file, on a record, or on a screen.

- A *data product code* is a data code that exists in a data product characteristic.

Data Refining Approach

Data refining is one step toward developing a mature data resource, as shown in Figure 8.1. Physical disparate data are refined to logical common data represented by the common data architecture. The logical common data are denormalized and deployed to physical databases within the common data architecture. The physical disparate data are moved to the new physical databases though a database transition process.

Data refining is not a data normalization process, because it does not bring disparate data into a normal form. It does not change disparate data in any way. Disparate data need to stay in their current form to support current applications. Refining data just cross references dis-

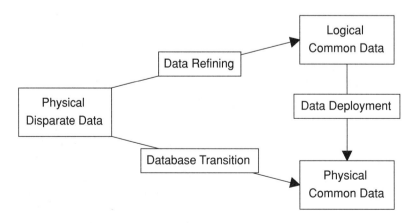

Figure 8.1 *Developing the mature data resource.*

parate data to the common data architecture. It is the common data architecture that is normalized by data subjects. In other words, data refining cross references existing data to a normalized common data architecture so that they can be readily understood.

Data refining is not a data denormalization process. Data denormalization is a formal process for converting a logical data resource model to a physical data resource model for a particular operating environment. It is used for deploying physical data throughout the organization or on a network. It is not involved in data refining.

Existing data are refined to a common data architecture.

Data refining is accomplished by identifying or creating common data characteristic variations and common data codes that represent data product characteristics and data product codes. Then cross references are made between the data product characteristics and common data characteristic variations, and between data product codes and common data codes. When the cross references are completed, the extent of data variability is determined. Data variability is analyzed by a team of knowledgeable people and official data variations are designated. Data translations are prepared between non-official and official data variations.

The formal data resource contains all data characteristic variations. The mature data resource is a subset of the formal data resource, and contains only the official data characteristic variations. The data translation schemes support short-term data sharing within the formal data resource and long-term evolution to the mature data resource.

Data refining is a complex process that requires looking at each piece of disparate data to determine its true content and meaning. It is a conversion from an application structure to a data subject structure. It is a physical-to-logical process that requires considerable thought and analysis. But the results are well worth the effort.

Discovery Process

Data refining is a discovery process. It requires knowledge, analysis, evaluation, thought, interpretation, reasoning, intuition, vision, an open mind, and some luck. It is a people-oriented process that takes the knowledge and synergy of people to find the true content and meaning of disparate data. It is people who understand the data and the business and make the discovery.

The real knowledge of disparate data is in people, not in documentation, programs, or dictionaries. The discovery process captures that knowledge and documents it in a common data architecture. The process cannot be performed by tools or automated applications. They can only support the process. Knowledgeable people must be involved.

People analyze disparate data piece by piece to determine the true content and meaning of those data. This analysis requires a real understanding and awareness of the common data architecture, the business activities of the organization, and the data that support those business activities. Just when it appears that the entire process is getting out of hand, the true content and meaning will never be determined, and cross references will never be made, everything collapses into a meaningful structure. Just when it appears that the job is insurmountable, the critical mass of information is achieved and disparate data fall into place within the common data architecture.

> *Developing a common data architecture and refining disparate data is a discovery process performed by people.*

Data refining cannot be automated because current automation techniques cannot identify true content and meaning. It is just not possible to run a program to scan data files or applications and dump the results into a data dictionary. The result will be as meaningless as the original documentation, and may be worse in some cases. Automation can assist the process, but it cannot undo the disparate data situation.

Data refining is not a precise process, because of the uncertainty involved in disparate data. It is a cyclic process that uses the techniques until certainty is achieved. It is an evolutionary process based on discovery and enhancement. It is not accomplished in one pass and it is not accomplished solely by top-down or bottom-up approaches.

Consensus Approach

A discovery process involving people requires a consensus approach to understanding disparate data, developing a common data architecture, and cross referencing disparate data to the common data architecture. Consensus is gained through a combination of individual interviews and group meetings. Individual interviews are best for collecting data to develop a draft document for a group meeting. They are also good in a conflict or adversary situation where individuals won't speak out in a group meeting, when participants are widely dispersed and it is difficult to get all participants together, or when limited participation is needed for detailed fact finding. Group meetings are best for consensus building and issue resolution, or for people who are close together.

> *Consensus is the best approach to developing a common data architecture and refining disparate data.*

There a few basic principles that make the consensus approach work. These principles are explained below.

- People work best with a draft document, particularly when the material is confusing or complex. It is easier to start modifying a draft than to build something from scratch. This is true for both individual interviews and group sessions. Therefore, a draft document should be prepared and distributed before interviews or group sessions.

- There must be an atmosphere of *no blame–no whitewash.* People who build and use disparate databases have a wealth of knowledge about the data in those databases. This knowledge base must be tapped if data refining is to be successful. There can be no blame about the existing disparate data situation. Blame polarizes people, leading to conflicts and disagreements, and resulting in failure of data refining. Whitewashing the disparate data situation does not break the disparate data syndrome, and instead merely perpetuates the current situation.

- No one should be criticized for input to the data refining process, as long as that input is constructive. Criticism also polarizes people, and the process can quickly become counterproductive. Similarly, no issue should be overlooked. All issues must be brought up and resolved constructively in the building of a stable common data architecture.

- Resolution of issues should not be forced. An unresolved issue should be documented and let sit for a period of time. Documentation of an issue raises the awareness of that issue, and time is required for answers. Many issues resolve themselves in time. Forcing resolution does not allow enough time for the proper answer, and therefore usually results in an answer that is not acceptable. Allow people time think through the issue before it is resolved.

- Conflicts and discrepancies occur during data refining. Although it is desirable to have a resolution to these conflicts and discrepancies during data refining, it is not necessary. It is necessary to identify and document the conflicts and discrepancies to make them known. Identification and documentation of conflicts and discrepancies allow people to review them and determine a resolution. If it is not possible to determine a resolution, at least the situation is documented so that people know it exists and can operate accordingly.

- Success is gained through a pattern of involvement, commitment, and acceptance. When people are involved, they become committed to the process. When people are committed to a process, their confidence is increased and there is a high degree of acceptance of the results of that process. When there is a high degree of acceptance, there is successful implementation of a formal data resource. Therefore, knowledgeable people must be involved in the data refining process.

- Data refining is based on consensus, not compromise. Compromise is a give and take situation until there is agreement on a particular topic. It leads to hidden strategies and often results in voting. This approach is not acceptable and usually does not result in a successful process. Consensus is a process of seeking the truth and agreeing to that truth. It is an iterative process that involves input from knowledgeable people until consensus is gained. Common data architectures built on consensus may take slightly longer, but are far more successful.

- There is no arbitrator in data refining. The typical approach in an organization is to move up the hierarchy to a point of commonality and get a decision when there is disagreement. This approach does not work with multiple autonomous organizations because there is not point of commonality. Consensus must be gained from the team.

Facilitated Approach

A consensus approach to refining data that involves a group of knowledgeable people requires facilitation to ensure that consensus is reached. Without facilitation there is constant discussion, but little progress toward consensus. Facilitation brings people together, combines individual thought with group synergy, and maximizes productivity.

Facilitation also helps resolve the problems of changing team membership. As data refining proceeds, people may join or leave a team, resulting in changing knowledge and changing views of the data. Facilitation ensures that these changes are incorporated into the data refining process without impacting the team's progress. In many situations, the facilitator will reach out and acquire people with additional knowledge to help the data refining process.

The steps below outline a facilitated approach to refining data. They may be modified or repeated as necessary to achieve consensus.

- The team facilitator or a knowledgeable member of the team prepares an initial common data architecture with an emphasis on preliminary data descriptions. It is prepared from laws, professional standards manuals, existing policies and standards, common usage, existing system documentation, dictionaries, personal knowledge, or any other form of documentation that exists.

- The preliminary data descriptions are sent to each member of the team. Each member reviews the data descriptions and makes comments. The review may be done individually by the team members, team members may meet for review, or the team leader may meet with team members. Regardless of the method of review, the comments are documented without altering the data descriptions.

- When the individual review process is completed, the preliminary data descriptions and all comments are sent to each member of the team for review and comment. The facilitator may adjust the comments to remove any personal bias or blame, and to make the comments objective and constructive.

- Frequently, a second review is necessary, particularly if there is wide disagreement over the data descriptions. This second round resolves many of the issues that were identified in the first round, indicating that consensus is being achieved.

- The revised data descriptions and all comments are sent to each team member for review. The comments may be adjusted by the facilitator as issues are resolved and suggested enhancements to the data descriptions are made.

- A general meeting is held for collective review of the preliminary data descriptions and comments. This meeting leads to acceptable data descriptions for most of the data.

- Remaining discrepancies or disagreements are identified as specific issues. Responsibilities are assigned for resolving these issues and additional meetings are set. By this point, usually fewer than five to ten percent of the data descriptions are at issue.

Generally, names and dates are put on comments to identify different views about the data. This technique allows individuals to express their opinions and perceptions about the initial common data architecture. It also helps to broaden understanding of the data. Once these opinions and perceptions are expressed, the synergy of a group meeting produces acceptable data descriptions. However, if there is concern over identifying the source of the comment, then it should be removed and made into a generic statement.

> *An initial common data architecture developed by consensus*
> *starts the data refining process.*

Team members should make liberal use of notes, comments, questions, and issues to document concerns, observations, discrepancies, suggestions, and issues. This technique helps to enhance the discovery process and helps the team achieve consensus on the data descriptions. Data refining can continue based on this initial common data architecture.

Common Data Architecture Size

The size of the common data architecture changes constantly, from the time its development begins until the point when a mature data resource is completed. The size changes in four different ways.

First, a common data architecture grows for each project until the disparate data are understood. It grows very rapidly during the initial confusion involved in understanding disparate data, and can look complex, insurmountable, and discouraging. Then, as additional information is gained and the disparate data are understood, it collapses to a minimum set of common data characteristic variations and common data codes that represent the disparate data. Organizations should plan for this situation and not be alarmed when it happens.

Second, a common data architecture grows as cross references between disparate data and the common data architecture are documented. Every time a new set of disparate data are refined within the common data architecture, the quantity of cross references increases. Eventually, as the mature data resource evolves and disparate data disappear, the quantity of cross references decreases. Cross references remain only for disparate data that are not part of the mature data resource. Organizations should plan for a rapid growth in cross references as long as products are being refined, with a slow decline as the mature data resource evolves.

Third, a common data architecture grows as new data variations are identified and documented. Each new set of disparate data brings new data variations that need to be documented in the common data architecture. As the formal data resource evolves to a mature data resource and disparate data disappear, the common data architecture will decrease in size to the official data variations. Organizations should plan for a common data architecture that continues to grow as disparate data are refined and new data variations are discovered, with a steady decrease as the mature data resource evolves.

Fourth, a common data architecture grows as derived data are identified and defined. Primitive data generally grow to a plateau and then remain constant, or grow slowly unless an organization enters a new business area that requires substantially different data. Derived data continue to grow steadily, often at an exponential rate, as organizations develop executive information systems and other forms of derived data. As existing data are understood and become available, derived data are developed at rapid rate. Organizations should plan for this continued increase in the size of a common data architecture from derived data.

▼ EVOLUTIONARY STAGES

There are five evolutionary stages an organization goes through to develop a common data architecture, build a formal data resource, and evolve to a mature data resource. Not all organizations progress at the same rate through the stages. Some organizations may linger in one stage before moving ahead, and some may skip a stage. Some organizations may be in more than one stage at the same time. Certainly all organizations are not in the same stage at the same time.

These five stages define an evolutionary pathway to assist organizations in their efforts to build a common data architecture. Knowing the evolutionary path provides a road map for organizations to develop a plan for achieving a common data architecture and the mature data resource.

Traditional Stage

The Traditional Stage is the first stage in the evolutionary path, characterized by a focus on building individual applications or information systems without concern for common data. It is the current environment in many organizations today.

> *The Traditional Stage is the current situation in most organizations today.*

There are considerable quantities of disparate data. Data redundancy is high and largely unknown. Documentation is poor, data names and definitions are inconsistent, and there is no formal data dictionary. There is no data architecture, data structure is minimal, and data quality is low. Primary data sources and major data flows are unknown. Any attempts at inventorying or integrating data usually fail. Data sharing is non-existent or occurs only between a few applications. There are usually no standards, no data administration, and no data management function in the organization.

Project Stage

The Project Stage is the second stage on the evolutionary path, characterized by a focus on integrating data for major projects that includes one or more information systems. It is the current environment in many organizations today. It is better than the Traditional Stage, but it is not the desired stage. Achieving the Project Stage requires a one-year to two-year horizon.

The Project Stage is the norm for many organizations.

There is an emphasis on common data at the project level, but minimal interest in common data at the organization level. Disparate data still exist, but baseline data are being refined within the common data architecture. Data redundancy is identified for baseline data and major data redundancy is resolved or managed. Formal names and comprehensive definitions exist for baseline data. A project or organization data dictionary is established and is being populated for project. CASE tools may be used at the project level.

Major projects usually have a data architecture at the project level, but not at the organization level. A formal data structure exists at the project level for new information systems and there is an emphasis on identifying data subjects within a project, but minimal effort toward integrating those data subjects across the organization. Data quality is improving for baseline data, but formal data integrity constraints are not implemented.

There is some initial sharing of baseline data between major information systems within an organization, but there is limited sharing between organizations. Data flows within major information systems are identified, as are some major data flows within the organization. Primary data sources are identified for major information systems. Attempts to inventory disparate data are physically oriented and usually fail.

There may be an organization initiative for formal data resource management, but must initiatives are at the project level. Initial standards exist at the project level, most newly developed data follow those standards, and there may be an informal data administration or data management function.

Organization Stage

The Organization Stage is the third stage on the evolutionary path, characterized by a focus on integrating data across the organization. It is the current environment in a few organizations today. It is an acceptable stage, but it is not the desired stage. It may evolve directly from the Traditional Stage without going through the Project Stage. Achieving the Organization Stage requires a three-year to five-year horizon.

> *The Organization Stage is an acceptable stage, but exists in only a few organizations.*

There is emphasis on common data across the organization, but minimal interest in common data between organizations. Formal names and comprehensive definitions exist for all new data. Most redundant data are identified and documented, and major data redundancies are resolved or properly managed. Formal data integrity rules are established from business rules, and formal data integrity constraints are beginning to be implemented. An organization-wide data dictionary is established and is being actively populated and used. CASE tools may be used and documentation is improving.

Data sharing occurs within the organization, but there is some limited data sharing between organizations. Major data flows within the organization and initial data flows between organizations are identified. Primary data sources within the organization and some primary sources outside the organization are identified. Data inventories within an common data architecture are successful, but physical data inventories usually fail. There is usually an organization initiative for formal data resource management.

Organization Cluster Stage

The Organization Cluster Stage is the fourth stage on the evolutionary path, characterized by a focus on integrating data across organizations that perform the same types of business activities. It is a rare environment today. It is a desired state that many organizations would like to achieve. It usually evolves from the Organization Stage. Achieving the Organization Cluster Stage requires a five-year to seven-year horizon.

> *The Organization Cluster Stage is a desired stage, but is rare today.*

A common data architecture is evolving for clusters of organizations, but there is limited effort for a common architecture between organization clusters. Formal names and definitions exist for most data. A formal data structure exists for all new information systems, and common data are identified for organization clusters. Formal data integrity rules are established on business rules and formal data integrity constraints are implemented. Decentralized data are common and are normally well managed.

Nearly all redundant data are identified and documented within an organization, and most redundant data are identified and documented within an organization cluster. Redundant data within an organization and major redundant data within organization clusters are resolved or managed. A comprehensive Data Resource Guide is evolving. The mature data resource may exist in some organizations.

Data sharing is common within the organization cluster, but is limited between organization clusters. Data flows and primary data sources within organization clusters are identified. Major data flows between organization clusters and primary data sources in other organization clusters are identified. Most data inventories are conducted within a common data architecture and are successful. Official data variations are routinely identified and data translation schemes are routinely developed. There is an initiative for cooperative data resource management for organizations in the cluster.

Common Data Architecture Stage

The Common Architecture Stage is the fifth stage on the evolutionary path, characterized by a focus on one common data architecture for all organization clusters. It does not exist today, but it is the ideal stage. It usually evolves from the Organization Cluster Stage. Achieving the Common Data Architecture Stage requires a ten-year horizon.

Organization cluster data architectures merge to form a common data architecture across all organizations and all business activities. The mature data resource is largely achieved, and there is one common data architecture and one comprehensive Data Resource Guide for all data. Information engineering routinely goes to the mature data resource to obtain data.

The Common Data Architecture Stage is the ideal stage.

All redundant data are known and are largely resolved or managed. All data are formally named and comprehensively defined. All data are properly structured and have formal data integrity rules. Data integrity constraints are routinely implemented and enforced. Data are routinely decentralized and move freely around the network. CASE tools are more robust and more client-friendly.

Data are easily identified and readily shared between organizations on open systems. All primary data sources and major data flows are identified and documented. Data resource management activities are embedded in the organization as a routine way of doing business. Organizations actively cooperate for data collection and data sharing.

▼ SUMMARY

Disparate data have been actively developed for many years. This process has created a disparate data syndrome that is difficult to break. The syndrome produces application data files that continue to perpetuate disparate data. Traditional attempts to break the syndrome failed because there was no common base for defining data. The common data architecture provides the common base for refining disparate data and allows the disparate data syndrome to be broken.

Refining data is much like remodeling an old house. It is a discovery process that starts with an initial common data architecture and some assumptions about existing data. The initial common data architecture is enhanced and the assumptions are proven or altered until data refining is complete. The result is an accurate model of disparate data and a better understanding of the data. Once the process is started it is easy to continue to completion. The biggest difficulty is getting started.

Data refining is a discovery process that involves knowledgeable people. These people analyze disparate data and cross reference them to the common data architecture. They develop a common data architecture from above, and place detail in that architecture from below through a consensus process. It is an evolutionary process that weaves the knowledge hidden in people and products into a common data architecture.

A consensus approach is used that is based on active involvement in a *no blame–no whitewash* atmosphere. No one is blamed for the existing state and the existing state is not covered up. People who are actively involved become committed and readily accept the resulting common data architecture. They work as a team to produce a successful data resource library.

There are five evolutionary stages that organizations pass through as they move from the disparate data situation, through a formal data resource, to the mature data resource. Knowing these stages helps organizations move through the stages more easily. It helps them increase their productivity, minimize impacts on the business due to a lack of data, and capitalize on the investments they already have in their existing data.

▼ QUESTIONS

The following questions are designed to provide a review of Chapter 8 and to stimulate thought about the concepts and approaches to refining disparate data and the evolutionary stages that organizations go through to achieve a mature data resource.

1. How are disparate data created?

2. What is the disparate data syndrome?

3. Why have traditional attempts to break the disparate data syndrome failed?

4. How can the disparate data syndrome be broken?

5. What is the base for refining disparate data?

6. Why is data refining not a precise process?

7. What is the general sequence of events for data refining?

8. Why is data refining not the same as data normalization or data denormalization?

9. Why is data refining a discovery process?

10. Why can data refining not be automated?

11. Why is a consensus approach necessary?

12. Why is facilitation of a consensus approach important?

13. Why does arbitration hamper the consensus process?

14. Why is it important to have a *no blame–no whitewash* approach?

15. How are individual interviews and group sessions used to gain consensus?

16. Why is it not appropriate to force resolution of issues?

17. How does the common data architecture size vary through data refining?

18. What are the evolutionary stages for developing the mature data resource?

19. Why is it difficult to get to the organization cluster and common data architecture stages?

20. Where is the real knowledge about disparate data?

▼
▼
▼

9

DISPARATE DATA DESCRIPTION

Describing disparate data properly is the key to understanding their true content and meaning.

Disparate data have widely varying names and definitions. Most names are short and abbreviated, and provide little insight into the content or meaning of the data. Most definitions are short, truncated sentences and phrases, if they exist at all. They range from an elongated name to data entry instructions, but seldom provide any real understanding of the data.

The challenge is to determine what disparate data represent in the real world. Each data product characteristic and data product code is analyzed to determine its true content and meaning, independent of its use. Once its true content and meaning are determined, it can be properly cross referenced to the common data architecture.

This chapter explains how the data naming taxonomy is used to name disparate data and common data. The techniques for identifying and uniquely naming disparate data are explained. The preparation of common data names to represent variations in disparate data is described. Documenting and enhancing disparate data definitions and aggregating those definitions to form comprehensive data definitions for the common data architecture are explained. The preparation of fundamental and derived data definitions is also explained.

▼ DATA NAMING TAXONOMY

The data naming taxonomy is used to uniquely identify all disparate data, all data in the common data architecture, and all deployed data, as shown in Figure 9.1. The data repository name, data subject name, and data characteristic name components are used to uniquely identify data products, data product subjects, and data product characteristics. The data subject name, data characteristic name, and data characteristic variation name components are used to uniquely identify data in the common data architecture. All four components are used to uniquely identify all data deployed within the common data architecture.

New data defined within the common data architecture use the techniques described in the Data Name and Data Definition chapters. An explanation of the formal naming of data deployed throughout an organization or on a network is beyond the scope of this book. The unique identification and definition of disparate data, along with the naming and definition of common data that represent those disparate data, are explained below.

▼ DISPARATE DATA NAMES

Disparate data names are usually short, inconsistent, and often meaningless. There are often many synonymous and homonymous names that do not uniquely identify each data characteristic or each data code.

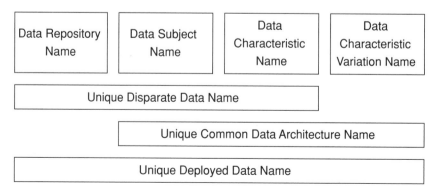

Figure 9.1 *Unique data names from data naming taxonomy.*

Making a cross reference to the common data architecture with these names provides only a one-way cross reference because it is impossible to uniquely identify all disparate data. Unique names for all disparate data are needed to provide a two-way cross reference with the common data architecture. Therefore, each data product, data product subject, data product data characteristic, and product data code must be uniquely identified within the scope of the common data architecture.

Data Product Names

Each data product must be uniquely named within the scope of the common data architecture. The unique naming of data products starts the hierarchy for uniquely naming all disparate data. Therefore, the ultimate scope of the common data architecture must be considered so that unique data product names are developed. For example, Health Department Data Dictionary, County Water Sampling Project, Financial Information System, and Traffic Investigation Unit are examples of unique data product names.

> *Uniquely naming data products sets the scope for uniquely identifying all disparate data.*

Data product names are developed when the data product is first identified. A unique data product name usually does not exist and needs to be developed so that all disparate data in that data product can be uniquely identified. Organizations must plan for unique data product identification from the beginning of the data refining effort. If the data product names are not unique, the identification of disparate data will not be unique and the data refining effort will not be successful. For example, using data product names like Health, County, Financial, and Traffic may initially be unique, but probably will not be unique as additional data products are identified.

Data Product Subject Names

Each data product subject must be uniquely named within a data product. The data product name provides uniqueness within the common data architecture and the data product subject name provides uniqueness within the data product.

Data product subject names must be unique within a data product.

Data product subject names are relatively easy to identify. For example, PERS.DATA.NEW, BUDGET.DATA, or IBM 3090 PERS.DATA.NEW are typical data file names. Daily Financial Transaction Report, Monthly Vehicle Accident Summary, and Water Sample Analysis Results are typical report or screen names. Water Sample, Accident, and Account are typical semi-structure data subject names. When these data product subject names are added to their data product names, a unique data product subject name is created. For example, Financial Information System - Daily Financial Transaction Report uniquely identifies a specific report.

Semi-structured data usually have a data subject name, or a similar data entity name, that becomes the data product subject name. These names may be close to the common data subject names, but they do not match the common data architecture exactly. Unstructured data may have a single record type that becomes the data product subject name, such as Vehicle. Unstructured data may also have multiple record types, such as Control Record, Summary Record, and Transaction Record, that become the data product subject names. Any major grouping of unstructured data could become a data product subject name.

Data Product Characteristic Names

A data product characteristic is uniquely identified by the data product name, the data product subject name, and the data product characteristic name. The data product characteristic name must be unique within the data product subject.

Data product characteristic names are very easy to identify because they already exist in the documentation. For example, field names in a data file like TYPE, CODE, STATUS, or DATE are data product characteristic names. When combined with the data product and data product subject names, each data product characteristic is uniquely named within the common data architecture. For example, Financial

Information System - Daily Financial Transaction Report - Status uniquely identifies a data field on a report.

The data product characteristic name must be unique within a data product subject.

Data product characteristic names are shown exactly as they appear in the data product. There is no alteration in their format, type font, or spelling. For example, if the data product characteristic name is fully capitalized, underscored, or abbreviated, it is shown in exactly that form. This is done both to represent the data product characteristic name as it appears in the data product and to gain client involvement. When clients see a data product characteristic name they recognize, they will become more involved in data refining.

Data Product Code Names

A data product code is uniquely identified by the data product name, the data product subject name, the data product characteristic name, and the data product code value. The data product code value must be unique within the data product characteristic.

Data product codes are uniquely identified by the value, not the name.

Data product code names can be very difficult to identify, and often do not exist. Data product codes always have a value; they may have definitions without names, or names without definitions, or neither name nor definition. Many times it is difficult to tell whether a phrase is the data product code name or a definition. Therefore, a data product code is identified by the data product code value rather than by the data product code name. For example, if there are financial status codes of N and A, the data product codes would be uniquely identified by Financial Information System–Daily Financial Transaction Report-Status–N and Financial Information System–Daily Financial Transaction Report-Status–A.

▼ COMMON DATA NAMES

Identifying common data names that represent disparate data is often a difficult task. It requires an understanding of the true content and meaning of disparate data and an understanding of the common data architecture. The techniques for naming common data were explained in the Data Name chapter. They are further clarified below for use in developing common data names to represent disparate data.

Common Data Subject Name

Common data subject names are developed within the common data architecture. Some input to the common data subject name may be obtained from the data product subject name, but the common data subject name is developed within the common data architecture.

Common Data Characteristic Name

Determining the common data characteristic name is often a difficult task. For example, determining that Traffic Investigation Unit–Vehicle File–TYPE is Vehicle Model Name, Traffic Investigation Unit–Vehicle File–CODE is the Vehicle Engine Type Code, Traffic Investigation Unit–Vehicle File–STATUS is Vehicle License Expiration Indicator, and Traffic Investigation Unit–Vehicle File–DATE is the Vehicle License Expiration Date is a difficult task. A major part of data refining is determining the common data characteristic name for data product characteristics.

> *A major part of data refining is determining data characteristic names that represent data product characteristics.*

The data product characteristic must be analyzed very carefully to determine its true content and meaning. Then a common data characteristic is located or created to match the data product characteristic.

Fully Qualified Data Characteristic Names

Common data characteristic names must be fully qualified to prevent any confusion about the exact content and meaning of a data product characteristic. The general guideline is to fully qualify common data characteristic names during data refining, even if there are no closely related common data characteristics. It is very likely that when additional disparate data are refined, there will be closely related common data characteristics. Always using fully qualified common data characteristic names prevents any confusion about what each common data characteristic represents, and avoids any later adjustment to make those names fully qualified. If there are no closely related common data characteristics, no harm is done with the fully qualified data name.

Common data characteristic names must be fully qualified.

For example, identifying a driver's name as Driver Name is not sufficient. That name could be complete or abbreviated. The common data characteristic name should be Driver Name Complete or Driver Name Abbreviated. The same might be true for a Well Depth. It could be Well Total Depth or Well Usable Depth. The person creating the common data characteristic name needs to be very perceptive about creating fully qualified names.

Common Data Characteristic Variation Name

Common data characteristic variations identify variations in content, meaning, or format of a common data characteristic. Each common data characteristic has at least one variation, and may have many. The general guideline is to assume data variability and always use common data characteristic variation names. This approach prevents adjustment of common data characteristic variation names when new variations are discovered, and helps designate official data variations after data cross referencing is completed.

Each common data characteristic has at least one common data characteristic variation.

For example, the common data characteristic name Lake Size provides little information about which size of a lake is being measured, such as area, volume, or depth. The common data characteristic variation name Lake Area Acres provides more information, but does not indicate how the area was obtained. Common data characteristic variation names like Lake Area Acres 1:24 Photo, meaning *acres interpreted from 1:24,000 aerial photographs*, and Lake Area Acres 1:4 Survey, meaning *acres determined by field survey on 1:4,000 maps*, provide much more information.

Many data product characteristics contain irregular data, such as different forms of an employee's name. Since the precise variation cannot be shown in the common data characteristic name, the common data characteristic variation word *Irregular* is used, as in Employee Name Irregular. It indicates that the contents of that data characteristic are irregular, and the data definition explains the irregularity.

Each data product characteristic must be analyzed very carefully to determine its true content, meaning, and format. Then a common data characteristic variation is located or created to match the data product characteristic. This is the point where data product characteristics will be connected to the common data architecture. To use a cliché: this is where the rubber meets the road. The success of data refining depends on proper connection between data product characteristics and common data characteristic variations.

Common Data Code Name

A common data code must have a unique value and a formal name. Data product codes usually have unique values, but seldom have formal names. Determining the common data code name is often as difficult as determining the common data characteristic and common data characteristic variation name.

For example, determining that Financial Information System–Daily Financial Transaction Report–Status–A represents Adjustment, and that Financial Information System–Daily Financial Transaction Report–Status–N represents New, might be difficult. The data product codes must be analyzed very carefully to determine their true meaning. Then a common data code name is formed that reflects that meaning. In this situation, Adjusted Financial Transaction and New Financial Transaction might be the common data code names.

Determining common data code values and names is another point where disparate data will be connected to the common data architecture. Like data characteristic variations, the data code values and data code names must be correct for the proper connection between data product codes and common data codes. Like the proper connection of data product characteristics and common data characteristic variations, the success of data refining depends on the proper connection between data product codes and common data codes.

Data Code Variations

There are many variations in product data code values. Different sets of data product code values may be used in different data products to represent the same thing. For example, a set of data product codes is identified in a motor pool maintenance system for the types of vehicles, such as A for Automobile, B for Motorcycle, C for Truck, and so on. Another set of data product codes is identified in a licensing system for the types of vehicles, such as 1 for Automobile, 2 for Motorcycle, and 3 for Truck.

Data code value variations are identified in the common data characteristic name.

A common data characteristic Vehicle Type Code is created for these vehicle type codes. Two common data characteristic variations are created for Vehicle Type Code Motor Pool and Vehicle Type Code License. The two data product characteristics will be cross referenced to these two common data characteristic variations. However, the two sets of data product codes are not defined in the common data architecture.

The data product codes for vehicle type are analyzed to determine the full set of data codes. Then an official set of data codes is either defined or designated from the existing sets of data product codes. Common data code names and common data code values are defined in the common data architecture to represent this official set of codes. For example, a new set of vehicle type codes was defined, such as A for Automobile, M for Motorcycle, and T for Truck. The common data characteristic variations for this set of common data codes could be Vehicle Type Code New and Vehicle Type Name New. The two sets of data product codes would be cross referenced to this official set of common data codes.

The data product characteristic representing a set of data product codes has a corresponding common data characteristic variation. All sets of data product codes representing the same set of properties, such as vehicle type, are analyzed, and an official set of common data codes is designated. Those official common data codes are defined in the common data architecture.

Questionable Data Characteristic Names

There may be uncertainty about a common data characteristic name during data refining. This situation is common because it is often difficult to determine the exact content, meaning, and format of a data product characteristic. If the exact content, meaning, and format cannot be determined, it is difficult to determine the common data characteristic name or the common data characteristic variation name.

If the common data characteristic name is only partially known, it is followed by dashes to indicate that the name is incomplete. For example, a common data characteristic is known to be an employee's name, but the exact contents and format of that name are unknown—it could be complete or abbreviated, normal or inverted. The common data characteristic name would be Employee Name –––– to indicate the name is incomplete. If the common data characteristic were known to be complete, but the format was unknown, the data characteristic name would be Employee Name Complete ––––. When the additional information is obtained, the data name is completed and the dashes are removed.

A common data characteristic name may be questionable during data refining. In this situation, the data characteristic name is followed by a question mark to indicate uncertainty about that common data characteristic. For example, Employee Name Complete Normal ? indicates that the data name is most likely the employee's complete name in normal sequence, but that this information is questionable for some reason. The uncertainty must be resolved before data refining is complete.

Incomplete and questionable data characteristic names must be identified during data refining.

These two conventions indicate the current understanding of data during data refining. For example, Employee Birth Date ―――― indicates that the common data characteristic is the employee's birth date, but the format is unknown. Employee Birth Date CYMD ? indicates that the common data characteristic is most likely the employee's birth date in CYMD format, but it is not known for sure. Both dashes and question mark indicate an incomplete name and uncertainty about what the data characteristic represents. For example, Employee Birth Date ――――? indicates that the data characteristic is most likely the employee's birth date, but it is not known for sure. It could represent a hire date, a promotion date, or an evaluation date. The dashes indicate that the format variation for date is not known.

▼ DATA DEFINITIONS

The task of finding a definition for disparate data is frustrating and confusing for most people. Most disparate data do not have good definitions, if they have any at all. However, developing a definition for disparate data is necessary for a thorough understanding of those data and development of comprehensive common data definitions.

Every common data subject, data characteristic, data characteristic variation, and data code must have a comprehensive definition that fully explains its true content and meaning. Disparate data definitions help form comprehensive common data definitions.

Disparate Data Definitions

It is a poor practice to assume that disparate data definitions are complete and accurate. They probably aren't. Most disparate data definitions were either developed early in a project and forgotten, or developed after the project was completed. Definitions developed early in a project were probably altered during the project, but were never enhanced. Definitions developed after the project were based on memory, which is poor at best.

Do not assume that disparate data definitions are complete and accurate.

Data product definitions generally do not exist and are usually developed during data refining. They must comprehensively define a data product and the scope of disparate data included in that data product.

Data product subject definitions usually do not exist because records, record types, screens, and reports do not have definitions. A good definition of a data product subject should be prepared to help people understand what the data product subject represents.

Data product characteristic definitions are usually short phrases or single sentences, and are usually oriented to the entry or use of the data. These definitions should be retained as they are stated in the original documentation. However, the definition can be extended as the data product characteristic is analyzed. These extended data product definitions will be combined to form a comprehensive definition for the common data characteristic and its variations.

An *extended data product definition* includes the original definition of a data product characteristic or data product code as it appears in the original documentation, followed by any additional information gained during analysis of the data product. For reference, the additional information should contain a date and the name of the person who added the information.

Data product code definitions are usually names or short phrases, and often do not exist at all. If a definition exists, it should be retained for reference. The definition can be extended as the data product codes are analyzed.

Data product characteristic and data product code definitions can be extended as information is gained.

Data product characteristic and data product code definitions are highly variable. They can have the same name with different content and meaning, or different names with the same content and meaning. There can be gaps and overlaps in the content and meaning. These situations should be recognized when preparing extended data product definitions.

The use of disparate data cannot be included in a comprehensive common data definition. However, since disparate data generally represent specific uses of data, that use can help identify and define the true content and meaning of those data. The expanded data product characteristic and data product code definitions may include the use of data to gain a better understanding about what those data represent.

Common Data Definition Approach

The general approach to developing comprehensive common data definitions that represent disparate data is to combine the extended data product definitions and add a real-world, use-free perspective to those data product definitions. The true content and meaning are determined and used to form a comprehensive common data definition.

Developing a comprehensive common data definition is an evolutionary process that requires constant review and rework throughout data refining. It is poor practice to just wait for a full data definition to happen, because it never will. Comprehensive data definitions are built incrementally by collecting information piece by piece and consulting knowledgeable people. This collection is a difficult task because of the uncertainty in disparate data. The general guideline is to be diligent and open-minded, and to build comprehensive data definitions incrementally.

> *Developing comprehensive data definitions is an evolutionary process that requires constant review and enhancement.*

A common data definition begins with aggregates from disparate data definitions plus short terms, phrases, and comments. When additional information is discovered, it is entered into the common data definition. Eventually, enough information is available to develop a tentative common data definition. As additional information is gained, the common data definition is constantly enhanced until it is complete and accurate. Notes, questions, comments, and issues can be added to assist with the development of a comprehensive common data definition.

If there is strong disagreement over a common data definition, there may be multiple common data subjects or common data characteristics included in one definition. An effort should be made to subdivide the definition until agreement is reached and then identify and name the individual components. It should not be assumed that disparate data always contain single components, because they don't.

For example, suppose that there is considerable disagreement and discussion about Building Value and consensus cannot be reached. On careful examination, there are three different building values: one for original acquisition cost, one for current value, and one for replacement cost. Three data characteristics are defined for Building Original Value, Building Current Value, and Building Replacement Cost, and the disagreement is resolved.

Data Subject Definitions

Common data subject definitions are built incrementally as information is gained from disparate data and from the real world. When a common data subject is first identified, an initial data definition is prepared. As disparate data are identified and cross referenced to the common data architecture, the definition is reviewed and adjusted as necessary. As new information is gained from knowledgeable people and the real world, the definition is further adjusted. Ultimately, a good common data subject definition evolves.

Data subject definitions are based on real-world objects.

A good approach is to determine what the common data subject represents in the real world. Identifying the real-world objects and defining those objects helps develop common data subject definitions. When a common data subject is first identified from disparate data, it may be useful to immediately identify the real-world objects represented by that common data subject to prepare the initial common data subject definition.

Data product subject definitions may provide information for defining common data subjects. Generally, data product subjects represent multiple common data subjects or part of a common data subject. However, their definitions can be useful for defining common data subjects.

Data Characteristic Definitions

Preparing common data characteristic definitions that represent disparate data is often difficult. The best approach is to work down from the common data subject and up from the common data characteristic variations. When the common data subject is defined, common data characteristics can be defined for features of the data subject. This top-down approach assures a real-world data definition. For example, a common data subject is defined for Vehicle. Any common data characteristics in Vehicle must define the features of a vehicle, such as a Vehicle Value.

Common data characteristics can be defined both from their data subject and from their data characteristic variations.

Data product characteristic definitions can be aggregated through the common data characteristic variations to form an initial common data characteristic definition. This bottom-up approach ensures that common data characteristics truly represent disparate data. For example, all the common data characteristic variations for Vehicle Value, which represent data product characteristics, can be aggregated to form an initial definition for a Vehicle Value.

Data Characteristic Variation Definitions

Any difference in the content or meaning of a data product characteristic results in definition of a common data characteristic variation. For example, several data product characteristics related to well location were identified in disparate data. Their equivalent common data characteristic variations are shown in Figure 9.2. Well Location is the common data characteristic. It has four common data characteristic variations: Public Land Survey to the nearest forty acres, latitude and

> Well Location
>   Well Location PLS 40 Acres
>   Well Location Lat/Lon 5 Degrees
>   Well Location SPC 50 Feet
>   Well Location Lat/Lon 1 Degree

Figure 9.2 *Data characteristic variations.*

longitude to the nearest five degrees, State Plane Coordinates to the nearest 50 feet, and latitude and longitude to the nearest one degree.

Each common data characteristics variation is comprehensively defined by inheriting the common data characteristic definition for Well Location and adding an definition of the specific location method. The definition of Well Location is placed in each data characteristic variation definition to make those definitions comprehensive.

Data Code Definitions

A comprehensive data definition is prepared for each common data code. Like common data characteristics, common data code definitions can be developed either from their parent data characteristic or from data product code definitions. When a set of common data codes is identified, such as Disability, all the properties of disability are identified and defined based on the disabilities that can be found in the real world, such as speech disabilities, hearing disabilities, and so on. The definitions of these properties become the common data code definitions. This top-down approach ensures that all the properties of disability are comprehensively defined.

> *Common data code definitions can be developed from real-world properties and from aggregated data product code definitions.*

Common data code definitions can also be developed from a combination of corresponding data product codes. This bottom-up approach ensures that the common data codes truly represent disparate data. For example, the definitions for each data product code representing a disability, such as speech, are aggregated from data product codes for an initial common data code definition.

In many situations, data codes have overlapping meanings. If the aggregated definitions for a common data code have different meanings, that difference must be raised as an issue and resolved. For example, the definition of a common data code for Developmental Disability may show a difference between a mental developmental disability and a physical developmental disability. This issue can be resolved by creating two common data codes for Mental Developmental Disability and Physical Developmental Disability.

Fundamental Data Definitions

Fundamental data are defined as the common data architecture is developed. A good place to start defining fundamental data is with dates and times. Fundamental data should be defined for century, calendar year, federal fiscal year, state fiscal year, and quarter for each of these years. Month should be defined within a calendar year, federal fiscal year, and state fiscal year. Day should be defined within each of those years and within month. Hours should be defined for both 12 and 24 hour days. Other fundamental data definitions can be added for people, addresses, and locations.

Fundamental data are actively defined to support specific data.

Development of fundamental data definitions is a continuous process. Any person refining data must constantly look for fundamental data. When fundamental data are identified, such as person, organization, chronology, address, phone, geographic location, and so on, they are defined and added to the existing fundamental data definitions. For example, location data characteristics are identified that use the Public Land Survey designations. Fundamental data definitions should be prepared for Public Land Survey Tier Number, Range Number, Section Number, Section Quarter Identifier, and Section Forty Identifier.

Hierarchies of fundamental data definitions can also be developed. For example, Century Number, Calendar Year Number, Month Number Calendar Year, and Day Number Month can be combined into Date CYMD. Date CYMD can be inherited by Person Birth Date CYMD, which can be inherited by Employee Birth Date CYMD or Student Birth Date CYMD.

Derived Data Definitions

Derived data are part of the formal data resource like primitive data, and must be named and defined in the same way. Many design methods ignore formal names and comprehensive definitions for derived data, such as summary data in executive information systems. The reason given is that derived data subjects and data characteristics are so dynamic and so prolific that it is impossible to name and define all of them. Although this may be true for ad hoc inquiries from executive information systems, it is not true for derived data that are stored and maintained.

All derived data must be formally named and comprehensively defined.

It is a poor practice to ignore the naming and definition of derived data during data refining, because doing so limits understanding of data available in the formal data resource. An organization must know all the data it has at its disposal, including derived data. All data, including derived data, must be formally named and comprehensively defined so that people understand what data are available to meet their business needs. Ideally, ad hoc data that are not stored in a database should be formally named and comprehensively defined so that people are sure what the data represent. Practically, however, data refining is limited to derived data that are stored in databases.

Derived data must be carefully reviewed to develop a comprehensive data definition. Identification of the contributing data characteristics and the derivation method adds considerable information to the definition. Information on the use of derived data also provides insight into the true content and meaning of those derived data, although the use is not part of the comprehensive data definition. The data derivation algorithm for each derived data characteristic is documented as part of the data definition, including the data characteristics involved in the derivation and the method of derivation.

A different derivation algorithm results in a different data subject or data characteristic variation.

Any contributing data characteristic identified in a derived data algorithm must exist in the common data architecture. It may or may not be listed in the cross reference between product data and common data. Any common data definition for derived data must identify all the contributing data characteristics. If those contributing data characteristics do not exist in the common data architecture, they must be added.

▼ SUMMARY

Disparate data have many synonymous and homonymous names that cannot be used for unique identification. The data naming taxonomy is used to provide unique identification for all disparate data within the scope of the common data architecture. Data product names, data product subject names, data product characteristic names, and data product code values are used to uniquely identify all disparate data. The data naming taxonomy is also used to provide formal data names within the common data architecture.

Disparate data also have poor definitions that do not meet the criteria for comprehensive definitions in the common data architecture. However, they do contain information that can be used to develop comprehensive common data definitions. Original disparate data definitions are extended with information gained from an analysis of disparate data. These extended data product definitions are aggregated in the common data architecture to help form common data definitions. Definitions from the real world and input from knowledgeable people are added to the aggregated disparate data definitions to form comprehensive data definitions.

The development of comprehensive data definitions is an evolutionary process. A comprehensive data definition usually starts with a short phrase. As information is gained, the definition is enhanced until a full comprehensive data definition is formed. The definition of fundamental data and development of a hierarchy of fundamental data helps the definition of specific data.

The benefits of unique identification of disparate data, and of formal naming and comprehensive definition of the common data that represent disparate data, are a better understanding of an organization's formal data resource and preparation for data cross referencing.

▼ QUESTIONS

The following questions are designed to provide a review of Chapter 9 and to stimulate thought about the unique identification of disparate data, and about the formal naming and comprehensive of common data representing those disparate data.

1. What is the real challenge to uniquely identifying disparate data?

2. Why must disparate data be uniquely identified?

3. How does the data naming taxonomy support unique identification of disparate data?

4. Why must common data names be fully qualified when refining disparate data?

5. How is an incomplete data name or uncertainty about a data name indicated?

6. Why do disparate data have short data definitions?

7. Why is it poor practice to assume that disparate data definitions are accurate?

8. How is a comprehensive common data definition developed?

9. How real-world definitions help develop common data definitions?

10. Why must common data characteristic variations be defined?

11. What constitutes a new data characteristic variation?

12. Why are there so many variations in disparate data?

13. What are the top-down and bottom-up approaches for developing comprehensive data definitions?

14. Why are product data codes so difficult to name and define?

15. How are variations in data code definitions managed?

16. What fundamental data definitions could be developed to support data refining?

17. How does a hierarchy of fundamental data definitions help data refining?

18. Why should derived data be formally named and comprehensively defined?

19. Why are derivation algorithms documented for derived data?

20. Why is developing common data definitions an evolutionary process?

10

DISPARATE DATA STRUCTURE

Disparate data are structured in a wide variety of different ways.

Disparate data are usually very poorly structured, if they are structured at all. Most disparate data never went through logical data modeling with data normalization or formal data denormalization. Any structure that does exist is a physical structure of data files developed to meet a specific need. Data relations that exist are based on primary keys or on the same data items that exist in different data files.

The author never ceases to be amazed at the different ways disparate data can be structured. Each new data refining project brings new insights into how physical data can be designed without the benefit of logical data modeling with data normalization or formal data denormalization. Data files have been developed in every imaginable way, and even in some unimaginable ways. Examples of disparate data structures could easily fill an entire book devoted to that topic alone.

One major effort in data refining is identifying the structure of disparate data. Knowing that structure makes it easier to create accurate cross references between disparate data and the common data architecture. This chapter begins with a definition of terms used in documenting the physical structure of data. Then the techniques for documenting the physical structure of disparate data are explained. The prominent structures that appear in disparate data are presented.

Finally, several logical data structures used to document the logical structure of disparate data are presented.

▼ PHYSICAL DATA STRUCTURE

The physical structure of data is documented with a data file diagram and a physical data structure chart. Each of these types of documentation is described below for data that have been through logical data modeling with data normalization and formal data denormalization. The variations for documenting the structure of disparate data are also explained.

Definitions

A *data file* is a physical file of data that exists in a database management system, as a computer file outside a database management system, or as a manual file outside a computer. It consists of a set of data records that contain data items. Ideally, a data file represents a data subject that has gone through a formal data denormalization process. For example, data files are developed for Employee, Position, and Equipment to match the data subjects for Employee, Position, and Equipment.

However, most data files containing disparate data never went through logical data modeling with data normalization or formal data denormalization. They were built to meet a specific need and often contain data from several data subjects. In many cases, the data from one data subject is split across many data files. This is one reason that data cross referencing is often difficult.

A *disparate data file* is a data file that did not go through logical data modeling with data normalization or data denormalization and does not represent one complete data subject. For example, a training data file contains data about students, training courses, training classes, and training facilities. An equipment data file contains data about equipment, equipment breakdowns, and equipment maintenance. Most disparate data files represent parts of several data subjects.

A *data record* is a physical grouping of data items that are stored and retrieved from a data file. It is the basic component of a data file. Ideally, a data record represents a single data occurrence. For example, the data occurrences in Employee for *John J. Jones*, *Sally S. Smith*, and *Marilyn M. McDonald* have corresponding data records in the Employee data file.

However, data records in disparate data files do not always represent one data occurrence. They may represent several data occurrences, or they may represent part of a data occurrence. In many situations, different data subjects are represented by different data record types in a single disparate data file, or a single data subject may be split between several data record types in a single disparate data file.

A *disparate data record* is a data record that does not represent one complete data occurrence of a data subject in a disparate data file. For example, an employee's personal data may be placed on one record type and professional data on another. An employee's data may also be split between an employee data file, a training data file, and an affirmative action data file. As explained above, a training data record may contain data about a student, a class that student took, the course that class represents, and the location of the class.

A *data item* is an individual field in a data record. It is the basic component of a data record. Ideally, a data item represents a single or combined data characteristic containing two or more closely related data characteristics. For example, data characteristics in the Employee data subject for Employee Name Complete Normal and Employee Birth Date CYMD have matching data items in the Employee data file.

However, data items in disparate data files do not always represent a single data characteristic or a combined data characteristic containing two or more closely related data characteristics. They may represent two or more unrelated data characteristics. This is another reason that data cross referencing is often difficult.

A *disparate data item* is a data item that represents two or more unrelated data characteristics. For example, a data item might contain an employee's name and birth date. A coordinate location data item might contain both a latitude and a longitude. A vehicle type data item might contain the manufacturer, make, and model.

A *disparate data code* is a data code in a disparate data item. It may represent a one or more common data codes. Several disparate data codes may represent one common data code.

A *data key* is one or more data items used as access to a data file to store or retrieve data. Data keys are normally defined from secondary keys on a logical data resource model during a formal data denormalization process. For example, the data keys defined for access to Employee data are Employee Social Security Number and Employee Name Complete Normal.

However, the data keys in most disparate data files were defined as they were needed without any formal data denormalization. In many cases, they were defined and maintained without any known need. Many disparate data files have numerous data keys defined that are maintained and never used.

A *disparate primary key* is any primary key defined in a disparate data file. It may or may not meet the criteria for a true primary key. It often contains redundant data items that are not necessary for unique identification of each data record. For example, the primary key for a vehicle might contain the vehicle's license number and the manufacture date.

A *disparate foreign key* is any foreign key defined in a disparate data file. It may or may not match the criteria for a true foreign key and may or may not match the disparate primary key in a parent data file. The general rule is that *anything goes* with primary and foreign keys in disparate data.

Data File Diagram

A *data file diagram* is a diagram that shows the data files and the data relations between those data files. It is developed from the formal denormalization of a data relation diagram defined during logical data modeling. Data subjects are converted to data files according to a formal set of criteria.

A data file diagram shows data files and the data relations between those data files.

Two symbols are used to prepare a data file diagram. These symbols are consistent with semiotics, which specifies the consistent use of symbols across all models. An oval represents a data file, and the name of the data file is placed inside the oval. A dashed line represents a data relation between data files. The data relation has an arrow on one end representing a one-to-many data relation, the most prominent data relation between data files, and no arrows representing a one-to-one data relation. There is no many-to-many data relation between data files.

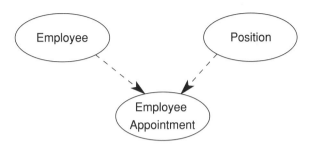

Figure 10.1 *Data file diagram for employee data.*

For example, a data file diagram containing three data files for Employee, Position, and Employee Appointment is shown in Figure 10.1. It was developed from the formal denormalization of a data relation diagram containing Employee, Position, and Employee Appointment data subjects.

Disparate Data File Diagram

A data file diagram normally represents data files developed from the formal data denormalization of a logical data resource model. However, disparate data files were developed without logical data modeling and formal data denormalization. A *disparate data file diagram* is a data file diagram representing the existing structure of disparate data files. It uses the same symbols described above, but it represents disparate data files and the data relations between them.

A data file diagram may or may not exist for data products that contain data files. If it does exist, it may be in any form the developer decided to use at that time. There are usually no consistent symbols or notations between data file diagrams, and often no consistent symbols or notations within a data file diagram. Developers used any symbols and notations that were useful to them at the time the diagram was developed.

> *A disparate data file diagram is prepared for any data product containing disparate data files.*

Even though a data file diagram does not have consistent symbols or notations, it does provide some insight into the structure of disparate data. The best approach is to prepare a disparate data file diagram for any data product that contains disparate data files, using whatever information exists. In many cases, an initial disparate data file diagram is prepared and is continually enhanced as additional information is gained about the structure of disparate data. The result is a complete disparate data file diagram using the standard symbols.

Physical Data Structure Chart

A *physical data structure chart* is a listing of the data keys and data items in each data file. It looks similar to a logical data structure chart, but shows data keys rather than primary keys and foreign keys. The data keys are usually named or numbered to match the naming convention required by the database management system where the data files are maintained. For example, the physical data structure chart for the Employee data file is shown in Figure 10.2.

Disparate Data Structure Chart

A physical data structure chart normally represents the physical structure of data from the formal data denormalization of a logical data

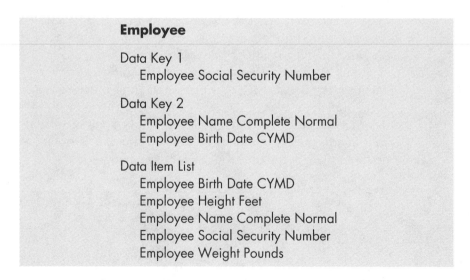

Employee

Data Key 1
    Employee Social Security Number

Data Key 2
    Employee Name Complete Normal
    Employee Birth Date CYMD

Data Item List
    Employee Birth Date CYMD
    Employee Height Feet
    Employee Name Complete Normal
    Employee Social Security Number
    Employee Weight Pounds

Figure 10.2 *Physical data structure chart for employee data.*

resource model. However, disparate data files were often developed in such a haphazard manner that a physical data structure chart would not be meaningful. A *disparate data structure chart* is a variation of the physical data structure chart for disparate data. It shows the disparate primary keys, disparate foreign keys, and data items in a disparate data file. It is not a logical data structure chart because it represents a data file, which could represent more than one data subject. It is not a physical data structure chart because it shows disparate primary and foreign keys rather than data keys.

For example, a disparate data structure chart for part of an Employee_File is shown in Figure 10.3. The data file and data item names are entered as they appear in the data file.

Usually there is no physical data structure chart for disparate data files. The closest thing is a listing of the data items. There may be some indication of primary keys or foreign keys on the list, but those indications may not truly represent the data file. The best approach is to prepare a disparate data structure chart for every data product containing data files. If a data product does not contain data files, a list of the data items is usually sufficient for preparing cross references to the common data architecture.

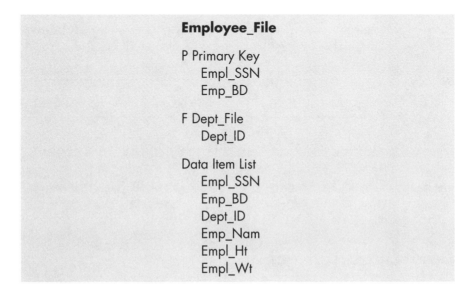

Figure 10.3 *Disparate data structure chart for employee data.*

▼ RECOGNIZING DISPARATE DATA STRUCTURES

Knowing the different ways disparate data can be structured helps people identify the structure of disparate data. When the structure of disparate data is determined, that structure can be aligned with the common data architecture. The prominent ways that disparate data can be structured are explained below. However, a complete explanation of all the possible ways disparate data could be structured is way beyond the scope of this book.

The structure of disparate data is best understood by developing a disparate data file diagram and a disparate data structure chart, as well as a data relation diagram and logical data structure chart representing the logical structure of disparate data files. Developing the data relation diagram and logical data structure helps people understand disparate data, and it makes cross referencing to the common data architecture easier.

Data Subjects

Disparate data files often represent multiple data subjects and partial data subjects. They frequently represent a combination of multiple and partial data subjects. For example, a disparate data file contains vehicle data, vehicle trip data, and vehicle maintenance data. These data actually represent three data subjects for Vehicle, Vehicle Trip, and Vehicle Maintenance. Any person refining disparate data must be aware that disparate data files usually represent multiple data subjects.

Disparate data files usually represent part of multiple data subjects.

Ideally, spatial data should be designed so that each data layer represents a single data subject, such as timber stand or soil unit. However, this is not always the situation with disparate spatial data. A single data layer may represent more than one data subject, just as disparate data files represent more than one data subject.

Data Characteristics

Disparate data items usually represent single data characteristics. However, there are many disparate data items that represent multiple data characteristics. If the multiple data characteristics are closely related, such as the data characteristics in a date, their combination is acceptable. If the multiple data characteristics are not closely related, their combination is not acceptable.

> *Disparate data items frequently have combined data characteristics.*

For example, the combination of century, year, month, and day into a date, and the combination of a person's individual, middle, and last names into a complete name are acceptable. However, the combination of a well depth, well casing diameter, and well casing thickness into one data item is not acceptable. Any person refining disparate data must watch for the combination of data characteristics in disparate data items and determine whether the combination is acceptable.

Data Codes

Disparate data codes are one of the most confusing things about disparate data, and one of the most difficult to understand and cross reference to the common data architecture. People have found many ways to invent data code structures that are very difficult to understand. Some of those ways are listed below.

- A disparate data code can represent a single common data code. For example, a vehicle type code in a data product characteristic matches a vehicle type code in a corresponding common data characteristic.

- A disparate data code can represent a partial common data code. For example, several vehicle type codes in a data product characteristic match one data code in a corresponding common data characteristic.

- A disparate data code can represent multiple common data codes. For example, a vehicle type code in a data product characteristic matches two or more data codes in a corresponding common data characteristic.

- A set of disparate data codes can represent a single set of common data codes in one common data subject. For example, a set of disability codes in a product data characteristic matches a set of disability codes in a corresponding common data characteristic.

- A set of disparate data codes can represent part of a complete set of common data codes in one common data subject. For example, a set of disability codes in a product data characteristic only match part of a complete set of disability codes in a corresponding common data characteristic.

- A set of disparate data codes can represent more than one set of common data codes in more than one common data subject. For example, a set of disability codes in a product data characteristic contains data codes matching data codes in a set of disability codes and data codes in a set of race codes.

Disparate data codes may have a hidden hierarchy. For example, the new Census Code is a set of three-digit numbers. However, there is a hidden three-level hierarchy in those codes. These three levels were defined as Census Race Category, Census Race Group, and Census Race. Census Race Category is identified by a range of 3-digit numbers, such as *653* through *699* for *Pacific Islander*. Census Race Group is identified by another range of 3-digit numbers within Census Race Category, such as *653* through *659* for *Polynesian*. Census Race is identified by a single 3-digit number within Census Race Group, such as *653* for *Hawaiian*.

Any person refining data must carefully review each set of disparate data codes and each disparate data code to determine what they represent in the common data architecture and if there is a hidden hierarchy in those data codes. If there is a hidden hierarchy, the levels must be identified and defined as separate data subjects. Common data subject words, such as *category, group,* and *class,* can be used to form the data subject names. The appropriate data relations and primary keys are defined for those new data subjects.

Primary Keys

Identifying disparate primary keys is not always an easy task, because they are not always readily apparent. In many cases, they may not even exist. Many databases were built without any concept of primary keys. Primary keys may be buried in a large control number and may be implied by their use. However, primary keys need to be identified and placed on a physical data structure chart to help people understand the data.

A prominent practice is to identify a primary key consisting of all the data characteristics that might ever be used for access. For example, a primary key defined for an employee data file might consist of the employee's name, social security number, birth date, seniority date, race, and disability. Clearly, not all of these data items are needed for uniqueness, but they are all used in some way for access.

Another prominent practice is to define all secondary keys that might ever be used for access. For example, secondary keys could be defined in an employee file for an employee's name and birth date, an employee's social security number, an employee's social security number and hire date, and so on. One of these secondary keys may be a primary key, such as the employee's social security number, but not defined as a primary key.

Some data files may have no primary key defined, if there was never any attempt to ensure the uniqueness of data records or to relate data records between data files. This situation is rare, but it does exist, particularly with databases that were not part of a database management system.

Different data files may have the same primary key. Since many data files were developed without logical data modeling and data normalization, several data files could have the same primary key. For example, a training data file, a payroll data file, and an affirmative action data file could all have a primary key of the employee's social security number. This situation is a good indication that the data files represent the same data subject.

Different data files representing the same common data subject could have different primary keys. For example, a vehicle purchase data file could have a primary key for the vehicle identification number and purchase date, a vehicle surplus data file could have a primary key for the vehicle license number and sale date, and a vehicle inventory data file could have a primary key for the vehicle license number. This situation leads to multiple primary keys for a common data subject.

Disparate primary keys frequently contain redundant data.

Disparate primary keys frequently contain redundant data. For example, a disparate primary key in the employee data file contains the employee's social security number, last name, and birth date. Traditionally, a unique control code was established, containing all the major data characteristics in a data file. This unique control code was considered the primary key, even though it contained redundant data. Any person refining data must review large control codes to identify the data items that form a true primary key.

Foreign Keys

Foreign keys are not easily identified in disparate data because they were never defined. They are usually identified indirectly by references to relations between data files, or to the location of data items with the same name in different data files. However, finding data items with the same name is not absolute proof that they represent the same data characteristic. Also, the foreign key data items in one data file may have completely different names than the primary key data items in the parent data file. This situation makes it very difficult to identify foreign keys. The person refining data must use any information available to determine whether data items represent the same data characteristic and whether they are a foreign key.

Foreign keys are usually not defined in disparate data.

A foreign key may be difficult to identify because it represents only part of the primary key in a parent data file. As mentioned above, primary keys in disparate data often contain redundant data items that are not required to make each data record unique. These redundant data items may not appear in subordinate data files. The best approach is to identify data items in a primary key that are required for uniqueness and then look for those data items in subordinate data files.

Another technique is to identify the foreign key in a subordinate data file and use those data items to identify the primary key in a parent data file. If the foreign key is easily identified, it may indicate the non-redundant data items in the primary key of a parent data file.

Indicators

Data items that represent a binary situation, such as true/false or yes/no, are common in disparate data. They identify the existence of another, often hidden, data subject. Whenever an indicator is identified during data refining, the data subject supporting the indicator must be identified and documented. Even if that data subject does not exist in the data resource, it must be identified and documented in the common data architecture to support the existence of an indicator. Identification of these hidden data subjects makes a richer data resource model.

Indicators represent another data subject that must be identified and defined in the common data architecture.

▼ USING DATA RELATION DIAGRAMS

Data relation diagrams are useful for understanding the logical structure of disparate data. However, several of the arrangements of data subjects that are used in data relation diagrams are very helpful for understanding the logical structure of disparate data. Three of these arrangements are explained below.

Data Categories

Data categories are very useful for understanding disparate data. Whenever separate data subjects are identified as having a one-to-one data relation with each other and being mutually inclusive, they become data categories of a common data subject. For example, separate data subjects are identified for Attorneys, Defendants, Witnesses, and Police Officers associated with court cases. A single person might exist in any of these data subjects, and could exist in more than one data subject. These data subjects become data categories of a common data subject for Court Case Associate, as shown in Figure 10.4.

Data categories may have different primary keys, such as Attorney State Bar Number, Defendant Identification Number, Witness Social Security Number, and Police Officer Badge Number. The primary keys are maintained for each data category. Ideally, there is one official primary key in the parent data subject, and each data category carries that primary key as a foreign key, such as Court Case Associate. However, this is not always true for disparate data, and the primary key of each data cate-

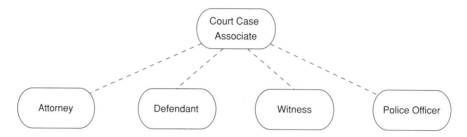

Figure 10.4 *Data category example.*

gory is maintained in the parent data subject for navigation to each data category.

Hierarchies

Data subject hierarchies are also very useful for understanding disparate data. They allow multiple perceptions of data to be integrated into one data structure. They provide a framework for bringing a jigsaw puzzle of disparate data subjects together and placing them in the proper perspective. Whenever separate data subjects that have a one-to-one data relation with each other and are mutually exclusive are identified, they form a data subject hierarchy.

> *Any data subjects that have a one-to-one data relation and are mutually exclusive form a data subject hierarchy.*

For example, different organizations track irrigation wells, geothermal wells, domestic wells, gas wells, and recharge wells. Each of these well types is a data subject, according to the organization, but the types also fit into a hierarchy of wells. The hierarchy of Wells might consist of Petroleum Wells and Water Wells, as shown in Figure 10.5. Petroleum Wells might consist of Oil Wells and Gas Wells. Water Wells might consist of Irrigation Wells, Domestic Wells, and Recharge Wells. This hierarchy puts the types of wells in their proper perspectives, and maintains each organization's original perception of its data subjects.

There is no limit to the number of levels in a data subject hierarchy, particularly in the documentation of disparate data. The data subject

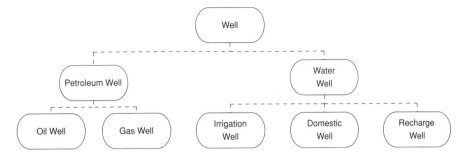

Figure 10.5 *Data subject hierarchy for wells.*

hierarchy may contain a virtual data subject, several true data subject levels, and several data subject type levels. These levels may collapse as further information becomes available.

The data subjects in a data subject hierarchy may have different primary keys. Data subject types usually have no primary keys; virtual data subjects never have primary keys. Ideally, a common primary key is identified for all true data subjects in a data subject hierarchy. However, this is not always true with disparate data, and separate primary keys may need to be defined for true data subjects during data refining.

Summary Data

Derived data, particularly summary data, often exist in disparate data. They usually do not appear in data files, but they appear in screens and on reports. Since data refining includes all data, whether in data files or on screens and reports, summary data must identified and defined.

Summary data are often ignored because they are more difficult to identify, name, and define than primitive data. However, they must be identified, named, defined, and included in the common data architecture so that people can understand how those data were derived and what they represent. A misunderstanding of derived data can be far more disastrous than a misunderstanding of primitive data.

Summary data subjects often have many parent data subjects that identify the level of summarization. For example, individual employee leave data may be summarized by Organization Unit, by Calendar Month, or by Leave Type. The data relation diagram in Figure 10.6 shows the Employee Leave Summary 1 data subject and the parent data subjects.

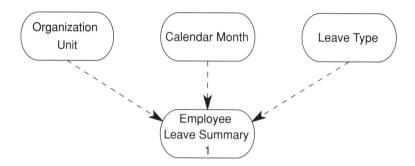

Figure 10.6 *Employee leave summarization.*

Several parent data subjects may be involved in defining a summary data subject. If different levels of summarization occur, different sets of parent data subjects may be involved. Mathematically, there are $2^n - 1$ possible summary data subjects for a set of parent data subjects. For example, if there were 5 parent data subjects, there would be 31 possible summary data subjects. Usually there are fewer, because some combinations of parent data subjects are meaningless.

When a set of parent data subjects is involved in defining summary data subjects, it is best to show all the parent data subjects in the same location around the summary data subject, whether or not they are involved in the summarization. This *summary data relation shell* gives people a better understanding of summary data subjects.

For example, the summarization of individual employee leave data is controlled by 5 parent data subjects, giving the possibility of 31 different summary data subjects. A summary data relation shell is prepared, as shown in Figure 10.7. That shell contains all five parent data subjects and an empty employee leave summary data subject. Each implementation of that shell contains only the data relations involved in characterizing a specific employee leave summary data subject. The example in Figure 10.8 shows only Organization Unit, Quarter, and Leave Type involved in characterizing the summary data subject.

A different algorithm, including different contributing data characteristics or different summarization methods, results in a different data characteristic. For example, hourly stream flow measurements can be accumulated to create daily, monthly, seasonal, and annual stream flow measurements. Algorithms are developed for converting stream

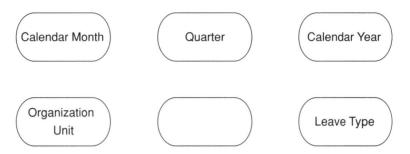

Figure 10.7 *Summary data relation shell for employee leave.*

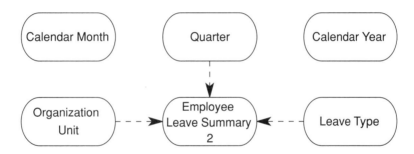

Figure 10.8 *Specific summary data subject for employee leave.*

flow to the volume of water flowing for each of these time periods and are documented with the data definitions. If different methods are used for determining the volume of water flowing, separate data characteristics are identified, and their definition contains a specific explanation of the method of derivation.

Many summary subjects exist only on reports and screens, or they may exist in databases, such as executive information systems. The techniques listed below explain how to identify, name, and define summary data.

- Identify and define data items that contain summary data. The definition should include the algorithm for deriving the data values.

- Identify and define the common data subject and data characteristics for the summary data items. A common data subject word, such as *Summary,* helps identify summary data subjects.

- Identify the primary key for the summary data subject. A primary key usually consists of data characteristics representing the primary keys of the parent data subjects.

- A different set of data characteristics in a primary key indicates a different summary data subject. The same set of data characteristics in a different sequence does not indicate different summary data subjects.

- Identify and define the parent data subjects.

- Prepare a summary data relation shell and specific data relation diagrams to help people understand the summary data.

Identifying and defining summary data is usually a difficult task, because most people are not familiar with defining and managing summary data. Identifying primary keys for summary data is also difficult, because there are usually many data items in the primary key, and those data items belong to several parent data subjects. There are usually very few non-key data items in a summary data.

▼ SUMMARY

Most disparate data never went through logical data modeling, data normalization, or data denormalization, and are usually very poorly structured. The are many different ways that disparate data can be structured. In the past, they were usually structured for a specific problem and a specific operating environment. Identifying and understanding the physical structure of disparate data is one of the most difficult tasks in refining data.

The best approach is to develop a disparate data file diagram and a disparate physical data structure chart for disparate data. A disparate data file diagram shows the data files and the data relations between those data files using common notations. A disparate physical data structure chart shows the structure of each data file on the disparate data file diagram, including the disparate primary keys and disparate foreign keys.

A data relation diagram and logical data structure chart can also be prepared for disparate data so their true logical structure can be better understood. They also help cross reference disparate data to the common data architecture.

Understanding some of the more prominent ways disparate data are structured helps people refine disparate data.

- The data items in disparate data files usually represent several common data subjects, and often do not represent all the common data characteristics in those data subjects. Disparate data files seldom represent all the data characteristics in a single common data subject.

- A data item usually represents a single common data characteristic. However, many data items represent the combination of common data characteristics that are not commonly used together.

- A disparate data code can represent a single common data code or multiple common data codes, or several disparate data codes may represent a single common data code.

- A set of disparate data codes may represent a single set of common data codes, part of a set of common data codes, or several sets of common data codes. Disparate data codes may have an implied hierarchy.

- Primary keys may not exist, may exist and not be readily identifiable, or may exist and be readily identifiable. They may contain many redundant data items. Different data files may have the same primary key, indicating that they represent the same common data subject, or data files representing the same common data subject may have different primary keys.

- Foreign keys are usually not defined in disparate data. However, their identification can help identify the non-redundant data items in a disparate primary key.

- Indicators identify the presence of hidden data subjects that need to be identified and defined.

Understanding the use of data relation diagrams to represent the logical structure of disparate data also helps people understand disparate data. Three of the most useful logical structures are listed below.

- Data categories help identify the relations between several data subjects that are in one-to-one relationships with each other.

- Data subject hierarchies help identify the hierarchy of data subjects defined by different organizations.

- Summary data structure shells help identify and understand relations between summary data subjects and their parent data subjects.

Disparate data are often very complex and very confusing. Documenting data file diagrams and physical data structure charts using consistent notation, and developing data relation diagrams and logical data structure charts, helps people understand disparate data, and helps them cross reference those data to the common data architecture.

▼ QUESTIONS

The following questions are designed to provide a review of Chapter 10 and to stimulate thought about the structure of disparate data and how that structure can be documented to help data refining.

1. Why are disparate data so poorly structured?

2. Why were logical data modeling and data denormalization never used with older data files?

3. How are data files, data records, and data items related?

4. What is a disparate primary key?

5. What is a disparate foreign key?

6. What does a data file diagram represent?

7. What is a disparate data file diagram?

8. What does a physical data structure chart represent?

9. What is a disparate data structure chart?

10. What is the usual relationship between disparate data files and common data subjects?

11. What is the usual relationship between disparate data items and common data characteristics?

12. Why do disparate data items sometimes represent multiple common data characteristics?

13. What is the relationship between disparate data codes and common data codes?

14. What is the relationship between sets of disparate data codes and sets of common data codes?

15. Why are there hidden hierarchies in disparate data codes?

16. What is the difference between a disparate primary key and a valid primary key in the common data architecture?

17. How can disparate foreign keys help identify disparate primary keys?

18. How do data categories and data subject hierarchies help people understand disparate data?

19. How can summary data subjects be documented so they can be easily understood?

20. Why is it necessary to thoroughly understand and document disparate data?

▾ 11

DISPARATE DATA QUALITY

Disparate data quality must be identified and documented to ensure that the formal data resource contains high quality data.

Disparate data have very poor quality. Their integrity is generally undefined and seldom maintained in a consistent manner. Their accuracy is unknown and highly variable. They may or may not be complete, but the completeness cannot be determined. This is a bad situation for most organizations.

However, the quality of existing disparate data can be identified and defined. The desired quality of the formal data resource can also be defined, and a plan to achieve that desired quality can be implemented. The best way to manage disparate data quality is to identify it and implement a plan to improve it.

This chapter explains techniques for identifying disparate data quality and for managing data quality across disparate data. Techniques for managing purchased applications, conflicting classification schemes, multiple data sources, and conflicting mandates are described.

▾ DISPARATE DATA QUALITY APPROACH

Data quality is a measure of how well data support the needs of an organization. It includes data integrity, data accuracy, and data completeness. The quality of disparate data is not well defined or well managed. Therefore, it is very difficult to maintain data quality while refining disparate data within a common data architecture. One of the major concerns of data refining is how to identify and maintain data quality through the data refining process. If data quality deteriorates because it is not closely controlled, the benefits of the data refining could be lost.

Existing data quality must be identified, documented, and maintained through the data refining process.

One major emphasis during data refining is to document and maintain existing data quality. Well-defined data quality forms a base for improving data quality during the development of a mature data resource. If the quality of existing data is not documented and maintained, it cannot be easily improved, and the mature data resource will not have the level of quality necessary to support an organization's business activities.

When the existing quality of disparate data is identified and documented within the common data architecture, it becomes part of the formal data resource. The desired data quality is also defined and documented and becomes part of the formal data resource. Desired data quality may be implemented at any time in the formal data resource, but it must be fully implemented for the mature data resource.

▼ DISPARATE DATA INTEGRITY

Most disparate data have incomplete, inconsistent, and highly variable data integrity rules that are not formally stated. *Disparate data integrity rules* are data integrity rules that actually exist for disparate data and may or may not be formally documented. Disparate data integrity rules must be identified and documented within the common data architecture to enable the development of comprehensive data integrity for the formal data resource.

Data Value Integrity

Disparate data value integrity is the data value integrity that actually exists for disparate data, whether or not it is documented. *Disparate data domains* are data domains that contain disparate data value integrity. *Official data domains* are data domains in the common data architecture that have been designated as official by the consensus of knowledgeable people for maintaining data quality in the formal data resource.

Disparate data frequently have several—often incomplete and conflicting—data domains for the same data characteristic, because data products were developed by different people for different uses. Disparate data domains must be aggregated to form an official data domain for every official data characteristic variation. An official data domain is developed by identifying the data domain for each data characteristic variation, aggregating those domains to the official data characteristic variation, and reviewing that data domain to define an acceptable data domain for the mature data resource.

> *Each official data characteristic variation must have an official data domain.*

A disparate data domain is identified and documented for each data product characteristic when that product is identified, even if the documentation does not contain a data domain. After data cross referencing is completed, the disparate data domains are aggregated to the common data characteristic variation. Any discrepancies are noted, along with any comments about how the discrepancies are resolved.

After the official data characteristic variations are designated, the data domains for each non-official data characteristic variation are aggregated with the data domain for the official data characteristic variation. All the discrepancies and potential resolutions are also aggregated, and additional discrepancies are noted. The discrepancies are then resolved by consensus and enhanced to provide an official data domain. Enhancements identified in the official data domain may be applied to existing data product characteristics to improve their integrity.

Documentation of disparate data domains is retained as long as disparate data exist, because it is often the only documentation available. However, maintenance of disparate data domains ceases as soon as the disparate data they represent are converted to the mature data resource.

Official data domains may be applied to disparate data to improve their integrity.

Disparate data frequently have a mixture of data rule domains and data value domains, which makes the aggregation of data domains difficult. The best approach is to determine whether a data rule domain or a data value domain is the best for a particular common data characteristic. Then all disparate data value integrity is converted to that form for aggregation. If it is difficult to select either a data rule domain or a data value domain during aggregation, both may be maintained until final acceptance of the official data domain. Then all data value integrity for a common data characteristic variation must be stated as either a data rule domain or a data value domain.

Conditional data value integrity for disparate data is managed in the same way as data value integrity. The data value domains or data rule domains are documented, aggregated to their corresponding common data characteristic variation, and then aggregated to the official common data characteristic variation.

Data Structure Integrity

Disparate data structure integrity is the data structure integrity that actually exists in disparate data, whether it is documented or not. *Official data structure integrity* is the data structure integrity that has been designated as official by a consensus of knowledgeable people for maintaining data quality in the formal data resource.

Disparate data relations are the data relations that actually exist in disparate data, whether they are documented or not. *Official data relations* are the data relations defined in the common data architecture. A *disparate data relation diagram* is a diagram that shows disparate data subjects and the relations between them. It may be shown as either a file relation diagram or a data relation diagram. An *official data relation diagram* is a data relation diagram in the common data architecture.

Disparate data also have different data structure integrity that must be aggregated to obtain the official data structure integrity for the mature data resource. The official data structure integrity is developed by identifying and documenting all the disparate data structure integrity, adding it to the common data architecture, and reviewing it to ensure completeness for the mature data resource.

Official data structure integrity must be determined for the mature data resource.

Disparate data structure integrity is determined by identifying data relations that exist in disparate data. This is often difficult because data relations are not readily visible and are usually not documented. Many developers of disparate data did not even attempt to maintain structural integrity, let alone document it. However, some data structure integrity exists in disparate data and must be documented.

The disparate data structure integrity and disparate data relation diagrams are maintained as long as the disparate data exist. When disparate data are converted to the formal data resource, the diagrams are no longer needed.

Reviewing disparate data structure integrity may lead to changing views of the real world, and adjustments may be made to common data subjects and data relations. If these adjustments are more than minor adjustments, common-to-common cross references are created and then collapsed, as described in the Data Cross Reference chapter. Although this approach is time-consuming, it provides the control necessary for managing detailed changes to the common data architecture, ensuring that data integrity is maintained.

Data Derivation Integrity

A *disparate data derivation algorithm* is a data derivation algorithm that actually exists for disparate data, regardless of when or how it is implemented and whether it is documented. A *disparate data derivation diagram* is a data derivation diagram that documents the way disparate data are actually derived. An *official data derivation algorithm* is a data derivation algorithm that documents the derivation of common data characteristics and has been designated as official by a consensus of knowledgeable people.

Disparate data often have different data derivation rules. Each data product characteristic is analyzed to determine whether it is derived. If a data product characteristic is derived, a disparate data derivation algorithm must be defined, and that algorithm must include the data characteristics contributing to the derivation. If there is a series of derivations, those derivations are defined on a disparate data derivation diagram.

Identifying derived data is relatively easy, but identifying the data derivation algorithm is often difficult. The algorithms may be buried in program code, or they may even be done outside an information and entered into an information system. Regardless of how or when the data are derived, the data derivation algorithm must be identified and documented.

> *Official data derivation algorithms and diagrams must be created for the formal data resource.*

After data cross referencing is completed, the disparate data derivation algorithms are aggregated to their respective data characteristic variations. When the official data characteristic variations are designated, the derivation algorithms are aggregated to the official data characteristic variations. Disparate data derivation diagrams are also aggregated to form official data variation diagrams. The different data derivation algorithms are then reviewed, discrepancies are resolved, and official data derivation algorithms are designated.

Aggregating disparate data derivation diagrams frequently leads to better ways to derive data. The data derivation algorithms are enhanced accordingly, and may be applied to disparate data to improve their integrity. Disparate data derivation algorithms and diagrams are maintained as long as the disparate data exist. When disparate data are converted to the mature data resource, the algorithms and diagrams are no longer needed.

Data redundancy is seldom identified, let alone consciously maintained, in disparate data. If data redundancy is identified and maintained in disparate data, the rules are documented and aggregated, like derived data algorithms. However, most of the identification of redundant data is done within the common data architecture through a review of all the data product characteristics that contribute to a common data characteristic. When redundant data are identified, the primary data version can be identified and rules can be established for maintaining the redundant versions.

Data Retention Integrity

A *disparate data retention rule* is an actual data retention rule that exists in disparate data, whether or not it is documented. An *official data retention rule* is a data retention rule that has been designated as official for the mature data resource by a consensus of knowledgeable people.

Disparate data may have many different data retention rules, but frequently have none at all. Generally, updating and deleting disparate data are done without regard for the data needs of other applications or the future need for historical data. This omission can result in the loss of critical data. Data may be retained manually by individuals or by programs that are unknown or undocumented. Any disparate data retention rules that exist must be identified and documented.

> *Official data retention must be determined for adequate support of all business activities.*

Disparate data retention rules are documented for each data product characteristic. After data cross referencing is completed, these rules are aggregated to the data characteristic variations, and any discrepancies are noted. When official data characteristic variations are designated, the data retention rules are aggregated to the official data characteristic variations and reviewed. The rules are adjusted and enhanced to official data retention rules for the mature data resource.

Disparate data retention rules are retained as long as the disparate data exist. However, maintenance of the disparate data retention rules ceases as soon as the disparate data are converted to the mature data resource.

Formal documentation of data retention rules often leads to a better understanding of how existing data might be retained to support future business activities. Changes are usually made to keep data for longer periods or to summarize data before they are deleted or updated. Data retention rules are enhanced accordingly, and are usually applied to disparate data in the formal data resource to prevent any further loss of critical data.

▼ DISPARATE DATA ACCURACY

Data accuracy indicates how well data represent the real world. It includes many things, such as precision, resolution, scale, granularity, significant digits, reliability, source, method of collection, type of equipment used, method of analysis, method of calculation or estimation, adjustments made, person or organization involved, and confidence.

Data accuracy must be known for all data in the formal data resource.

Disparate data have widely different degrees of accuracy, although the accuracy is frequently unknown and not readily apparent. The accuracy cannot be changed or improved during data refining. It can only be identified and documented to increase understanding of the data. People knowledgeable about the disparate data can usually help identify and document data accuracy.

Data accuracy can be documented as a single common data characteristic with the accuracy shown in the variation name. For example, Lake Size Acres Estimated 1:24000 Photo means the size of a lake was estimated from 1:24,000 scale aerial photographs, and Lake Size Acres Surveyed means the size of the lake was surveyed. Data accuracy can also be identified with paired common data characteristics. One data characteristic contains the value, such as Lake Size Acres, and the other data characteristic contains the accuracy, such as Lake Size Accuracy Code or Lake Size Determination Code.

Data accuracy is shown in data characteristic variation names or as paired data characteristics.

A single common data characteristic is best when there are only a few possibilities for different data accuracy and those are used frequently. For example, if there were only three levels of accuracy for the size of a lake and there were usually values for one or two of those data characteristics, three single common data characteristics would be used. Paired common data characteristics are best when there are many possibilities for accuracy, but only one exists in any data occurrence. For example, if there were 20 different methods of determining the size of a lake and only one of those was used, paired data characteristics would be used.

The accuracy of each data product characteristic must be determined and documented. Cross references are made to the common data architecture with either the single data characteristic or the paired data characteristic techniques. After the cross references are completed, the data accuracy variations are reviewed to help designate the official data variations.

For example, a data product characteristic may contain a lake size, as determined by 1:24,000 aerial photo interpretation. This size can be cross referenced to a single data characteristic for Lake Size Acres Estimated 1:24000 Photo, as shown at the top of Figure 11.1. It can also be cross referenced to paired data characteristics for Lake Size Acres and Lake Size Determination Code, as shown at the bottom of Figure 11.1. The specific code for lake accuracy for the product data characteristic is shown in parentheses.

When official data characteristic variations are being designated, it may be desirable to aggregate several single common data characteristics from different sources into paired common data characteristics. This is one approach to putting several different levels of accuracy into two data characteristics. The single common data characteristics are abandoned and the data product characteristics are cross referenced to the paired common data characteristics, as shown in the example above.

Data accuracy also includes the instance of time the data value represents and volatility of the data. These are usually contained in the data definition. However, if the instance and volatility are variable between data occurrences, they need to be documented either as a single common data characteristic or as paired common data characteristics. Accuracy may also vary over time, as with data collected by different methods. These accuracy variations may be documented by either single data characteristics or paired data characteristics.

Lake
    Size   Lake Size Acres Estimated 1:24,000 Photo

Lake
    Size   Lake Size Acres
    Lake Size Acres Determination Code (3)

Figure 11.1 *Documenting data accuracy.*

Data accuracy is documented at the most detailed level.

Data accuracy is identified and documented at the most detailed level. Clients can determine for themselves what levels of accuracy they should combine to meet their needs. It is a poor practice to combine different levels of data accuracy during data refining, because future needs may require specific accuracy. Therefore, the most detailed level of data accuracy should be documented during data refining.

▼ DISPARATE DATA COMPLETENESS

Data completeness ensures that the data resource contains all the data that is necessary to support business activities. Generally, data product characteristics have many different data uses. When defining disparate data, the use—or potential use—of each data characteristic is identified and defined. If a current or potential use of a data characteristic cannot be determined, that data characteristic may be a candidate for elimination.

The techniques for determining data completeness are explained in more detail the Data Completeness chapter. Data needs surveys, data needs inventories, data resource surveys, and data resource inventories are used to determine what data are needed to support business activities and what data is available. Data that are available can be used, and data that are not available can be acquired.

▼ MANAGING DISPARATE DATA QUALITY

Managing the quality of disparate data is a challenging task. When disparate data have been identified, documented, and cross referenced to the common data architecture, their quality can usually be maintained better than it was before data refining. A few techniques for managing purchased applications, multiple data sources, conflicting classification schemes, and conflicting mandates are described below.

Purchased Applications

The mature data resource contains only official data variations. Although this is the ideal for many organizations, it is not always possible to achieve. Many organizations maintain purchased applications and legacy systems that do not match the official data variations. It's a reality that cannot be ignored.

High quality data are maintained in purchased applications by cross referencing data in the purchased applications to the common data architecture and developing data translation schemes if the data do not represent the organization's official data variations. In many cases, the understanding of purchased applications is increased by data refining, and data quality can be ensured by proper translation to data in other information systems.

Data quality in purchased applications and legacy systems can be maintained through data refining.

One approach to maintaining data quality in purchased applications is to propagate data definitions from the common data architecture back through the data cross references to the data product characteristics in the purchased application. These data definitions can be used to develop data entry instructions to ensure that proper data values are entered. For example, the data definitions for an Employee Name Complete Normal, Employee Birth Date CYMD, and Employee Social Security Number can be applied to their respective data product characteristics. Data entry instruction can be prepared for these product data characteristics to ensure that data are entered properly.

The same process can also be used with any data integrity rules. The official data integrity rules can be propagated back through the data cross references to the purchased application and used to maintain data integrity. For example, data domains for the three common data characteristics in the example above can be applied to their respective data product characteristics. Appropriate data integrity routines can be implemented within the purchased application, or prior to entering data into the purchased application to maintain data integrity.

These approaches are very useful for purchased applications that have generic data fields with no data entry instructions or data integrity rules. Developing data entry instructions and data integrity rules before the databases in purchased applications are populated ensures that those databases remain high quality. If the data quality has already deteriorated, the data integrity rules can be applied in whatever manner is appropriate for the purchased application to improve the data quality. It is very difficult to describe the exact implementation procedure because of the proprietary nature and variability of many purchased applications.

Multiple Data Sources

Existing applications frequently have multiple data sources through feeds and bridges from other applications. This situation leads to many sources for a single data product characteristic in the receiving application. Since the data quality in these multiple sources can be quite variable, the data sources must be documented to ensure high quality data in the receiving application.

Multiple data sources are documented through the data refining process. The data product characteristics in each source and in the receiving application are cross referenced to the common data architecture. Then a *data feed table* is developed to show the source data product characteristics, their common data characteristic equivalent, and the corresponding data product characteristic in the receiving application or database.

A data feed table ensures data integrity from multiple data feeds.

For example, there are several problem-tracking systems containing data that are fed into a central problem-tracking system. The feeds from the individual problem-tracking systems and the central problem-tracking system are cross referenced to the common data architecture and a data feed table is developed, as shown in Figure 11.2. Field 1 and Field 2 in File A are moved directly into the central problem-tracking system. Field 3 needs to be translated from Priority Code Alpha to Priority Code Numeric before it is placed in the central problem-tracking system. All three fields in File B are moved directly into the central problem-tracking system. Field 1 in File C is moved directly to the central problem-tracking system, but Priority Name is translated to Priority Code Numeric.

The offset common data characteristic names, such as Priority Code Alpha and Priority Code Numeric, indicate that a data translation is

Source	Common	Central System
File A		
Field 1	Person Name Complete Normal	Prob:Name
Field 2	City Name Complete	Prob:Cty-Name
Field 3	Priority Code Alpha	
	Priority Code Numeric	Prob:Prio
File B		
Field 1	Priority Code Numeric	Prob:Prio
Field 2	Problem Date CYMD	Prob:Prob-Dt
Field 3	Resolution Date YMD	Prob:Resl-Dt
File C		
Field 1	City Name Complete	Prob:Cty-Name
Field 2	Priority Name	
	Priority Code Numeric	Prob:Prio

Figure 11.2 *Data feed table for problem-tracking.*

needed. If both of these common data characteristics were non-official data variations, a non-official data translation scheme is developed. This is one situation where a non-official data translation scheme is acceptable.

If there are several sources for the same data product characteristic and there is conflicting data in those sources, the most appropriate source is identified. If the appropriate source data product characteristics are consistent in all situation, they can be shown in the data source table. However, if the source data product characteristics are not consistent, additional process logic or intervention of knowledgeable people is needed.

Source data product characteristics that are not used can still appear in the data feed table as documentation. For example, there might be a Field 3 in File C that is not involved in feeding the central problem-tracking system. It could appear in the data feed table but have no corresponding entry for a common data characteristic or for the central problem-tracking system.

The same situation is true for data product characteristics in the receiving application that do not receive data from the data feed. They can appear in the receiving application and have no corresponding entry for a common data characteristic or for the source application. For example, there might be a Prob:Person-Name in the central problem-tracking system that is not populated through a data feed. It would not have a corresponding entry under the source or the common data characteristic.

The information in the data feed table could be rearranged into a *data source table* that shows all the possible sources for each data characteristic in the receiving application or database. This table is useful for determining the most appropriate source for each data characteristic. For example, the data feed table in Figure 11.2 is rearranged to a data source table in Figure 11.3.

The same process can be used for developing the mature data resource. Data feed tables and data source tables are prepared to show the movement and translation of data from disparate databases to the mature data resource. These tables are maintained until the disparate data are converted to the mature data resource, and then the tables are discarded.

Conflicting Classification Schemes

When disparate data are refined, multiple classification schemes are often identified. These classification schemes represent the same real-

Prob:Name	Person Name Complete Normal
	File A:Field 1
Prob:Cty-Name	City Name Complete
	File A:Field 2
	File C:Field 1
Prob:Prio	Priority Code Numeric
	File A:Field 3 Priority Code Alpha
	File B:Field 1
	File C:Field 2 Priority Name
Prob:Prob-Dt	Problem Date CYMD
	File B:Field 2
Prob:Resl-Dt	Resolution Date YMD
	File B:Field 3

Figure 11.3 *Data source table for problem-tracking.*

world objects, but they conflict with each other. There are three techniques for resolving conflicting classification schemes.

The first technique is to designate one of the existing classification schemes as official and cross reference all other classification schemes to it. For example, there are many different land use classification schemes. One of those classification schemes can be designated as official and all the others can be cross referenced to that official classification scheme. This technique is useful when the conflicting classification schemes cover the same objects and have similar structures.

The second technique is to create a new official classification scheme and cross reference all other classification schemes to it. For example, there are many classification schemes for surface water bodies, such as lakes, springs, and streams. None of those classification schemes covers all surface water bodies. However, a new official classification scheme can be created to encompass all surface water bodies, and the existing schemes can be cross referenced to that new classification scheme. This technique is useful when the conflicting classification schemes do not cover all objects or have different structures.

The third technique is to keep all classification schemes as peers—that is, as, multiple official classification schemes. Every classification scheme is cross referenced to every other classification scheme. For example, several classification schemes are in use for diagnosis and treatments in veterinary medicine. None of these classification schemes is used predominantly, and each covers nearly all diagnoses and treatments. A cross reference is developed between all classification schemes. This technique is useful when each classification scheme covers all objects and all are in prominent use.

If conflicting classification schemes represent spatial data, they are defined as different layers in a geographic information system. The layers are compared for differences in classification. Any of the above three techniques can be used to manage the differences in conflicting classification schemes for spatial data.

The best approach to conflicting classification schemes is to formally name and comprehensively define each classification scheme so that people are aware there are different schemes. This allows people to state which classification scheme they are using and avoids any confusion arising from a non-specific name. For example, there are several classification schemes for wetlands. Each of these schemes is formally named, such as Wetland Class Federal 1:12,000 Field or Wetland Class

Planning 1:24,000 Photo, and each is comprehensively defined. Whenever people use a wetland classification scheme, they use a specific name to avoid confusion.

Conflicting Data Mandates

Organizations frequently receive mandates for data standards from regulatory authorities. These mandates usually do not conform to any common data architecture. In fact, they often conflict, which creates problems for the organization receiving those mandates. Many of these mandates are nothing more than glorified physical data descriptions. *Conflicting data mandates* is the situation where mandates for data standards from two or more regulatory authorities cover the same data and they conflict. Mandates for data standards are often enforced through the appropriation of funds so that an organization must use the mandate to obtain funding.

For example, one regulatory authority mandates data standards for a 40-character complete employee's name in the normal sequence and an employee's birth date as year, month, and day. Another regulatory authority mandates data standards for a 48-character abbreviated employee's name in an inverted order and an employee's birth date as month, day, and year. The organization needs to manage these conflicting data mandates in order to obtain funding.

> *Conflicting data mandates are managed within a common data architecture.*

Most mandated data standards cause more problems than they cure. There is usually no formal naming convention, and most data names are abbreviated or truncated, often inconsistently. Data definitions are often oriented toward use of the data, and frequently contain only formats or data entry instructions for a specific system. They are seldom comprehensive or based on content and meaning. The structure is usually a physical file structure rather than a formal, normalized logical data structure. There are seldom any data integrity rules. In short, mandated data standards generate another set of disparate data.

Most conflicting data mandates are for sharing data, not for storing data. They are usually mandates for supplying data in a certain form. These mandates can be met by identifying and cross referencing them to the common data architecture. The mandated data variations are compared to the organization's official data variations. Data translation schemes are developed if the mandates are non-official data variations. This approach allows an organization to store data in its own official data variation and still meet the requirements of the mandate.

For example, the mandates in the example above are cross referenced to the common data architecture to become Employee Name Complete Normal 40 and Employee Birth Date YMD for the first regulatory authority and Employee Name Abbreviated Invented 48 and Employee Birth Date M/D/Y for the second regulatory authority. The organization's official data variations are Employee Name Complete Normal 50 and Employee Birth Date CYMD. The organization stores the data according to its official data variations, and data translation schemes are used to convert the data prior to reporting to a regulatory authority.

If conflicting data mandates pertain to data storage and the mandates are non-official data variations, the organization must make a decision. It can either change its official data variation to match the mandate, or it can store both data variations. However, this is usually not the case: most organizations can store data according to their official data variations and translate the data to meet mandates.

Regulatory authorities should develop data standards within a common data architecture.

Ideally, mandated standards should be prepared as part of a common data architecture. They should have formal data names according to a naming taxonomy and comprehensive definitions based on true content and meaning. They should have a formal, normalized data structure and comprehensive data integrity rules. Mandated standards should be developed through the designation of official data variations. Organizations involved in implementing mandated data standards should be directly involved as part of the base of knowledgeable people developing those standards.

▼ SUMMARY

Data quality is how well data meet business needs, and includes data integrity, data accuracy, and data completeness. The quality of disparate data is usually not well defined or well managed. However, it should be documented and maintained throughout the data refining process. The existing data quality forms a base for improving data quality in the mature data resource.

Data value integrity is maintained by the identification of disparate data integrity, and by aggregation through the cross references to the official data variations. It is then reviewed and enhanced to meet an organization's needs. Data structure integrity is maintained through disparate data relation diagrams and official data relation diagrams. Like data value integrity, both data derivation integrity and data retention integrity are maintained by aggregation through the cross references to the official data variations. Any enhancements to data integrity can be applied to the existing data to prepare for transition to the mature data resource.

Data accuracy is documented either in the data characteristic variation name or through paired data characteristics that contain the value and an indication of the accuracy of that value. Data completeness is the assurance that the formal data resource contains all data necessary to support business activities. Techniques for defining and ensuring data completeness are described in the Data Completeness chapter.

The data in purchased applications and legacy systems are managed through data cross references and translation schemes. Multiple data feeds to central applications are documented and managed through data feed tables and data source tables. Conflicting classification schemes are documented for increased awareness, and may be resolved by designating one of those classification schemes as official, by creating a new classification scheme and cross referencing all other classification schemes to it, or by treating all classifications schemes as official. Conflicting data mandates are managed through data cross references to the common data architecture and data translation schemes.

▼ QUESTIONS

The following questions are designed to provide a review of Chapter 11 and to stimulate thought about disparate data quality, how it is documented, and how it can be maintained and improved in the formal data resource.

1. Why do disparate data have low data quality?

2. How is disparate data value integrity documented?

3. How is disparate data structure integrity documented?

4. How is disparate data derivation integrity documented?

5. How is disparate data retention documented?

6. How is disparate data retention integrity documented?

7. What are the two techniques for documenting data accuracy?

8. How are data in purchased applications and legacy systems managed?

9. How are multiple data feeds managed?

10. What is the difference between a data feed table and a data source table?

11. How are conflicting classification schemes managed?

12. How are conflicting data mandates managed?

13. How should mandates for data standards be prepared?

14. How is data quality improved in the formal data resource?

15. Why is it important to maintain data quality during data refining?

▼▼▼ 12

DATA CROSS REFERENCE

Cross referencing disparate data to the common data architecture is a major step in understanding and managing disparate data.

Major problems with managing disparate data are the data's inherent variability and users' uncertainty about the data's content and meaning. All other problems are minor compared to the problems associated with uncertainty and variability. They are the major stumbling blocks for integrating data and developing a formal data resource. If the uncertainty and variability of disparate data were reduced, the formal data resource could be easily developed.

The common data architecture is the base for reducing the uncertainty and variability of disparate data. All disparate data are identified and cross referenced to the common data architecture. Cross referencing disparate data to the common data architecture is the most important task in the entire data refining process. It is a simple task, but considerable thought and analysis are needed to determine their true content and meaning before the cross reference is made. Once the cross reference is made, the other tasks of determining the variability, designating official data variations, and developing translation schemes are relatively easy.

This chapter explains data cross referencing concepts and describes techniques for cross referencing disparate data to the common data architecture. It begins with an explanation of the concepts of cross referencing. Then the techniques for cross referencing data subjects, data characteristics, and data codes are explained. Finally, techniques for managing data cross references for large projects are explained.

DATA CROSS REFERENCE CONCEPT

The key to refining disparate data is cross referencing disparate data to the common data architecture. It is a difficult and time consuming task, but it is not impossible. Considerable thought and analysis are needed to determine the true content and meaning of disparate data before cross references are made. The concepts below provide a base for describing the data cross reference techniques.

Data Variability

The content, meaning, and format of disparate data are highly variable. The more disparate data an organization maintains, the greater the degree of variability. Also, the more geographically dispersed or functionally diverse an organization is, the greater the degree of variability. The greater the variability of disparate data, the more difficult it is to gain control of those data and develop a formal data resource.

Cross referencing disparate data to the common data architecture helps in gaining control of disparate data and developing the formal data resource. It identifies the variability that exists, and begins the process of short-term sharing and long-term transition to a mature data resource. Developing cross references begins with an explanation of how data are cross referenced to the common data architecture and how those cross references are documented.

Data Cross Referencing Approach

Cross referencing data is more challenging than developing formal data names and comprehensive data definitions. It is a critical process that requires a thorough understanding of both data products and the common data architecture. It also requires tremendous patience and diligence to make sure that appropriate data cross references are made. Failure to make appropriate data cross references affects the designation of official data variations, the development of translation schemes, data sharing, and the development of a formal data resource. It is not a task to be taken lightly or done hastily.

An *alias* is an alternate name for a single piece of data. Every piece of data has a primary data name based on the data naming taxonomy and data naming vocabulary. Any other data name, whether it exists in a data file, on a screen, in a document, or on a report, is an alias of the primary data name.

A *data cross reference* is a link between data names. That link may be between an alias data name and the primary data name, between two alias data names, or between two primary data names. A *primary cross reference* is a data cross reference between data product names and primary data names in the common data architecture. A *secondary cross reference* is a data cross reference between two data product names or between two primary data names in the common data architecture. Cross references are used to support very complex data refining projects.

Data cross references are not data translation schemes, but they form the base for defining data translation schemes. This process is described in the Data Translation chapter.

Data cross references work in both directions so that all the data product names can be identified for a primary data name, and the primary data name can be identified for any data product name. This two-way cross reference helps people sort through masses of disparate data and identify data more quickly.

Some data cross references are determined very easily, and others require considerable searching and analysis before their true counterpart in the common data architecture can be determined. The best approach is to make data cross references as soon as there is enough information available to make the cross reference with reasonable certainty. Generally, the majority of data cross references are easy to make once the true content and meaning of data are determined. However, there are always a few cross references that are very difficult to determine.

The determination of a data cross reference is based on reasoning, definitions, and knowledge about data products. A data product characteristic definition is reviewed and the common data architecture is searched for an appropriate common data characteristic variation. If a match is not found, a new common data characteristic variation is defined and the data cross reference is made. Data cross referencing may take many iterations and many reviews with knowledgeable people to determine the appropriate cross reference.

When a new common data subject, common data characteristic, or common data code is created, it must be not be a synonym or homonym of an existing data subject, data characteristic, or data code. It must be entirely new and unique to ensure that the common data architecture remains stable. It is often tempting to create a new component in the common data architecture to provide a data cross reference without determining whether an appropriate component already exists. A review of data definitions and primary keys for data subjects, along with a well-maintained data resource thesaurus, helps in determining whether an appropriate component exists.

When a candidate common data characteristic variation is found, the data product characteristic is reviewed to make sure it fits within the common data characteristic variation description, and the common data description is reviewed to make sure it encompasses the data product description. If the common data description is not acceptable, it may need to be changed.

However, changing a common data definition must be done carefully, and only after reviewing all other data cross references. If the change is an enhancement or clarification of the existing definition, it can be made with minimal concern. If the change is an alteration of the existing definition, more care should be taken. If the component is *Proposed* status, the change can be made with minimal concern. If the component is *Interim* status, more care should be taken, because there are other cross references to—or uses of—that component. If the component is *Accepted* status, the change must be made according to whatever criteria are used for the common data architecture.

Data Cross Reference Types

There are four types of data cross reference, as shown in Figure 12.1. The normal cross reference is between the primary data product and the desired common data architecture. However, there are situations where secondary data products are cross referenced to primary data products, and where interim common data architectures are used as a step toward the desired common data architecture.

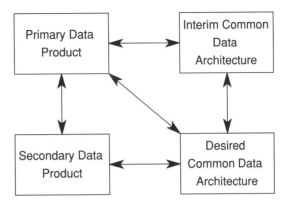

Figure 12.1 *Data cross reference types.*

A *primary data product* is a data product that contains considerable information about disparate data, such as a database listing, a program, or a data dictionary. A *secondary data product* is any other data product that contains ancillary information about disparate data, such as a report, screen, document, or other form of documentation.

A *desired common data architecture* is the common data architecture used for identifying data variations, developing data translation schemes, and building the mature data resource. An *interim common data architecture* is any intermediate, temporary common data architecture used as a step toward the desired common data architecture.

A *product-to-common cross reference* is a data cross reference between a primary data product and either the interim or the desired common data architecture. It is also known as a *primary cross reference*. A *product-to-product cross reference* is a data cross reference between a secondary data product and a primary data product. It is also known as a *secondary cross reference*. A *common-to-common cross reference* is a data cross reference between an interim common data architecture and a desired common data architecture. It is also known as an *interim cross reference*.

Data refining usually starts with cross references between primary data products and the desired common data architecture, as shown in Figure 12.2. Multiple primary data products are cross referenced to the desired common data architecture. As data refining projects increase in complexity, or as the common data architecture grows, the other types of data cross references are used.

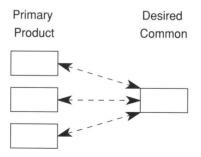

Figure 12.2 *Product-to-common, or primary, cross reference.*

▼ DATA SUBJECT CROSS REFERENCE

A *data subject cross reference* is a data cross reference between a data product subject and a common data subject. Data product subjects are usually not cross referenced to common data subjects because they seldom represent complete, single data subjects. Making a data cross reference between data subjects implies that all data characteristics in that data product subject belong to the same common data subject, which is not true in most cases. Therefore, data cross references are seldom made between data product subjects and common data subjects.

> *Data product subjects and common data subjects are seldom cross referenced.*

When there is a one-to-one relationship between a data product subject and a common data subject and all data product characteristics belong in the same common data subject, a data subject cross reference may be defined. The data product subject name can also be placed in the data resource thesaurus as a reference to the common data subject.

When geographic information systems are cross referenced to the common data architecture, each database is usually defined as a data product, and each data layer in the database is usually defined as a data product subject. The data layers may be cross referenced to common data subjects if they match those common data subjects. Otherwise, the data product characteristics in each data layer are cross referenced to common data characteristic variations.

▼ DATA CHARACTERISTIC CROSS REFERENCE

A *data characteristic cross reference* is a data cross reference between a data product characteristic and a common data characteristic variation. All data product characteristics are cross referenced to the common data characteristic variations during the process of data refining. These data characteristic cross references show the common data characteristic variation that represents each data product characteristic.

The cross references are made to common data characteristic variations, not to common data characteristics. Since there is considerable variability in disparate data, the cross references must be to common data characteristic variations so that the variability can be identified. Therefore, each common data characteristic has at least one variation for any cross references. This approach allows an organization to plan ahead for multiple variations of the same common data characteristic.

Each data product characteristic is cross referenced to a common data characteristic variation during the data refining process.

A *data characteristic cross reference diagram* consists of rectangles representing data characteristics, with the name of the corresponding data characteristic inside each rectangle. The rectangles are connected with dashed lines that have an arrowhead on each end indicating a two-way cross reference. For example, a data characteristic cross reference diagram for Equipment Identification Number is shown in Figure 12.3. Data charac-

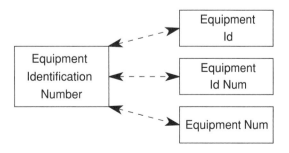

Figure 12.3 *Data characteristic cross reference diagram.*

teristic cross reference diagrams are good for showing two-way cross reference in pictorial form, although they take more space than an outline.

A *data characteristic cross reference list* is the usual form for documenting data characteristic cross references. The list shows data product characteristics on the left exactly as they appear in the data product, including sequence, spelling, capitalization, and punctuation. Headings show data products and subheadings show data product subjects. The corresponding common data characteristic variations are shown on the right. This format is used to help clients understand how their data fit into the common data architecture. A typical data characteristic cross reference list is shown in Figure 12.4.

Data characteristic cross references can also be placed on a logical data structure chart so that people can see both the data product characteristics and the common data characteristic variations, as shown in Figure 12.5.

Data characteristic cross references are placed in a database to provide a two-way cross reference between data product characteristics and

Water Right File

Control Number
    TYPE WATER   Water Resource Category Code
    OLD NEW   Water Right Number Status Code
    ASSIGNED NUMBER   Water Right Number
    STAGE   Water Right Stage Code
    RECORD MODIFIER   Water Right Record Modifier

AA Transaction
    TRANS CODE   Water Right Transaction Code
    STATUS   Water Right Status Code
    NAME   Water Right Processor Name Variable
    NUMBER OF POD/W   Water Right Removal Site Count
    REPEAT POD/W   Water Right Removal Repeat Count
    LOCATION OF POD/W   Water Right Removal Location Detail
    WRIA   Water Resource Inventory Area Number
    SECTION   Water Right Section Number
    TOWNSHIP   Water Right Tier Number
    RANGE   Water Right Range Number

Figure 12.4 *Data characteristic cross reference list.*

Equipment

Primary Key
    Equipment Identification Number   Equip_Id

Equipment
    Equipment Owner Name Complete   Ownr_Name

Data Characteristic List
    Equipment Identification Number   Equip_Id
    Equipment Owner Name Complete   Ownr_Name
    Equipment Manufacturer Date CY   Equip_Yr

Figure 12.5 *Logical data structure chart with data cross references.*

common data characteristic variations. All data product characteristics can be listed for each common data characteristic variation. The common data characteristic variation names are listed alphabetically within a document for quick reference. For example, the Equipment Identification Number cross references shown above are shown in Figure 12.6.

Common data characteristics can also be listed for each data product characteristic. The data product names are listed alphabetically for quick reference. For example, the Equipment Identification Number data cross references are shown in Figure 12.7.

Equipment Identification Number
    EquipId
    Equip Id Num
    Equipment Num

Figure 12.6 *Common data characteristic cross reference list.*

EquipId   Equipment Identification Number
Equip Id Num   Equipment Identification Number
Equipment Num   Equipment Identification Number

Figure 12.7 *Data product characteristic cross reference list.*

Combined Data Characteristics

The examples above show data cross references for data characteristics that are a one-to-one match. However, this is not always the case with disparate data. Data product characteristics frequently represent more than one elemental common data characteristic. A *combined data product characteristic* represents more than one elemental common data characteristic.

There are two techniques for cross referencing combined data product characteristics. The first technique is to list all elemental common data characteristic variations for each combined data product characteristic. For example, if a data product characteristic Veh-Id consists of Vehicle License Number and Vehicle Identification Number, both of these common data characteristic variations are listed in the cross reference, as shown in Figure 12.8. This technique is best when the elemental data characteristics have no relation to each other.

The second technique is to create a combined common data characteristic variation that is cross referenced to the combined data product characteristic. The definition of the combined common data characteristic variation contains references to all of the elemental common data characteristics. For example, Ship_Dt consists of year, month, and day and is cross referenced to Equipment Ship Date YMD. This technique is best when the combined data characteristics are related to each other.

It is not a good practice to use the second technique for data characteristics that are not related to each other. For example, the Veh-Id example above could be cross referenced as shown in Figure 12.9. The data definition shows the elemental data characteristic variations and has a status of *Limited*. This technique is poor because the data cross reference does not show the elemental common data characteristic variations represented by the data product characteristic, and it creates an unnecessary common data characteristic.

Veh-Id   Vehicle License Number
              Vehicle Identification Number

Figure 12.8 *Cross reference to elemental common data characteristics.*

> **Emp-Id   Employee Identifier**
>
> Employee Identifier is a combined data characteristic consisting of **Employee Name Complete Normal** and **Employee Birth Date MDY**.
>
> Status: Limited

Figure 12.9 *Data cross reference to combined common data characteristic.*

Irregular Data Characteristics

Data product characteristics frequently contain irregular data. An *irregular data product characteristic* does not have a consistent content or format. Irregular data product characteristics are cross referenced to an irregular common data characteristic variation that has a status of *Obsolete*.

For example, Emp-Nam contains an employee's name in an irregular format and is cross referenced to Employee Name Irregular. The common data characteristic variation is labeled *Obsolete* so that it will not be propagated any further. A suitable official data characteristic variation is designated to replace the obsolete data characteristic variation, such as Employee Name Complete Normal, and data are ultimately converted to that data characteristic.

Variable Data Characteristics

Data product characteristics often contain variable data. A *variable data product characteristic* contains different data characteristics under different situations. In most situations, a record type indicates the data product characteristic that exists in a particular field. For example, suppose that a file contains data about computer hardware. Since each hardware component does not contain the same data characteristics, separate record types are created for computers, controllers, and modems. Different data product characteristics may be placed in the same physical field in different record types.

The data cross references are made using a record type, as shown in Figure 12.10. Record type *1* is a *Computer* record and Field_1 contains

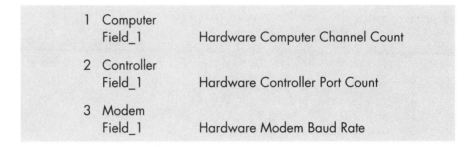

Figure 12.10 *Variable data characteristic cross reference.*

Hardware Computer Channel Count. Similarly, record type *2* is a *Controller* record and Field_1 contains Hardware Controller Port Count.

The criteria for cross referencing data product characteristics to common data characteristics and validating those cross references are shown in Appendix D.

▼ DATA CODE CROSS REFERENCE

A *data code cross reference* is a data cross reference between data product codes and common data codes. Data product codes do not need to be cross referenced to common data codes if they are the same as the common data codes. Only the data product characteristic containing the data codes needs to be cross referenced to the common data characteristic variation. However, data product codes must be cross referenced to common data codes if they are different from the common data codes.

Data product codes are cross referenced to common data codes if they are different.

The criteria for cross referencing data product codes to common data codes and validating those cross references are shown in Appendix D.

Cross Referencing Data Codes

A *data code cross reference list* shows the common data code values that correspond to the data product code values. The data product code is

Product Code	Common Code	Common Name
1	T	Truck
2	C	Car
3	B	Bus
4	M	Motorcycle

Figure 12.11 *Data code cross reference.*

listed on the left, followed by the common data code value and the common data code name. For example, Vehicle Type Codes represent *Trucks*, *Cars*, *Buses*, and *Motorcycles*, as shown in Figure 12.11. The data product code values are *1* through *4* and are cross referenced to common data code values. The data product characteristic containing the data codes is cross referenced to the corresponding common data characteristic variation as explained above.

Usually there is only a data product characteristic representing the data code value. A common data characteristic variation is created for the data code name but has no cross reference. However, if a data product characteristic exists for the data code name, it is cross referenced to a common data characteristic variation for the data code name.

If a data product characteristic contains data code names, those names are placed in the data code cross reference list. For example, if the data product contained data code names, they would be placed in the data code cross reference list, as shown in Figure 12.12. This format can be used when the data code values are the same and the data code names are different, when the data code names are the same and the

Product Code	Product Name	Common Code	Common Name
1	Truck	A	Truck
2	Auto	B	Car
3	Bus	C	Bus
4	M/C	D	Motorcycle

Figure 12.12 *Data code cross reference with names.*

data code values are different, or when both data code names and data code values are different.

The example above is a *simple data code set*, because there is one set of data product codes that is cross referenced to one set of common data codes. *Multiple data code sets* exist when there are many sets of data product codes that are cross referenced to the same set of common data codes. They are cross referenced like the examples above, with one data code cross reference list prepared for each set of data product codes.

Splitting Data Code Sets

Combined data code sets exist when a set of data product codes represents two or more sets of common data codes. This situation occurs when two or more separate sets of properties are combined into one set of data product codes. For example, a data product characteristic contains codes for a person's height and weight. A 1 means *Tall* height and *Light* weight, a 2 means *Tall* height and *Heavy* weight, and so on.

In this situation, the data product characteristic is cross referenced to two common data characteristics for Employee Height Code and Employee Weight Code. Then the data product codes are cross referenced to the common data codes, as shown in Figure 12.13. The combined data product codes are split into two different sets of common data codes. The common data code names can be added to the list if desired.

A similar situation exists when data product codes have different meanings. For example, there may be 39 counties in a state, coded *1* through *39*. The data product code set identifies revenue recipients by these county codes, and includes counties *40* and *41* to represent *State government* and *Federal government*, respectively.

Product Code	Product Name	Employee Height Code	Employee Weight Code
1	Tall, Light	T	L
2	Tall, Heavy	T	H
3	Short, Light	S	L
4	Short, Heavy	S	H

Figure 12.13 Splitting combined data code sets.

In this situation the data product characteristic is cross referenced to two common data characteristics for County Code and to Revenue Recipient Code. The data product code values are cross referenced to common data codes, as shown in Figure 12.14. The only difference from the example above is that there are no corresponding county codes for State and Federal revenue recipients.

Combining Data Code Sets

Data products often split one set of common data codes across several sets of data product codes. *Split data code sets* exist when the data product codes in different data product characteristics belong to the same set of common data codes. For example, vehicle horsepower is divided between two data product characteristics for large vehicles and small vehicles, but belongs to one set of common data codes.

In this situation, each data product characteristic is cross referenced to the same common data characteristic variation. Then the data product code values are cross referenced to the common data code values, as shown in Figure 12.15.

Splitting Data Code Values

Data products often contain combined data codes. A *combined data code* exists when a data product code represents more than one data property. For example, data product codes exist for new students and for

Rev_Cd	County Code	Revenue Recipient Code	Revenue Recipient Name
1	1	C	County
2	2	C	County
			etc.
39	39	C	County
40		S	State
41		F	Federal

Figure 12.14 Splitting revenue recipient codes.

Sml_Veh_HP		Vehicle	Horsepower
Below 100	A	1	Below 100
100–199	B	2	100–199
200–349	C	3	200–349
350–499	D	4	350–499
Lrg_Veh_HP			
500–749	1	5	500–749
750–999	2	6	750–999
1000–1499	3	7	1000–1499
1500+	4	8	1500+

Figure 12.15 *Combining data code sets.*

continuing or returning students. The latter data code represents two properties: continuing students and returning students.

In this situation, the data product characteristic is cross referenced to the common data characteristic variation. Then each data product code is cross referenced to a common data code, as shown in Figure 12.16. The data product code value for *Continuing or Returning Student* is split into two common data codes. Additional information or the involvement of knowledgeable people is usually required to make this split.

Product Value	Product Name	Common Value	Common Name
1	New Student	N	New Student
2	Continuing or Returning Student	C	Continuing Student
		R	Returning Student

Figure 12.16 *Splitting data code values.*

Combining Data Code Values

Several data product codes may represent the same common data code. This situation usually occurs when there are more codes in the data product than are desired in the common data architecture, and therefore several data product codes need to be combined into the same common data code. For example, sales orders can be classified by region, as shown in Figure 12.17. These eight original regions are combined into three larger regions in the common data architecture, as shown on the right side of the table.

Mutually Exclusive Data Code Values

Data products often contain data codes that are mutually exclusive. *Mutually exclusive data codes* exist when data product codes are placed in separate data product characteristics. For example, separate data product characteristics exist for shipping packages by air, bus, or truck. If a package was shipped by air, the data product characteristic for air contains a *Y* and the others are blank.

In this situation, each data product characteristic is cross referenced to the same common data characteristic variation, as shown in Figure 12.18. Then the data code values of each data product characteristic are cross referenced to the common data code values, as shown in Figure 12.19.

Property	Reg_Code	Sales Region Code	Sales Region Name
Northeast	1	E	East
East Central	2	E	East
Southeast	3	E	East
Southern Midwest	4	M	Midwest
Central Midwest	5	M	Midwest
Northern Midwest	6	M	Midwest
Southwest	7	W	West
Northwest	8	W	West

Figure 12.17 *Combining data code values.*

Air	Shipping Type Code
Bus	Shipping Type Code
Truck	Shipping Type Code
Rail	Shipping Type Code
Postal	Shipping Type Code

Figure 12.18 *Mutually exclusive data product characteristics.*

Product Characteristic	Product Value	Common Value
Air	Y	A
Air		
Bus	Y	B
Bus		
Truck	Y	T
Truck		
Rail	Y	R
Rail		
Postal	Y	P
Postal		

Figure 12.19 *Mutually exclusive data codes.*

Irregular Data Code Values

Data products also contain irregular data codes. *Irregular data codes* exist when many different data product code values are allowed for the same data property. For example, different data product codes exist for a data product characteristic representing priority, such as *1, A,* and *H,* all meaning *High Priority.* In this situation, the data product characteristic is cross referenced to the common data characteristic, as described above. Then each data product code value is cross referenced to the proper common data code value, as shown in Figure 12.20.

Subset 1	Subset 2	Subset 3	Common
1	A	H	1
2	B		2
3	C	M	3
4			4
		L	5

Figure 12.20 *Irregular data codes.*

▼ PRODUCT-TO-PRODUCT CROSS REFERENCE

All data product characteristics must be cross referenced to common data characteristic variations to determine the full scope of data variability. Knowing the full scope of data variability helps in the designation of official data variations, the development of data translation schemes, and the construction of the formal data resource. If the full scope of data variability is not known, the appropriate official data variations may not be designated and the formal data resource may not be built properly.

> *All data product characteristics must be cross referenced to the common data characteristic variations.*

Product-to-product cross references are created within data product groups to facilitate the data refining process. A *data product group* is set of related data products, such as those found in a purchased application, that contain both primary and secondary data products. Usually, there are only a few primary data products and many secondary data products in a data product group. A primary data product is selected, such as a database in a purchased application. Secondary data products, such as screens, documents, and reports, are cross referenced to the primary data product, as shown in Figure 12.21.

The format for product-to-product cross references is the same as the product-to-common cross references described above. For example, an employee's birth date may be captured on a screen, stored in a database, or displayed on a report. The database is identified as the primary

Secondary Product   Primary Product

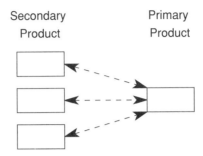

Figure 12.21 *Product-to-product cross reference scheme*

data product, and the screen and report are identified as secondary data products. The secondary data products are cross referenced to the primary data product, as shown in Figure 12.22.

Many product-to-product cross references already exist and only need to be changed to the appropriate format. However, these existing cross references may not be correct. The best approach is to assume that existing product-to-product cross references are not correct until they are verified. Most incorrect product-to-product cross references result from not recognizing data characteristic variations. A data product characteristic may be entered on a screen differently from the way it is stored in the database or printed on a report. These variations are hidden in programs or database management systems. They need to be stated explicitly during cross referencing.

All existing product-to-product cross references must be verified for correctness.

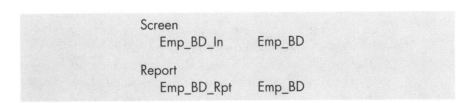

Screen
    Emp_BD_In   Emp_BD

Report
    Emp_BD_Rpt   Emp_BD

Figure 12.22 *Product-to-product cross references.*

Screen
    Emp_BD_In   Employee Birth Date YMD

Database
    Emp_BD   Employee Birth Date CYMD

Report
    Emp_BD_Rpt   Employee Birth Date M/D/CY

Figure 12.23 *Conversion to product-to-common cross references.*

For example, the employee's birth date example above appears to be correct. However, on closer inspection, it becomes clear that the birth date is captured as Employee Birth Date YMD, stored in the database as Employee Birth Date CYMD, and displayed as Employee Birth Date M/D/CY. Therefore, the existing cross references are not correct and should not be maintained because they can only cause confusion. The data product characteristics must be cross referenced to the common data characteristic variation, as shown in Figure 12.23.

Product-to-common cross references can be generated from valid product-to-product cross references. This technique is useful for cross referencing data product characteristics in secondary data products to the common data characteristic variations. For example, the estimated value of a piece of equipment is captured as Equip_Val_Est and is stored on a database as Eq_Val. Equip_Val_Est is cross referenced to Eq_Val, as shown in Figure 12.24. Eq_Val is cross referenced to Equipment Estimated

Secondary to Primary Product
    Equip_Val_Est   Eq_Val

Primary Product to Common
    Eq_Val   Equipment Estimated Value Dollars

Secondary Product to Common
    Equip_Val_Est   Equipment Estimated Value Dollars

Figure 12.24 *Creating secondary product-to-common cross references.*

Value Dollars in the common data architecture. The product-to-product cross reference is verified as correct and is used to create a cross reference between Equip_Val_Est and Equipment Estimated Value Dollars.

Valid product-to-product cross references may be retained on an interim basis until they can be converted to product-to-common cross references, or they may be retained permanently to support management of data in a product.

Product-to-product cross references are not defined if the data product code values are the same in all secondary data products. However, product-to-product cross references are created if the data product code values are different in the secondary data products. These data code cross references are made as described above.

▼ COMMON-TO-COMMON CROSS REFERENCE

Normally, data products are cross referenced to the desired common data architecture. However, on very large and complex data refining projects, this is not always possible. Interim common data architectures are developed for one or more data product groups. The interim common data architectures are then reviewed and cross referenced to the desired common data architecture, as shown in Figure 12.25.

Interim common data architectures are useful for refining segments of disparate data, since the names and definitions may change when all cross references are known. They are an interim step to the desired common data architecture, allowing major segments of disparate data

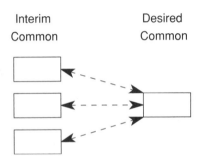

Figure 12.25 *Common-to-common cross reference scheme.*

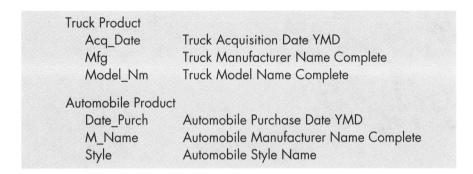

Figure 12.26 *Product-to-interim common cross reference for vehicles.*

to be cross referenced to the common data architecture without knowing what the desired common data architecture will contain.

For example, one data product contains data for automobiles that are cross referenced to an interim common data subject for Automobile, and another data product contains data for trucks that are cross referenced to an interim common data subject for Truck, as shown in Figure 12.26.

When the interim common data architectures are complete, the desired common data architecture is developed, based on information contained in the interim common data architectures. Common-to-common cross references are made between the interim common data architecture and the desired common data architecture. New data subjects, data characteristics, data characteristic variations, and data codes may be added to the desired common data architecture to support the cross reference.

For example, a desired data subject for Vehicle is defined to include both automobiles and trucks. Common-to-common cross references are made from Automobile to Vehicle and from Truck to Vehicle, as shown in Figure 12.27.

When the desired common data architecture is accepted, the common-to-common cross references are collapsed so that data products are cross referenced directly to the desired common data architecture. Collapsing common-to-common cross references is relatively easy. Each product-to-interim common data architecture cross reference is adjusted to become a product-to-desired common data architecture cross reference. The interim common data architecture is then discarded.

Truck
Truck Acquisition Date YMD	Vehicle Purchase Date YMD
Truck Manufacturer Name Complete	Vehicle Manufacturer Name Complete
Truck Model Name Complete	Vehicle Style Name Complete

Automobile
Automobile Purchase Date YMD	Vehicle Purchase Date YMD
Automobile Manufacturer Name Complete	Vehicle Manufacturer Name Complete
Automobile Style Name	Vehicle Style Name Complete

Figure 12.27 *Common-to-common cross reference for vehicles.*

---

*Common-to-common cross references are collapsed when the
desired common data architecture is complete.*

Using the example above, each cross reference from the data product to Automobile is changed to Vehicle and each cross reference from the data product to Truck is change to Vehicle, as shown in Figure 12.28. The common-to-common cross references are then discarded.

Common-to-common cross references can be developed for both data characteristics and data codes. Designing a desired common data architecture often results in changes to both data characteristics and data codes, in addition to changes made during product-to-desired common cross references. Therefore, both data characteristics and data codes may be included in common-to-common cross references.

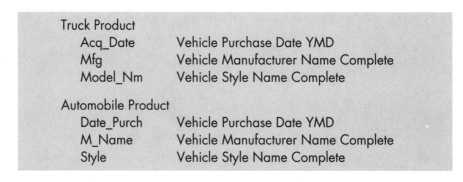

Truck Product
    Acq_Date   Vehicle Purchase Date YMD
    Mfg   Vehicle Manufacturer Name Complete
    Model_Nm   Vehicle Style Name Complete

Automobile Product
    Date_Purch   Vehicle Purchase Date YMD
    M_Name   Vehicle Manufacturer Name Complete
    Style   Vehicle Style Name Complete

Figure 12.28 *Product-to-desired common cross reference for vehicles.*

Common-to-common cross references are not normally developed for data subjects. However, if an interim data subject name is useful for identifying the desired common data subject name, it is placed in the data resource thesaurus. In the example above, both Truck and Automobile would be placed in the data resource thesaurus with references to Vehicle.

▼ MANAGING DATA CROSS REFERENCES

Refining large quantities of disparate data and developing a desired common data architecture requires management of many data cross references. The data cross references often become very complex because of the uncertainty and variability in disparate data. The cross referencing techniques described above are useful for managing these complex cross references. The diagram in Figure 12.29 shows an overview of complex cross references.

On large data refining projects, data product groups are identified, and primary and secondary data products are established in those data product groups. Existing product-to-product cross references are formally documented, and new product-to-product cross references are made between the secondary and primary data products.

Next, product-to-interim common cross references are created between the primary data products and an interim common data architecture. These cross references are based on the current understanding of the disparate data and the existing common data architecture. The interim common data architectures are reviewed, and common-to-common cross references are created between the interim common data architecture and the desired common data architecture.

When the desired common data architecture is complete, the common-to-common cross references are collapsed to product-to-desired common cross references, and the interim data architectures are abandoned. Finally, product-to-product cross references are collapsed to product-to-common cross references. The result is cross references between all data products and the desired common data architecture.

▼ SUMMARY

Disparate data have high variability, and their content and meaning are very uncertain. This situation is preventing most organizations from

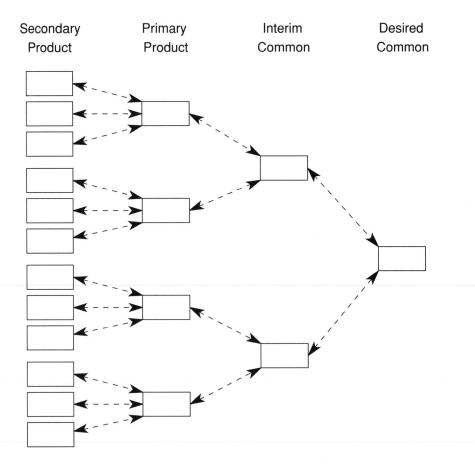

Figure 12.29 *Complex cross reference management.*

converting their disparate data to a formal data resource. It also makes management of the existing data very difficult. The lack of a formal data resource and difficult management of existing disparate data severely hinder the efficient and effective development of information systems.

The common data architecture provides a base for refining disparate data within a common context. It helps people understand the true content and meaning of disparate data and the extent of their variability. Once the uncertainty is removed and the variability is understood, disparate data can be used more effectively and efficiently, and the formal data resource can be built.

Cross referencing disparate data begins by defining data product groups, data products, data product subjects, data product characteristics, and data product codes. Data product characteristics and data product codes are cross referenced to the common data architecture. These data cross references are initially documented in cross reference lists designed to encourage direct client involvement.

There are many different types of data cross references; their use depends on the nature of the disparate data. A data product characteristic can be cross referenced to a single common data characteristic variation or split into more than one common data characteristic variation. Irregular and variable data product characteristics are cross referenced in a manner that readily identifies these situations.

A data product code set may be split between two or more common data code sets or several data product code sets may be combined into one common data code set. A data product code value may be split into two or more common data codes or several data product code values can be combined into one common data code. Mutually exclusive and irregular data product codes are cross referenced in a manner that resolves those situations.

Product-to-product cross references may be created for data product characteristics. If those cross references are valid, they are useful for managing disparate data and generating product-to-common cross references. Interim common data architectures can be created for data product groups to facilitate development of the desired common data architecture. These interim common data architectures are cross referenced to the desired data architecture and then collapsed to provide cross references from primary data products to the desired common data architecture.

Data refining uses a set of data cross referencing techniques to manage the variability and uncertainty of disparate data. These techniques enable an organization to begin reviewing its disparate data and start building its formal data resource.

▼ QUESTIONS

The following questions are designed to provide a review of Chapter 12 and to stimulate thought about cross referencing disparate data to the common data architecture.

1. Why is there so much uncertainty about disparate data?

2. Why are disparate data so variable?

3. How does data cross referencing help reduce uncertainty and resolve variability?

4. How are disparate data structured for cross referencing?

5. What are the major types of data cross references?

6. Why are data subjects seldom cross referenced?

7. How are data characteristics cross referenced?

8. What are the techniques for cross referencing combined data product characteristics?

9. How do irregular data product characteristics differ from variable data product characteristics?

10. How are data codes cross referenced?

11. How are data product code sets split?

12. How are data product code sets combined?

13. How are data product code values split?

14. How are data product code values combined?

15. How are mutually exclusive data product codes cross referenced?

16. How are irregular data product codes cross referenced?

17. What is the advantage of product-to-product cross references?

18. Why must existing product-to-product cross references be verified?

19. What is an interim common data architecture?

20. How are interim common data architectures useful?

21. What are common-to-common cross references?

22. Why are common-to-common cross references collapsed when the desired data resource is accepted?

23. Why are product-to-product cross references ultimately converted to product-to-common cross references?

24. How are complex cross references managed?

25. How do data cross references help develop the formal data resource?

▼ 13

DATA TRANSLATION

Data translation enables data sharing within the common data architecture.

Data cross referencing connects disparate data to the common data architecture. It is a major step in the data refining process, but it is not the only step. The next step is to determine the variability of disparate data, designate official data variations, and develop data translation schemes.

When data cross referencing is completed, the extent of data variability is determined by reviewing primary keys and data characteristic variations. Official primary keys and official data characteristic variations are designated by the consensus of knowledgeable people. Data translation schemes are developed to promote short-term data sharing and to assist the long-term evolution to a mature data resource.

This chapter explains techniques for determining data variability, designating official data variations, and developing data translation schemes.

▼ DATA VARIATIONS

After data cross referencing is complete, common data subjects, primary keys, common data characteristic variations, and common data codes are analyzed to determine the extent of data variability. The results of this analysis are used for designating official data variations.

Data Subject Variations

Much of the work of developing a common data architecture is in identifying different views of the real world. These different views cannot be discarded or radically changed. They must be incorporated into a common view of the real world so that everyone understands the complete picture of the real world and where he or she fits into that picture. It is a process that increases awareness and understanding.

Disparate data represent many different data subjects because information system developers had different views of the real world. A *data subject variation* is a data product subject that does not exactly match a common data subject. It may represent a smaller scope than a common data subject, it may represent a larger scope, or it may represent several common data subjects.

> *Data subject hierarchies are useful for documenting variability when disparate data subjects closely match common data subjects.*

Data subject hierarchies are the most useful technique for documenting data subject variations. However, they are only useful when data product subjects represent supersets or subsets of common data subjects. They are not useful when there is a poor match between data product subjects and common data subjects. This latter situation is prominent in disparate data; it is the reason that most cross referencing is done with data characteristics.

Primary Keys

Primary keys that exist in disparate data can be documented during data cross referencing or after data cross referencing is complete. They are documented on the logical data structure chart. Generally, they are documented after data cross referencing is complete, because then all cross references have been made and considerable information is available about the true content and meaning of the disparate data. This information helps identify which common data subjects the primary keys represent.

Disparate data subjects often contain more than one primary key, resulting in *multiple primary keys* for a common data subject. These primary keys must be documented and reviewed to determine their range and uniqueness, and whether they contain redundant data characteristics. Primary keys in disparate data frequently have a limited range of uniqueness and often have redundant data characteristics. These situations must be documented so that an official primary key can be designated.

Multiple primary keys are analyzed within the common data architecture.

The *range of uniqueness* for a primary key is the range of data occurrences for which the primary key provides uniqueness. For example, four primary keys identified for Vehicle are shown in Figure 13.1. Their range of uniqueness is shown on the right. The first one is unique for all vehicles. The second is unique for all vehicles in the United States

Vehicle

Primary Key Vehicle Identification Number	Unique for all Vehicles.
Primary Key State Code ANSI Vehicle License Number	Unique for Vehicles in the United States.
Primary Key Vehicle License Number	Unique for Vehicles in a specific State
Primary Key Vehicle License Number Vehicle Model Name Complete	Unique for Vehicles in a specific State. Redundant

Figure 13.1 *Primary key variability for vehicles.*

because it contains a license number and a state code. The third is unique for all vehicles in a specific state, because there is no state code. The forth is also unique for all vehicles in a specific state, but has a redundant data characteristic.

A *primary key matrix* shows the common data characteristics that comprise the primary keys. It is useful for analyzing primary keys between data subjects to determine whether they represent the same data subjects, different data subjects, or different data subject types. Data subjects are listed across the top, and the data characteristics are listed down the left side. For example, the unique identification of people that are drivers, employees, inmates, and welfare recipients is shown in Figure 13.2.

Foreign Keys

Disparate data often contain more than one foreign key, resulting in *multiple foreign keys* for the same parent data subject. Foreign keys can be documented during data cross referencing or after data cross referencing is complete. Generally, they are documented at the same time primary keys are documented. They are documented on the logical data structure chart, just like primary keys.

	Driver	Employee	Inmate	Welfare Recipient
Social Security Number		X		
Driver's License Number	X			
State Identifier			X	
Person Name Complete				X
Person Birth Date				X

Figure 13.2 *Primary key matrix.*

Data Characteristic Variations

Disparate data characteristics contain many variations. Data characteristic variations represent differences in content or meaning of a data characteristic. Differences in content can include format and length variations. Data characteristics variations that have content, meaning, and format variations are *data characteristic content variations*. Data characteristics with length variations are *data characteristic length variations*.

Data characteristic content variations are documented in *data characteristic content variation outline* that lists data characteristic variations under their parent data characteristic. The data characteristic content variation outline for a person's name is shown in Figure 13.3.

Data characteristic length variations are documented in a *data characteristic length variation matrix* that shows the lengths used by different data products. Data characteristic variations are listed on the left, and the data products are listed across the top. The actual lengths are listed in the body of the matrix. The data characteristic length variation matrix for a person's name is shown in Figure 13.4.

Person Name
Person Name Complete Normal
Person Name Complete Inverted
Person Name Abbreviated Normal
Person Name Abbreviated Inverted

Figure 13.3 *Data characteristic content variation outline.*

	Education	Health	Justice
Person Name Complete Normal	60	48	55
Person Name Complete Inverted	55		48
Person Name Abbreviated Normal		30	20
Person Name Abbreviated Inverted	26	26	

Figure 13.4 *Data characteristic length variation matrix.*

Person Name
   Person Name Complete Normal
      Person Name Complete Normal 60
      Person Name Complete Normal 48
      Person Name Complete Normal 55
   Person Name Complete Inverted
      Person Name Complete Inverted 55
      Person Name Complete Inverted 48
   Person Name Abbreviated Normal
      Person Name Abbreviated Normal 30
      Person Name Abbreviated Normal 20
   Person Name Abbreviated Inverted
      Person Name Abbreviated Inverted 26

Figure 13.5 *Data characteristic length variation outline for a person's name.*

Data characteristic length variations can also be documented in a *data characteristic length variation outline* when the data product identification is not needed. The data characteristic variations are listed under their respective data characteristics, and the length variations are listed under the data characteristic variations. The data characteristic variation name is formed by adding the length variation to the end of the data characteristic variation name. The data characteristic length variation outline for a person's name is shown in Figure 13.5.

If there are no data characteristic content variations, data characteristic length variations are listed under their respective data characteristics. The data characteristic length variation outline for Vehicle Model Name is shown in Figure 13.6.

Vehicle Model Name
   Vehicle Model Name 50
   Vehicle Model Name 35
   Vehicle Model Name 28

Figure 13.6 *Data characteristic length variation outline for vehicle model name.*

The outline format can also be used for showing statistics about each data characteristic, such as frequency of occurrence or frequency of use. The statistics are shown to the right of the data characteristic variation names. They are useful for designating official data characteristic variation.

Data Code Value Variations

Disparate data also contain many data code variations. A *data code variation* is a data property, such as Sight Disability, that is represented by more than one data code value, such as 2 and S. Each different set of properties, such as Disability or Vehicle Type, is defined as a separate data subject. Each different set of data codes for the same set of properties, such as Disability Code School and Disability Code Employment, or Vehicle Type Code Motor Pool and Vehicle Type Code License, is defined as a separate data characteristic variation.

> *Data code variations are managed at the data characteristic level.*

Data code values and name lengths may both vary. These length variations are identified and managed as data characteristic variations. Data characteristic variations are defined for each length variation. For example, the Vehicle Type Code License was found in two different information systems. One system used two-digit codes and one system used one-digit codes. The data characteristic variations names are Vehicle Type Code License 1 and Vehicle Type Code License 2. The code names were also different lengths, and were defined as Vehicle Type Name License 20 and Vehicle Type Name License 16.

A *data code matrix* contains all the data code sets for one set of data properties. It identifies the variability between sets of data code values and names. The names of the variations are listed across the top of the matrix, and the individual data code values and names are listed under each data subject. For example, different sets of disability data codes for School, Employment, and Health are shown in Figure 13.7.

This matrix is built by aggregating all the data product codes according to their corresponding data characteristic variations. In the example above, there are three data characteristic variations for three different

	School		Employment		Health
10	Sight	A	Seeing	V	Vision
20	Hearing	H	Hear	S	Sound
30	Physical	P	Physical	A	Accidental
40	Developmental	D	Developed	G	Genetic

Figure 13.7 *Data code matrix with paired names and values.*

sets of data product characteristics: Disability Code School and Disability Name School, Disability Code Employment and Disability Name Employment, and Disability Code Health and Disability Name Health.

A data code matrix may also have one set of data code names and several sets of data code values. The property name is listed on the left and the data code values are listed on the right. For example, the disability codes shown above may have only one property name and several sets of data codes, as shown in Figure 13.8.

▼ OFFICIAL DATA VARIATIONS

A data subject may have more than one primary key, a data characteristic may have more than one variation, and a set of data properties may have more than one data code variation. When the extent of data variability is determined, an official primary key is designated for each data subject, an official data characteristic variation is designated for each data characteristic, and a set of official data codes is designated for each data property. An *official data variation* is a data variation that has been

Property	School	Employment	Health
Sight	10	A	V
Hearing	20	H	S
Physical	30	P	A
Developmental	40	D	G

Figure 13.8 *Simple data code matrix.*

accepted by consensus for short-term data sharing and long-term evolution to the mature data resource. A *non-official data variation* is a data variation that was not designated as an official data variation.

---

*Official data variations are designated for each primary key,
each data characteristic, and each data property.*

Official data variations are designated by consensus of a team of knowledgeable people. The frequency of existence, frequency of use, data definitions, formats, and desires of the organization for the mature data resource are considered, and an appropriate data variation is designated as the official data variation. The official data variations hold their status, and the non-official data variations become *Limited* or *Obsolete* so they are no longer perpetuated.

Official Primary Keys

When all primary keys have been identified for a data subject, they become candidate primary keys. They are reviewed by knowledgeable people, and an official primary key is designated for each data subject. More than one official primary key may be designated, but that practice is discouraged. Ideally, there should be only one official primary key for each data subject that survives to the mature data resource.

A *candidate primary key* is any primary key that originates from disparate data. All primary keys that originate from disparate data are candidate primary keys until their range of uniqueness is determined. An *official primary key* is a primary key whose value is unique for all data occurrences within the scope of the common data architecture, and that has been designated as the primary key for long-term evolution to the mature data resource.

The candidate primary keys that are not designated as official primary keys are *non-official primary keys*. These become either alternate primary keys, limited primary keys, or obsolete primary keys. An *alternate primary key* is a primary key whose value is unique for all data occurrences in the common data architecture, but that has not been designated as the official primary key. A *limited primary key* is a primary key whose uniqueness is limited to a subset of the data occurrences within the scope of the common data architecture. An *obsolete primary key* is a primary key that is no longer used because it has lost its uniqueness or is not appropriate for some reason.

> *One official primary key must be designated for each data subject in the mature data resource.*

For example, the primary keys listed for Vehicles in Figure 13.1 become candidate primary keys, as shown in Figure 13.9. They are reviewed to determine the official primary key. Since a unique identifier was needed for the United States, the first candidate primary key was selected as the official primary key. The second candidate primary key became an alternate primary key because it is also valid for the United States. The third candidate primary key is a limited primary key because it is valid only within a specific state. The last candidate primary key became obsolete because it was the same as the third primary key when the redundant data characteristic was removed.

Generally, an official primary key is the one that is used predominantly in an organization. However, in a common data architecture that spans multiple organizations, there can be many primary keys that are all in predominant use by different organizations. Ideally, one of the candidate primary keys is selected as the official primary key, in a

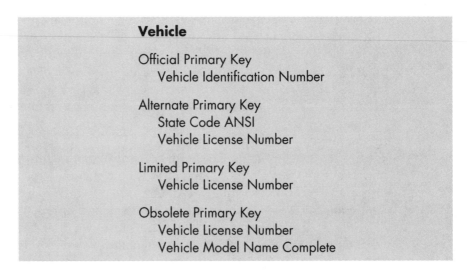

Vehicle

Official Primary Key
    Vehicle Identification Number

Alternate Primary Key
    State Code ANSI
    Vehicle License Number

Limited Primary Key
    Vehicle License Number

Obsolete Primary Key
    Vehicle License Number
    Vehicle Model Name Complete

Figure 13.9 *Official primary key for vehicles.*

similar process to that within an organization, but the selection is based on consensus rather than on predominance of use.

The techniques for designating an official primary key are listed below.

- Each existing primary key becomes a candidate primary key, and the range of uniqueness is determined.

- Each candidate primary key is reviewed for redundant data characteristics. Any redundant data characteristics are identified.

- Each candidate primary key is compared to the primary key criteria to determine whether it is valid. If it is a valid primary key, and it is unique within the scope of the common data architecture, it remains a candidate primary key. If it is a valid primary key, but has limited uniqueness, it is designated a limited primary key. If it is not valid as a primary key, it is designated an obsolete primary key.

- The official primary key is designated from the remaining candidate primary keys. If there are several candidate primary keys, the most appropriate one is designated as the official primary key. If there is only one candidate primary key, it is designated as the official primary key. If no candidate primary keys remain, or none of the remaining candidates are acceptable, an official primary key is created.

- Any remaining candidate primary keys become alternate primary keys.

Official Foreign Keys

When the official primary key is designated, foreign keys are adjusted to match the official primary key. An *official foreign key* is the foreign key that matches the official primary key in a parent data subject. An *alternate foreign key* is a foreign key that matches an alternate primary key in a parent data subject. A *limited foreign key* is a foreign key that matches a limited primary key in a parent data subject. An *obsolete foreign key* is a foreign key that matches an obsolete primary key in a parent data subject.

The techniques for adjusting foreign keys are listed below.

- An official foreign key is designated to match the official primary key in each parent data subject.

- An alternate foreign key may be defined as necessary to match an alternate primary key in a parent data subject.

- A limited foreign key may be defined as necessary to match a limited primary key in a parent data subject.

- An obsolete foreign key may be defined as necessary to match an obsolete primary key in a parent data subject.

Generally, it is not difficult to identify which primary key is being referenced by a foreign key. The data subject name in the foreign key reference identifies the data subject. The data characteristic names in the foreign key match the data characteristic names in the primary key, and the sequence of data characteristics is the same in both the primary key and the foreign key. However, if any difficulty is found, the primary keys may be numbered in the parent data subject, such as Primary Key 1, Primary Key 2, and so on. That primary key number is placed after the data subject name in the foreign key of a subordinate data subject, such as Employee 1, Employee 2, and so on.

Official primary keys and official foreign keys are used to define the mature data resource. Alternate and limited primary and foreign keys are only maintained as long as disparate data exist.

Official Data Characteristic Variations

When the range of data characteristic variability is determined, official data characteristic variations are designated. An *Official data characteristic variation* is a data characteristic variation that has been selected by consensus and accepted as the official variation for short-term data sharing and long-term evolution to the mature data resource. All data characteristic variations are reviewed for each data characteristic and an official data characteristic is designated. If an existing variation is not acceptable as an official data variation, a new data characteristic is defined and designated as the official data variation.

One official data characteristic variation is designated for data sharing and the mature data resource.

More than one official data characteristic variation may be designated on an interim basis. The extra ones may be used to promote data

Employee Birth Date
    Employee Birth Date CYMD*
    Employee Birth Date YMD
    Employee Birth Date MDY
    Employee Birth Date DMY

Figure 13.10 *Designation of official data characteristic variations.*

sharing, or kept only until additional information is gained to designate one official data variation. However, one official data variation must be designated before the mature data resource is developed. The mature data resource cannot contain more than one official data variation for each data characteristic.

For example, four employee birth dates were identified during data cross referencing, as shown in Figure 13.10. After the variations were reviewed and the approach of a new century was considered, Employee Birth Date CYMD was designated the official data characteristic variation. It is identified with an asterisk and is placed at the top of the data characteristic variation list. The other data characteristic variations become non-official variations.

The criteria listed below help in the designation of official data characteristic variations.

- If there is only one data characteristic variation and it is acceptable, it is designated as the official data characteristic variation.

- If there are multiple data characteristic variations and one is acceptable, it is the official data characteristic variation.

- If there is only one data characteristic variation and it is not acceptable, a new data characteristic variation is identified, defined, and designated as the official data characteristic variation.

- If there are multiple data characteristic variations and none is acceptable, a new data characteristic variation is identified, defined, and designated as the official data characteristic variation.

Official Data Codes

After the data code variations are identified and documented, one set of data codes in each data subject is designated as the official set. An *official data code set* is a set of data codes that has been designated by consensus and accepted as the official variation for short-term data sharing and long-term evolution to the mature data resource. If an existing data code set is not acceptable as the official data variation, a new set of data codes is defined and designated as the official set. All other data code sets become non-official.

More than one data code set may be designated as official on an interim basis. It may be used to promote data sharing or until additional information is gained to designate one set as official. However, one set of data codes must be designated as official before the mature data resource is developed.

One official set of data codes must be designated for the mature data resource.

For example, the sets of data codes listed above were reviewed. Disability Name School and Disability Code Employment were designated as official, as shown in Figure 13.11.

▼ DATA TRANSLATION SCHEMES

When official data variations are designated, data translation schemes are developed between data variations. A *data translation scheme* is a translation between common data characteristic variations when those data characteristic variations represent measurements for format varia-

Disability Name School	Disability Code Employment
Sight	A
Hearing	H
Physical	P
Developmental	D

Figure 13.11 *Official data code value variation designation.*

tions. Data translation schemes are usually developed between official and non-official data variations. An *official data translation scheme* translates data between non-official variations and official variations. However, data translation schemes may also be developed between non-official data variations if absolutely necessary. A *non-official translation scheme* translates data between non-official variations.

> *Data translation schemes are developed between official and non-official data variations.*

A *fundamental data translation scheme* is a data translation scheme that applies to many specific data characteristics, such as the translation of different date formats. A *specific data translation scheme* is a data translation scheme that applies to only one data characteristic, such as a translation between sets of laboratory analysis method codes.

A data translation scheme is developed by a consensus of people who are knowledgeable about the relevant data characteristics and data codes. Data translation schemes are used to translate disparate data until the mature data resource is developed. Data translation schemes will be eliminated or substantially reduced as the mature data resource is completed.

Data Characteristic Translation

A *data characteristic translation scheme* translates data between variations of the same data characteristics. They are not the same as data derivation algorithms, which create data characteristic values from contributing data characteristics. Data characteristic translation schemes are developed only for format and value variations, not for meaning, content, or accuracy variations. For example, a data translation scheme can be developed between Well Depth Estimated Feet and Well Depth Estimated Yards. However, a data translation scheme cannot be developed between Well Depth Estimated Meters and Well Depth Measured Feet because there is a different accuracy involved.

> *Data characteristic translation schemes are developed only for format and value variations, not for accuracy or meaning variations.*

Data characteristic translation schemes are usually developed between official and non-official data characteristic variations. However, they may be developed between non-official data characteristic variations if there is a definite reason. It is not appropriate to develop translation schemes between all non-official data characteristic variations of a data characteristic because of the volume of translations that need to be created and maintained.

For example, Employee Birth Date CYMD can be designated as the official data characteristic variation. Data translation schemes are then developed between Employee Birth Date CYMD and Employee Birth Date MDY, Employee Birth Date YMD, and Employee Birth Date DMY. They are not developed between the non-official data variations.

Fundamental data translation schemes are usually developed for fundamental data. They can be applied to specific data translations without developing many identical data translation schemes. For example, fundamental data translation schemes are developed for all date translations. The examples above use these fundamental data translation schemes rather than defining specific data translation schemes.

> *Translation schemes are developed each way between data characteristic variations.*

Data characteristic translation schemes are created both ways between data characteristics because translation usually occurs both ways. For example, six different data translation schemes would be developed for the employee birth dates, as shown in Figure 13.12.

```
Employee Birth Date YMD ——> Employee Birth Date CYMD
Employee Birth Date YMD <—— Employee Birth Date CYMD

Employee Birth Date MDY ——> Employee Birth Date CYMD
Employee Birth Date MDY <—— Employee Birth Date CYMD

Employee Birth Date DMY ——> Employee Birth Date CYMD
Employee Birth Date DMY <—— Employee Birth Date CYMD
```

Figure 13.12 *Data translation schemes for employee birth dates.*

Well Depth Yards times 3 equals Well Depth Feet
Well Depth Feet divided by 3 equals Well Depth Yards.

Figure 13.13 *Data translation schemes for well depth.*

Data characteristic translation schemes can be very simple, such as the translation between units of measurement. For example, the translation between feet and yards is simple, as shown in Figure 13.13.

Data characteristic translation schemes can also be more complex. For example, translation of a person's name from Person Name Complete Normal to Person Name Complete Inverted involves a set of instructions to parse and rearrange the name components. Many of these complex data translation schemes can be fundamental data translation schemes that apply to many specific translations.

Data translation schemes between data characteristic length variations are relatively simple. If a shorter variation is translated to a longer variation, the data values are moved and aligned right or left as necessary. However, if a longer variation is translated to a shorter variation, the values may be too long. Some additional criteria must be supplied, such as truncation right or left, to handle data values that are too long for the receiving data characteristic variation. Justification translations, such as right and left justified, are easy to define.

Data translation schemes can also be complex for variable and irregular data characteristics, such as translating Person Name Irregular to Person Name Complete Normal. Additional information is usually required to make these data translations, and knowledgeable people are usually required to review the data values and make the determinations. Expert systems may be able to provide some assistance with variable or irregular data translations.

> *Variable and irregular data characteristics require additional information for translation.*

Data translation schemes between a combined data characteristic and elemental data characteristics are relatively easy. For example, translation between Person Name Complete Normal and Person Name

Individual, Person Name Middle, and Person Name Family requires parsing and movement. Translation from the individual elements to the combined data characteristic is simply a concatenation.

It is not acceptable to chain data translation schemes together. Too much integrity is lost in successive data translations. For example, it is not acceptable to translate Well Depth Inches to Well Depth Meters through two successive translations from inches to yards and then from yards to meters. Therefore, individual data translation schemes must be developed for each set of data characteristics.

Data Code Translation

A *data code translation scheme* translates data between data code sets. Data code translation schemes, like data characteristic translation schemes, can be very simple where there is a one-to-one relation between data values. For example, the data translation scheme for disability codes is the table shown in Figure 13.8. No additional translation schemes are necessary.

Data code translations may combine many disparate codes into one official code. These one-to-many translation schemes are also easy to define. However, the reverse translation is impossible without additional information. For example, disparate data contain many detailed data codes for the termination of an employee's employment. These data codes are combined into fewer data codes for the mature data resource, as shown in Figure 13.14. Translation from the left to the right is easy, but translation from the right to the left is impossible without additional information.

Employee Termination Code A	Employee Termination Code B
10 through 13	1
14	3
21 through 23	3
40 through 44	2
45	3
46 through 47	2

Figure 13.14 *Data code value translation scheme.*

Data translation schemes for variable and irregular data codes are developed by listing all the possible values that could occur in the disparate data characteristic and their equivalent in the official data characteristic variation. A many-to-one data translation scheme is then developed like the one shown above.

Data translation schemes for splitting data codes requires additional information. Documentation of these translation schemes is more detailed, and the format is dependent on the type of additional information required. Data translation schemes may be automated with traditional systems or with expert systems, or they may require intervention of knowledgeable people. Fortunately, there are not too many situations that require splitting disparate data code values.

▼ SUMMARY

Cross referencing disparate data to a common data architecture identifies those data in a common context. When cross referencing is completed, the extent of variability is determined and official data variations are designated. Data translation schemes are then developed between the official and the non-official data variations. These data translation schemes facilitate short-term data sharing and enable long-term evolution to the mature data resource.

Data subject variations usually result from different views of the real world that were held when the disparate data were developed. They are documented on a data subject hierarchy if they are subsets or supersets of common data subjects. If they are widely different from common data subjects, all documentation is done through the data characteristics.

Each candidate primary key is reviewed to determine the range of its uniqueness. Official primary keys are designated based on their uniqueness within the scope of the common data architecture. Limited primary keys are valid for a limited range of uniqueness. Obsolete primary keys are no longer useful. All other candidate primary keys become alternate primary keys. Official, alternate, and limited foreign keys are designated based on their corresponding official primary keys.

Disparate data characteristics usually have many content and length variations. Disparate data codes also have many data code value and data code name variations. These variations are documented and official variations are designated by consensus. Data translation schemes are developed and maintained until disparate data are converted to the mature data resource, or until the disparate data no longer exist.

▼ QUESTIONS

The following questions are designed to provide a review of Chapter 13 and to stimulate thought about data variability, the designation of official data variations, and data translation schemes.

1. How are data subject variations documented?

2. How are primary key variations documented?

3. How are data code variations documented?

4. Why is it important to identify the range of uniqueness for a primary key?

5. How are data characteristic content and length variations documented?

6. How are data code variations documented when both codes and names are different?

7. How are official primary keys designated?

8. What is the difference between an alternate, a limited, and an obsolete primary key?

9. How are foreign keys aligned with primary keys?

10. How are official data characteristics designated?

11. How are official data code sets designated?

12. What is the difference between an official and a non-official data translation scheme?

13. What is the difference between a fundamental and a specific data translation scheme?

14. Why are data characteristic translation schemes developed both ways?

15. How is a data code translation scheme documented?

14

MATURE DATA RESOURCE

The concepts and techniques of data refining provide a formal
process for moving from disparate data to a mature data resource.

A mature data resource is developed by refining data within the common data architecture to create a formal data resource. The data still exist in their original data files, but they are named and defined within a common context that represents the formal data resource. The official data variations in the formal data resource define the mature data resource, which is the ideal that organizations are trying to achieve. When the mature data resource is defined, the data translation schemes are used to convert data from their original data files into new data files, thus forming the mature data resource.

The concepts and techniques for data refining are explained in the previous chapters. Those concepts and techniques are put into a formal process for achieving a mature data resource. This formal process gives organizations a general plan for moving from disparate data to a mature data resource. They can use this general plan to develop specific projects for refining disparate data.

Most organizations agree on the advisability of refining disparate data, particularly when they understand the benefits of evolving to a mature data resource. Most organizations want to build a formal data resource and evolve to a mature data resource, but are concerned about how to make the changes on-the-fly with minimum impact on business operations. Most organizations must make the change to survive. They just don't have a process for making the change.

This chapter explains the process for refining data to create a formal data resource and evolve to a mature data resource. It explains the general plan for understanding disparate data, promoting data sharing, and building a formal data resource. It begins with an overview about achieving a mature data resource. Then each phase of the data refining process is described.

▼ MATURE DATA RESOURCE OVERVIEW

The mature data resource is developed by the formal data refining process shown in Figure 14.1. Disparate data are identified, defined, and cross referenced to a common data architecture. The cross referencing defines disparate data within a common context and creates a formal data resource. The disparate data still exist in their original data files, but they are defined within a common context so their true content and meaning is known.

Data cross referencing identifies a wide range of data variability. The variability is analyzed, official data variations are designated, and data translation schemes are defined. The formal data resource, using official data variations and data translation schemes, is used to facilitate short-term data sharing. It is also used to define the mature data resource based on official data variations.

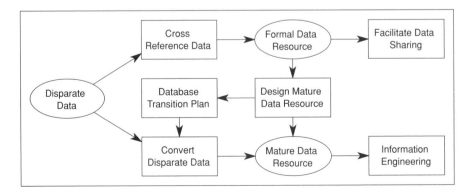

Figure 14.1 *Formal data refining process.*

A database conversion plan is developed to convert disparate data to the mature data resource using the data translation schemes. When the plan is developed, the disparate data are converted and placed in the mature data resource. The data are actually moved to new data files structured by data subjects within the common data architecture. The mature data resource becomes a true data library that information engineering can use to produce information.

Building a mature data resource is not a precise process because of the uncertainty involved in disparate data. It is a cyclical process that uses the data refining concepts and techniques until certainty is achieved. It is an evolutionary process based on discovery and enhancement that is done by people, not by tools. It cannot be accomplished in one pass and it cannot be done overnight. It often seems like an insurmountable task, but it is possible.

The mature data resource process consists of six phases, shown in Figure 14.2. The data refining process begins with a Data Preparation Phase, which establishes the scope of the project, identifies the data products to be refined, identifies people who are knowledgeable about the data, and defines an initial common data architecture. It is followed by a Data Product Phase, which identifies and defines each component in each data product within the given scope. Next, a Data Cross Reference Phase cross references all data products to the common data architecture.

When data cross referencing is completed, the Data Variability Phase determines the extent of data variability, designates official data variations, and develops data translation schemes. The Data Sharing Phase facilitates data sharing while the disparate data are being converted to

Mature Data Resource Process

Data Preparation Phase
Data Product Phase
Data Cross Reference Phase
Data Variability Phase
Data Sharing Phase
Mature Data Resource Phase

Figure 14.2 *The phases of the mature data resource process.*

the mature data resource. The Mature Data Resource Phase builds a data resource model for the mature data resource, develops a database conversion plan for converting data into the mature data resource, and implements that plan.

▼ DATA PREPARATION PHASE

The Data Preparation Phase establishes the data refining scope, identifies the data products within the scope, identifies the people who are knowledgeable about the data, develops the initial common data architecture, and prepares the tools to support the data refining process. It includes any project management activities involved in running a successful project. The schedule should not be too rigid, because data refining is a discovery process.

> **Data Preparation Phase**
>
> Establish Scope
> Identify Data Products
> Identify Knowledgeable People
> Develop Initial Common Data Architecture
> Identify Supporting Tools

Establish Scope

Data refining begins by establishing the scope of the process. The scope can be so small that it is meaningless, such as the process of documenting the depreciation equations for fixed assets, or it can be so large that it is unmanageable, such as the process of documenting all education data for an entire state. An acceptable method for defining the scope is to refine baseline data within a critical area, such as educational curriculums for kindergarten through the 12th grade.

Identify Data Products

All existing data products within the scope are identified, and any existing documentation about those data products is collected. The data products should include all applications and all databases that may be involved in sharing data or developing the mature data resource. Existing documentation includes file listings, application listings, reports, documents, data dictionaries, or any other documentation that might provide information about the data products.

Identify Knowledgeable People

People who have a working knowledge of the data and of the business activities involved in producing or using the data products are identified. They form a knowledge base that provides information about disparate data and helps ensure the success of data refining. They are briefed on the data refining process and the part they will play in that process.

There is usually no limit on the number of people forming the knowledge base. It is more important to have adequate knowledge about the data and adequate representation for the organizations involved than to have a fixed number of people. Usually, five to twenty-five people can provide a sufficient knowledge base for data refining.

Develop Initial Common Data Architecture

An initial common data architecture is developed for the scope of data refining. This initial architecture expands throughout the data refining process to include all data subjects, data characteristics, data characteristic variations, and data codes within the scope.

If no common data architecture exists, major data subjects are defined by identifying major objects in the real world. For example, if kindergarten through 12th grade education were the scope, the major data subjects might be Student, Employee, School District, Vehicle, Building, Curriculum, Class, Equipment, and so on. Generally, ten to twenty major data subjects are sufficient to form an initial common data architecture. A formal name and comprehensive definition are developed for each major data subject, and initial data relations are identified. Each major data subject is reviewed by knowledgeable people, and prominent data characteristics are identified, named, and defined. Generally, five to ten prominent data characteristics for each major data subject are enough to get started.

Identify Supporting Tools

Tools that support data refining are identified and prepared. For example, a data resource glossary, data resource thesaurus, and data name lexicon should be established if they do not already exist. A text processor and utility diagrammer are identified and made available to the appropriate people. Generally, existing CASE tools are not robust enough to handle the rigors of data refining and should not be considered. They can play a prominent role after the mature data resource is developed and information engineering begins drawing data from the mature data resource.

▼ DATA PRODUCT PHASE

The Data Product Phase documents the data products within the data refining scope. It determines the sequence in which data products will be refined, names and defines each data product, develops a data file diagram and physical data structure chart for the data products, identifies unused data, defines data product characteristics and data product codes, and documents existing data quality.

> **Data Product Phase**
>
> Determine Data Product Sequence
> Prepare Data Product Descriptions
> Prepare Data File Diagram
> Prepare Physical Data Structure Chart
> Identify Unused Data
> Define Data Product Characteristics
> Define Data Product Codes
> Document Data Product Quality

Determine Data Product Sequence

The sequence for refining data products is determined before data refining begins. The first data products to be refined are primary data products, because they are the most complete, most recognized, and most comprehensive. Usually, major data file documentation or applications containing the structure of major data files are refined first, because they provide the most information about existing data. Other data products, such as screens, documents, and reports, are secondary data products and are refined later.

The objective is to get the most and best information possible as early as possible. This approach maximizes people's understanding of disparate data and enhances the common data architecture in a timely manner. It is a poor practice to select data products that are small, incomplete, less informative, or represent secondary data products, because it often results in many changes to the data cross references and an increase in frustration.

Prepare Data Product Descriptions

Each data product is uniquely identified so that each data product subject, data product characteristic and data product code can be uniquely identified. The unique name may include an organization name, a location name, a computer name, a database name, or any other name that makes the data product name unique. The data product names must be unique within the common data architecture, not just within the current scope.

Each data product is defined to help people understand what it contains or represents. Initial data product definitions should be retained exactly as they appear in the original product. The initial definition may be extended to provide additional information.

Prepare Data File Diagram

A data file diagram and physical data structure chart are prepared for each data product if it represents a database, such as a dictionary listing or a file structure in a program. A data flow diagram is prepared if the data product is a screen, document, report, or other non-database product. It is a good practice to prepare a general data flow diagram of the existing system so that people understand all of the components involved in data refining.

Each data product is reviewed for major data groupings, such as data files, record types, or screens. Each major grouping becomes a data product subject that is named, defined, and placed on either the data file diagram or the data flow diagram. Any data relations between data product subjects are shown on the data file diagram.

The data file diagram and data flow diagram are adjusted as more information is gained about the data product. However, extensive effort to prepare a data file diagram is not the most productive use of time. When enough information is gained to identify the data product and data product subjects, no further effort is needed. The effort is better spent refining other data products or enhancing the common data architecture.

Prepare Physical Data Structure Chart

A physical data structure chart is prepared for each data product, showing all the data product subjects and data product characteristics. Usually, the outline format is used, because it is best for documenting cross references to the common data architecture. Primary keys for each data product subject are also documented if the data product subject represents a physical file.

Data names are entered exactly as they appear in the data product, including upper- and lower-case, underscores, and so on, not as they appear in the common data architecture. Indentation is useful for indicating nesting, hierarchies, repeating groups, or record types. If there is more than one data name, the complete or most meaningful name is used.

The data product structure chart may be enhanced as more information is gained. However, extensive effort should not be spent on developing a precise data product structure chart. When enough information is gained to identify the data product characteristics in enough detail that they can be cross referenced to the common data architecture, no further effort is required. The effort is better spent enhancing the common data architecture.

Identify Unused Data

Any data product characteristics that are not used and have a low probability of use are identified. Unused data usually occur in purchased applications that have capabilities beyond those that the organization is using. It is usually unproductive to spend time identifying, defining, and cross referencing data product characteristics that have a low probability of use. If they were to be used in the future, they could be easily identified, defined, and cross referenced to the common data architecture at that time.

A good practice is to list each data product characteristic that is unused and indicate *Not Used* in the data cross reference. This approach shows all data product characteristics available and indicates whether they are used. The unused data product characteristics that are available for future use are readily visible.

Define Data Product Characteristics

When the physical data structure chart is completed, a definition is prepared for each data product characteristic that is used. The definition may come from the data product, a related data product, or people familiar with the data product. The initial definition should be exactly as it appears in the data product. If the initial definition is extended, the initial definition should remain intact, and the additional information should follow that initial definition. This approach retains the original definition for reference.

The definition must ultimately reflect the true content and meaning of the data product characteristic. This is usually a difficult process, because there is usually minimal information about the content and meaning of data product characteristics. Most information, if it exists at all, is about the format and use of data. Knowledgeable people provide considerable insight into the data. However, their input should only be necessary if there is difficulty in developing a data cross reference to the common data architecture. If the data cross reference is easy to determine, the effort is best spent enhancing the common data architecture.

Define Data Product Codes

An initial definition is prepared for each data product code. Like the data product characteristic definitions, the data product code definition may come from the data product, a related data product, or knowledgeable people. The initial definition should be shown exactly as it appears in the data product. If the initial definition is extended, the initial definition should remain intact and the additional information should follow that initial definition. This approach retains the original definition for reference.

Applications often contain hard-coded tables, constants, literals, and messages. It is often assumed that all data are contained in data files and those are the only data products included in data refining. This assumption is false, and it results in a considerable quantity of data being missed.

This is one reason that data products other than data files are included in data refining. If a considerable quantity of data is hard-coded in applications, those applications should be included in the data refining process.

Like data product characteristic definitions, a data product code definition must ultimately reflect its true content and meaning. This is usually a more difficult process than determining the true content and meaning of data product characteristics, because there is less information available. In many cases, there is no information about data product codes, and many do not even have names. People knowledgeable about data product codes can provide enough information to make a cross reference to the common data architecture.

Document Data Product Quality

Any data integrity constraints that exist in the data product must be documented. It is best to capture existing data integrity constraints as they are discovered, rather than later. However, a major effort to identify data integrity constraints should not be made. People involved in data refining should not assume that data integrity exists in a data product, because many existing databases have no data integrity constraints. They should not document desired data integrity constraints, because comprehensive data integrity rules will be defined within the common data architecture.

Data accuracy is documented for each data product characteristic. Determination of data accuracy is usually a difficult task because the true accuracy of disparate data is often unknown. People knowledgeable about the data can help determine data accuracy. A major effort may need to be made to identify the data accuracy so it can be aggregated to the common data architecture.

▼ DATA CROSS REFERENCE PHASE

The Data Cross Reference Phase cross references data product characteristics and data product codes to common data characteristic variations and common data codes. It then validates those data cross references, maintains the data resource glossary, thesaurus, and lexicon, and maintains fundamental data. The objective is to develop a cross reference for every data product characteristic and data product code that is used.

Unused data product characteristics and data product codes are not cross referenced to the common data architecture.

Data Cross Reference Phase

Cross Reference Data Subjects
Cross Reference Data Characteristics
Cross Reference Data Codes
Validate Data Cross References
Maintain Data Resource Glossary
Maintain Data Resource Thesaurus
Maintain Data Naming Lexicon
Maintain Fundamental Data

Cross Reference Data Subjects

A data cross reference between data product subjects and common data subjects is optional. If the data product is well structured and the data product subject closely aligns with a common data subject, even though the name may be different, a data cross reference can be made. If the product represents an application data file containing multiple data subjects, a data cross reference is not made.

Cross Reference Data Characteristics

Each data product characteristic is cross referenced to one or more corresponding common data characteristic variations. The data product characteristic descriptions are reviewed, and a search is made for a corresponding common data characteristic variation. A good data characteristic thesaurus helps identify appropriate common data characteristic variations.

Cross Reference Data Codes

Each data product code value is cross referenced to one or more corresponding common data code values. The data product code names and descriptions are reviewed, and a search is made for a corresponding common data code value.

Data code cross references are usually very difficult to make, because they have limited names and definitions. They are also difficult because data properties are often split between data product codes or combined into one data product code. Each data product code value must be cross referenced to a common data code value that represents a single property.

Validate Data Cross References

When a data cross reference has been made, it is reviewed to make sure it is valid. Every data characteristic and data code cross reference must be validated before data refining is complete.

Data cross reference validation may be done at the time a data cross reference is made, at any time during data refining, or at the end of data refining. Since data refining is a discovery process, a data cross reference can be validated whenever sufficient information is gained to ensure that the cross reference is valid. If the information is available when the data cross reference is made, it can be validated. If the information is not available, the data cross reference remains *Proposed* until the information is available. The person involved in data refining should not get sidetracked trying to validate a cross reference when sufficient information is not available. The information will become available in due time.

If a data cross reference passes the criteria, the status is changed from *Proposed* to *Verified*. If it does not pass these criteria, the cross reference remains *Proposed*, and additional information is obtained to identify a data cross reference that passes the criteria.

Any new component in the common data architecture becomes *Proposed*. When a data cross reference is verified for that component, the status is elevated to *Interim* because it represents existing data. The status is then elevated to *Accepted* by whatever criteria are used within the common data architecture. Validating a data cross reference to a new component does not automatically raise it to *Accepted* status.

Maintain Data Resource Glossary

Any terms and abbreviations identified during data refining are defined in the data resource glossary. The glossary is built incrementally as terms and abbreviations are found, not after data refining is completed. The best time to start building a glossary is when terms and abbreviations are first identified, even if the definition is tentative or incomplete. The definitions will be refined as more information is gained. It is a bad practice to wait until data refining is nearly complete before developing a glossary.

Developing a comprehensive data resource glossary helps draw out the knowledge of people familiar with the data. As they see definitions unfolding, they tend to enhance those definitions and add new definitions. When this knowledge is placed in the glossary, it is available to other people who are using, or may want to use, the data for their business activities. A comprehensive data resource glossary also facilitates data sharing.

Maintain Data Resource Thesaurus

When a new common data subject or data characteristic is created, any synonyms, similar names, or keywords for that name are added to the data resource thesaurus. These entries may be made as they are identified, or there may be a separate task at the end of data refining that reviews all names and makes entries into the thesaurus. Usually, both approaches are used to develop a robust thesaurus. This incremental development provides a viable data resource thesaurus that helps with future cross reference activities.

A robust data resource thesaurus helps people identify existing common data and establish data cross references. It also provides a base for expert systems to find appropriate data based on client inquires. When data refining is substantially underway or completed, expert systems can identify data and assist in data sharing based on a client's request, using terms that clients understand and use in their own environments.

Maintain Data Naming Lexicon

Any new common words that are used to support the data naming taxonomy must be placed in the data naming lexicon. Whenever a newly formed data name contains a word that could be defined as a common word for the data naming taxonomy, that word is placed in the data naming lexicon. This incremental development of the lexicon ensures consistent use of common words and promotes more meaningful names. It also supports the use of expert systems, in conjunction with a data resource thesaurus, in locating and sharing data.

Maintain Fundamental Data

Any new fundamental data are defined and documented. As new common data subjects and data characteristics are identified and defined, they should be analyzed to determine whether there could be a fundamental data definition. If a fundamental data definition is appropriate, one is prepared and placed in the Data Resource Guide, and it is used to support the naming and definition of specific data.

▼ DATA VARIABILITY PHASE

The Data Variability Phase identifies the extent of data variability, designates official data variations, and prepares data translation schemes. This information is used to facilitate data sharing and reduce variability in the mature data resource.

> **Data Variability Phase**
>
> Designate Official Data Characteristic Variations
> Designate Official Primary Keys
> Develop Data Translation Schemes

Designate Official Data Characteristic Variations

Disparate data are highly variable. Data refining identifies and documents the extent of data variability and the frequency of use for each common data characteristic variation. Official data characteristic variations are designated for every common data characteristic based on the extent of data variability, the frequency of existence, the frequency of use, and practicality.

Data characteristic variability is identified through a listing of the data characteristic variations for each data characteristic. The frequency of existence and frequency of use for each data characteristic variation is listed next to the data characteristic variation. Knowledgeable people review the data characteristic variations and designate an official one for each data characteristic. If an existing data characteristic variation is not acceptable, a new one is defined and designated as the official variation.

Data code variability is identified by placing all the sets of data codes for a set of data properties in a table. The frequency of existence and frequency of use are listed for each set of data codes. Knowledgeable people review the variation information and identify an official set of data codes. If none of the existing data code sets is acceptable, a new data code set may be created and designated as the official data code set.

The official data characteristic variation and the official set of data codes become *Accepted*. The other non-official data characteristic variations become *Limited*, and ultimately become *Obsolete* as applications and databases are converted to the official data characteristic variations. Each data code in the official set is also reviewed to determine whether it is acceptable. Acceptable codes become *Accepted*, and the others become *Interim* until enough information is gained to make them *Accepted*.

It is not always possible to select one official data characteristic variation, so several may need to be designated on an interim basis. The number of official data characteristic variations should be kept to a minimum for an efficient formal data resource, and should be considerably less than the full range of data variability. It is a poor practice to designate a large number of official data characteristic variations.

Designate Official Primary Keys

An official primary key is designated for each common data subject. That primary key must be unique within the scope of the common data architecture. Knowledgeable people review each candidate primary key for each data subject and designate an official primary key. In some situations, none of the existing candidate primary keys is acceptable and a new primary key is defined.

Any other candidate primary key that provides unique values across the entire range of data occurrences becomes an alternate primary key. Any candidate primary key that provides unique values for only some of the data occurrences becomes a limited primary key. Any candidate primary key that does not provide uniqueness or is not acceptable for other reasons becomes an obsolete primary key.

The foreign keys in each subordinate data subject are adjusted to match the primary keys in their parent data subjects. Foreign keys become official, alternate, limited, and obsolete to match the parent data subjects primary keys.

Develop Data Translation Schemes

Data translation schemes are developed between non-official data variations and official data variations for every common data characteristic and common data code that has official and non-official variations. These data translation schemes provide support for short-term translation, which assists with data sharing and with converting disparate data to the mature data resource.

A data translation scheme is developed between the non-official and the official data characteristic variation for each data characteristic. If there is more than one official data characteristic variation, a data translation scheme is developed from each non-official data characteristic variation to each official data characteristic variation. A data translation scheme is also developed from each official data characteristic variation to every other official data characteristic variation within the same data characteristic. This is one reason that the quantity of official data characteristic variations must be kept to a minimum.

A data translation scheme is developed between each non-official set of data codes and the official set of data codes in each code table data subject. If there is more than one official set of data codes, data translation schemes are developed from each non-official set to each official set, and between each official set and every other official set.

Generally, data translation schemes are not developed between non-official data variations because it results in an increased workload and defeats the purpose of sharing data using official data variations. However, if there is a profound reason for creating data translation schemes between non-official data variations, they may be developed.

▼ DATA SHARING PHASE

The Data Sharing Phase develops a formal data resource model and facilitates data sharing after data refining is completed. The objective is to facilitate data sharing through development of a formal data resource model and enhancement of the Data Resource Guide.

Data Sharing Phase

Develop Formal Data Resource Model
Facilitate Data Sharing

Develop Formal Data Resource Model

When data refining is completed, a logical data resource model is developed for the formal data resource within the chosen scope. The logical data resource model consists of data descriptions for data subjects, data characteristics, data characteristic variations, and data codes, along with data relation diagrams, logical data structures, and comprehensive data integrity rules. Developing comprehensive data integrity rules is usually the most difficult and time-consuming task because only minimal information is gained from data refining.

Data descriptions should be in place following the data cross referencing. However, those descriptions should be reviewed again in the context of a complete logical data resource model to ensure they are complete and accurate. Adjustments are made to the data definitions within the criteria for changing data definitions, and the status of those definitions may be changed based on established criteria.

Data relation diagrams are developed to include all data subjects within the project scope. A logical data structure is developed for every data subject within the scope. The primary keys are listed for each data subject. Foreign keys are listed for every data relation to a parent data subject. A complete data characteristic list shows all the data characteristics available in that data subject.

Data rule domains or data value domains are defined for each data characteristic. Relations between data characteristics are defined in a data value domain or a data rule domain. Conditional data relations and cardinalities are documented. Data derivation, data redundancy, and retention are documented.

Facilitate Data Sharing

The Data Resource Guide is enhanced with the logical data resource model, data cross references, data translation schemes, glossary, thesaurus, and lexicon. The Data Resource Guide facilitates data sharing by helping people identify data they need, locate those data, and acquire data in the desired form. The common data architecture provides the framework for integrating and sharing data, and the Data Resource Guide provides the means to identify and locate those data.

Expert systems can facilitate data sharing when a common data architecture is developed, data cross references are identified, official data variations are designated, and data translation schemes are in place. People indicate what data they need and expert systems search through the thesaurus, lexicon, and cross references to find appropriate data. When appropriate data are located, expert systems can implement appropriate data translation schemes and move data from the source to the destination in the form desired. This is the point where the data refining effort really provides benefits to an organization.

▼ MATURE DATA RESOURCE PHASE

The Mature Data Resource Phase develops a logical data resource model for the mature data resource, resolves any data cross references, develops a database conversion plan, and builds the mature data resource. The objective is to develop a mature data resource that directly supports information engineering.

> **Mature Data Resource Phase**
>
> Develop Mature Data Resource Model
> Resolve Data Cross References
> Develop Database Conversion Plan
> Build Mature Data Resource

Develop Mature Data Resource Model

The mature data resource is defined with a *mature data resource model*, which is a logical data resource model of the mature data resource. The mature data resource model represents the desired state. It represents an aggregate of the different views of the real world that existed in disparate data. It represents a true conversion from the application data structure to a subject data structure that is independent of application use.

The mature data resource model only includes official data variations. There is only one official data variation for each data characteristic, data code, and primary key. If there is more than one, every effort should be made to identify a single official data variation before developing the mature data resource model. Only in extreme cases should multiple official data variations be allowed in the mature data resource.

The mature data resource model includes only data that have *Interim* or *Accepted* status. Data that have *Limited* or *Obsolete* status must not be included in the mature data resource model because their use cannot be perpetuated. Data that have *Proposed* status should be carefully reviewed before being included in the mature data resource model. If it is likely that their status will become *Interim* or *Accepted,* they can be included. If it is likely that their status will become *Limited* or *Obsolete,* they should not be included.

All data must be formally named and comprehensively defined before they can be included in the mature data resource model. It is best to review the data names and definitions of all data included in the mature data resource to ensure that they comply with naming and definition criteria.

Comprehensive data integrity rules must be defined for all data included in the mature data resource model. These rules may be defined before or after data are included. However, the mature data resource model is not complete until all data integrity rules are formally defined.

Resolve Data Cross References

Creation of a mature data resource model often requires creation of interim common data architectures and development of common-to-common cross references. These data cross references must be collapsed to product-to-common cross references so that database conversion plans can be developed for moving data from disparate data files to the mature data resource. Any product-to-product cross references are also collapsed if they are involved in database conversion.

Develop Database Conversion Plan

When the mature data resource model is complete, a database conversion plan is developed to convert existing disparate data to the mature data resource. The *database conversion plan* is a plan for building a mature data resource according to the mature data resource model.

Database conversion is usually done as a separate project from data refining. However, it must be done after data refining is completed for all areas of data involved in the transition. A full explanation of database conversion is beyond the scope of this book, but a few guidelines are listed below. A complete description of database conversion techniques is provided in a previous book (Brackett, 1990).

- Identify the scope of database conversion, including the data files and applications involved in the transition.

- Prepare a cross reference of all applications and the data they use to identify the sequence and priority of database conversion.

- Prepare a data flow diagram of the existing and desired data files and related applications within the project scope.

- Locate the data converters between applications and data files. These can convert data until the mature data resource is built and all applications are connected to the mature data resource.

- Locate the database converters between application data files and the mature data resource so application data can be converted to the mature data resource.

- Establish a sequence and priority for implementing data converters and database converters for database conversion.

- Arrange fall-back and recovery procedures to the original database if problems arise.

Data feed tables and data source tables help identify data that are being converted to the mature data resource. A matrix of applications and data is also helpful for developing database conversion plans. An equally critical part of database conversion is identifying the applications that contain data within the application. When an application contains hard-coded data, it is a repository for data and must be involved in the database conversion plan. Developing a matrix requires extensive analysis to identify all data created or used by every application. This difficulty explains why most organizations do not change their existing application data files to subject data files.

If every application and every data file involved in database conversion were a data product that went through the data refining process, all data would be known and cross referenced to the common data architecture. The data cross reference becomes a detailed matrix of applications and data and can be used to develop a database conversion plan. Therefore, the best practice is to include every application and every data file that will be involved in database conversion in the data refining process. In other words, the scope of the data refining process must include all data products that are involved in database conversion.

Database conversion can include deployment of data on a network. Generally, deploying data on a network is done as a separate project after the mature data resource is developed. It is very difficult to convert existing disparate data to a mature data resource and deploy those data on a network at the same time. The odds are in favor of failure. It is much better to convert disparate data to the mature data resource and adjust applications accordingly in one step, then deploy the mature data resource on a network with appropriate application adjustment in a second step.

Build Mature Data Resource

When the database conversion plan is completed, it can be implemented. If the data refining process was correct and the database conversion plan was complete, the conversion of disparate data to the mature data resource will be successful. The ultimate goal of data refining will be achieved and the full benefits of a mature data resource will be realized. Data can be readily shared and fully utilized.

▼ SUMMARY

Data refining is a process that involves identifying and defining disparate data, cross referencing them to the common data architecture, and developing a mature data resource model. Official data variations are designated and data translation schemes are developed between official and non-official data variations. The Data Resource Guide is enhanced, and data sharing is facilitated by the information it contains. Database conversion plans are developed for converting disparate data files to the mature data resource.

A good practice for people involved in data refining is not to rush ahead or make rash decisions. The data refining process is a discovery process that requires thought, analysis, intuition, and patience. People knowledgeable about data must take the time to build a good mature data resource. They must keep an open mind about the way things existed in the past, the way they are today, and the way they should be in the future, so the organization can support itself in a dynamic business environment.

▼ QUESTIONS

The following questions are designed to provide a review of Chapter 14 and to stimulate thought about the formal process of developing a formal data resource that can evolve to a mature data resource.

1. What is the objective of data refining?

2. Why is data refining a discovery process?

3. Why is it difficult to automate the data refining process?

4. What does the Data Preparation Phase accomplish?

5. Why should the scope of data refining include all applications and all data files that will be involved in database conversion?

6. Why is it important to have a base of knowledgeable people to support the data refining process?

7. What does the Data Product Phase accomplish?

8. Why is it important to establish a sequence for refining data products?

9. What does a data file diagram represent?

10. What does a physical data structure chart represent?

11. Why is it important to identify unused data?

12. What types of data integrity rules are usually available for disparate data?

13. Why are data codes difficult to cross reference?

14. Why are cross references validated?

15. Why should a glossary, thesaurus, and lexicon be maintained?

16. Why is it important to identify official data variations?

17. What data translation schemes are developed?

18. How is data sharing facilitated?

19. What is a mature data resource model?

20. What is a database conversion plan?

▼ ▼ ▼ 15

DATA COMPLETENESS

---

*Data completeness is achieved by identifying data needs and
ensuring that data are available to meet those needs.*

Data completeness is the component of data quality that ensures
that a mature data resource contains all the data necessary to support
an organization's business activities. Data completeness can be ensured
by identifying the data needed to support business activities, determining whether those data exist inside or outside the organization, and
acquiring existing data through data sharing. Data that are needed to
support the business, but that do not exist and cannot be acquired
from another organization, must be collected.

Data sharing is a common theme in many organizations today.
Organizations are finding that sharing existing data, exchanging existing data, and cooperating on data collection is a cost-effective way to
obtain data to support their business activities. As resources become
more limited, data sharing will play a major role in ensuring completeness of the mature data resource.

This chapter explains how data completeness is achieved through
data sharing. The identification of broad groupings of data needed to
support business strategies and the identification of broad groupings of
existing data are explained. The identification of detailed data needed
to support business activities and the identification of detailed data
that exist are also explained. The use of templates for identifying existing data and designing new databases is described. The identification of

primary data sources and major data flows is explained. Finally, the problems with sharing and combining data are presented.

▼ DATA COMPLETENESS OVERVIEW

Organizations need data to support their business activities. Identifying those data and ensuring that they are available requires careful planning. Organizations need to begin, or extend, their research operations (institutional research, enterprise analysis, and so on) to analyze and understand their businesses and identify the data needed to support those business activities.

Most organizations have an information system portfolio, a financial portfolio, a client portfolio, and so forth. They need to develop a portfolio of data that are available both inside and outside the organization. A *data portfolio* is meta-data about the data that exist inside and outside the organization that can be accessed and used to support business activities. A comprehensive data portfolio is developed through general data surveys and detailed data inventories.

Inventory Analogy

A traditional data inventory within an organization or across many organizations does not work. It only produces lists of data items based on the organization's view of the real world when the data items were developed. These individual inventory lists cannot be combined into a single data inventory because there is no common base for integration.

Traditional data inventories do not work because there is no common base for integration.

For example, there are several different organizations that keep inventories of plumbing items. Organization A installs plumbing systems and deals with only one-inch pipe, valves, and unions. It is implied within the organization that all items are one-inch steel and that all valves are gate valves. Organization B carries all types of valves, and its interest is only in the types (e.g., gate or ball) and sizes of the valves. It is implied within the organization that all items are steel valves. Organization C carries all types of pipe, and its interest is in size and composition (e.g., steel or copper). It is implied within the organization that all items are pipe.

A traditional inventory of plumbing items from these three organizations would produce three lists that could not be integrated. Organization A's inventory would list the number of pipes, valves, and unions, but would show nothing about size or material. Organization B's inventory would list quantities by size and type of valve, but indicate nothing about the material. Organization C's inventory would list quantities of pipe by size and material, but show nothing about the item. Finding the proper plumbing item from these lists would be difficult and would require additional information. There would be a delay and a loss of productivity.

A common nomenclature provides a base for identifying plumbing parts and for inventorying the items in each organization. Each organization's inventory shows the type of item, the size, the material, and the quantity. The individual inventory lists are easily combined to identify the existence of plumbing items. Development of a common nomenclature requires the participation of all three organizations. It also requires that each organization cross reference its item descriptions to the common nomenclature before the inventories are developed.

Data Inventories

The same situation exists for data. Each organization has its own data naming, data definition, and data structuring conventions. Any data inventories these organizations produce cannot be integrated into a common data inventory, any more than the plumbing inventories above could be integrated. Sharing data from these individual inventories would be as difficult as locating plumbing parts from the individual plumbing inventories.

The common data architecture provides the base for conducting data inventories. It provides formal data names, comprehensive data definitions, and consistent data structure. Data inventories that are conducted within a common data architecture can be easily integrated. Data inventories that are conducted without a common data architecture are less than fully effective and ultimately fail. They may even be detrimental by causing confusion and lowering productivity.

*The common data architecture provides a base for integrating
data inventories.*

There are two levels of data inventories. The highest level is a general *data resource survey* that provides a high-level identification of data needs and data that already exist. It identifies the data needs and existing data by broad data groupings, such as census data, medical data, transportation data, and education data. The lowest level is a detailed *data resource inventory*, which is a detailed inventory of data needs and data that already exist. It identifies specific data subjects and data characteristics, such as the specific data subjects and data characteristics for census data.

A general data resource survey is usually done first to set priorities for conducting detailed data resource inventories. A detailed data resource inventory follows the general data resource survey to identify data needs and existing data in greater detail. These two processes often uncover a hidden data resource of which the organization was not aware, and many of those hidden data could be readily available to the organization.

Data Resource Survey

A data resource survey consists of a data availability survey, a data needs survey, and a data survey analysis. It provides information about broad groupings of data needed to support an organization's business strategies and broad groupings of data that currently exist. Information obtained from the data availability survey is placed in the Data Resource Guide. Information obtained from the data needs survey is compared with information from the data availability survey and used to develop initial data acquisition plans. The diagram in Figure 15.1 shows the data resource survey process.

A data resource survey is a discovery process. Through that process, an organization learns more about its business strategies and the data needed to support those business strategies. It also learns that there are more data available than originally expected. It is easier and less expensive to use existing data than to collect the same data again, even if the existing data are disparate data. It is also easier and less expensive to cooperate with other organizations for collecting new data.

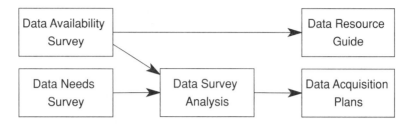

Figure 15.1 *Data resource survey process.*

---
*A data resource survey identifies data needs and existing data
by broad data groupings and business strategies.*

The data resource survey narrows the initial scope of data needs to high-priority baseline data. An organization's total data needs are usually so broad that those needs cannot all be met in the short term. The initial scope of data needs must be narrowed to the critical data that support high-priority business strategies so that available resources can be used to the organization's advantage.

Broad Data Groupings

A general data resource survey is done by broad data groupings. The *broad data groupings* are the categorical levels of data classification. Broad data groupings are used because it is just too difficult to start identifying an organization's data needs and existing data at the data subject and data characteristic levels. There are too many disparate data for people to get involved with when they are trying to identify critical data needs and set priorities. Starting with broad data groupings also helps people understand their data needs better than they would if they started at the data subject and data characteristic level.

---
*The categorical levels of data classification provide the broad
data groupings.*

A portion of the broad data groupings for a water resource survey is shown in Figure 15.2. The Stream Data Area represents all data about

Stream Data Area
    Stream Descriptive Data Group
    Stream Quantity Data Group
    Stream Quality Data Group
        Stream Biological Quality Data Class
        Stream Chemical Quality Data Class
        Stream Physical Quality Data Class

Figure 15.2 *Example of broad data groupings.*

streams and includes data groups for descriptive data, quantity data, and quality data. The Stream Quality Data Group contains data classes for biological data, chemical data, and physical data. Similar classifications exist for other water bodies, such as lakes and reservoirs.

Broad data groupings are identified and defined within the scope of the data resource survey. Usually, two or three levels are sufficient for a data resource survey. The typical data resource survey contains two levels of broad data groupings. Having more than three levels makes the survey more difficult to conduct. It also makes the results more difficult to compile and interpret.

Data Needs Survey

A *data needs survey* identifies an organization's business strategies and the broad groupings of data needed to support those business strategies. Priorities of the business strategies, the data needed to support those strategies, and the degree to which those data needs are met are used to identify critical data, plan the acquisition of data, and develop the organization's data resource. High-priority data needs that support major business strategies become critical data needs, and are further defined in a more detailed data needs inventory. A *critical data need* is a broad grouping of data needed to support a high-priority business strategy that is unmet or only partially met.

A data needs survey identifies business strategies and the broad groupings of data needed to support business strategies.

A data needs survey begins with a definition of the survey scope. The scope includes definition of the business strategies and broad data groupings, and identification of the organizations to be surveyed. A single organization may be involved in the survey, or many organizations may be involved. The business strategies are developed based on mandates, mission, goals, plans, and desires. All organizations, regardless of their missions, have business strategies that can be identified and defined.

A matrix is developed for business strategies and broad data groupings within the scope of the survey. Each cell in the matrix contains an indication of the priority of the data need (high, medium, or low) and the degree to which the data need is already met (fully, partially, or not at all). All data needs, whether or not they are currently met, must be included in the survey. It is a bad practice to exclude data needs that are already met, because data needs change with changing business strategies. Limiting the data resource survey to only data needs that are not met limits the effectiveness of the survey.

Data Availability Survey

A *data availability survey* identifies broad groupings of data that currently exist inside or outside the organization and obtains general information about those data. A data availability survey may be conducted before, during, or after a data needs survey. However, both the data needs survey and the data availability survey must be completed before the data survey analysis begins.

The scope of the data availability survey includes the same broad data groupings used in the data needs survey, because those are the base for comparing data needs with existing data. The organizations to be surveyed should be primary sources of data, and are not always the same organizations as those involved in the data needs survey.

Specific questions are developed within the scope of the data availability survey. The questions are oriented toward the content and meaning of the data, not the formats or physical storage parameters. Information about what the data represent is far more important for identifying critical data than physical are parameters about data storage. The specific questions may vary with the type of survey, but the general approach is the same. Sample questions for a data availability survey are listed in Appendix E.

> *Information collected during a survey must show the content
> and meaning of data, not physical storage parameters.*

During the data availability survey, the broad data groupings may be refined, or new data groupings may be identified. Organizations that indicated any substantial changes in the definitions of their data must be re-surveyed to ensure that their response was correct. If there are new data groupings, any organizations already surveyed must be re-surveyed to determine whether they have data in the new data groupings.

Data Survey Analysis

The *data survey analysis* compares the data needs with the data available to identify groups of data that already exist and groups of data that need to be acquired. It identifies critical data needs based on the priorities identified in the data needs survey. Any data need that is high-priority and unmet is a critical data need. These critical data needs are used to prepare initial data acquisition plans.

> *The data survey analysis identifies critical data that need to be
> acquired for the data resource.*

If all of the data needs are critical, then the data needs survey was not effective because it did not narrow the scope. People who perform data resource surveys must be aware that the survey is a prioritization process to identify critical data needs. Those critical data needs must be less than the total data needs for an organization.

▼ DATA RESOURCE INVENTORY

A data resource inventory consists of a data availability inventory, a data needs inventory, and a data inventory analysis. It provides detailed information about what data are needed to support business activities and what data currently exist. Information obtained from the data availability survey is placed in the Data Resource Guide. It is then compared to information obtained from the data needs inventory and

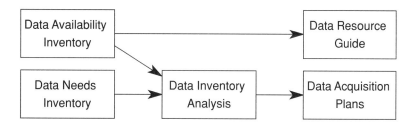

Figure 15.3 *Data resource inventory process.*

used to develop detailed data acquisition plans. The diagram in Figure 15.3 shows the data resource inventory process.

The data groupings used in the data resource inventory are the data subjects and data characteristics that support the critical data needs identified in the data resource survey. They are the baseline data needed to support business activities in the high priority business strategies. They are the first set of data needed to assure completeness of the data resource.

> *A data resource inventory identifies data subjects and characteristics needed to support business activities and indicates the availability of those data.*

A data resource inventory, like a data resource survey, is a discovery process. An organization can discover many more data than it ever expected, both inside and outside the organization, and can then begin to understand how those data can be used to support business activities.

Data Needs Inventory

A *data needs inventory* identifies data subjects and data characteristics needed to support an organization's business activities. Priorities of the business activities, the data needed to support those activities, and the degree to which those data needs are met are used to develop detailed data acquisition plans and populate the organization's data resource. The data needs inventory ensures that baseline data are in the data resource.

> *A data needs inventory identifies and prioritizes the data
> subjects and data characteristics needed to support high-priority
> business activities.*

The scope of the data needs inventory includes the business activities in the high-priority business strategies, the data subjects and characteristics in the broad data groupings that support those strategies, and the organizations that have data available in those broad data groupings. A matrix of these factors is developed. Each cell in the matrix contains an indication of the priority of the data and the degree to which the data need is met.

Data Availability Inventory

A *data availability inventory* identifies the existence of data subjects and data characteristics and obtains detailed information about them. A data availability inventory may be conducted before, during, or after a data needs inventory. However, both the data needs inventory and the data availability inventory must be completed before the data inventory analysis begins.

The scope of the data availability inventory includes identification and definition of data subjects and data characteristics, the business activities supporting high priority business strategies, and the organizations that indicated that they have data. The data subjects and data characteristics are the same as those used in the data needs inventory, because they are the base for comparing data needs against the data available.

When the scope is defined, a few specific questions can be developed. The questions may vary with each survey, but guidelines for generating the questions are listed in Appendix E. The major effort in a data availability survey is in identifying the data needed to support business activities and the existing data, and in defining them with the common data architecture. All of the techniques described earlier for developing a common data architecture and cross referencing existing data to that architecture are also used in this case.

> *The data availability inventory identifies data needs and
> existing data within the common data architecture.*

There is frequently a question as to whether a complete inventory of all data is needed or whether an inventory of existing inventories is better. If the objective is to identify all data within the context of a common data architecture, a complete data resource inventory is necessary. All data are cross referenced to the common data architecture so they can be easily identified and readily shared. However, if the objective is to identify primary data sources and then contact those locations for additional information, an inventory of inventories is appropriate. This approach is often used when there are limited resources that need to be used to maximum benefit.

Data Inventory Analysis

The *data inventory analysis* compares the data needs inventory with the data availability inventory to determine which data subjects and data characteristics exist and which need to be acquired. It identifies baseline data needs based on the priorities identified in the data needs inventory. Any data characteristics that are high-priority and are not available must be acquired to ensure completeness of the data resource.

The data inventory analysis is usually more difficult than the data survey analysis; it requires considerable thought. The detailed data needs are usually summary or derived data with a few primitive data. The existing data are usually primitive data with a few summary or derived data. It helps the data inventory analysis to identify summary data, define the derivation of those summary data, and develop data derivation diagrams. This is one reason that the common data architecture must include all primitive and derived data.

▼ DATA RESOURCE TEMPLATES

Templates can be designed for inventorying existing data, or for designing a new data resource based on official data variations. A *template* is a pattern for forming an accurate copy of an object or shape, or for categorizing an object or shape. A *data template* is a template used to identify existing data in terms of the common data architecture, or to design data based on official data variations.

The process of collecting information through data availability surveys and data availability inventories can be laborious and time-consuming. In many cases, the people who provide the information are busy and don't have time to provide good information. The last thing most people need is another survey form to complete. Therefore, many data resource surveys and inventories are never completed or are completed superficially.

One way to solve these problems is to visit each organization personally and conduct an interview. Visiting people is effective, but it is time-consuming and costly for the collector, and the scope of the project is usually narrowed accordingly. Another way to solve these problems is to develop data templates that can assist people in documenting their data.

Data templates are a good way to get maximum results in a short period of time and at a minimum expense. They increase the awareness and understanding of the person using the template, with respect to both their own data and the ways those data fit into a common context. Data templates are a good technique for leveraging limited resources to achieve a common data architecture.

Data Survey Templates

A *data survey template* is a set of broad data groupings used for data resource surveys. People review their data needs and existing data and check for a match with the broad data groupings. If a match is found, they provide the appropriate information. If a match is not found, the broad data grouping definitions may be enhanced or new broad data groupings may be defined.

Any enhancements or additions to the broad data groupings are only suggestions, and must be reviewed by the lead data architect. The suggestion is compared with suggestions from other organizations and the common data architecture. If the suggestion is valid, it is included in the common data architecture. If it is not valid, it is not included in the common data architecture and the contributor is notified.

> *The broad data groupings should be as complete as possible within the scope of a data resource survey.*

The initial broad data groupings should be as complete as possible. If there are too many missing broad data groupings within the scope of the survey, respondents become discouraged and the survey is not fully effective. It is better to have too many definitions in the data survey template than too few. However, the template should not be so large that it discourages the respondent by the sheer volume of broad data groupings to review. Therefore, the broad data groupings included in the data survey template should be as complete as possible within the scope of the data being reviewed by the respondent.

Data Inventory Templates

A *data inventory template* is a set of common data subject, data characteristic, and data characteristic variation definitions, along with a supporting data thesaurus used for data resource inventories. It is used to identify data needs and existing data in terms of the common data architecture. In some situations, it is helpful to have the cross references between prominent data products and the common data. Many people have already related their data to prominent data products, and including those cross references helps them identify their data in terms of the common data architecture.

People review their data needs and existing data and check for a match with the common data subjects, data characteristics, and data characteristic variations. If a match is found, a cross reference is made between the data and the common data architecture. If a match is not found, a new data subject, data characteristic, or data code is created and the appropriate cross reference is made.

Any additions to the common data architecture are only suggestions, and must be returned to the lead data architect for verification. The lead data architect reviews the suggested additions, checks for similar additions from other organizations, and checks for a match with the common data architecture. If the suggested addition is valid, it is added to the common data architecture. If it is not valid, the appropriate adjustment is made and the contributor is advised of the change. In many cases, the data characteristic or data codes already exist, and the suggestion is simply a variation. Generally, as a data resource inventory progresses, there are fewer new data characteristics and data codes and more variations.

Data Design Templates

A *data design template* is a set of data subjects, official data characteristic variations, and official data codes used to design a specific database.

The template minimizes the effort required to design and develop applications and databases, assists the conversion to official data variations, and increases productivity. It also prevents further proliferation of disparate data and facilitates data sharing. The data design template is packaged in a manner that helps people quickly select data needed for their database and design that database with a minimum of effort.

> *Official data variations provide templates for designing applications and databases.*

Most people are willing to accept existing data definitions rather than prepare new ones. Most people are willing to design their applications and databases based on official data variations. Most people are willing to design their data so they can be shared. Data design templates based on official data variations facilitate development of databases and data sharing.

Data design templates utilize available resources by providing official data variations that eliminate the need to develop things from scratch. They also eliminate the need for additional cross referencing to the common data architecture after the design is complete. When people develop applications and databases that are independent of the common data architecture, they eventually need to cross reference them to the common data architecture. Data design templates are a proactive approach for preventing creation of additional disparate data and facilitating data sharing.

▼ DATA TRACKING

Data tracking is the process of tracking data from their origin to their ultimate destination. Data can be tracked into an information system, between storages and processes within an information system, and out of an information system. They can also be tracked between information systems within an organization and between organizations. Data tracking within information systems is relatively easy with data flow diagrams. Data tracking within large organizations and between organizations is more difficult.

Data tracking within large organizations and between organizations involves the identification of primary data sources, secondary data sources, and major data flows. As data become more readily available and more data are shared, it becomes increasingly important to know the source of data and their true content and meaning. Data tracking shows where data originate, their original content and meaning, and any changes that occur to those data as they move between organizations.

Data Sources

All data originate from a primary data source. A *primary data source* is an organization that initially collects, modifies, or creates data. The primary data source is the record of reference; it is the official version of data. A *secondary data source* is an organization that acquires data from another organization and stores those data without alteration or modification.

Primary data sources are the originators of data.

Data resource surveys and data resource inventories identify primary data sources. Identifying primary data sources encourages people to acquire data from the originator. Acquiring data from the originator ensures consistency of the data and helps prevent any misinterpretation resulting from alteration.

Major Data Flows

A *major data flow* is a data flow between organizations or between major segments of a large organization. Each data flow represents a set of data characteristics moving between organizations at a point in time. Data flows within information systems, and between information systems within an organization, are not identified and documented. They add nothing to the documentation of major data flows.

The data sources and major data flows are documented on a major data flow diagram. A *major data flow diagram* is a variation of the traditional data flow diagram: it represents sets of data moving between major organizational units in a large organization, or between organizations. It does not show processes that create or manipulate data.

Two symbols are used on a major data flow diagram to identify business entities and major data flows. These symbols conform to semiotics and the use of consistent symbols across all models. Primary data sources are identified with bold hexagons, and secondary data sources are identified with normal hexagons. A solid line with an arrow on one end represents a major data flow between organizations. Each major data flow must be uniquely named within the scope of the common data architecture. Each major data flow is documented with a logical data structure chart.

For example, the major data flows among five organizations are shown in Figure 15.4. Each major data flow is uniquely named and the contents of that major data flow are defined with a logical data structure. That logical data structure always contains the common data names, but may also contain the data product names.

A common misconception is that major data flows are linear and that it is therefore relatively easy to track data from the primary data source to their various uses. However, major data flows, particularly in large organization or between organizations, are not linear. They form a network where sets of data are moving in all directions between organizations. A *major data flow network* is a set of major data flows among many organizations, or among many segments of a large organization. It can be used to analyze the flow of data and arrange better data flows from primary data sources. It can also be used to identify multiple points of data derivation and to prevent redundant data derivation.

A major data flow network is not stable: the sets of data are constantly changing. Data are continually being added and removed from major data flows. Documentation of major data flows must be kept current to ensure adequate support of data sharing.

A major data flow network is not the same as an electronic communications network. A major data flow network represents the movement of data between organizations independently of the medium for

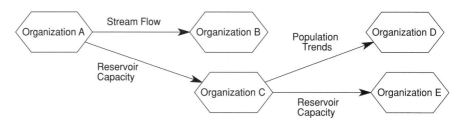

Figure 15.4 *Major data flow diagram.*

that movement. The medium may be a communications network, documents, diskettes, tapes, or any other form of data transfer.

A major data flow network is initially developed during data resource surveys. As organizations are surveyed, their data are identified, defined, and placed on a major data flow network. The primary data sources and major data flows are identified, defined, and added to the major data flow network. As additional major data flows and data storages are identified, or as major data flows change, they are added to the major data flow network. The result is a current, comprehensive major data flow network.

▼ DATA SHARING

The main reason for a common data architecture is to define data in a common context so they can be readily shared. Data sharing helps ensure completeness of an organization's data resource. However, the emphasis on most data sharing today is on the movement of the data, not on the content of the data.

The Medium and the Message

There are two aspects to data sharing: the medium and the message. The *data sharing medium* is the electronic or mechanical method of moving data, such as communication lines, system software, magnetic tapes, diskettes, or paper. It represents the *how* of data sharing. The *data sharing message* is the content and meaning of the data being moved. It represents the *what* of data sharing.

Most data sharing efforts today concentrate on the data sharing medium. They emphasize the mechanism by which data are stored and shared, such as standard database management systems, electronically compatible communications, or tape formats. They emphasize hardware and electronic standards, and assume that when these problems are solved, data will be readily shared. The data sharing medium is emphasized because it is easily comprehensible.

However, the problem with sharing data is not with the data sharing medium. Data sharing is more than electronics, transmission lines, computers, and storage media. Hardware and electronic problems are resolved relatively easily today, and these resolutions will be even easier with open systems and interoperability. Emphasizing the hardware and electronic aspects of data sharing avoids the real problem. The real problem is the data sharing message—what data are being shared.

The data sharing medium is not a major problem.

Current data sharing efforts ignore the content and meaning of data being shared. The situation is much like the installation of a state-of-the-art telephone system between countries where the people do not speak the same language. There is only noise on the line and no information is being exchanged. The problem can be resolved only by using a common language with translations at strategic points.

The real problem is in determining what data are being shared.

Data sharing should be done using official data variations, as explained in the Shared Data Vision chapter. If the contributing and receiving organizations both maintain their data according to the official variations, the data are sent over the sharing medium without change, as shown in Figure 15.5.

If one or both organizations maintain their data in a form other than the official data variations, the data must be translated to the official variations for sharing, as shown in Figure 15.6. Data are translated to the official data variations with the appropriate translation scheme, moved to another organization as official data variations, and translated to the non-official data variations.

It is a bad practice to share data by sending meta-data ahead of the real data. A common approach today is to send meta-data describing the real data, rather than sending data according to the official data variations defined within a common data architecture. The initiating organization prepares meta-data that defines the data being shared.

Figure 15.5 *Sharing official data variations.*

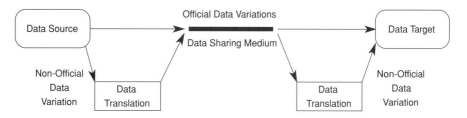

Figure 15.6 *Sharing non-official data variations.*

The receiving organization reads the meta-data and uses it to interpret the actual data.

Data should not be shared based only on accompanying meta-data.

The problem with this approach is that standards need to be established for the meta-data that are sent with the data. This approach can be pursued to absurdity by developing meta-meta-data that defines the meta-data, and so on. The process is very confusing and time-consuming, and can get out of control very quickly. It begs the issue of designating official data variations and sharing data through those official data variations. It allows organizations to ignore their responsibility for developing common data architectures and sharing data within those architectures.

Combining Data

Combining data is a form of data sharing where data from different databases are combined into a single database. Combining data is a trend that will increase as organizations rightsize their hardware, merge, and convert their application databases to subject databases. Even though decentralization and open systems are the trend, well-managed decentralization and robust open systems are not yet available. Central databases still provide the means for accessing large volumes of data from many sources.

Combining data is more than just moving data from existing databases to the new database. It is more than hardware and database man-

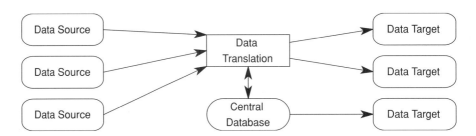

Figure 15.7 *Creating a central database.*

agement system connectivity. Those tasks are relatively easy. Combining data requires careful planning and coordination to ensure that high-quality data are available to meet business needs.

Data are combined through official data variations and data translation schemes. Ideally, the receiving database is structured according to the official data variations. Any data going into that database are translated to the official data variations, as shown in Figure 15.7. If the receiving database is not structured according to the official data variations, it should be buffered by a set of translation schemes so that data coming out of that database are automatically translated to the official data variations to support business activities. Buffering a combined database containing non-official data variations with data translation schemes allows the use of official data variations for business activities, and helps achieve the long-term objective of a mature data resource.

Many contributors to combined databases are concerned about the correct translation of their data to official data variations. They want their variations included in the combined database along with the official variations, just to be sure that the translation was done correctly. Addition of contributors' variations increases the size of that database, and thereby increases the cost of developing and maintaining the database. It also adds a level of confusion because there are two variations of data in the database: the contributor's variation and the official variation. People accessing the database must access the official variation, or the whole concept of a combined database fails.

A combined database must be developed within a common data architecture and with full participation of the contributors.

One approach to solving this problem is to develop a combined database within a common data architecture and involve the contributors in that development. When contributors are involved in developing the combined database within a common data architecture, they understand where their data fits into the overall scheme. When contributors are involved in developing the translation schemes from their data variations to the official data variations, they are more willing to accept the official data variations and less likely to want their own data variations in the combined database. The result is a smaller and more functional combined database.

Preferred Development

The preferred development for new information systems, both databases and applications, is shown in bold in Figure 15.8. Logical models are developed by extracting data definitions and structure from the common data architecture. The common data architecture is enhanced by any new data definitions and structures identified during logical modeling. The logical model is denormalized to a strong physical model that uses common abbreviations for data names. The physical model is then implemented as a structured system. The physical model does not need to be cross referenced to the common data architecture, because the data names can easily be converted back to the formal data names used in the common data architecture.

If denormalization uses independent abbreviations for data names, a weak physical model is developed. It is still implemented as a structured system, but the data need to be cross referenced to the common data architecture so they can be defined in a common context. Data

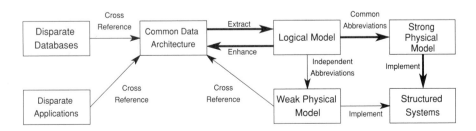

Figure 15.8 *Creating a central database.*

defined in another database or applications developed independently of the common data architecture are considered disparate data; they need to be cross referenced to the common data architecture to ensure that they are defined in a common context. Since cross referencing results in extra work, produces additional documentation, and takes longer for people to understand, the preferred development approach is to build structured systems within the common data architecture.

▼ SUMMARY

Data completeness is an important component of data quality. It ensures that all the data needed to support an organization's business activities are readily available in the data resource. Sharing data is one viable way to ensure the completeness of an organization's data resource.

Ensuring data completeness begins with a high-level data resource survey to identify critical data needs and data available to support those needs. Business strategies and broad data groupings are defined and organizations to be surveyed are identified. The priority of data needs and information about existing data are determined for each business strategy and broad data grouping. Analysis of the data resource survey results in an understanding of the data that are available and the development of initial data acquisition plans.

When the critical data needs are identified, a detailed data resource inventory identifies high priority baseline data to support high priority business strategies. Organizations that have critical data needs identify the data subjects and data characteristics, and organizations that have data available to meet critical data needs identify the data subjects and data characteristics they have available. Analysis of the data resource inventory results in a better understanding of the data available and the development of detailed data acquisition plans.

Data resource templates provide a mechanism for conducting data resource surveys and inventories, as well as for designing databases. Data tracking provides a mechanism to identify primary data sources and major data flows, and to prepare a major data flow network within a large organization or between organizations. This major data flow network is used to plan and manage the acquisition of data in the most productive manner so that completeness of the data resource can be ensured.

Data sharing includes both the the data being shared and the medium by which it is shared. Most efforts concentrate on the sharing medium. However, the sharing medium is not the real problem. The content and meaning of the data being shared are the problem. Effective data sharing efforts must concentrate on the true content and meaning of the data being shared and should be based on the official data variations.

The process of ensuring data completeness should not be ignored. The best data names, data definitions, data structure, data integrity, and data accuracy will fail to produce an effective and efficient data resource if that data resource does not contain all the data needed to support the organization's business activities. An organization must make every effort to analyze its data needs and acquire the data necessary to support those needs.

▼ QUESTIONS

The following questions are designed to provide a review of Chapter 15 and to stimulate thought about sharing data and ensuring the completeness of the mature data resource.

1. Why is data completeness important?

2. Why is it important to identify business strategies?

3. What is a data portfolio?

4. Why have traditional data inventories failed?

5. How can the failure of traditional data inventories be corrected?

6. Why is a data resource survey considered a discovery process?

7. What are broad data groupings?

8. How is a data needs survey conducted?

9. How is a data availability survey related to a data needs survey?

10. How is a data resource inventory related to a data resource survey?

11. What does a data resource inventory provide?

12. What does data tracking provide?

13. What is the difference between a primary and a secondary data source?

14. Why should people go to a primary data source to obtain their data?

15. What is a major data flow?

16. Why do major data flows form a network rather than linear flows?

17. How are data templates useful for promoting data sharing?

18. How are data combined into a central database?

19. What are the two aspects of data sharing?

20. What are the benefits of sharing data?

▼▼▼ 16
SHARED DATA REALITY

People, not technology, make shared data a reality.

This book began with an explanation of the current disparate data situation and the presentation of a shared data vision. The next 14 chapters provided concepts and techniques for achieving the shared data vision and resolving the disparate data situation. This chapter explains how the shared data vision can become a reality.

Data sharing is not really about sharing data. It's about people understanding each other's views of data and the real world those data represent. It's about people using common data to meet different and changing business needs. It's about people working together to refine disparate data into a formal data resource and developing a mature data resource. It's about people combining available resources to meet high demands for information.

The business environment today is very dynamic and very complex. Information needs are high and change rapidly. Financial resources are limited, and most organizations cannot afford to recapture data that already exist, even if they have the necessary resources. Most organizations cannot afford to spend time understanding their own data or someone else's data. The only alternative is to share the knowledge about existing data, build a formal data resource, and share existing data within a common data architecture.

Most of us learned to share in kindergarten, and we have not really forgotten how. We have been victims of circumstances, because the capability to share data wasn't available in the early days of data processing. Without the ability to share data, there was no need to understand someone else's data. Once we were hooked on our own data, it was difficult to start sharing those data because there was no common framework within which to define and share data.

Data sharing is what a common data architecture is all about, and people are what data sharing is all about. This chapter explains how people make data sharing a reality. It's about visions of the future, how people make those visions, and how people achieve those visions. It's about people making data sharing a reality.

▼ PEOPLE AND THE FUTURE

Data sharing can become a reality if people are involved in defining their own futures and developing the technology they need to achieve those future states. People can become involved in defining their futures by understanding the relationships between people and technology, by learning how to invent the future, by understanding the willingness to change and the resistance to change, and by developing clear visions and reasonable horizons.

People and Technology

The biggest problem in information technology today is that technology is advancing too fast for people to keep up. It is time to get people back in sync with technology. It is time to emphasize people at least as much as technology. An emphasis on people does not mean concentrating solely on people and ignoring technology. It means integrating people and technology properly for success.

> *Successful data sharing requires the proper integration of people and technology.*

Most of this book presents the technology for understanding and refining data into a formal data resource, sharing data, and developing a mature data resource. However, there is an underlying theme about the involvement of people in the technology. Business strategies and different views of the real world are people issues, not technology issues.

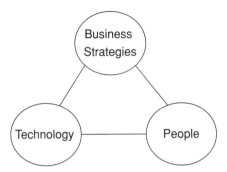

Figure 16.1 *People and technology supporting business strategies.*

Techniques for involving people in the data refining process were presented with an emphasis on drawing people into the data refining process and helping them understand and use their data appropriately.

The diagram in Figure 16.1 shows both people and technology supporting business strategies. The best technology will not support business strategies without the involvement of people, and people cannot carry out business strategies without the support of technology. People can create and improve technology, but technology cannot solve people issues. There needs to be an integration of knowledgeable people and sound technology for the proper support of business strategies.

Inventing the Future

There are only four ways to deal with the future. You can attempt to prevent it or block it, usually with little success. You can simply accept the future and adapt to it. You can predict it, prepare for it, and take advantage of it. Or, you can invent the future you prefer. The latter is the best approach.

There is an old story that planning is the art of uncovering the inevitable, determining how to exploit it, and then taking credit for having brought it all about. Planning the future requires determining what is—or is becoming—obsolete and what will inevitably replace it, and then determining how to make that happen.

Making a real change requires breaking traditional approaches. Real change is not accomplished by squeezing more out of existing technology or by making cosmetic changes. Inventing the future allows people to think the unthinkable and consider new options or alternatives. Considering alternative approaches that help people invent the future they desire is often referred to as *breakthrough thinking*.

Willingness to Change

Most people want to change their current disparate data situation. They see the need for change and would willingly participate in the change. They understand the benefits of change and can usually find the time to contribute to the change. In most situations, they can even find the money to make a change. They just don't know how to make the change without adversely affecting the business.

> *Most people want to change, but don't know how to do it*
> *without adversely affecting the business.*

Most people have the same basic problems with their data. They understand the disparate data syndrome so well that they don't want to hear about it again. They know that the syndrome does not and cannot solve their data problems. They want a better approach without any more failures or any further delays. They just don't know how.

People are caught between *stop the world so we can change in an orderly manner* and *we can't change because we don't have time*. The first of these is not possible, because no organization can stop its business activities for any length of time to get its data organized. The second is not possible either, because the disparate data will only get worse— much, much worse. Organizations must be able to refine their disparate data on-the-fly to survive. In most cases, when people are shown the techniques and are given the skills to use those techniques, they can refine their data into a formal data resource and develop a mature data resource on-the-fly without impacting business operations.

> *Organizations must change their data on-the-fly and must*
> *have short-term cost-effective benefits.*

Changing data on-the-fly is an evolutionary process. It requires a reasonable vision, an acceptable horizon for that vision, and incremental steps to achieve it. The incremental steps must provide tangible, cost-effective benefits to keep the process going and to maintain enthusiasm. A common phrase today is *incrementally cost-effective*, which means that any new approach must pay its own way. Incremental steps also provide the opportunity for small mid-course corrections. An evolutionary approach is contrary to the traditional high-cost, long-term approach that has few intermediate benefits.

Resistance to Change

Even though people are willing to change, there is always some resistance to change. The resistance exists because most people are unsure of new approaches, particularly new information technology approaches, and this uncertainty usually causes anxiety and apprehension. There have been so many "snake-oil cures" and so much vendor hype in information technology without significant results that most people are very skeptical of any new approaches.

> *Resistance to change is due to uncertainty about the outcome of new approaches.*

People do not want to be pioneers again, because pioneers get arrows. Most people have already had enough arrows during their information technology careers. They come up with many excuses for why their data cannot be shared. Most of these excuses are symptoms of a more basic problem: resistance to change. Resistance to change is due to uncertainty about the outcome of approaches, and uncertainty is a very frightening thing to most people. Therefore, acceptance of any new approach must begin with a thorough understanding of that approach and what it will accomplish.

People are comfortable with existing approaches, and that comfort keeps them from seeing what is really happening today and what could happen in the future. If existing technology is successful, it can block a vision of the future and the development of new approaches. In many ways, existing technology is like an old pair of shoes that fit well and are comfortable, but need to be replaced.

Most people don't understand new approaches because the outcome of the new ideas usually does not match their expectations. New approaches create uncertainty, anxiety, and apprehension. There is a concern that they will slow things down or bring them to a stop. The successes, large or small, of existing technology guarantee nothing about new approaches or future outcomes. New approaches can also create expectations that exceed the capabilities of those approaches. Any plan to implement a new approach must deal with both uncertainty and expectations.

Visions of the Future

A thorough understanding of a new approach begins with a vision of the future. Most people are overwhelmed by the future. Many people are so overwhelmed by the present that they can't even think of the future, let alone be overwhelmed by it. However, the future isn't something that just happens. It is something that people invent and make happen.

A new approach can block its own implementation by being unclear. People must have a clear vision and understanding of where a new approach is taking them. They must understand the concept and the process to achieve a preferred future. The vision must increase discomfort with the current approach and increase the desirability of a new approach so that the new approach is the path of least resistance to the future.

> *Understanding a new approach begins with a clear vision of the future.*

Inventing the future requires thinking in the future tense and preparing a vision of the future desired state. The vision is an image of what things will be like when we get there. It is a real, vivid, colorful picture of the outcome of a new approach. It begins by unfolding new concepts and reducing uncertainty about a new approach. It eases people through a new approach by building successes, thus increasing enthusiasm to overcome resistance to change. A good, clear vision attracts proponents who help achieve the vision.

A good vision provides clear outcomes of a new approach and starts a plan to achieve those outcomes. It describes the current state, the future state, and the incremental steps to get from the current state to the future state. A vision is periodically enhanced and the steps are constantly adjusted to achieve the vision. Barriers and roadblocks are frequently encountered, and day-to-day shifts are needed to achieve the vision. These small corrections at frequent intervals provide greater benefits than quantum corrections at infrequent intervals.

Horizons

Painting a clear vision of the future is only the first step to achieving that vision. The next step is establishing a reasonable horizon for the vision. A horizon can be too close or too far away. If the horizon is too close, it is assumed to be rigid, and there is little effort to make a change because the future is inevitable. If the horizon is too far away, it is fantasy, and there is little effort to make the change because it is not achievable. A good horizon must be far enough away to be challenging and close enough to be realistic.

Establishing a reasonable horizon is not always easy, because each person's horizon is different. A horizon that challenges one person may be inevitable for another person. A horizon that is realistic and achievable for one person may be unrealistic and unachievable for another person. Establishing a reasonable horizon is difficult, but must include as many people as possible.

> *Picking the proper horizon for a vision is a difficult but crucial task.*

A reasonable horizon for achieving any information technology vision is between five and ten years. Generally, people find it easy to think five years in the future, but difficult to think ten years in the future. A good guideline is to pick a horizon that matches what people can easily remember about the past. If people cannot remember the environment ten years ago, they generally cannot understand the future ten years away. If people can readily remember the environment five years ago, they can easily understand the future five years away.

Another approach is to develop two horizons. The nearest horizon is more realistic and more detailed, but is not inevitable. The farthest horizon is more challenging and less detailed, but still realistic. A good guideline for implementing a common data architecture and building a mature data resource is to have a five-year horizon and a ten-year horizon. Most people can perceive the future within the time frame between those two horizons.

▼ GETTING PEOPLE INVOLVED

There are several ways to get people involved in understanding and accepting a new approach. One way is to paint a vivid vision of the future and establish a reasonable horizon for that vision. Other ways are to use acceptable terms, acceptable documentation, and acceptable support tools to help people understand and use a new approach.

Acceptable Terms

Success of a new approach is enhanced with the use of terms that are acceptable to people. The wrong term can turn people away and lead to failure, and the correct term can draw people in and lead to success. Throughout this book, terms acceptable to most people were used.

> *Terms that attract people and increase understanding should be used.*

Data subject and *data characteristic* are used rather than *data entity* and *data attribute* to emphasize the development of a common data architecture and a formal data resource that are based on subjects in the real world. *Data product* is used to refer to all products that have been developed that reference data in some way, such as programs, reports, screens, databases, and data dictionaries.

Client is used rather than *user*. There are only two cultures left where the term *user* is common: data processing and drugs. If you think about it, there are many similarities between the two cultures. Changing the term can break the similarities and help implement a new approach.

Approved, adopted, and *standard* represent a formal review process and a finality that does not allow change. They suggest mandates from a regulatory authority and are not used. *Accepted, common,* and *official* represent the best information available and the option to change when additional information is available. They suggest concurrence from below and are more acceptable terms. These latter terms also avoid the potential problem of making mandates from a regulatory authority a non-standard. The mandate still remains a standard, but is considered non-official in the common data architecture.

Re-engineering suggests the need for a strong mathematical background and a college degree. It also implies that something was engineered in the first place, which may not be true. *Remodeling* is more acceptable to most people because they have probably remodeled something in their own lives, such as a house, deck, car, or boat. They know how to approach a remodeling task, and they often know the problems and uncertainties involved in a remodeling effort. *Refining* is even more acceptable because it more accurately represents the situation of converting crude data into unique products that can be stored and used when needed.

The words used in data names should also reflect the current environment. For example, *gender* should be used rather than *sex*, *race* should be used rather than *ethnicity*, and *disability* should be used rather than *handicap*. The use of current words in data names helps draw people into the common data architecture.

People involved in implementing a common data architecture and developing a mature data resource should be aware of terms and use them appropriately. They should pick terms that promote understanding and acceptance. They should avoid terms that turn people away.

Acceptable Documentation

Acceptable documentation of the common data architecture and the formal data resource helps overcome uncertainty and resistance. Acceptable documentation draws people in, and unacceptable documentation turns people away. Having documentation that is acceptable to people is just as important as having technically correct documentation. If documentation is technically correct but unacceptable, it will not be used, and data sharing will therefore be less than completely successful.

Documentation must be technically correct and acceptable to people for data sharing to be successful.

The whole purpose of good documentation is to provide information to people about their data. However, much of the documentation produced today, although technically correct, is very difficult to understand. People spend more time deciphering the documentation than they do working with their data. This situation must be changed if data sharing is to become a reality.

Paper is an acceptable form for documentation, although it may be bulky and difficult to manage. When people are beginning to understand and refine their data, paper documentation is an excellent way to start. They can copy it, refer to it, write on it, and take it with them. Far more people still use Webster's dictionary in book form than in electronic form.

When people understand their data and the data refining process, the documentation can be maintained by some tool, such as a Data Resource Guide. However, the documentation tool must be *client-friendly*. People should not have to purchase expensive hardware and software and undergo extensive training just to access documentation. Also, a documentation tool must not be viewed as a cure-all for disparate data. People must understand that disparate data cannot just be dumped into a documentation tool and automatically refined.

Documentation tools are only support tools, not a panacea.

The best approach is to select a documentation tool that helps people get enthused, involved, and committed to refining and sharing data. Then, as people understand their data and the data refining process, documentation can be automated in a form that is more efficient. The orientation should be toward getting people involved in data refining and data sharing, rather than letting them do their own thing and create more disparate data.

A good documentation tool should have a variety of features to help people get involved. It should provide data descriptions, data variations, cross references, and data structure. It should include models and diagrams, as well as text. It should provide a way for people to browse the documentation at their leisure to get an understanding of the common data architecture. It should provide a thesaurus to locate specific data, a lexicon of common words used to name data, and a glossary of words, terms, and abbreviations. It should provide tutorials and on-line help to guide people through the documentation.

> *Acceptable documentation of the common data architecture is*
> *mandatory to the realization of a shared data reality.*

Development of good documentation is the responsibility of the data architect, who should have substantial input from the client community. The data architect must be the facilitator and coordinator for the acquisition and dissemination of the data documentation. He or she must provide training on the documentation and how to effectively use that documentation to understand and share data, and must ensure that the documentation is readily available to everyone.

Development of good documentation must involve people with good interpersonal communication skills. These people must be able to use text and diagrams to provide information about an organization's data resource. They must be able to build navigation mechanisms to assist people in using the documentation. They must maximize the transfer of knowledge from the documentation tool to clients.

Acceptable Tools

Computer aided system engineering (CASE) tools are prominent in many organizations for developing information systems and managing data. However, they are not a panacea for achieving the shared data reality. CASE is often viewed as a quick-fix solution to existing problems. People believe they can just dump in the required data and CASE will automatically maintain all the applications and databases, requiring no more maintenance and no more backlog.

The situation is reminiscent of an anecdote about a lady who entered a department store and saw an advertisement about a new product that cut housewives' work in half. She immediately ran to the counter and bought two.

CASE is leading people who don't know where they are going. CASE is only effective if it supports a formal approach that helps people understand what is being accomplished. Without a formal approach and an understanding of the outcome, CASE only perpetuates past practices faster than before.

CASE is expensive to acquire, implement, and use. Hardware and software must be purchased and people must be trained. Many CASE products are labor-intensive, not easy to use, and require a long learning curve. Many CASE products are too rigid and do not allow for the discovery that produces meaningful results in a reasonable time. Many projects take too long and produce poor results because people are concentrating on the tool, not on the business and the data needed to support the business.

CASE is getting better, but it is not complete. It works well for developing new databases and new applications at the project level in a structured environment. It does not work well for refining the disparate data or for developing organization-wide or inter-organization data architectures. In most organizations, 80 percent or more of the effort is maintenance of existing systems and databases that are unstructured or semi-structured. CASE does not provide support for this effort.

CASE does not provide support for refining disparate data.

A new set of Computer Assisted Data Engineering (CADE) tools needs to be developed to assist the data engineering effort. The Shared Data Vision chapter explained the concept of data engineering and information engineering. It presented the concept of CASE for supporting information engineering and CADE for supporting data engineering. The development of robust CADE tools to support data refining is the only way that disparate data can be refined into a formal data resource and data sharing can become a reality.

▼ ACHIEVING A SHARED DATA REALITY

A shared data reality is achieved when people understand the current situation, invent the future, and get involved in making the future happen. It is achieved when they understand the business and the data needed to support the business, involve knowledgeable clients in defining and developing a formal data resource, and combine from-above and from-below approaches to achieve a win–win situation.

Business Understanding

The business activities and the data needed to support business activities must be thoroughly understood to make data sharing a reality.

Terms like *business driven, business focused, business oriented,* and *business supporting* all require essentially the same thing: an understanding of the business. The data resource must be developed based on business needs derived from the business strategies. A strategic data resource plan must directly support a strategic business plan.

However, there are situations where no strategic business plan exists. It is easy to rationalize that if there is no business plan, there is no reason to develop a formal data resource. However, this rationalization does not work. It only allows the current disparate data situation to get worse. It is better to develop a formal data resource to meet critical data needs and extend that data resource as necessary when a strategic business plan is available. In many situations, a good data resource plan helps initiate development of a strategic business plan, because it gives people a better understanding of the business world.

A thorough business understanding helps achieve a shared data reality.

Another approach to developing a formal data resource when there is no strategic business plan is to determine what information is required to meet a need or resolve an uncertainty and what data are needed to produce that information. This determination requires an analysis of current data needs. Then, the existing data that meet those data needs are identified through data resource inventories and data resource surveys. The unmet data needs identify data that need to be acquired or collected.

This *data needs approach* is effective if the proper business activities are included in determining business data needs. Ideally, critical or strategically important business areas are selected first. A business data needs approach is not effective if non-strategic or non-critical business areas are selected.

An excellent way to ensure that data sharing becomes a reality is to establish a partnership between information technology and the business. The partnership develops business strategies and defines initiatives to carry out those strategies. It allows adjustment of the strategies to meet the dynamic business environment. It creates a belief in the business that acts as a self-fulfilling prophecy to ensure the success of that business.

The theme of a successful partnership is that *you must understand my business to get my business.* That is the basic problem with many data administration units today. They do not understand the business, nor do they want to. Their approach is a data technology, and the business must fit within that technology. These units will continue to fail until they use data technology to support the business in terms that clients understand. They must not hide their data technology in jargon and mystique.

A partnership should also be established between data engineering and information engineering. Data engineering must be oriented toward identifying disparate data and refining them to a formal data resource within a common data architecture. Information engineering must be oriented toward using the formal data resource to produce information to meet a changing business environment. A strong partnership between data engineering and information engineering ensures that the proper data are available in the formal data resource to support information engineering.

Client Involvement

Achieving a business orientation requires a *client-focused approach.* A client focus requires direct involvement of people to fully utilize the knowledge they have about business activities and data that support those activities. It follows the principle that *involvement leads to commitment, which leads to acceptance, which leads to success.* When clients are directly involved, they develop a common data architecture to meet their business needs, they understand that architecture, and they readily accept it and use it to accomplish their business activities.

Direct client involvement is one key to a shared data reality.

When clients are directly involved in developing a common data architecture and building a formal data resource, they begin to convert their data more quickly than when mandates are issued. If clients are not directly involved, they begin to block the efforts at change, effectively promoting continuation of the existing disparate data situation. Clients who are not involved can find many reasons that a formal data resource cannot be developed. Therefore, clients must be encouraged to become involved in development of a common data architecture to ensure the project's success.

From-Above and From-Below

A formal data resource is developed using both from-above and from-below approaches. A *from-above approach* provides the strategic directions through identification of organization clusters and critical areas within each cluster. It establishes priorities and ensures the effectiveness of the common data architecture and the mature data resource, as shown in Figure 16.2. The *from-below approach* provides the baseline data for the critical areas. It fills in the detail and ensures efficiency by gaining consensus from people knowledgeable about the data. Both approaches enhance the common data architecture, leading to development of the mature data resource.

One approach to developing a common data architecture is to identify organizational clusters that have similar business activities and share similar data. These clusters may be within one large organization or across multiple organizations. Critical areas are identified in each organizational cluster, based on problems that are affecting business operations. Baseline data are identified in each critical area, and a common data architecture is built for those baseline data. This approach provides the 20 percent of the data that meets 80 percent of the business needs.

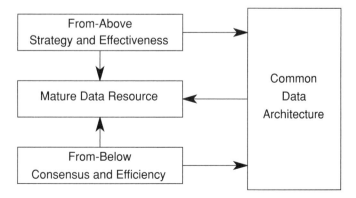

Figure 16.2 *Combining from-above and from-below approaches.*

*Strategy from above and consensus from below help achieve a
shared data reality.*

This *critical area approach* provides the short-term, cost-effective benefits that make the common data architecture successful. It provides the success necessary to reduce resistance and increase enthusiasm about a common data architecture. It produces a strategic data architecture because the critical areas represent core business activities. The strategic data architecture also provides an incentive to start developing a strategic business plan or develop a better strategic business plan.

A Win–Win Situation

Combining the from-above approach and the from-below approach ensures a win–win situation, as shown in Figure 16.3. If a mandate is issued from a regulatory authority, it is a win for that authority, but a loss for clients because they were not involved and their knowledge was not considered. A mandate increases resistance. If independent actions are allowed, it is a win for clients because they get exactly what they want in the short term, but a loss for the organization because an understanding of the business and support for business strategies are lost. Combining strategic direction from above and implementation from below ensures a win for both the organization and the clients.

Although a mandate may appear to work, it has a lower probability of success, and will usually fail in the long term because it does not involve a consensus of knowledgeable people. Including consensus may take longer, but it has a higher probability of being successful. Therefore, a combination of from-above strategy and from-below consensus ensures success.

	Executive	Client
Mandate	Win	Lose
Consensus	Win	Win
Independence	Lose	Win

Figure 16.3 *Creating a win–win situation.*

▼ ROBUST DATA SHARING ARCHITECTURE

The common data architecture contains components for formally naming and comprehensively defining data, for properly structuring data, for assuring high-quality data through integrity, accuracy, and completeness, and for adequately documenting data. These four components are also applied to the new approach for data refining and data sharing. A whole new set of concepts, terms, and techniques were developed to establish a common data architecture, refine disparate data to a formal data resource within that common data architecture, develop a mature data resource, and make data sharing a reality.

The concepts, terms, and techniques introduced in this book are formally named and comprehensively defined, both in the text and in the Glossary. The techniques are properly structured to provide a formal process for refining disparate data into a formal data resource and for developing a mature data resource starting with critical data needs. A high-quality data resource is ensured by maintaining the integrity of the data refining process, making sure that disparate data are accurately represented in the common data architecture, and providing a data refining process that leads from disparate data to a mature data resource. The whole approach is adequately documented in this book and is readily available to anyone interested in making data sharing a reality.

▼ SUMMARY

Data sharing is really about people, not data. People use data, people need data, and people share data. Traditional data sharing efforts do not concentrate on people. They do not concentrate on the content and meaning of data that people need to use the data properly. They do not concentrate on business needs and client involvement. They concentrate on hardware, database management systems, and media for data sharing.

To change this tradition and concentrate on people sharing data to meet their needs, a new approach was developed. However, implementing the new approach is difficult because of the comfort with the existing approach and the uncertainty of a new approach. Many people are unwilling to change because of this uncertainty. Successfully implementing a new approach requires a clear vision, a reasonable horizon, and an explanation of the outcome that reduces the uncertainty and increases the willingness to change.

The common data architecture is an approach that makes shared data a reality. Ensuring the success of that shared data reality requires a business understanding. Business strategies must drive development of an organization's data resource if it is to support the business. A client focus ensures a business understanding, because people perform the business activities. Acceptable terms help draw people into the new approach and reduce uncertainty. Acceptable documentation also helps people understand the new approach, and to use the common data architecture to its full advantage. Acceptable support tools ensure that people design, develop, and manage data properly within the common data architecture.

People cannot continue operating efficiently or effectively with the existing disparate data situation because it will only get worse. There is a window of opportunity to implement a new approach before the volume of disparate data gets any larger. The window of opportunity extends from today until open systems and interoperability are common. When open systems and interoperability are readily available, data will be rapidly decentralized in whatever form they exist at that time. If that form is disparate data, the disparate data situation may never be corrected.

The common data architecture and the data refining process provide a base for solving the disparate data situation and achieving a shared data reality. They provide a foundation for managing data within and between organizations. They allow autonomous development of databases and information systems within a common framework. They help people achieve a preferred future, utilize available resources to achieve that future, and ensure early returns on their investment in that future.

Achieving a shared data reality requires executive support, an architect with vision, and engineers to manage the details. It requires visionaries, architects, engineers, change agents, cheerleaders, facilitators, coordinators, integrators, champions, executives, managers, and clients to move from disparate data to a mature data resource. It requires a partnership of people working together.

▼ QUESTIONS

The following questions are designed to provide a review of Chapter 16 and to stimulate thought about making shared data a reality.

1. What is data sharing all about?

2. Why has traditional data sharing not been successful?

3. What is necessary to make data sharing successful?

4. Why are most people willing to change?

5. What is keeping most people from changing?

6. Why are people resistant to accepting a new approach?

7. How can this resistance be overcome?

8. How does a vision help overcome resistance?

9. How are a vision and a horizon related?

10. Why is a reasonable horizon important?

11. What are acceptable horizons for a vision?

12. How does a understanding the business help achieve the vision?

13. How does client involvement help achieve the vision?

14. Why are acceptable terms important?

15. Why is acceptable documentation important?

16. What is meant by acceptable support tools?

17. What is the difference between a from-above and a from-below approach?

18. How is a win–win situation created?

19. Why is there such a strong emphasis on people?

20. How are the data architecture components applied to the new approach?

▼ POSTSCRIPT
▼
▼

There is considerable talk today about the establishment of standards for using information technology within an organization. There is also considerable talk about using information technology to enhance creativity and innovation. The problem faced by many organizations is that overly rigid standards limit creativity and innovation, while an absence of standards allows creativity and innovation but leads to fragmentation and incompatibility.

Rigid standards imply mandates, compliance, and penalties. They limit creativity and innovation by making everyone conform to a set way of doing things. Without the opportunity to try new technology, experiment, and learn, there is no advancement and no competitive advantage. However, a lack of standards causes fragmentation and increased maintenance, and a loss of productivity. It also limits creativity by allowing too many possibilities and options.

How can an organization control fragmentation, prevent incompatibility, improve productivity, promote creativity and innovation, and increase its competitive advantage, all at the same time?

The answer lies in creating enough standards to provide a foundation for productivity, creativity, and innovation. The standards must set a nominal base and limit experimentation by the mainline workforce so the workforce can accomplish its tasks in a productive manner. They must also create a positive environment for creativity and innovation through experimentation by selected individuals. The right level of standards increases competitive advantage by ensuring the productivity of the workforce and allowing new technology to be explored.

Organizations must constantly review and adjust their standards so that those standards ensure the desired competitive advantage and productivity. They must find the right level of technology and rate of introducing new technology to meet their missions. Organizations that find the right level of standards are those that will compete and succeed.

▼ APPENDIX A
DATA RESOURCE LEXICON

▼ DATA SUBJECT WORDS

Common words can be defined for data subject names. These common data subject words are largely dependent on the type of data an organization has in its data resource, and will vary between organizations. Below is a list of common data subject words that can be defined by an organization.

Account A data subject for tracking and managing Moines, such as Customer Account.

Activity A data subject for actions or transactions that are pending, such as Customer Account Activity. Generally, a subordinate data subject.

Authority A data subject for approval or delegation, such as Expenditure Authority.

Authorization A data subject showing approval or delegation, such as Employee Account Authorization.

Budget A data subject for planned monetary or effort expenditure, such as Yearly Budget.

Category A data subject representing a classification or grouping of objects, usually higher than Class or Group, such as Equipment Category. The hierarchy should be common for the organization, such as Category, Group, Class.

Class   A data subject representing a class of objects, such as Facility Class. The hierarchy should be common for the organization, such as Category, Group, Class.

Detail   A data subject containing details about a parent data subject, such as Customer Account Activity Detail.

Exemption   A data subject containing an exclusion or different situation, such as Tuition Exemption.

Expense   A data subject for expenses, such as goods or services, or for Moines expended, such as Equipment Expense.

Group   A data subject representing a specific grouping of objects, such as Building Group. The hierarchy should be common for the organization, such as Category, Group, Class.

History   A data subject for historical information, such as Customer Account History.

Image   A data subject containing graphic images of documents in an imaging system, such as Purchase Order Image. Generally not used for remote sensing or satellite imaging.

Income   A data subject for income data, such as Client Income.

Integrity   A data subject containing integrity rules for a corresponding data subject, such as Employee Integrity.

Inventory   A data subject for tracking and managing objects, such as Part Inventory.

Item   A data subject of individual objects that are part of another object, such as Purchase Order Item.

Layer   A data subject representing a specific layer of data in a geographic information system (GIS) consisting of lines, points, and polygons, such as Soil Layer.

Month   A data subject representing data for a month, such as Employee Month.

Project   A data subject for grouping events, tasks, people, Moines, and so on, such as Service Project.

Quarter   A data subject representing data for a quarter, such as Equipment Maintenance Quarter.

Rate   A data subject representing monetary or other rates, such as Service Rate.

Revenue   A data subject for income or Moines received, such as Sales Revenue.

Status   A data subject representing the status of objects, such as Project Status.

Summary   A data subject of summary data above a detailed operational level, such as Employee Leave Summary. Usually used in an executive information system (EIS).

Suspense   A data subject for items held for a specific purpose or action, usually pending resolution of a problem, such as Account Activity Suspense.

Text   A data subject containing textual information that can be searched in a variety of ways for words, phrases, content, meaning, conclusions, and so on, such as Contract Text. Usually used in a text information management system (TIMS).

Type   A data subject representing types of objects, such as Equipment Type.

Validation   A data subject for verification or proof of a combination of objects, such as Equipment Part Validation.

Week   A data subject representing data for a week, such as Project Week.

Year   A data subject representing data for a year, such as Equipment Year.

▼ DATA CHARACTERISTIC WORDS

Common words can be defined for data characteristic names. These common data characteristic words are more common between organizations and are not as dependent on the type of data an organization has in its data architecture. The list below is an example of common data characteristic words that can be defined by an organization.

Altitude The distance above or below a specific datum (reference point), such as sea level.

Amount A monetary quantity in some type of currency, such as dollars. Not a count or a capacity.

Area A two-dimensional measurement of an object. Not a region, district, or other geographical area.

Balance The quantity or amount remaining, such as dollars in an account or parts in an inventory.

Capacity The maximum content of an object. Similar to Volume. Not used for monetary quantities.

Centuries A time interval, elapsed time, or duration in centuries. Not a point in time.

Code Alphabetic or numeric coded data values that indicate the existence of a code table data subject. Should not be used if data values are not coded.

Comment A textual comment about an object. Similar to Description, Explanation, Remark, and Text.

Constant A numerical value that does not change over time or circumstances and is used in one or more calculations. Not the same as a Literal.

Count The number of objects that exist or have occurred. Not the same as Amount or Number.

Date A point in time.

Day A number representing a point in time.

Days A time interval, elapsed time, or duration in days.

Depth A one-dimensional measurement below a specified plane, such as below the ground. Not the same as Altitude.

Description A textual description of an object. Similar to Comment, Explanation, Remark, and Text.

Distance   A one-dimensional measurement between two points.

Duration   A time interval or duration representing an elapsed time or the length of time an event lasted.

Explanation   A textual explanation about an object. Similar to Comment, Description, Remark, and Text.

Flag   An indication that some event has happened or should happen. A binary situation, such as on/off, true/false, 0/1, or yes/no. Similar to Indicator.

Height   A one-dimensional measurement above a specified plane, such as a person's height. Not the same as Altitude.

Hour   A number representing a point in time. Must have an associated date for meaning.

Hours   The time interval, elapsed time, or duration in hours.

Identifier   A unique alphanumeric identification of an object. Generally not just a number.

Indicator   An indication of two possible conditions. A binary situation, such as on/off, true/false, 0/1, or yes/no. Similar to Flag.

Label   A textual phrase that provides a distinctive designation for an object. Similar to Name and Title.

Length   A one-dimensional measurement of an object.

Literal   An alpha or alphanumeric value that does not change over time or circumstances. Not the same as a Constant.

Minute   A number representing a point in time. Must have an associated hour and date to be meaningful.

Minutes   A time interval, elapsed time, or duration in minutes.

Month   A number representing a point in time.

Months   A time interval, elapsed time, or duration in months.

Name   A textual phrase that provides a distinctive designation for an object. Similar to Label and Title.

Number   A number that identifies an object. Not an Amount, Capacity, Code, or Quantity.

Percent   A number that represents a ratio between two objects, based on 100.

Price   A monetary amount charged for an object.

Quantity   The capacity or amount of something other than money. Not a Value, Amount, or Number.

Quarter   A number representing a point in time.

Quarters   A time interval, elapsed time, or duration in quarters.

Ratio   A number that represents a ratio between two objects. Not the same as Percent.

Remark   A textual remark about an object. Similar to Comment, Description, Explanation, and Text.

Second   A number representing a point in time. Must have an associated date, hour, and minute to be meaningful

Seconds   A time interval, elapsed time, or duration in seconds.

Sequence   A word showing the sequence of a set of objects. Usually used with another common word, such as Number or Character.

Size   A number indicating the extent of an object.

Status   A textual remark about the status of an object.

Text   A free-form string of text, usually unstructured or unformatted. Similar to Comment, Description, Explanation, and Remark. It may be implied in other common words like Description, Explanation, and so on.

Title   A textual phrase that provides a distinctive designation for an object. Similar to Label and Name.

Value   A monetary value that indicates the worth of something in some type of currency. Not the same as Amount.

Volume   The capacity of an object. Similar to Capacity.

Week   A number representing a point in time.

Weeks   A time interval, elapsed time, or duration, in weeks,

Width   A one-dimensional measurement of the breadth of an object.

Year   A number representing a point in time.

Years   A time interval, elapsed time, or duration in years.

▼ DATA CHARACTERISTIC VARIATION WORDS

Common words can be defined for data characteristic variations. These common data characteristic variation words are common between organizations and are not dependent on the type of data an organization has in its data architecture. Below is a list of common data characteristic variation words that can be defined by an organizlation.

Acres, **Square Feet**, **Hectares**, and so on, for variations to areas.

Complete, **Abbreviated**, **Short**, **Long**, and so on, for different lengths of names, titles, labels, and so on.

Cubic Inches, **Gallons**, **Yards**, and so on, for variations in volumes.

Dollars, **Yen**, and so on, for variations to monetary data characteristics, such as Amount, Price, Value, and so on.

Estimated, **Measured**, **Actual**, and so on, for variations in method of determining values.

Inches, **Feet**, **Miles**, **Meters**, and so on, for variations to lengths, distances, heights, widths, and so on.

Irregular   Indicates a data characteristic whose contents have no consistent format or meaning—that is, it varies from one data characteristic to another.

Multiple   Indicates that the contents may have multiple values, such as several dates or several people's names.

Normal, **Inverted**, and so on, for different sequences within a data characteristic.

Variable for a data characteristic that contains different data characteristics depending on the circumstances.

▼ DATA DEFINITION WORDS

Common words can be defined for data definitions. These common data definition words are common between organizations. Below is a list of common data definition words that can be defined by an organization.

Code Table   Used with a data subject definition to indicate that it contains a set of data codes, such as *A code table data subject...* .

Combined   Indicates that a data characteristic is formed from a combination of two or more single data characteristics, such as *A combined data characteristic consisting of....*

Maximum   Indicates that a data characteristic format has a maximum number of positions, but that all do not need to be used, such as *A maximum 32-character name....* If Maximum is not used, it implies that all positions must be filled.

Parent   Used with a data subject definition to indicate that it is a parent of a subtype, such as *It is the parent of....*

Subtype   Used with a data subject definition to indicate that it is a subtype of a parent data subject, such as *It is a subtype of....*

Virtual   Used with a data subject definition to indicate a virtual data subject, such as *A virtual data subject....*

▼ APPENDIX B
DATA DEFINITION EXAMPLES

▼ DATA SUBJECT AND CHARACTERISTIC

EMPLOYEE

Any **Person** who works for another in exchange for financial compensation. A State Employee is any person employed by the State who receives compensation directly from the State. A State Employee is normally required to follow merit system rules, unless the **Position** held is specified as being exempt from such rules. Each occurrence represents a Person employed by the State.

Employee Anniversary Date CYMD

The **Date CYMD** the Employee originally entered State service. For DOP Employees this date is adjusted forward by leave without pay.

Employee Birth Date CYMD

The **Person Birth Date CYMD** of an Employee.

Employee Last Separation Date CYMD

The **Date CYMD** on which the Employee was last separated from State service—that is, the most recent separation from State Service.

Employee Name Abbreviated Normal

The **Person Name Abbreviated Normal** for an Employee.

Employee Name Complete Inverted

The **Person Name Complete Inverted** for an Employee.

Employee Name Complete Normal

The 20-character **Person Name Complete Normal** for an Employee.

Employee Personal Holiday Indicator

A 1-character indicator showing whether an Employee has taken his/her Personal Holiday for the **Calendar Year**.

- Y indicates that he has taken his Personal Holiday

- N indicates that he has not taken his Personal Holiday.

Employee Phone Number Complete Home

The **Phone Number Complete** where an Employee resides.

Employee Phone Number Complete Work

The **Phone Number Complete** where an Employee works.

Employee Social Security Number

The **Person Social Security Number** for an Employee. This number is required for all State employees.

POSITION

A specific post of employment. A group of duties and responsibilities normally assigned to an **Employee**. A Position may be filled or vacant, full-time or part-time, seasonal, temporary, or permanent. Each occurrence represents a specific Position in a **State Agency**.

Position Established Date CYMD

The **Date CYMD** the position was established and available for assignment.

Position Number

A four-digit number assigned to identify a specific position within a State merit system. Every Position within a specified **State Agency** and a specified State merit system has a four-digit number that is unique to that position within a specific agency and merit system. Only merit systems number one (DOP) and five (MARINE) currently use Position Numbers within the State.

Position Seasonal FTE

The number of Full Time Equivalents (FTEs) allowed for a seasonal Position.

Position Seasonal Start Month

The **Month Number Calendar Year** that a seasonal Position is available for employment.

Position Title

The maximum 35-character title of the Position as assigned by the State Agency. This data characteristic may be different than the Job Class Name.

Position Vacant Date CYMD

The **Date CYMD** the Position was vacant and available for assignment.

MILITARY VETERAN STATUS

The status of a military veteran or the widow of a military veteran. A military veteran is any individual who has one or more years of active military service in any branch of the armed forces of the United States, or who has less than one year's service and is discharged with a disability incurred on the line of duty, or who has less than one year's service and is killed on the line of duty, or who is discharged at the convenience of the government and who, upon termination of such service, has received an honorable discharge, a discharge for physical reasons with an honorable record, or a release from active military service with evidence of service other than that for which an undesirable, bad conduct, or dishonorable discharge is given. Each occurrence represents a specific Military Veteran Status.

Military Veteran Status Code

A 1-character code uniquely identifying a Military Veteran Status.

Military Veteran Status Name

The maximum 35-character unique name of a Military Veteran Status.

SEPARATION ACTION TYPE

A **Code Table** containing a set of codes designating the type of action that caused the separation of an **Employee** from State service. Each occurrence represents a specific type of separation action.

Separation Action Type Code

A 2-digit number uniquely identifying a Separation Action Type.

Separation Action Type Name

The maximum 35-character unique name of a Separation Action Type.

▼ DATA CODES

MILITARY VETERAN STATUS

N **Not A Veteran**—The individual is reported not to be a veteran.

0 **Veteran Status Not Reported**—Veteran status was not reported and is unavailable.

1 **Disabled Veteran**—The individual is a veteran with a disability that is stated to be a "service connected disability" because it was incurred in the line of military duty. The Veterans Administration will provide any veteran, or spouse of a veteran, who has a "service connected disability" with a letter, on request, stating the type of disability and the rating, in percentage form, that was assigned to the disability by the VA for benefit purposes.

2 **Spouse of Totally Disabled Veteran**—The individual was the person legally married to a military veteran at the time when that veteran received a service connected permanent and total disability.

3 **Nondisabled Veteran**—The individual is a veteran who did not incur a disability in the line of duty while serving in the military. This individual may have a disability, but it is not considered to be a "service related disability."

4 **Unremarried Spouse of Deceased Veteran**—The individual was the person legally married to a military veteran at the time when the military veteran passed away, regardless of whether the military veteran's death occurred during the period of service or at a later time, and the individual is not currently remarried.

SEPARATION ACTION TYPE

0 **Employee Not Separated**—The employee has not been separated from his/her assigned position.

1 **Involuntary Separation Layoff**—The employee's separation from his/her assigned position was involuntary due to an employer's action of layoff.

2 **Voluntary Separation Resignation**—The employee's separation from his/her assigned position was voluntary due to the employee's action of resignation.

3 **Termination of Employee**—The employee's separation from his/her assigned position was due to an employer's action of termination.

4 **Termination of Position**—The employee's separation from his/her position was due to an employer's action of terminating the position.

5 **Voluntary Separation Disability**—The employee's separation from his/her position was due to an employee action because of a disability.

6 **Voluntary Separation Retirement**—The employee's separation from his/her position was due to an employee action of retirement.

7 **Death of Employee**—The employee's separation from his/her position was due to the employee's death.

8 **Register Reversion**—The employee's separation from his/her position was due to an employee action of register reversion.

▼ FUNDAMENTAL DATA

ADDRESS

The logical or physical location where a person or organization can be located or contacted. Address is used in the broad sense to include any location where a person or organization can be reached. It does not include **Geographic Locations**, such as **Latitude Longitude**.

Address Box Identifier

The post office box, drawer, or pouch number at a public or private post office, or the box number of a rural route or star route, such as P.O. Box 92 or Box 44A (on Route 6).

Address Common Postal Code

A 9-digit data characteristic that contains any postal code, including both the United States ZIP codes and **Address Foreign Postal Code**.

Address Foreign Postal Code

The ZIP code equivalent for a foreign country. This data characteristic does not contain a United States ZIP code.

Address Line 1

A 30-character combined data characteristic for **Address Street Identifier**, **Address Lot Identifier**, **Address Route Identifier**, **Address Box Identifier**, **Address Room Identifier**, and **Address Mail Stop Identifier**, as appropriate. This data characteristic is not to be used for city names, state names, ZIP codes, or country names. This data characteristic is equivalent to the Delivery Address Line standard of the U.S. Postal Service, except that it may include punctuation.

Address Line 2

A 30-character combined data characteristic if additional information is needed that cannot be contained in **Address Line 1**. This data characteristic is not to be used for city names, state names, ZIP codes, or country names. This data characteristic is equivalent to the Alternate Location Line standard of the U.S. Postal Service, except that it may include punctuation.

Address Lot Identifier

The actual lot number or building number assigned to a specific Address, such as house number 124 on Circle Loop, or 14587 on Turnpike South.

Address Mail Stop Identifier

A 10-character unique mail-stop other than a **Address Room Identifier**, **Address Zip Base**, or **Address Zip Suffix**, such as MS: 11-D.

Address Room Identifier

The apartment, room, or suite identification at a specific **Address Street Identifier** and **Address Lot Identifier**, such as Suite 12A or Apartment 16.

Address Route Identifier

The rural or star route identification when route and box numbers are used, such as Route 6 or Star Route A.

Address Street Identifier

A combined data characteristic consisting of **Address Street Title**, **Address Street Type**, and **Cardinal Direction Abbreviation**, such as Johnson Boulevard S or 123rd Ave SW.

Address Zip Base

The basic 5-digit ZIP code for the United States, such as 98507 for post office boxes in Olympia, Washington. This data characteristic does not contain an **Address Foreign Postal Code**.

Address Zip Complete

The 9-character complete ZIP code for the United States. such as 985071144 for P.O. Box 1144 in Olympia. This data characteristic contains the **Address Zip Base** and **Address Zip Suffix**, but does not contain an **Address Foreign Postal Code.**

Address Zip Complete Format

The 10-character complete ZIP code for the United States, such as 98507-1144 for P.O. Box 1144 in Olympia. This data characteristic contains the **Address Zip Base**, **Address Zip Suffix**, and hyphen, but does not contain an **Address Foreign Postal Code.**

Address Zip Suffix

The 4-digit extension of the basic ZIP code for the United States, such as 1144 for P.O. Box 1144 in Olympia, Washington. This data characteristic does not contain an **Address Foreign Postal Code.**

CALENDAR YEAR

A period of consisting of 12 consecutive Months from January through December, such as January 1, 1988, through December 31, 1988 for calendar year 1988.

Calendar Year Days Remaining

A maximum 3-digit number of full days remaining in a Calendar Year beginning with the day after the current day, such as 241 for August 28, 1992.

Calendar Year Identifier

A 4-digit combined data characteristic containing **Century Number** and **Calendar Year Number**, such as 1989 for the Calendar Year from January 1, 1989, through December 31, 1989.

Calendar Year Number

A 2-digit number (00 through 99) representing the sequence of the **Calendar Year** within a **Century**, such as 89 for Calendar Year 1989. A **Century Number** is required for unique identification of a Calendar Year.

COUNTRY

A Geographic Area representing a territory with specific boundaries that is sovereign and recognized as a separate and distinct nation in its own right.

Country Code ANSI ISO 2

A 2-character code uniquely identifying a particular Country as defined in ANSI Z39.27-1984 or its revision. These codes are specified in ISO 3166-1981 and are the same as **Country Code FIPS ISO 2.**

Country Code ANSI ISO 3

A 3-character code uniquely identifying a particular Country as defined in ANSI Z39.27-1984 or its revision. These codes are specified in ISO 3166-1981 and are the same as **Country Code FIPS ISO 3.**

Country Code FIPS ISO 2

A 2-character code uniquely identifying a particular Country using the ISO Alpha-2 Code as defined in FIPS 104-1, May 12, 1986, such as AF for Afghanistan or US for United States. The codes are specified in ISO 3166-1981 and are the same as **Country Code ANSI ISO 2.**

Country Code FIPS ISO 3

A 3-character code uniquely identifying a particular Country using the ISO Alpha- Code as defined in FIPS 104-1, May 12, 1986, such as AFG for Afghanistan or USA for United States. The codes are specified in ISO 3166-1981 and are the same as **Country Code ANSI ISO 3.**

Country Name Abbreviation

The 4-character abbreviation of the **Country Name Complete**. The U.S. Postal Service does not accept abbreviations of country names.

Country Name Complete

The 35-character commonly accepted, completely spelled out name of the country, such as Saudi Arabia or Dominican Republic. Abbreviations are not included.

DAY

A period of consisting of 24 consecutive Hours beginning at midnight, and considered to be a normal calendar day.

Day Name Abbreviated

A 3-character abbreviated common name of a specific Day of the Week. The first three characters of the complete name of the Day are always used for the abbreviation. The abbreviation is capitalized and does not include a period.

Mon	Wed	Fri	Sun
Tue	Thu	Sat	

Day Name Complete

The maximum 9-character completely spelled out, capitalized, common name of a Day of the Week.

Monday	Wednesday	Friday	Sunday
Tuesday	Thursday	Saturday	

Day Number Calendar Year

A 3-digit number (001 through 366) representing the sequence of a Day within a specific **Calendar Year** without reference to Quarters, Months, or Weeks, such as 123 for the 123rd day in a Calendar Year.

Day Number Federal Fiscal Year

A 3-digit number (001 through 366) representing the sequence of a Day within a specific **Federal Fiscal Year** without reference to Quarters, Months, or Weeks, such as 123 for the 123rd day in a Federal Fiscal Year.

Day Number Month

A 2-digit number (01 through 31) identifying the sequence of the Day within a **Month** starting with 01 for the first Day in a Month, such as 05 for the fifth day of the Month.

Day Number Quarter

A 2-digit number (01 through 93) identifying the sequence of the Day within a **Quarter** starting with 01 for the first Day in a Quarter, such as 05 for the fifth day of the Quarter.

Day Number State Fiscal Year

A 3-digit number (001 through 366) representing the sequence of a Day within a specific **State Fiscal Year** without reference to Quarters, Months, or Weeks, such as 123 for the 123rd day in a State Fiscal Year.

PERSON

A Person is an individual human being of any age, living or deceased.

Person Age Years

A Person's age represented in years as of his/her last **Person Birth Date**.

Person Name Abbreviated Inverted

A Person's abbreviated name in the sequence **Person Name Family**, **Person Name Individual**, and **Person Name Middle Initial**. The middle initials may be eliminated, the first name may be shortened, and the extension is eliminated, such as Jackson, Bob for Robert E. Jackson III.

Person Name Abbreviated Normal

A Person's abbreviated name in the sequence **Person Name Individual**, **Person Name Middle Initial**, and **Person Name Family**. The middle initials may be eliminated, the first name may be shortened, and the extension is eliminated, such as Bob Jackson for Robert E. Jackson III.

Person Name Complete Inverted

A Person's complete legal name in the inverted sequence for that person, such as of **Person Name Family**, **Person Name Individual**, **Person Name Middle** or **Person Name Middle Initial**, and **Person Name Extension**. It does not include **Person Name Prefix** or **Person Name Suffix**.

Person Name Complete Normal

The 30-character Person's complete legal name in the natural sequence, such as **Person Name Individual**, **Person Name Middle** or **Person Name Middle Initial**, **Person Name Family**, and **Person Name Extension**. This complete name does not include any prefix or suffix.

Person Name Extension

The legal extension or qualification of a Person's name, such as Jr. or Sr., including a period if is part of the legal name. This extension does not include **Person Name Prefix** or **Person Name Suffix**. The extension is not the same as the Person Name Suffix because the extension is given at birth or inherited rather than earned.

Person Name Family

The legal family name of a Person, which may contain one or more separate words, and is commonly referred to as "last name" or "surname," such as Smith or Van Der Walker. However, some naming conventions place the family name first and the individual name last, and there can be confusion over the meaning of "surname." To prevent wrong names, the term "family" is used rather than "last name" or "surname."

The use of hyphenated family names resulting from the concatenation of two or more family names is becoming common, such as Smith-Jones. Hyphenated family names, regardless of the number of words in that name, are treated as one family name, and the hyphen is included in the name. Native American names, such as Running Bear, are considered family names.

Person Name Individual

The legal individual name of a Person, commonly referred to as "first name," "given name," or "Christian name," such as Robert or Sally. However, some naming conventions place the family name first, and the individual name last. To ensure proper individual names, the term "individual" is used rather than "first name" or "Christian name."

Person Name Middle

The legal middle name or names of a Person, excluding **Person Name Family** and the **Person Name Individual**. Some individuals may have no middle name, while others may have multiple middle names. When multiple middle names occur, all of the names are included.

Person Name Prefix

The prefix to a Person's name, such as Mr., Mrs., Ms., Dr., Father, and so on, including the period if appropriate. The prefix is not included in the **Person Name Complete Normal** and **Person Name Complete Inverted** data characteristics.

Person Name Suffix

The suffix to a Person's name, such as Ph.D., D.V.M., M.D., D.D.S., and so on, including periods if appropriate. The suffix is usually a degree that is earned by the person. The suffix is not included in the **Person Name Complete Normal** and **Person Name Complete Inverted** data characteristics. The suffix is not the same as the **Person Name Extension** because the suffix is earned rather than inherited.

Person Social Security Number

A 9-digit number assigned to each individual by the Federal government to allow an assessment from the Person's earnings, as well as from the employer. This number uniquely identifies each Person and is used for identification purposes by State government and Employers.

▼ BROAD DATA GROUPINGS

CLIMATE DATA SUBJECT AREA

Climate is the meteorological conditions, including temperature, precipitation, wind, barometric pressure, evaporation, and transpiration, that prevail in a specific area or region. *Weather* is the meteorological conditions at a specific location or in an area, at a specified time or during a time interval. Climate includes glacier data but excludes snow pack data.

The Climate Data Subject Area includes any data pertaining to either the prevailing meteorological conditions of an area or region, or the specific meteorological conditions at a particular location and time.

Estuary Data Subject Area

An *estuary* (estuarine environment) is a surface water body that is semi-enclosed by land but has open, partly obstructed, or sporadic access to open salt water. It is at least occasionally diluted by fresh water, resulting in appreciably reduced salinity, and salinity may periodically increase higher than that of ocean waters due to evaporation. Estuaries continue upstream to the point where salinity measures less than 0.5 o/oo of average annual low flow. An estuary is any estuarine environment and may include wetland and deep water components. Puget Sound is considered an estuary, not an ocean.

The Estuary Data Subject Area includes any data pertaining to the location, identification, description, quantity, quality, or use of estuary water.

Ground Water Data Subject Area

Ground water is that part of the State's water resource that exists beneath the earth's surface, or beneath the bed of any stream, lake, reservoir, or other body of surface water, or in the pores or fractures of rocks or unconsolidated material. Ground water may be static, or it may flow, percolate, or move in some manner.

The Ground Water Data Subject Area includes any data pertaining to the location, identification, description, quantity, quality, or use of ground water.

Ground Water Descriptive Data Subject Group

Any location, identification, or description data about ground water, or other data about ground water that do not fit into the other data subject groups.

Ground Water Quality Data Subject Group

The condition of ground water, including its purity; types of biological, physical, and chemical substances; its usefulness for specific purposes; its vulnerability to pollutants; any treatments to improve water quality; and the water quality history, patterns, trends, and changes.

Ground Water Quantity Data Subject Group

Any data pertaining to the capacity, flow, and volume, or the history, patterns, trends, or changes of those data for any ground water.

Ground water quantity data show the supply of ground water, including artificial recharge of ground water.

Ground Water Use Data Subject Group

Any data pertaining to the use of ground water in place below the earth's surface, or the collective or summarized use of ground water, excluding the specific use of ground water. The specific uses are included in the method of withdrawal, such as Water Wells, Springs, and Water Systems.

LAKE DATA SUBJECT AREA

A *lake* (lacustrine environment) is a surface water body of any size that is situated in a natural topographic depression, including all lacustrine environments, such as ponds, pools, and so on, where the salinity is below 0.5 o/oo. A lake includes permanently flooded lakes and tidal lakes up to the high water lines, but excludes areas of abnormal flooding. A lake may have wetland and deep water components.

A wide portion of a stream where the width and depth are significantly increased and the water flow is significantly reduced is considered to be a lake. A lake differs from a reservoir in that it occurs naturally rather than as a man-made structure. If any portion of a lake is within the State, that lake is considered part of the State's water resource.

The Lake Data Subject Area includes any data pertaining to the identification, location, description, quantity, quality, or use of lake water.

Lake Descriptive Data Subject Group

Any location, identification, or description data about a lake, or other data about lakes that do not fit into the other data subject groups.

Lake Quality Data Subject Group

The condition of lake water, including its purity; types of biological, physical, and chemical substances; its usefulness for specific purposes; its vulnerability to pollutants; any treatments to improve water quality; and quality history, patterns, trends, and changes.

Lake Quantity Data Subject Group

Any data pertaining to the capacity, flow, and volume, or the history, patterns, trends, or changes of those data for any lake. Lake quantity data represent the water supply in a lake. Monitoring stations are included as lake quantity data.

Lake Resource Data Subject Group

Any biological, physical, or chemical resource that exists in a lake or has a high dependency on a lake.

Lake Use Data Subject Group

The use of water in a lake or removed from a lake. Lake use data include points of diversion, quantities, frequency, duration, and points of return, and any quality changes resulting from use. Lake water use data do not include data about Water Systems or the specific offbody use of water, but include summarized data about offbody water use.

SPRING DATA SUBJECT AREA

A *spring* is a surface water body in the form of a natural flow of water from below the earth's surface to the earth's surface, including natural artesian and man-made springs, but excluding artesian wells, regardless of the period of time, frequency, or length of time that water flows. A spring is also defined as the natural intersection of ground water with the earth's surface. Springs may be visible or they may be hidden beneath other water bodies, such as lakes or streams.

The Spring Data Subject Area includes any data pertaining to the identification, location, description, quantity, quality, or use of a spring or spring water.

Spring Descriptive Data Subject Group

Any location, identification, or description data about springs, or other data about springs that do not fit into the other data subject groups.

Spring Quality Data Subject Group

The condition of spring water, including its purity; types of biological, physical, and chemical substances; its usefulness for specific purposes; its vulnerability to pollutants; any treatments to improve water quality; and quality history, patterns, trends, and changes.

Spring Quantity Data Subject Group

Any data pertaining to the capacity, flow, and volume, or the history, patterns and trends of those data for any spring, excluding the use of water from a spring. Spring quantity data represent the water supply in springs.

Spring Resource Data Subject Group

Any biological, physical, or chemical resource that exists in a spring or has a high dependency on a spring.

Spring Use Data Subject Group

The use of water in a spring or removed from a spring. Spring use data include points of diversion, quantities, frequency, and duration, and any quality changes resulting from use. Spring use data do not include data about Water Systems or the specific offbody use of water, but include summarized data about offbody water use.

▼ APPENDIX C
▼ DATA STRUCTURE CRITERIA
▼

▼ PRIMARY KEY CRITERIA

- A primary key must uniquely identify each data occurrence in a data subject, regardless of the scope of that data subject. If the scope changes, the primary key must still uniquely identify each data occurrence to remain valid.

- A primary key must be robust enough to identify all data occurrences that may be found over time. It must allow for future growth.

- A primary key must have a definite value for every data occurrence. Null values are not allowed in a primary key.

- A primary key must not contain redundant data. If a data characteristic is not needed for unique identification, it must be removed from the primary key.

- A primary key must be known when the data occurrence is created. It cannot be identified and added later.

- A primary key value must not change over the life of the data occurrence. It must have long-term stability.

- A primary key must be legal to use, and cannot disclose any privileged information.

- A primary key must be known, understandable, and assessable by clients. It must not be a hidden, surrogate key.

- A primary key must be within the organization's control, and from a designated source within the organization. There is a risk if the primary key cannot be controlled. This requirement is somewhat controversial because many primary keys, such as Social Security Number, are outside the control of an organization. Therefore, the control need not be within the organization.

- A more controversial requirement is that a primary key must not contain any facts, or be intelligent in any way, because facts change. This requirement necessitates identification of a meaningless primary key, which is another data characteristic to manage. It is more reasonable to pick a primary key that meets all the other requirements as well as containing a fact. Only in the situation that such a primary key cannot be found, should a meaningless primary key be identified.

▼ DATA RELATION DIAGRAM CRITERIA

- The major data subjects and data relations forming the backbone of the data structure should be placed on a separate page. This page should be the first page that a reader views.

- Subordinate data subjects and data relations should be placed around major data subjects, or placed on separate pages. These pages are usually placed behind the major data subjects.

- Data subjects forming a sequence or hierarchy should be placed vertically with the one-to-many data relations point down.

- One-to-many data relations should generally point down and in or down and out. One-to-many data relations pointing up should be avoided.

- Data relations should not cross or take a roundabout path. This usually indicates a diagram that is too detailed and needs to be divided into two or more diagrams. A data subject may appear more than once on a diagram to keep the data relations short.

- Code tables qualifying a major data subject should be placed on a separate page, particularly when there are many code tables. The code table data subjects should surround the data subject being qualified by the code tables.

- Summary data subjects with their qualifying data subjects should be placed on a separate page, particularly when there are many qualifying data subjects. The qualifying data subjects should surround the summary data subject. If there a set of related summary data subjects with different qualifying data subjects, a common diagram should be prepared showing all the qualifying data subjects even if they are not used.

- A data subject hierarchy should be placed on a separate page and should be independent of any data relations to the data subjects in that hierarchy.

- Data categories and their parent data subject should be placed on a separate page and should be independent of any other data relations to those data subjects.

▼ DATA STRUCTURE CHART CRITERIA

- When a primary key is identified, it is added to the data structure chart. The data characteristics are added to the data characteristic list if they are not already listed.

- When a one-to-many data relation to a parent data subject is defined, a foreign key is identified and added to the data structure chart. The data characteristics forming the foreign key are added to the data characteristic list if they are not already listed.

- When a one-to-one data relation is defined, a foreign key is identified and placed in each data subject involved in the relation. The data characteristics forming the foreign key are added to the data characteristic list if they are not already listed.

- Foreign keys are listed in alphabetical sequence by data subject name for easy reference.

- When a data characteristic is defined, it is placed in the data characteristic list.

- The data characteristics are listed in alphabetical sequence for easy reference.

- When a primary key is removed, the data characteristics are removed from the data characteristic list unless their existence is verified.

- When a foreign key is removed, the data characteristics are removed from the data characteristic list unless their existence is verified.

▼ APPENDIX D
DATA CROSS REFERENCE CRITERIA

▼ DATA CHARACTERISTIC CROSS REFERENCE CRITERIA

- If the data product characteristic is a single data characteristic and a matching common data characteristic variation is found, a cross reference is made.

- If a data product characteristic is a single data characteristic and that variation is not defined, a new common data characteristic variation is created and listed as the cross reference.

- If the data product characteristic is a combined data characteristic and matching common data characteristic variations are found, list the corresponding common data characteristic variations in the sequence in which they occur in the data product characteristic.

- If a data product characteristic is a combined data characteristic and one or more matching common data characteristic variations are not found, new common data characteristic variations are created and listed as the cross references.

- If a new common data characteristic variation is the first data characteristic variation of a common data characteristic, a new common data characteristic is created.

- If a new common data characteristic is the first data characteristic in a common data subject, a new common data subject is created.

- If the new common data characteristic contains data codes, a code table data subject is defined containing data characteristics for the data code value and data code name.

- If the product data characteristic contains data codes, each of those data codes is cross referenced to common data codes.

- If a new common data subject, data characteristic, or data characteristic variation is created, it is formally named and comprehensively defined according to the data description criteria.

▼ DATA CHARACTERISTIC CROSS REFERENCE VALIDATION CRITERIA

- Does the data product characteristic correspond to the common data characteristic variation?

- Does the common data characteristic variation adequately represent the variation of the data product characteristic?

- Does the common data characteristic variation definition adequately cover the data product characteristic?

▼ DATA CODE CROSS REFERENCE CRITERIA

- If a data product characteristic contains a set of data codes, it is cross referenced to a common data characteristic variation in a code table data subject.

- If an appropriate common data characteristic variation is not found, a new common data characteristic variation is created and the data product characteristic is cross referenced to it. A new code table data subject may need to be created.

- If a data product code represents a single data property, it is cross referenced to the appropriate common data code.

- If a data product code represents multiple data properties, it is split between two common data code values. Additional information is needed to make the proper split.

- If a data product code represents a partial data property, it is cross referenced to the appropriate common data code.

- If a corresponding common data code cannot be found, a new common data code is created and used as the cross reference.

- If a new common data code is created, it is named and defined according to the data description criteria.

▼ DATA CODE CROSS REFERENCE VALIDATION CRITERIA

- Does the data product code correspond to the common data code?

- Does the common data code definition adequately cover the data product code?

▼ APPENDIX E
DATA SURVEY QUESTIONS

▼ DATA AVAILABILITY SURVEY QUESTIONS

General questions for the data availability survey:

- Are there any changes to the broad data grouping definitions?

- Are there any new broad data groupings that need to be defined?

- What are the organization's plans for collecting additional data in the next five years?

- Who should be contacted for follow-up information about the survey?

Specific questions for each broad data grouping:

- Are the data collected by the organization or acquired from another organization?

- If data are collected, what is the frequency of collection? Does the frequency of collection vary over time?

- If data are collected, what time frame is covered, such as the last year or the last 10 years?

- If data are acquired, what organization are they acquired from and who is the contact in that organization?

- Are the acquired data modified or altered in any way? If so, how are they modified or altered?

- What is the geographic extent of the data, such as city, county, state, or geographic area?

- What location scheme or schemes are used for data objects, such as geographic reference schemes?

- Are the data in tabular form or non-tabular (spatial, image, remote sensing, voice, text, etc.) form?

- What is the accuracy of the data, such as precision, resolution, scale, or units of measure? Does the accuracy vary over time?

- How is each real-world object uniquely identified?

- What is the level of detail or summarization of the data? Does the level of detail or summarization vary over time?

- Who should be contacted in the organization for acquiring data?

- Are there any special conditions for acquiring data from the organization?

- What are the organization's plans for continuing to collect these data in the next five years?

- What other organizations might have data in this broad data groupings? Who should be contacted about these data and how can they be contacted?

▼ DATA AVAILABILITY INVENTORY QUESTIONS

General questions for the data availability inventory:

- Are there any changes to the definitions of the data subjects and data characteristics?

- Are there any data subjects and data characteristics that need to be defined within the scope of this survey?

- What are the organization's plans for collecting additional data in the next five years?

- Who should be contacted in the organization for follow-up information about the survey?

Specific questions for each data subject or database:

- The same questions that appear in the data availability survey, but oriented to data subjects rather than broad data groupings.

- Are the data in manual or automated form?

- If the data are in automated form, what is that automated form?

- What are the formats for the data characteristics?

- What are the definitions for data subjects, data characteristics, and coded data values?

- What is the structure of the data?

- What are the data integrity rules?

- What documentation is available for the data?

▼ GLOSSARY

Acceptable Documentation   Documentation that is acceptable to people as well as technically correct.

Accuracy   *See* Data Accuracy.

Accuracy Assurance   *See* Data Accuracy Improvement.

Accuracy Control   *See* Data Accuracy Control.

Acquired Data Relation   A Data Relation that exists between two data subjects only when it is defined to meet a business need. It does not exist by reason of the definition of a Data Subject. *See also* Inherent Data Relation.

Active Data   Data that still exist and whose values can change. *See also* Static Data.

Active Data Definition Reference   A formal connection between the contributing Data Definition and the receiving Data Definition, such as hypertext. *See also* Passive Data Definition Reference.

Active Derived Data   Data that are derived from contributing Data Characteristics that still exist and whose values can change. *See also* Static Derived Data.

Actual Data Value   A Data Value that is an actual measurement, value, or description of a trait or feature of a Data Subject. It represents facts or measurements collected about a Data Subject. *See also* Coded Data Value, Data Code.

Algorithm   *See* Data Derivation Procedure.

Alias   An alternate or assumed name. *See* Alias Data Name.

Alias Data Name   An alternate name, or different name, for the same piece of data. Any Data Name other than the Primary Data Name. It does not represent a Data Characteristic Variation.

Alternate Foreign Key   A Foreign Key that matches an Alternate Primary Key in a Parent Data Subject. *See also* Limited Foreign Key, Obsolete Foreign Key, Official Foreign Key.

Alternate Primary Key   A Primary Key that is valid for all Data Occurrences of a Data Subject in the Common Data Architecture, but has not been designated as the Official Primary Key. *See also* Candidate Primary Key, Limited Primary Key, Obsolete Primary Key.

Architecture   The art, science, or profession of designing and building structures. Also, the structure or structures collectively, or the general style of structure. *See* Data Architecture.

Baseline Data   The basic core data upon which the organization's business depends for its very existence. The 20 percent of the data needed 80 percent of the time to directly support business activities. The highest priority data for an organization.

Behavioral Entity   Entities in the business world that behave and respond to the business rules of an organization.

Box with Bulging Sides   The symbol used to represent a data subject on a Data Relation Diagram. Conforms to Semiotic Theory.

Broad Data Groupings   The Categorical Levels of Data Classification that are used in Data Resource Surveys.

Business Activity Framework   A framework in the Information Technology Infrastructure that represents the business activities of an organization and the automation of those activities into business processes. *See also* Data Resource Framework, Information Systems Framework, Platform Resource Framework.

Business Data Needs Approach   An approach to developing a Common Data Architecture based on the data required to support business activities. *See also* Critical Area Approach.

Business Oriented Information Engineering   An approach to Information Engineering that is oriented to supporting business strategies and business activities.

CADE *See* Computer Aided Data Engineering.

Can-Also-Be The mutually inclusive situation between Data Categories. *See also* Can-Only-Be.

Can-Only-Be The mutually exclusive situation between Data Subjects in a Data Subject Hierarchy. *See also* Can-Also-Be.

Candidate Primary Key A Primary Key that has been identified in disparate data but has not been reviewed for validity and has not been designated as an Alternate Primary Key, Limited Primary Key, Obsolete Primary Key, or Official Primary Key.

CASE *See* Computer Aided System Engineering.

Categorical Levels of Data Classification Abstract groupings of data above the Working Levels of Data Classification that provide a broader perspective of data.

Characteristic List A list of data characteristics at the bottom of a Logical Data Structure Chart.

Class Word A component of traditional data naming conventions that provides a set of standard words for data characteristics. Not used in the Data Naming Taxonomy.

Classification A method or scheme to arrange things in classes according to some established criteria. *See* Conflicting Classification Scheme, Data Classification Scheme.

Classification Scheme *See* Conflicting Classification Scheme, Data Classification Scheme.

Clearinghouse *See* Data Resource Clearinghouse.

Client The preferred word that replaces User. Refers to anyone who is a client, customer, partner, or anyone else who uses information technology.

Client Databases Data files controlled by a database management systems and organized for rapid search and retrieval, not for high volume transactions. Generally used for ad hoc inquiries and unstructured problem solving.

Client Focused Approach An approach to developing a Formal Data Resource that includes direct client involvement. Based on the principle that involvement leads to commitment, which leads to acceptance, which leads to success. *See also* Data Needs Approach.

Client Involvement   The direct involvement of clients in developing an organization's data resource. *See* Client Focused Approach.

Client/Server   A technology that allows multiple clients to access shared data stored on one or more databases on a server.

Closed Recursive Data Relation   *See* One-to-One Recursive Data Relation.

Cluster   *See* Organization Cluster, Organization Cluster Stage.

Code Table   A table containing a set of related Data Codes. *See* Code Table Data Subject.

Code Table Data Subject   A Data Subject containing a set of related Data Codes.

Combined Data   A concatenation of one or more pieces of Elemental Data. *See also* Combined Data Characteristic, Elemental Data, Elemental Data Characteristic.

Combined Data Characteristic   A Data Characteristic that is a practical, useful combination of two or more closely related Elemental Data Characteristics. *See also* Elemental Data Characteristic.

Combined Data Code   A Data Product Code that represents more than one Data Property.

Combined Data Code Sets   The situation where a set of Data Product Codes represents two or more sets of Common Data Codes.

Combined Data Product Characteristic   A Data Product Characteristic that contains more than one elemental Common Data Characteristic.

Combining Data   A process where data from different databases are combined into a single database. A form of data sharing.

Comment   *See* Data Definition Comment.

Common Data Architecture   The common context within which all data are defined. The common context for identifying the true content and meaning of data and improving the value of data.

The base for refining and integrating disparate data and new data into the Formal Data Resource.

Common Data Architecture Stage The fifth Evolutionary Stage characterized by a Common Data Architecture across all organizations and all business activities. It is the ideal stage. *See also* Organization Stage, Organization Cluster Stage, Project Stage, Traditional Stage.

Common Data Characteristic A Data Characteristic in the Common Data Architecture.

Common Data Characteristic Variation A Data Characteristic Variation in the Common Data Architecture.

Common Data Code A Data Code in the Common Data Architecture.

Common Data Subject A Data Subject in the Common Data Architecture.

Common Word A set of words that are used consistently in the formation of Data Names. *See also* Data Naming Vocabulary.

Common-to-Common Cross Reference A Data Cross Reference between an Interim Common Data Architecture and a Desired Common Data Architecture. Also known as an Interim Cross Reference.

Completeness *See* Data Completeness.

Component *See* Information Technology Framework, Data Management Component, Data Architecture Component, Data Availability Component.

Comprehensive Data Definition A formal data definition that provides a complete, meaningful, easily read, readily understood, real-world definition of the true content and meaning of data.

Computer Aided Data Engineering A set of tools and techniques for analyzing and documenting both new and disparate data within a Common Data Architecture, and assisting the Data Refining process.

Computer Aided System Engineering A set of tools and techniques for using computers to aid the information system engineering effort. Often erroneously referred to as Computer Aided Software Engineering.

Conditional Data Structure Integrity Data Integrity that specifies the cardinality for data relations: whether data structure integrity is required, optional, or prevented under certain conditions. *See* Conditional Data Structure Integrity Rule, Conditional Data Structure Integrity Table.

Conditional Data Structure Integrity Table A table showing Conditional Data Structure Integrity.

Conditional Data Structure Integrity Rule A rule defining Conditional Data Structure Integrity.

Conditional Data Value Integrity Data Integrity that specifies whether data values are required, optional, or prevented under certain conditions.

Conditional Data Value Integrity Table A table containing Conditional Data Value Integrity criteria.

Conflicting Classification Schemes The situation where different classification schemes exist for the same data subject.

Conflicting Data Mandates The situation where mandates for data standards are received from two or more regulatory authorities, cover the same data, and conflict.

Connotative Meaning The idea or notion suggested by a Data Definition. What a person interprets from the definition in addition to what is explicitly stated. *See also* Denotative Meaning.

Conversion The process of changing something from one form to another form. Usually a rapid change, may occur one or more times, and may be in any direction. *See* Data Conversion, Database Conversion.

Conversion Plan *See* Database Conversion Plan.

Converters *See* Data Converters, Database Converters.

Cooperative Database A database that exists on two or more logically, and often physically, different locations. They cooperate to provide data to clients.

Critical Area A subset of an Organization Cluster that is critical to the success of the organization.

Critical Area Approach   An approach to developing a Formal Data Resource containing Baseline Data that provides short-term benefits and makes development of the Formal Data Resource cost-effective. *See also* Business Data Needs Approach.

Critical Data Need   A broad grouping of data needed to support a high priority business strategy that is unmet or only partially met. *See also* Broad Data Grouping.

Cross Reference   *See* Data Cross Reference.

Cyclic Data Subjects   The two Data Subjects resulting from resolution of a Many-to-Many Recursive Data Relation.

Dashed Line   The symbol used to represent a Data Relationship between Data Subjects on a Data Relation Diagram or between Data Files on a Data File Diagram. Conforms to Semiotic Theory. *See also* Solid Line.

Data   The individual facts with a specific meaning at a point in time or for a period of time. they include Primitive Data and Derived Data, and Elemental Data and Combined Data. *See also* Information.

Data Accuracy   The part of Data Quality that describes how well data in the Formal Data Resource represent the real world. *See also* Collection Frequency, Data Instance, Data Volatility, Precision, Resolution, Scale.

Data Accuracy Assurance   The proactive process of ensuring that data in the Formal Data Resource represent the real world as closely as the organization desires for support of its Business Activities.

Data Accuracy Control   The reactive process of determining how well data in the Formal Data Resource represent the real world.

Data Alias   *See* Alias Data Name.

Data Architecture (1)   The component of the data resource framework that contains all activities, and the products of those activities, related to the identification, naming, definition, structuring, quality, and documentation of the data resource for an organization.

Data Architecture (2)   The science and method of designing and constructing a data resource that is business driven, based on real-world subjects, and implemented in appropriate operating environments. The overall structure of a data resource that provides a consistent foundation across organizational boundaries to provide easily identifiable, readily available, high-quality data to support business activities.

Data Architecture Component   One of the three components of the Data Resource Framework that contains all the activities related to describing, structuring, maintaining quality, and documenting the data resource. *See also* Data Management Component, Data Availability Component.

Data Attribute   *See* Data Characteristic.

Data Availability Component   One of the three components of the Data Resource Framework that contains all activities related to making data available while properly protecting and securing those data. *See also* Data Management Component, Data Architecture Component.

Data Availability Inventory   A detailed inventory of Data Subjects and Data Characteristics that currently exist inside or outside the organization. One type of Data Resource Inventory. *See also* Data Needs Inventory.

Data Availability Survey   A survey to determine the broad groupings of data that currently exist inside or outside the organization. One type of Data Resource Survey. *See also* Broad Data Groupings, Data Needs Survey.

Data Category   A Data Subject that is in a mutually inclusive relation with other peer Data Subjects, all of which are subordinate to a parent Data Subject. A Can-Also-Be situation.

Data Characteristic   An individual feature or trait about a data subject. A data subject is described by a set of data characteristics. Also known as a Data Attribute.

Data Characteristic Content Variation   A Data Characteristic Variation due to format, content, or meaning. *See also* Data Characteristic Length Variation.

Data Characteristic Content Variation Outline   An outline that lists the Data Characteristic Content Variations under their parent Data Characteristics.

Data Characteristic Cross Reference   A Data Cross Reference between a Data Product Characteristic and a Common Data Characteristic Variation.

Data Characteristic Cross Reference Diagram   A diagram that shows Data Characteristic Cross References.

Data Characteristic Cross Reference List   A list that shows Data Characteristic Cross References.

Data Characteristic Definition   The Data Definition for a Data Characteristic.

Data Characteristic Length Variation   A Data Characteristic Variation due to length variations. *See also* Data Characteristic Content Variation.

Data Characteristic Length Variation Matrix   A matrix that shows the different lengths of Data Characteristics used by different Products.

Data Characteristic Length Variation Outline   An outline that lists the different lengths of Data Characteristics when Data Product identification is not needed.

Data Characteristic Matrix   A matrix showing the Data Characteristics that are valid for each Data Subject Type in a Data Subject Hierarchy.

Data Characteristic Name   The formal name consisting of the Data Subject Name followed a Data Characteristic Name that uniquely identifies a Data Characteristic within that Data Subject.

Data Characteristic Translation Scheme   A Data Translation Scheme that translates data between variations of the same Data Characteristic.

Data Characteristic Variation   The same Data Characteristic that exists in more than one form because of differences in format, content, meaning, or length.

Data Characteristic Variation Definition   The Data Definition for a Data Characteristic Variation.

Data Characteristic Variation Name   An extension of the Data Characteristic Name that indicates a specific variation of that Data Characteristic.

Data Characteristic Variation Substitution   A Data Characteristic Name that represents a variety of format variations.

Data Classification Scheme   A scheme for classifying data that progresses from general levels to specific levels. It includes Categorical Levels of Data Classification and Working Levels of Data Classification.

Data Code   A Data Value that is coded in some way. *See also* Actual Data Value, Data Code Name, Data Code Value.

Data Code Cross Reference   A Data Cross Reference between Data Product Codes and Common Data Codes.

Data Code Definition   The definition of a Data Code.

Data Code Cross Reference List   A list Showing the Common Data Code Values that correspond to the Data Product Code Values.

Data Code Name   The formal name that uniquely identifies a Data Code within the Common Data Architecture. *See also* Data Code Value.

Data Code Set   A set of Data Codes that are closely related. *See also* Code Table Data Subject.

Data Code Translation Scheme   A Data Translation Scheme that translates data between variations of Data Codes.

Data Code Value   An Actual Data Value that has been codified in some way. The value of a Data Code. *See also* Data Code Name.

Data Code Matrix   A matrix of all related Data Codes Sets for one set of data properties.

Data Code Variation   The same data property represented by more than one Data Code.

Data Completeness   The part of Data Quality that ensures that all the data needed to support business activities are available in the Formal Data Resource. It represents how available data are to support the business needs of an Organization.

Data Completeness Assurance   The proactive process of analyzing the data needs of an organization's business activities and ensuring that those data are available when needed.

Data Completeness Control   The reactive process of determining what data are available and how completely they support an organization's business activities.

Data Conversion   The process of converting data from one structure to another structure. Conversion can take place from the common data architecture to the structure of existing data, or from existing data to the structure of the common data architecture. It is usually a change in value or form and may be done many times until existing data are converted to the common data architecture. *See also* Database Conversion.

Data Converters   Routines for converting data between applications and data files.

Data Cross Reference   A link between data names. The link may be between an Alias Data Name and the Primary Data Name, between two Alias Data Names, or between two Primary Data Names. It is not the same as a Data Translation Scheme.

Data Cross Reference List   *See* Data Code Cross Reference List, Data Characteristic Cross Reference List.

Data Cross Reference Phase   The third phase of the Mature Data Resource Process. Links Data Product Characteristics and Data Product Codes to their counterparts in the Common Data Architecture.

Data Cross Reference Status   The status of a Data Cross Reference, such as Proposed or Verified.

Data Cross Reference Validation   The process that validates data cross references.

Data Cross Reference Validation Criteria   A set of criteria for determining the validity of a Data Cross Reference.

Data Definition   *See* Comprehensive Data Definition.

Data Definition Comment   An entry in a Data Definition that contains a comment about that definition from a person reviewing data definitions.

Data Definition Common Word   A word that is commonly used in data definitions to provide consistent meaning to data definitions.

Data Definition Inheritance   The situation where some portion of a data definition is received from another data definition.

Data Definition Inheritance Diagram   A diagram showing the inheritance of data characteristic definitions.

Data Definition Issue   Something about a Data Definition that needs further analysis or a decision.

Data Definition Note   An entry in a Data Definition that provides additional information or reference to other information pertaining to that Data Definition.

Data Definition Question   An entry in a Data Definition that contains a question that must be answered before the Data Definition is completed.

Data Definition Reference   A connection between two data definitions so that one data definition can be clarified by the other data definition or both data definitions can be mutually clarified by each other.

Data Deluge   A situation where massive quantities of data are being captured and stored at an alarming rate. *See also* Data Pollution, Data Proliferation.

Data Denormalization   The formal process of taking the Logical Data Resource Model and adjusting it to operate on the Information Technology Platform without compromising that logical model. It produces a Physical Data Resource Model. *See also* Data Normalization.

Data Deployment   The formal process of placing data in databases on a network or open system in an optimal manner to meet an organization's needs.

Data Derivation Diagram   A diagram for documenting Derived Data.

Data Derivation Procedure   An algorithm, equation, logical expression, or matrix that specifies the procedure for deriving data.

Data Derivation Integrity   Data Integrity that specifies the procedure for maintaining derived data and redundant data in the Formal Data Resource.

Data Description   The first activity in the Data Architecture component of the Data Resource Framework that includes the formal naming and comprehensive definition of all data.

Data Design Template A Data Template for designing a specific database based on Official Data Variations. *See also* Data Inventory Template, Data Survey Template.

Data Dictionary *See* Data Resource Dictionary.

Data Documentation The fourth activity of the Data Architecture component of the Data Resource Framework, which provides complete, accurate, readily available documentation about the data resource. It documents the other three activities in the Data Architecture component.

Data Domain A Data Subject that contains Data Integrity Values or Data Integrity Rules. *See* Data Value Domain, Data Rule Domain.

Data Engineering The discipline that designs, builds, and maintains the Formal Data Resource and refines data into that data resource. The formal discipline for identifying disparate data, bringing them into the organization's data resource, and making them available to Information Engineering. *See also* Information Engineering.

Data Entity *See* Data Subject.

Data Feed Table A table that shows the source of Data Product Characteristics, their Common Data Characteristic equivalents, and the corresponding Data Product Characteristics in the receiving application or database. *See also* Data Source Table.

Data File A physical file of data that exists in a database management system, such as a computer file outside a database management system or a manual file outside a computer. *See also* Data Repository.

Data File Diagram A Diagram that shows the Data Files and the Data Relations between those Data Files. It represents the physical structure of data.

Data Flow *See* Data Flow Diagram, Major Data Flow, Major Data Flow Diagram, Major Data Flow Network.

Data Flow Diagram A diagram showing the data flowing between processes within an information system, or data flowing into and out of an information system.

Data Flow Network *See* Major Data Flow Network.

Data Groupings   *See* Broad Data Groupings.

Data Index   *See* Data Resource Guide Index.

Data Instance   The time frame that data represent in the real world. The period of time for which data are valid. Part of Data Accuracy. It is not the same as a Data Occurrence.

Data Integrity   The part of Data Quality that deals with how well data are maintained in the Formal Data Resource. The formal definition of comprehensive rules and the consistent application of those rules to assure high-quality data in the Formal Data Resource. *See* Data Derivation Integrity, Data Integrity Rules, Data Retention Integrity, Data Structure Integrity, Data Value Integrity.

Data Integrity Assurance   The proactive process of ensuring that the Formal Data Resource contains the appropriate data integrity. *See* Data Integrity Control.

Data Integrity Constraints   Specific Data Integrity Rules that are implemented for Data Files and Data Items. Derived from denormalization of Specific Data Integrity Rules.

Data Integrity Control   The reactive process of determining the existing level of Data Integrity for the Formal Data Resource. *See* Data Integrity Assurance.

Data Integrity Inheritance   The situation where Data Integrity is obtained from parent Data Subjects and related Data Characteristics.

Data Integrity Rule   A statement that defines the Actual Data Values or Data Code Values that are allowed in the Formal Data Resource.

Data Integrity Value   An Actual Data Value or Data Code Value that is allowed in the Formal Data Resource.

Data Inventory   *See* Traditional Data Inventory, Data Resource Inventory.

Data Inventory Analysis   A process that compares detailed data needs from the Data Needs Inventory with the detailed data available from the Data Availability Inventory to determine what data exist and what data need to be acquired.

Data Inventory Template   A Data Template for identifying existing Data Subjects and Data Characteristics in terms of the Common

Data Architecture. *See also* Data Design Template, Data Survey Template.

Data Item   An individual field in a Data Record. The basic component of a Data Record.

Data Key (1)   A set of one or more Data Characteristics that have special meaning and use in addition to describing a feature or trait of a Data Subject. *See* Primary Key, Foreign Key, Secondary Key.

Data Key (2)   One or more Data Items that are used to access a data file to store or retrieve data.

Data Layer   A specific grouping of data in a Geographic Information System. Ideally, it consists of one Data Topic. *See* Derived Data Layer, Primitive Data Layer.

Data Management Component   One of the three components of the Data Resource Framework that contains all activities related to management of the data resource. *See also* Data Architecture Component, Data Availability Component.

Data Mandate   Data standards that are mandated by a regulatory authority outside the organization that must adhere to those mandates.

Data Model   The mathematical construct of a database management system, such as hierarchical, network, inverted, or relational. *See also* Data Resource Model.

Data Name   A label for a data repository, data subject, data characteristic, data characteristic variation, or data code.

Data Name Abbreviation   An Alias Data Name developed by a formal or informal abbreviation of the Primary Data Name.

Data Name Alias   *See* Alias Data Name.

Data Name Substitution   The technique of substituting a Specific Data Characteristic Name for a Generic Data Characteristic Name. The Generic Data Characteristic Name is enclosed in parentheses.

Data Naming Convention   A formal method to name data that evolved from Traditional Data Names. Replaced by the formal Data Naming Taxonomy.

Data Naming Lexicon   *See* Data Resource Lexicon.

Data Naming Taxonomy   A Taxonomy for arranging data into related groups and uniquely naming them consistently throughout the Common Data Architecture. It provides a common language for naming data.

Data Naming Vocabulary   A set of common words for each component of the Data Name. The common words used in the Data Naming Taxonomy. *See also* Class Word, Common Word.

Data Needs Approach   The approach to developing a Mature Data Resource based on an analysis of data needs. *See also* Client Focused Approach.

Data Needs Inventory   A detailed inventory of Data Subjects and Data Characteristics needed by an organization to support its business activities. One type of Data Resource Inventory. *See also* Data Availability Inventory.

Data Needs Survey   A survey to determine the broad groupings of data needed to support an organization's business strategies. One type of Data Resource Survey. *See also* Broad Data Groupings, Data Availability Survey.

Data Normalization   The process to bring data into normal form by Data Subjects. It produces a Logical Data Resource Model. *See also* Data Denormalization, Normalized Data.

Data Occurrence   A logical record that represents one existence of a Data Subject in the real world. It is not the same as a Data Instance.

Data Overload   The overloading of a recipient with too much data for that recipient to absorb through Messages that contain noise rather than Information. *See also* Information Overload.

Data Portfolio   A portfolio of meta-data about data available inside and outside an organization to support business activities. The Data Resource Guide contains the data portfolio for an organization.

Data Pollution   The situation resulting from an exponential increase in the capture and storage of Disparate Data. *See also* Data Deluge, Data Proliferation.

Data Preparation Phase   The first phase in the Mature Data Resource Process. Establishes the scope of the data refining project.

Data Product   A major, independent piece of documentation of any type that contains the names and/or definitions of Disparate Data.

Data Product Characteristic   An individual element of data in a Data Product Subject.

Data Product Characteristic Definition   The Data Definition for a Data Product Characteristic.

Data Product Characteristic Description   The Data Description of a Data Product Characteristic consisting of a unique Data Product Characteristic Name and a Data Product Characteristic Definition.

Data Product Characteristic Name   The unique Data Name of a Data Product Characteristic.

Data Product Code   A Data Code that exists in a Data Product.

Data Product Code Definition   The Data Definition of a Data Product Code.

Data Product Code Description   A Data Description for a Data Product Code that consists of a Data Product Code Value, Data Product Code Name, and Data Product Code Definition.

Data Product Code Name   The Data Name of a Data Product Code.

Data Product Definition   The existing Data Definition of a Data Product.

Data Product Description   The Data Description of a Data Product that consists of a unique Product Name and a Product Definition.

Data Product Group   A set of related Data Products that contains both Primary Data Product and Secondary Data Products.

Data Product Name   The unique Data Name of a Data Product.

Data Product Phase   The second phase of the Mature Data Resource Process. Identifies and defines the Data Products within the project scope.

Data Product Reference   A component of the Data Resource Guide that contains the definitions, integrity rules, and structure of disparate data, and all references between disparate data and the common data architecture.

Data Product Subject   A major grouping of data within a Data Product, such as a record, screen, report, or data subject.

Data Product Subject Definition   The Data Definition of a Data Product Subject.

Data Product Subject Description   The Data Description of a Data Product Subject consisting of a unique Data Product Subject Name and a Data Product Subject Description.

Data Product Subject Name   The unique Data Name of a Data Product Subject.

Data Property   A feature or trait of a data characteristic that supports a Data Code.

Data Proliferation   The process of continuing to capture and store massive quantities of disparate data. *See also* Data Deluge, Data Pollution.

Data Quality   The third activity in the Data Architecture Component of the Data Resource Framework that represents how well data in the Formal Data Resource support the Business Activities of an organization. It includes Data Integrity, Data Accuracy, and Data Completeness.

Data Quality Assurance   The proactive process of ensuring that data in the Formal Data Resource adequately support Business Activities. It ensures effectiveness of the Formal Data Resource. It includes Data Accuracy Assurance, Data Completeness Assurance, and Data Integrity Assurance.

Data Quality Control   The reactive process of determining how well data in the Formal Data Resource support Business Activities. It ensures completeness and correctness of the Formal Data Resource. It includes Data Accuracy Control, Data Completeness Control, and Data Integrity Control.

Data Reality   *See* Shared Data Reality.

Data Record   A physical grouping of Data Items that are stored and retrieved from a Data File. The basic component of a Data File.

Data Redundancy   The existence of the same Data Characteristic in two or more locations.

Data Redundancy Diagram   A diagram for documenting Data Redundancy Integrity.

Data Redundancy Integrity   Data Integrity that specifies proper maintenance of consistent values in each existence of a Redundant Data Characteristic.

Data Redundancy Table   A table for documenting Data Redundancy.

Data Reengineering   *See* Computer Aided Data Engineering, Data Refining.

Data Refinery   Applications that assist with the conversion of crude data to a comprehensive data resource library. *See also* Computer Aided Data Engineering.

Data Refining   The process of taking crude disparate data, refining them within the Common Data Architecture, and storing them in the Formal Data Resource for future use. Part of Data Engineering. *See* Refining.

Data Relation   An association between Data Occurrences in different Data Subjects or within the same Data Subject. They provide the connections between Data Subjects for building the structure of the Common Data Architecture. *See* Acquired Data Relation, Explicit Data Relation, Implicit Data Relation, Inherent Data Relation.

Data Relation Diagram   A diagram that shows the arrangement and relationship of Data Subjects in the Common Data Architecture, but does not show any of the contents of a Data Subject. Also known as an Entity-Relationship Diagram. *See also* Data Structure Chart.

Data Remodeling   *See* Data Refining.

Data Repository   A specific location where data are stored, such as a filing cabinet, computer file, or database management system. *See also* Data File.

Data Repository Definition   The Data Definition for a Data Repository.

Data Repository Name   The formal name that uniquely identifies a Data Repository in the Common Data Architecture.

Data Resource   The data resource of an organization. *See* Formal Data Resource, Mature Data Resource, Total Data Resource.

Data Resource Architecture   An Architecture of the Data Resource for an organization.

Data Resource Availability   A component of the Data Resource Guide that contains data about Primary Data Sources.

Data Resource Clearinghouse   A component of the Data Resource Guide that contains information abut projects that are completed, in progress, or planned for the documentation of existing data, or for the collection and development of new data.

Data Resource Dictionary   A component of the Data Resource Guide that provides an alphabetical list of Data Repositories, Data Subjects, Data Characteristics, Data Characteristic Variations, and Data Codes in the Formal Data Resource with comprehensive definitions about their content and meaning.

Data Resource Directory   A component of the Data Resource Guide that provides information about who has data and how those data can be acquired.

Data Resource Framework   A framework in the Information Technology Infrastructure that contains a discipline for the complete management of the data resource. It consists of three components for Data Management, Data Architecture, and Data Availability. *See also* Business Activity Framework, Information Systems Framework, Platform Resource Framework.

Data Resource Geography   A component of the Data Resource Guide that contains references to the existence of spatial data.

Data Resource Glossary   A component of the Data Resource Guide that provides an alphabetical listing of words, terms, and abbreviations used in data definitions in the Common Data Architecture.

Data Resource Guide   A repository for detailed meta-data about the organization's Data Resource and the Common Data Architecture. It provides extensive information about all data in the Formal Data Resource.

Data Resource Guide Index An index to components in the Data Resource Guide.

Data Resource Guide Tutorial A tutorial for using the Data Resource Guide and an on-line help facility.

Data Resource Integrity A component of the Data Resource Guide that contains all the Data Integrity Rules for the Formal Data Resource.

Data Resource Inventory A detailed inventory of data needed to support business strategies and data that already exist. *See* Data Needs Inventory, Data Availability Inventory.

Data Resource Lexicon A component of the Data Resource Guide that contains a special vocabulary of common words used to form Data Names and their definitions, and a list of words and their abbreviations for formally abbreviating Data Names.

Data Resource Library A Library containing an organization's formal data resource, organized by data subject independently of the way people use the data, and cross referenced in a variety of ways.

Data Resource Management The business activity responsible for designing, building, and maintaining the data resource of an organization and making data readily available for developing information.

Data Resource Model A comprehensive model of an organization's Formal Data Resource, including both the logical and physical design. *See also* Data Model.

Data Resource Structure A component of the Data Resource Guide that contains Data Relation Diagrams, Logical Data Structure Charts, Data File Diagrams, and Physical Data Structure Charts.

Data Resource Survey A high-level data inventory that determines both data needs and data availability by Broad Data Groupings. *See* Data Needs Survey, Data Availability Survey.

Data Resource Thesaurus A component of the Data Resource Guide that provides a set of data name synonyms to help people locate the particular data they need. It provides a reference between similar names or business terms and the true data names.

Data Restructuring The process of changing the structure of data from application files to the Data Resource Library. It is one component of the Data Refining process.

Data Retention Integrity Data Integrity that specifies the criteria for preventing the loss of critical data through updates or deletion.

Data Retention Integrity Statement A statement that specifies exactly what is done to existing Data Occurrences before they are deleted and to Data Characteristics before they are updated.

Data Retrodocumentation The process of documenting existing data in terms of the Common Data Architecture. It is a process to collect and store meta-data, but does not improve the quality or structure of data.

Data Rule Domain A Data Domain containing Data Integrity Rules. *See* Data Value Domain.

Data Sharing A process where data are shared between organizations or major segments of a large organization. Consists of a Data Sharing Medium and a Data Sharing Message.

Data Sharing Medium The medium over which data are shared, such as a network, a tape, a diskette, or other mechanism for sharing data. Generally not a major problem for sharing data. *See also* Data Sharing Message.

Data Sharing Message The content and meaning of data being shared over a Data Sharing Medium. *See also* Data Sharing Medium, Message.

Data Sharing Phase The fifth phase of Mature Data Resource Process. Facilitates data sharing after the official data variations are designated.

Data Sharing Strategy A strategy to share data that consists of determining data needed to support Business Activities, locating those data, and then acquiring them.

Data Source The organization providing data used in data sharing. *See* Primary Data Source, Secondary Data Source. *See also* Data Target.

Data Source Table A table that shows all the possible sources for each data product characteristic in the receiving application or database. *See also* Data Feed Table.

Data Structure (1)   The second activity in the Data Architecture component of the Data Resource Framework. Includes the arrangement, relationship, and contents of data subjects, including logical and physical data, and working and categorical levels of data classification.

Data Structure (2)   A representation of the arrangement, relationship, and contents of data subjects and data files. It includes both the logical and physical data, and both the working levels and categorical levels of data classification.

Data Structure Chart   A chart showing the contents of each data subject, but not the arrangement or relationship of those subjects. *See also* Data Relation Diagram.

Data Structure Outline   The preferred format for a Logical Data structure Chart.

Data Structure Integrity   Data Integrity that specifies rules pertaining to Data Relations.

Data Structure Integrity Diagram   A diagram showing Data Structure Integrity.

Data Structure Integrity Matrix   A matrix showing Data Structure Integrity.

Data Structure Integrity Table   A table showing Data Structure Integrity.

Data Subject   A person, place, thing, event, or concept about which an organization collects and manages data. Described by a set of Data Characteristics. Also known as a Data Entity.

Data Subject Cross Reference   A Data Cross Reference between a Data Product Subject and a Common Data Subject.

Data Subject Definition   The Data Definition for a Data Subject.

Data Subject Form   Different forms of a Data Subject. *See* Data Subject Type, True Data Subject, Virtual Data Subject.

Data Subject Hierarchy   A hierarchical structure of Data Subjects with branched one-to-one Data Relations. It represents a mutually exclusive, or can-only-be, situation. Previously known as an Entity Type Hierarchy.

Data Subject Name   The formal name that uniquely identifies a Data Subject in the Common Data Architecture and indicates the structure of the formal data resource.

Data Subject Type   A breakdown of a True Data Subject that either has no data characteristics of its own, or Data Characteristics that inherit their data names and definitions directly from a True Data Subject. *See also* Virtual Data Subject, True Data Subject.

Data Subject Variation   A Data Product Subject that does not exactly match a Common Data Subject.

Data Suitability   How suitable data are for a specific purpose. A part of Data Quality.

Data Survey Analysis   A process that compares data needs from a Data Needs Survey with the data available from an Data Availability Survey to identify data that already exist and data that need to be acquired.

Data Survey Template   A Data Template consisting of Broad Data Groupings for conducting Data Resource Surveys. *See also* Data Design Template, Data Inventory Template.

Data Target   The organization receiving data from data sharing. *See also* Data Source.

Data Template   A Template for either identifying existing data in terms of the Common Data Architecture or designing data based on Official Data Variations. *See* Data Design Template, Data Inventory Template, Data Survey Template.

Data Theme   Specific groupings of data for a specific purpose. They can cross the categorical Levels of the Data Classification and can easily change. They may cross Broad Data Groupings in the Data Classification Scheme.

Data Topic   One or more closely related data characteristics used in a Geographic Information System. *See also* Data Layer.

Data Tracking   The process of tracking data from their origin to their ultimate destination.

Data Translation   *See* Data Translation Scheme.

Data Translation Scheme   A translation between common data characteristic variations when those data characteristic variations represent measurements or format variations. *See* Fundamental Data Translation Scheme, Official Data Translation Scheme, Non-Official Data Translation Scheme, Specific Data Translation Scheme.

Data Translation Schemes   A component of the Data Resource Guide that contains Data Translation Schemes between data characteristic variations.

Data Value   The individual facts and figures contained in Data Characteristics. *See* Actual Data Value, Coded Data Value.

Data Value Domain   A Data Domain containing Data Integrity Values. *See also* Data Rule Domain.

Data Value Integrity   Data Integrity that specifies the allowable values for each Data Characteristic and each relation between data characteristics in the Formal Data Resource. *See* Data Integrity Rule, Data Integrity Value.

Data Variability   The degree of variability in the meaning, content, and format of Disparate Data.

Data Variability Phase   The fourth phase of Mature Data Resource process. Identifies the extent of data variability, designates official data variations and official primary keys, and prepares data translation schemes.

Data Variation   The variations in format, content, or meaning of data. Not the same as a Data Version. *See* Data Characteristic Variation, Data Code Variation, Non-Official Data Variation, Official Data Variation.

Data Version   A different set of data values representing a different Data Instance. A later Data Version is a more up-to-date version of the data. Not the same as a Data Variation.

Data Volatility   How quickly data in the real world change. Part of Data Accuracy.

Database   A set of one or more Data Files. May or may not be in a database management system.

Database Conversion   The process of converting data from a database with one structure to a database with another structure. *See also* Data Conversion.

Database Converters   Routines for converting data in Disparate Data Files to the Mature Data Resource Library.

Database Conversion Plan   A plan for building the Mature Data Resource from Disparate Data Files.

Denormalization   *See* Data Denormalization.

Denormalized Data   Data that are denormalized for implementation into a specific operating environment. They are represented by a Physical Data Resource Model. *See also* Normalized Data, Denormalized Data.

Denotative Meaning   The direct, explicit meaning in a Data Definition. *See also* Connotative Meaning.

Deployment   *See* Data Deployment.

Derivation Procedure   *See* Data Derivation Procedure.

Derived Data   Data that are derived from other data and are not obtained by direct measurement or observation. *See also* Active Derived Data, Primitive Data, Static Derived Data.

Derived Data Characteristic   A Data Characteristic whose value is derived, generated, summarized, or otherwise formed by some algorithm. *See also* Primitive Data Characteristic.

Derived Data Integrity   Data Integrity that specifies rules for maintaining derived and redundant data.

Derived Data Layer   A Data Layer containing two or more Data Topics. *See also* Primitive Data Layer.

Desired Common Data Architecture   The Common Data Architecture used for identifying Data Variations and Data Translation Schemes, and for building the Mature Data Resource. *See also* Interim Common Data Architecture.

Detail Data Relation Diagram   A Data Relation Diagram that shows all the data subjects in the Common Data Architecture and their relationships. *See also* Strategic Data Relation Diagram and Tactical Data Relation Diagram.

Dictionary An alphabetical list of words in a language, with definitions, meaning, origin and development, pronunciations, usage guidelines, and other information. *See* Data Resource Dictionary.

Directory A book of directions or a listing of names and locations for a specific group of people or organizations. *See* Data Resource Directory.

Discovery Process A process where new information is continuously being discovered. Data Refining is a discovery process.

Disparate Refers to things that are essentially not alike, or are distinctly different in kind, quality, or character. They are fundamentally different and are often incompatible.

Disparate Data Data that are essentially not alike, or are distinctly different in kind, quality, or character. They are fundamentally different and are often incompatible. They are unequal and cannot be readily integrated. Data that exist in a variety of locations, on a variety of different databases, with a variety of different structures, and a variety of documentation. They are generally inconsistent, unreliable, incompatible, incomplete, inaccurate, and expensive to maintain and access. They are heterogeneous data.

Disparate Data Characteristic Names The unique names of disparate data characteristics formed from the Data Naming Taxonomy.

Disparate Data Code A Data Code in a Disparate Data Item.

Disparate Data Derivation Algorithm The Data Derivation Algorithm that actually exists for Disparate Data, whether or not it is implemented and whether or not it is documented. *See also* Official Data Derivation Algorithm.

Disparate Data Derivation Diagram A Data Derivation Diagram documenting the derivations in Disparate Data.

Disparate Data Domains Data Domains that contain Disparate Data Value Integrity. *See also* Official Data Domain.

Disparate Data File A Data File that did not go through logical data modeling with data normalization or denormalization and does not represent one complete data subject.

Disparate Data File Diagram   A Data File Diagram representing the structure of Disparate Data Files.

Disparate Data Integrity Rules   The Data Integrity Rules that actually exist for Disparate Data and may or may not be formally documented.

Disparate Data Item   A Data Item that represents two or more unrelated data characteristics.

Disparate Data Record   A Data Record that does not represent one complete Data Occurrence of a Data Subject in a Disparate Data File.

Disparate Data Relation   A Data Relation that actually exists in Disparate Data, whether or not it is documented. *See also* Official Data Relation.

Disparate Data Relation Diagram   A Data Relation Diagram that shows Disparate Data Relations. *See also* Official Data Relation Diagram.

Disparate Data Retention Rule   The actual Data Retention Rule that exists in Disparate Data, whether or not it is documented. *See also* Official Data Retention Rule.

Disparate Data Structure Chart   A variation of the Physical Data Structure Chart for documenting Disparate Data.

Disparate Data Structure Integrity   The Data Structure Integrity that actually exists in Disparate Data, whether or not it is documented. *See also* Official Data Structure Integrity.

Disparate Data Syndrome   A set of signs and symptoms about an organization's data that form an identifiable pattern of disparate data.

Disparate Data Value Integrity   The Data Value Integrity that actually exists for Disparate Data, whether or not it is documented.

Disparate Foreign Key   Any Foreign Key defined in a Disparate Data File.

Disparate Primary Key   Any Primary Key defined in a Disparate Data File.

Domain   *See* Data Domain, Data Rule Domain, Data Value Domain.

Downsizing The process of moving all or part of an application or database to smaller, lower-cost computers. *See also* Rightsizing.

DRM *See* Data Resource Management.

EDI *See* Electronic Data Interchange.

EIS *See* Executive Information Systems.

Electronic Data Interchange The electronic exchange of standard data between two or more applications, often in two or more hardware environments, without manual intervention.

Elemental Data Individual facts that cannot be subdivided and retain any meaning. *See also* Combined Data, Combined Data Characteristic, Elemental Data Characteristic.

Elemental Data Characteristic An atomic level Data Characteristic that cannot be further subdivided and retain any meaning. *See also* Combined Data, Combined Data Characteristic, Elemental Data.

Engineering The science of putting scientific knowledge to practical use in the planning, design, construction, and management of something. *See also* Data Engineering, Information Engineering.

Entity *See* Data Entity, Behavioral Entity.

Entity Type Hierarchy The traditional term for a Data Subject Hierarchy.

Entity-Relationship Diagram The traditional name for a diagram that shows the arrangement and relationship of data subjects. *See* Data Relation Diagram.

ER Diagram *See* Entity-Relationship Diagram.

ESS *See* Executive Support System.

Everybody's Information System *See* Executive Information Systems.

Evolutionary Stages A series of five stages an organization goes through to achieve an integrated Common Data Architecture and a Mature Data Resource. *See* Common Data Architecture Stage, Organization Cluster Stage, Organization Stage, Project Stage, Traditional Stage.

Executive Information Systems Applications that provide financial, marketing, operational, personnel, and competitive information to executives in summary form. Becoming known as Everybody's Information System.

Executive Support Systems A broad group of systems that support executives, including electronic mail, scheduling, calendaring, decision support systems, executive information systems, and so on.

Explicit Data Relation A Data Relation that is shown explicitly on a Data Relation Diagram. *See also* Implicit Data Relation.

Extended Data Product Definition A definition of a Data Product, Data Product Subject, Data Product Characteristic, or Data Product Code that includes the original definition as it appears in the original documentation, followed by any additional information gained during analysis of the data product.

Foreign Data Characteristic A Data Characteristic that exists in a Data Subject other than the one it characterizes. *See also* Home Data Characteristic.

Foreign Key The Primary Key of a parent Data Subject that is placed in a Subordinate Data Subject. Its value identifies the Data Occurrence in the Parent Data Subject that is the parent of the Data Occurrence in the Subordinate Data Subject. *See also* Primary Key, Secondary Key.

Formal Data Resource An integrated, comprehensive data resource that makes data readily identifiable and easily accessible by Information Engineering. A subset of the Total Data Resource that contains data identified within the Common Data Architecture. *See also* Mature Data Resource.

Forward Engineering Denormalizing a Logical Data Resource Model to a Physical Data Resource Model, following Reverse Engineering.

Framework *See* Data Resource Framework, Zachman Framework.

Frequency of Collection How often data are collected. Part of Data Accuracy.

From-Above Approach An approach to developing a Formal Data Resource based on strategic direction through identification of Organization Clusters and Critical Areas. *See also* From-Below Approach.

From-Below Approach   An approach to developing a Formal Data Resource that provides Baseline Data. *See also* From-Above Approach.

Fully Qualified Data Characteristic   A Data Characteristic whose name contains a sufficient number of words so that there is no confusion as to what that Data Characteristic represents.

Fundamental Data   Data that do not exist in databases and are not used in applications, but support the definition of Specific Data.

Fundamental Data Integrity Rules   Data Integrity Rules that apply to Fundamental Data. *See also* Specific Data Integrity Rules.

Fundamental Data Translation Scheme   A Data Translation Scheme that applies to many Specific Data Characteristics. *See also* Specific Data Translation Scheme.

Geographic Information System   A system for storing, manipulating, and retrieving large quantities of spatial data.

Geography   *See* Data Resource Geography.

GIS   *See* Geographic Information Systems.

Glossary   An alphabetical listing of words and abbreviations. *See* Data Resource Glossary.

Guide   *See* Data Resource Guide.

Heritage Systems   Information systems that have been in place for many years, support a critical business function, and are performing satisfactorily. *See also* Legacy Systems.

Heterogeneous   Consisting of dissimilar or unlike ingredients or constituents, or having a dissimilar structure or composition. *See also* Homogenous.

Heterogeneous Data   Another term for disparate data. *See also* Homogenous Data.

Hexagon   A symbol that represents a business entity on diagrams.

Hidden Data Resource   The large quantities of data that are largely unknown, unavailable, and unused because they are not easily identified, understood, or located.

Hidden Data Subject A Data Subject that is not readily visible, but is indicated by the presence of an Indicator.

Hierarchy *See* Data Subject Hierarchy.

High Quality Data Data that adequately support Business Activities. *See also* Low Quality Data.

Home Data Characteristic A Data Characteristic that exists in the Data Subject it characterizes. *See also* Foreign Data Characteristic.

Homogenous Consisting of the same or similar ingredients or constituents, or having a uniform structure or composition. *See also* Heterogeneous.

Homogenous Data Data that have the same structure, content, and meaning regardless of the database management system or operating environment where they reside. *See also* Disparate Data.

Horizon A point in the future that a Vision represents.

Identifier *See* Unique Identifier, Primary Key.

Implicit Data Relation A Data Relation that exists between Data Subjects by the existence of Data Characteristics in the Primary Key, but is not shown on a Data Relation Diagram. *See also* Explicit Data Relation.

Index *See* Data Resource Guide Index.

Indicator A Data Characteristic that identifies a binary situation, such as 0/1, on/off, yes/no, or true/false.

Information A collection of data in the form of a Message that is relevant to the recipient at a point in time. It must be meaningful and useful to the recipient at a specific time for a specific purpose. *See also* Data.

Information Base A situation that does not exist with the current definition of Information because information cannot be stored; only data can be stored. *See also* Database.

Information Engineering The discipline for developing information systems to produce Messages that provide information to the recipient. A manufacturing process that uses data as the raw material to construct and transmit a Message. *See also* Data Engineering.

Information Overload A situation that does not exist with the current definition of Information because recipients cannot be overloaded with information that is relevant to them. *See also* Data Overload.

Information Quality The degree to which Data are transformed into Information to resolve uncertainty or meet a need. *See also* Data Quality.

Information Refinery Applications that perform Information Refining.

Information Refining The process that takes undifferentiated raw data, extracts the content into elemental units, and recombines them into usable information.

Information Resource Management Traditionally, the management of Information as a resource. In the new approach it does not exist, because the relevance to a recipient cannot be managed as a resource.

Information System The integration of business activities, the data resource, and the platform resource.

Information System Framework A framework in the Information Technology Infrastructure that represents the integration of business activities, the data resource, and the platform resource to support an organization's business strategies. *See also* Business Activity Framework, Data Resource Framework, Platform Resource Framework, Zachman Framework.

Information Technology Infrastructure An Infrastructure consisting of the four Information Technology Frameworks for business activities, the data resource, the platform resource, and information systems. *See* Business Activity Framework, Data Resource Framework Information Systems Framework, Platform Resource Framework.

Infrastructure An underlying foundation or framework for a system or an organization. *See* Information Technology Infrastructure.

Inherent Data Relation A Data Relation that exists between two Data Subjects based on the definition of those Data Subjects. *See also* Acquired Data Relation.

Inheritance   The situation where something is received from a predecessor, ancestor, or other type of contributor. *See* Data Definition Inheritance.

Instance   *See* Data Instance.

Integrity   *See* Data Integrity.

Intelligent Databases   Databases with applications, usually expert systems with an associated knowledge base, that search intelligently for patterns, trends, and other information of importance to the organization.

Interim Common Data Architecture   Any intermediate, temporary Common Data Architecture used as a step toward the Desired Common Data Architecture.

Interim Cross Reference   Same as Common-to-Common Cross Reference. *See also* Primary Cross Reference, Secondary Cross Reference.

Interoperability   A form of Cooperative Processing that allows systems to communicate across previously incompatible groups of hardware and software without human intervention.

Inventory   *See* Data Availability Inventory, Data Inventory, Data Needs Inventory, Data Resource Inventory, Traditional Data Inventory.

IRM   *See* Information Resource Management.

Irregular Data Codes   The situation where many different Data Product Code Values are allowed for the same data property.

Irregular Data Product Characteristic   A Data Product Characteristic containing data that does not have consistent content or format.

Issue   *See* Data Definition Issue.

Just-in-Time Data   Data that are available just when they are needed to produce information.

Just-in-Time Information   Information that is available just when it is needed to support business activities and meet information needs.

Key   An unqualified term. *See* Data Key, Foreign Key, Primary Key, Secondary Key.

Keyword   *See* Common Word.

Knowledgeable People People who have knowledge about the disparate data being refined and/or knowledge about the business.

Legacy Systems Information systems that have been in place for many years, support a critical business function, but are not performing satisfactorily and need to be replaced. *See also* Heritage Systems.

Lexicon A special vocabulary of a particular author or field of study. *See* Data Resource Lexicon.

Library A place where literary, musical, artistic, or reference materials are available for use, but are not for sale. A resource of works organized by subject and cross referenced by subject, title, and author. *See* Data Resource Library.

Limited Foreign Key A Foreign Key that matches a Limited Primary Key in a Parent Data Subject. *See also* Alternate Foreign Key, Obsolete Foreign Key, Official Foreign Key.

Limited Key A Primary Key that is valid for a limited set of Data Occurrences and does not uniquely identify all Data Occurrences in a Data Subject within the Common Data Architect. *See also* Alternate Key, Candidate Key, Obsolete Key, Official Key.

Limited Primary Key A Primary Key whose uniqueness is limited to a subset of the Data Occurrences within the scope of the Common Data Architecture. *See also* Alternate Primary Key, Candidate Primary Key, Obsolete Primary Key, Official Primary Key.

Logical Data References to data that appear on a data resource model, in a data architecture, or other documentation about the data resource. They represent the existence of Physical Data or a plan for development of physical data.

Logical Data Resource Model A logical model of the Data Resource. *See also* Physical Data Resource Model.

Logical Data Structure The Data Structure representing logical data. Part of a Logical Data Resource Model. *See also* Physical Data Structure.

Logical Data Structure Chart A Data Structure Chart showing the primary keys, foreign keys, secondary keys, and data characteristics contained in a Data Subject. *See also* Physical Data Structure Chart.

Low Quality Data Data that do not adequately support Business Activities. *See also* High Quality Data.

Major Data Flow A data flow between organizations or major segments of a large organization. Represented by a solid line between two business entities with an arrow on one end.

Major Data Flow Diagram A Data Flow Diagram showing Major Data Flows. A variation of the traditional data flow diagram that represents data moving between business entities.

Major Data Flow Network A set of Major Data Flows between many organizations, or many segments of a large organization that form a network rather than a set of linear flows.

Mandate *See* Data Mandate, Conflicting Data Mandates.

Many-to-Many Data Relation A Data Relation where a Data Occurrence in one Data Subject is related to more than one Data Occurrence in the second Data Subject, and each Data Occurrence in the second Data Subject is related to more than one Data Occurrence in the first Data Subject. Shown by a Dashed Line with an arrowhead on each end.

Many-to-Many Recursive Data Relation A Many-to-Many Data Relation within a Data Subject where each Data Occurrence can be related to many other Data Occurrences in that Data Subject. Results in Cyclic Data Subjects.

Mature Data Resource A subset of the Formal Data Resource that contains all Official Data Variations. The ultimate goal for an organization's Data Resource. *See also* Total Data Resource.

Mature Data Resource Model A Data Resource Model of the Mature Data Resource.

Mature Data Resource Phase The sixth, and last, phase of Mature Data Resource Process. Develops a Mature Data Resource.

Mature Data Resource Process A process consisting of six phases that lead from Disparate Data to a Mature Data Resource.

Meaning *See* Connotative Meaning, Denotative Meaning.

Medium *See* Data Sharing Medium.

Message Information: A communication containing a collection of data in some order and format. Data Sharing: The actual data being shared, independent of the sharing medium. Generally a much greater problem that the sharing medium.

Meta-Data Data about the data. They include names, definitions, logical and physical data structure, data integrity, data accuracy, and any other data about the organization's data resource. Specifically, these data concern the Common Data Architecture and the Formal Data Resource.

Multiple Data Code Sets The situation where there are many sets of Data Product Codes cross referenced to one set of Common Data Codes. *See also* Simple Data Code Set.

Multiple Data Sources The situation where the same data may be received from two or more sources.

Multiple Foreign Keys The situation where there are is than one Foreign Key in a Data Subject for the same Parent Data Subject. *See also* Multiple Primary Keys.

Multiple Primary Keys The situation where a Data Subject contains two or more Primary Keys. *See also* Multiple Foreign Keys.

Mutually Exclusive The Data Relations between Data Subjects in a Data Subject Hierarchy. *See* Can-Only-Be.

Mutually Exclusive Data Codes The situation where individual Data Product Codes are placed in separate Data Product Characteristics.

Mutually Exclusive Parents The situation where a Data Subject has two or more parent Data Subjects that are mutually exclusive.

Name Abbreviation *See* Data Name Abbreviation.

Naming Convention *See* Data Naming Convention.

No Blame–No Whitewash An approach used with the Modified Delphi Technique to ensure client participation and obtain maximum information about an organization's data.

Non-Official Data Code Set A Data Code Set that has not been designated as official. *See also* Official Data Code Set.

Non-Official Data Characteristic Variation A Data Characteristic Variation that has not been designated as official. *See also* Official Data Characteristic Variation.

Non-Official Data Translation Scheme A Data Translation Scheme that translates data between Non-Official Data Variations. *See also* Official Data Translation Scheme.

Non-Official Data Variation A Data Variation that has not been designated as an Official Data Variation. *See also* Official Data Variation.

Non-Official Primary Key A Candidate Primary Key that has not been designated as the Official Primary Key.

Non-Tabular Data Data that do not exist in tabular form, such as images, spatial data, remote sensing, voice, and text. *See also* Tabular Data.

Normalization *See* Data Normalization.

Normalized Data The way data are stored by Data Subject in the Formal Data Resource. The data that are represented by a Logical Data Resource Model. *See also* Data Normalization, Denormalized Data, Unnormalized Data.

Note *See* Data Definition Note.

Obsolete Foreign Key A Foreign Key that matches an Obsolete Primary Key in a Parent Data Subject. *See also* Alternate Foreign Key, Limited Foreign Key, Official Foreign Key.

Obsolete Primary Key A Primary Key that no longer uniquely identifies each Data Occurrence in a Data Subject within the Common Data Architecture. *See also* Alternate Primary Key, Candidate Primary Key, Limited Primary Key, Official Primary Key.

Of Language An early attempt to put structure and formality into a data name by progressing from specific to general and placing "of" between consecutive words.

Official Data Characteristic Variation A Data Characteristic Variation that has been designated by consensus and accepted as the official variation for long-term evolution to the Mature Data Resource. *See also* Non-Official Data Characteristic Variation.

Official Data Code Set   A set of Codes that has been designated by consensus and accepted as the official variation for long-term evolution to the Mature Data Resource. *See also* Non-Official Data Code Set.

Official Data Derivation Algorithm   A Data Derivation Algorithm that has been designated by the consensus of knowledgeable people as official for the Formal Data Resource. *See also* Disparate Data Derivation Algorithm.

Official Data Domain   A Data Domain in the Common Data Architecture that has been designated by the consensus of knowledgeable people as official for maintaining data quality in the formal data resource.

Official Data Relation   A Data Relation defined in the Common Data Architecture. *See also* Disparate Data Relation.

Official Data Relation Diagram   A Data Relation Diagram in the Common Data Architecture. *See also* Disparate Data Relation Diagram.

Official Data Retention Rule   The Data Retention Rules that have been designated by consensus as official for the Mature Data Resource. *See also* Disparate Data Retention Rules.

Official Data Structure Integrity   The Data Structure Integrity that has been designated as official by the consensus of knowledgeable people for maintaining data quality in the Formal Data Resource. *See also* Disparate Data Structure Integrity.

Official Data Translation Scheme   A Data Translation Scheme that translates data between Non-Official Data Variations and Official Data Variations. *See also* Non-Official Data Translation Scheme.

Official Data Variation   A Data Variation that has been designated by the consensus of knowledgeable people as the data variation to be used for short-term data sharing and long-term evolution to the Mature Data Resource. *See also* Non-Official Data Variation.

Official Foreign Key   A Foreign Key that matches the Official Primary Key in a Parent Data Subject. *See also* Alternate Foreign Key, Limited Foreign Key, Obsolete Foreign Key.

Official Key   A Primary Key that is designated as the dominant, outstanding, or preferred Primary Key for a Data Subject in the Mature Data Resource. It is valid for all Data Occurrences of a Data Subject in the Common Data Architecture. *See also* Alternate Key, Candidate Key, Obsolete Key, Primary Key.

Official Primary Key   A Primary Key whose value is unique for all Data Occurrences within the scope of the Common Data Architecture and has been designated as official for long-term evolution to the Mature Data Resource. *See also* Non-Official Primary Key.

One-to-Many Data Relation   A Data Relation where a Data Occurrence in one Data Subject is related to more than one Data Occurrence in the second Data Subject, but each Data Occurrence in the second Data Subject is related to only one Data Occurrence in the first Data Subject. Shown by a Dashed Line with an arrowhead on one end.

One-to-Many Recursive Data Relation   A One-to-Many Data Relation within a Data Subject where a Data Occurrence is related to two or more other Data Occurrences in that Data Subject. Also known as an Open Recursive Data Relation.

One-to-One Data Relation   A Data Relation where a Data Occurrence in one Data Subject is related to only one Data Occurrence in the second Data Subject, and that Data Occurrence in the second data subject is related to only one Data Occurrence in the first Data Subject. Shown by a Dashed Line with no arrowheads.

One-to-One Recursive Data Relation   A One-to-One Data Relation where a Data Occurrence in one Data Subject is related to only one other Data Occurrence in that Data Subject. Also known as a Closed Recursive Data Relation.

Open Recursive Data Relation   *See* One-to-Many Recursive Data Relation.

Open Systems   An open architecture that allows seamless integration across different platforms and gives people unlimited ability to produce new and innovative applications.

Optional Data Integrity Rules   Specific Data Integrity Rules that are optional or may be applied in certain situations. *See also* Required Data Integrity Rules.

Organization Cluster A group of organizations performing the same, or essentially the same, types of Business Activities and sharing similar data.

Organization Cluster Stage The fourth Evolutionary Stage, characterized by a Common Data Architecture evolving for organization clusters, but minimal effort between organization clusters. It is the desired stage for many organizations, but not the ideal stage. *See also* Common Data Architecture Stage, Organization Stage, Project Stage, Traditional Stage.

Organization Stage The third Evolutionary Stage, characterized by commonality at the organization level, but minimal interest in commonality between organizations. It is an acceptable stage, but not the desired stage. *See also* Common Data Architecture Stage, Organization Cluster Stage, Project Stage, Traditional Stage.

Oval The symbol used on a Data File Diagram to represent a Data File.

Overload *See* Data Overload, Information Overload.

Parent Data Subject A Data Subject that has one or more Subordinate Data Subjects.

Passive Data Definition Reference No formal connection between the contributing Data Definition and the receiving Data Definition. *See also* Active Data Definition Reference.

Phase *See* Preparation Phase, Data Product Phase, Data Cross Reference Phase, Data Variability Phase, Data Sharing Phase, Mature Data Resource Phase.

Physical Data Data that actually exist in a data file, database, database management system, or manual storage. *See also* Logical Data.

Physical Data Resource Model A physical model of the Data Resource. *See also* Logical Data Resource Model.

Physical Data Structure The Data Structure representing Physical Data Part of the Physical Data Resource Model. *See also* Logical Data Structure.

Physical Data Structure Chart A Data Structure Chart showing the Data Keys and Data Items contained in a Data File.

Platform Resource Framework   A framework in the Information Technology Infrastructure that represents the hardware and system software in an organization or between organizations. *See also* Business Activity Framework, Data Resource Framework, Information Systems Framework.

Portfolio   *See* Data Portfolio.

Pragmatics   The part of Semiotic Theory dealing with the relation between signs and symbols and their users, specifically the usefulness of those signs and symbols. It requires that everything have a practical value. *See also* Semantics, Syntatics.

Precision   How precisely a measurement was made and how many significant digits are in the measurement. Part of Data Accuracy.

Preparation Phase   The first phase of Mature Data Resource Process. Establishes the scope of the project, identifies knowledgeable people, develops the initial data architecture, and prepares support tools.

Proliferation   *See* Data Proliferation.

Primary Cross Reference   A Data Cross Reference between data product names and Primary Data Names in the Common Data Architecture. *See also* Primary Cross Reference, Product-to-Common Cross Reference, Secondary Cross Reference.

Primary Data Name   The official, real-world, fully spelled out Data Name that is not codified or abbreviated in any way and is not subject to any length restrictions. *See also* Alias Data Name.

Primary Data Product   A Data Product that contains considerable information about Disparate Data, such as a database listing, a program, or a data dictionary. *See also* Secondary Product.

Primary Data Source   An organization that initially collects data, modifies data, or creates data. The record of reference. *See also* Data Source, Secondary Data Source.

Primary Key   A set of one or more Data Characteristics whose values uniquely identify a Data Occurrence in a Data Subject. Also known as a Unique Identifier.

Primary Key Criteria   A set of criteria for determining the validity of a Primary Key.

Primary Key Matrix   a matrix for showing the Data Characteristics comprising the Primary Keys for a Data Subject.

Primitive Data   Data that are obtained directly from an object. *See also* Derived Data.

Primitive Data Characteristic   A Data Characteristic whose value represents a feature or actual measurement of a feature or trait of a Data Subject. *See also* Derived Data Characteristic.

Primitive Data Layer   A Data Layer consisting of a single Data Topic. *See also* Derived Data Layer.

Product-to-Common Cross Reference   A Data Cross Reference between a Primary Data Product and either the Interim Common Data Architecture or the Desired Common Data Architecture. Also known as a Primary Cross Reference.

Product-to-Desired Common Cross Reference   A Data Cross Reference between a Primary Data Product or Secondary Data Product and the Desired Common Data Architecture.

Product-to-Interim Common Cross Reference   A Data Cross Reference between a Primary Data Product or Secondary Data Product and the Interim Common Data Architecture.

Product-to-Product Cross Reference   A Data Cross Reference between a Secondary Product and a Primary Product. Also known as a Secondary Cross Reference.

Project Stage   The second Evolutionary Stage characterized by an orientation to major projects in an organization. The normal stage for most organizations today. *See also* Common Data Architecture Stage, Organization Stage, Organization Cluster Stage, Traditional Stage.

Purchased Application   Any application that is purchased or otherwise acquired by an organization, where the organization does not have access to or control of the code or data structure.

Quality   *See* Data Quality, Information Quality.

Quality Assurance   *See* Data Quality Assurance.

Quality Control   *See* Data Quality Control.

Question   *See* Data Definition Question.

Questionable Data Characteristic Name   A data characteristic name that is incomplete or questionable. An incomplete name contains a dash and a questionable name contains a question mark.

Range of Uniqueness   The range of Data Occurrences for which values of the Primary Key provide uniqueness.

Reality   *See* Shared Data Reality.

Recursive Data Relation   A Data Relation between Data Occurrences in the same Data Subject.

Redundant Data   Data Items that exist in two or more locations and carry, or are supposed to carry, the same data values at the same point in time.

Redundancy   *See* Data Redundancy.

Referential Integrity   The part of Data Structure Integrity that ensures a parent Data Occurrence exists for each subordinate Data Occurrence.

Refinery   *See* Data Refinery, Information Refinery.

Refining   The process of removing impurities from crude or impure material to form useful products. *See* Data Refining, Information Refining.

Remodeling Data   *See* Data Refining.

Repository   *See* Data Repository.

Required Data Integrity Rules   Specific Data Integrity Rules that must be applied in all situations. *See also* Optional Data Integrity Rules.

Resolution   The degree of granularity of data, or how small an object can be represented with the current Scale and Precision. Part of Data Accuracy.

Retrodocumentation   The process of documenting something that already exists in terms of a new or current set of standards. Usually a prerequisite for Data Refining. *See* Data Retrodocumentation.

Reusable   Describes something that can be used again in the same form.

Reusable Data   Data that can be used again in the same form. They are data that can be used for more than one purpose. Many of the existing Disparate Data are reusable if their true content and meaning are known. Defining data in terms of a Common Data Architecture makes data reusable.

Reverse Engineering Normalizing a previously denormalized Physical Data Resource Model to a Logical Data Resource Model. Done prior to Forward Engineering to another Physical Data Resource Model.

Rightsizing The process of moving applications or databases to the right size and mix of computers. *See also* Downsizing.

Scale The ratio of real-world distance to map distance. Part of Data Accuracy.

Secondary Cross Reference A Data Cross Reference between two data product names or between two Primary Data Names in the Common Data Architecture. *See also* Product-to-Product Cross Reference, Primary Cross Reference.

Secondary Data Product Any Data Product that contains ancillary information about Disparate Data, such as reports, screens, documents, or other forms of documentation. *See also* Primary Data Product.

Secondary Data Source An organization that acquires data from another organization and stores those data without alteration or modification. *See also* Data Source, Primary Data Source.

Secondary Key A set of Data Characteristics that provide physical access to a Data File. *See also* Foreign Key, Primary Key.

Semantics The part of Semiotic Theory dealing with the relation between signs and symbols and what they represent, specifically their meaning. It includes both Denotative Meaning and Connotative Meaning. *See also* Pragmatics, Syntatics.

Semi-Structured Disparate Data Data that have been structured by Data Subjects at the project or organization level, but do not conform to the structure of the Common Data Architecture. *See also* Unstructured Disparate Data.

Semiotic Data Resource Model A Data Resource Model developed according to Semiotic Theory that includes equal emphasis on Syntax, Semantics, and Pragmatics.

Semiotic Theory The branch of philosophy dealing with the theory of signs, symbols, and their use in expression and communication. Composed of Syntatics, Semantics, and Pragmatics.

Semiotics The general theory of signs and symbols and their use in expression and communication. *See* Semiotic Theory.

Shared Data Reality The Vision for defining data in a common context so they can be readily shared. It has a five- to ten-year Horizon and is based on the Common Data Architecture.

Sharing *See* Data Sharing.

Shell *See* Summary Data Subject Shell.

Simple Data Code Set The situation where one set of Data Product Codes is directly cross referenced to one set of data codes in the Common Data Architecture. *See also* Multiple Data Code Set.

Solid Line The symbol used to represent a flow between two objects, such as a data flow on a data flow diagram. Conforms to Semiotic Theory. *See also* Dashed Line.

Specific Data Data that exist in databases and are used in applications. They may inherit Fundamental Data definitions.

Specific Data Integrity Rules Data Integrity Rules that apply to Specific Data. A subset, or further qualification, of Fundamental Data Integrity Rules.

Specific Data Translation Scheme A Data Translation Scheme that applies to only one Data Characteristic. *See also* Fundamental Data Translation Scheme.

Split Data Code Set The situation where the Data Product Codes in different Data Product Characteristics belong to the same set of Common Data Codes.

Stage *See* Evolutionary Stages, Traditional Stage, Product Stage, Organization Stage, Organization Cluster Stage, Common Data Architecture Stage.

Standard Word *See* Common Word.

Static Data Data that exist and have values that cannot change. *See also* Active Data.

Static Derived Data Derived data that will never change because their contributing data characteristics either are static or no longer exist. *See also* Active Derived Data.

Strategic Data Relation Diagram A Data Relation Diagram that shows the Common Data Architecture on a page or two and usually represents behavioral entities. *See also* Tactical Data Relation Diagram, Detail Data Relation Diagram.

Structure Chart *See* Data Structure Chart.

Subject Data Data that are organized by subjects as perceived by the organization. Subject data are defined independently of business activities or the use of those data.

Subject Databases Data Files that are organized by subjects independently of specific applications.

Subordinate Data Subject A Data Subject that is subordinate, or a child of, another Parent Data Subject.

Substitution *See* Data Name Substitution

Suitability *See* Data Suitability.

Summary Data Data that are summarized or aggregated in some manner. One type of Derived Data.

Summary Data Structure Shell A template that shows all the Parent Data Subjects involved in developing a set of Summary Data Subjects, regardless of whether they are involved in the summarization.

Summary Data Subject A Data Subject containing summary data and identified by a Primary Key that consists of the Primary Keys of the Parent Data Subjects.

Survey *See* Data Availability Survey, Data Needs Survey, Data Resource Survey.

Syndrome A group of signs or symptoms that usually occur together and characterize a particular abnormality. A set of concurrent things that usually form an identifiable pattern. *See* Disparate Data Syndrome.

Syntatics The part of Semiotic Theory dealing with the relation between signs and symbols and their interpretation, specifically the rules of syntax for those signs and symbols. *See also* Semantics, Pragmatics.

Syntax   *See* Syntactics.

Tabular Data   Data that can be stored and displayed in tabular form. *See also* Non-Tabular Data.

Tactical Data Relation Diagram   A Data Relation Diagram that shows the major data subjects in the Common Data Architecture and their relationships. *See also* Strategic Data Relation Diagram, Detail Data Relation Diagram.

Taxonomy   The science of classification and a system for arranging things into natural, related groups based on common features. *See* Data Naming Taxonomy.

Template   A pattern for forming an accurate copy of an object or shape, or for categorizing an object or shape. *See* Data Template. *See also* Data Resource Template, Data Design Template, Data Inventory Template, Data Survey Template.

Theme   *See* Data Theme.

Thesaurus   A book containing a store of words, specifically a book of synonyms and antonyms. A book of selected words or concepts, often for a given field, for use in information retrieval. *See* Data Resource Thesaurus.

Topic   *See* Data Topic.

Total Data Resource   The total of all data available to the organization. *See also* Formal Data Resource, Mature Data Resource.

Tracking   *See* Data Tracking.

Traditional Data Name   Data names that were formed by abbreviations and truncations as programs were written or data files were developed. They preceded Data Naming Conventions.

Traditional Data Inventory   A data inventory based on separate lists of physical data items. It is an approach that seldom works or produces meaningful results. *See* Data Inventory.

Traditional Stage   The first Evolutionary Stage characterized by fragmented islands of data. An undesirable stage. *See also* Common

Data Architecture Stage, Organization Stage, Organization Cluster Stage, Project Stage.

Translation The process of changing to a different substance, form, or appearance. *See* Data Translation Scheme.

Translation Scheme *See* Data Translation Scheme.

True Data Subject A Data Subject that contains one or more Data Characteristics that describe that Data Subject. *See also* Virtual Data Subject, Data Subject Type.

Tutorial *See* Data Resource Guide Tutorial.

Unique Identifier Another name for a Primary Key.

Unnormalized Data Data that are not structured by Data Subjects according to the Data Architecture. The way data are used in the real world. *See also* Denormalized Data, Normalized Data.

Unstructured Disparate Data Disparate data that do not conform to any type of naming, definition, structure, or quality criteria and have no similarity to the Common Data Architecture. *See also* Semi-Structured Data.

User A slang term that has been replaced with Client.

Validation *See* Cross Reference Validation.

Value *See* Data Value.

Variability *See* Data Variability.

Variable Common Data Characteristic A Data Characteristic in the Common Data Architecture that contains different data characteristics under different situations.

Variable Data Product Characteristic A Data Product Characteristic that contains different data characteristics under different situations.

Variation *See* Data Variation.

Version *See* Data Version.

Virtual Data Subject A Data Subject that has no Data Characteristics and represents a broad classification of Data Subjects. *See also* True Data Subject, Data Subject Type.

Vision   An image of what things will be like. A very vivid picture of the future.

Vocabulary   A set of words or phrases used for a particular purpose. *See* Data Naming Vocabulary.

Volatility   *See* Data Volatility.

Win-Win Situation   The successful development of a Common Data Architecture based on a combination of the From-Above Approach and the From-Below Approach.

Working Levels of Data Classification   The lower three levels of the Data Classification Scheme: Data Subjects, Data Characteristics, and Data Characteristic Variations. *See also* Categorical Levels of Data Classification.

Zachman Framework   A Framework for Information Systems Architecture developed and promoted by John Zachman. *See also* Information Systems Framework.

▼ BIBLIOGRAPHY
▼
▼

Brackett, Michael H. *Developing Data Structured Information Systems.* Topeka, Kans.: Ken Orr and Associates, Inc., 1983.

———. *Developing Data Structured Databases.* Englewood Cliffs, N.J.: Prentice-Hall, 1987.

———. *Practical Data Design.* Englewood Cliffs, N.J.: Prentice-Hall, 1990.

Bruner, J.S. *In Search of Mind.* New York: Harper and Row, 1983.

Campbell, Jeremy. *Grammatical Man: Information, Entropy, Language, and Life.* New York: Simon and Schuster, 1982.

Conner, Daryl. *Managing at the Speed of Change: How Resistant Managers Survive and Prosper While Others Fail.* New York: Villard Books, 1993.

Covey, Stephen R. *The 7 Habits of Highly Effective People.* New York: Simon and Schuster, 1989.

Davies, P.C.W. *The Cosmic Blueprint: New Discoveries in Nature's Creative Ability to Order the Universe.* New York: Simon and Schuster, 1988.

Frankl, Viktor E. *Man's Search for Meaning.* New York: Pocket Books, 1985.

Glick, James. *Chaos.* New York: Viking Press, 1987.

Gilbraith, Robert D. *Forward Thinking.* New York: McGraw-Hill, 1987.

Hammer, Michael. *Reengineering the Corporation: A Manifest for Business Revolution.* New York: Harper Business, 1993.

Harrington, N.J. *Business Process Improvement: The Breakthrough Strategy for Total Quality, Productivity, and Competitiveness*. New York: McGraw-Hill, 1981.

Heisenberg, Werner. *The Uncertainty Principle and Foundations of Quantum Mechanics*. New York: Wiley, 1977.

Kaye, Harvey. *Decision Power: How to Make Successful Decisions with Confidence*. Englewood Cliffs, N.J.: Prentice Hall, 1992.

Koestler, Arthur. *The Ghost in the Machine*. New York: Macmillan, 1968.

Kosslyn, S.M. *Ghosts in the Mind's Machine: Creating and Using Images in the Brain*. New York: W.W. Norton, 1983.

Kuhn, Thomas S. *The Structure of Scientific Revolution*. Chicago: University of Chicago Press, 1962.

Minski, Marvin. *The Society of Mind*. New York: Simon and Schuster, 1986.

Pagels, Heinz. *The Cosmic Code*. New York: Bantam Books, 1983.

———. *Perfect Symmetry*. New York: Bantam Books, 1986.

———. *The Dreams of Reason*. New York: Simon and Schuster, 1988.

Porter, Michael E. *Competitive Advantage: Creating and Sustaining Superior Performance*. New York: Free Press, 1985.

———. *The Competitive Advantage of Nations*. New York: Free Press, 1990.

Sowa, J.F. *Conceptual Structures: Information Processing in Mind and Machine*. Reading, Mass.: Addison-Wesley, 1984.

VonNeumann, J. *The Computer and the Brain*. New Haven, Conn.: Yale University Press, 1958.

Zachman, John A. "A Framework for Information Systems Architecture," *IBM Systems Journal* 26, no. 3 (1987): 276–292.

▼ INDEX